Marx, a French Passion

Historical Materialism Book Series

The Historical Materialism Book Series is a major publishing initiative of the radical left. The capitalist crisis of the twenty-first century has been met by a resurgence of interest in critical Marxist theory. At the same time, the publishing institutions committed to Marxism have contracted markedly since the high point of the 1970s. The Historical Materialism Book Series is dedicated to addressing this situation by making available important works of Marxist theory. The aim of the series is to publish important theoretical contributions as the basis for vigorous intellectual debate and exchange on the left.

The peer-reviewed series publishes original monographs, translated texts, and reprints of classics across the bounds of academic disciplinary agendas and across the divisions of the left. The series is particularly concerned to encourage the internationalization of Marxist debate and aims to translate significant studies from beyond the English-speaking world.

For a full list of titles in the Historical Materialism Book Series available in paperback from Haymarket Books, visit: www.haymarketbooks.org/ series_collections/1-historical-materialism.

Marx, a French Passion

The Reception of Marx and Marxisms in France's Political-Intellectual Life

Edited by
Jean-Numa Ducange
Antony Burlaud

Translated by
David Broder

Haymarket Books
Chicago, IL

First published in 2023 by Brill Academic Publishers, The Netherlands
© 2023 Koninklijke Brill NV, Leiden, The Netherlands

Published in paperback in 2024 by
Haymarket Books
P.O. Box 180165
Chicago, IL 60618
773-583-7884
www.haymarketbooks.org

ISBN: 979-8-88890-211-0

Distributed to the trade in the US through Consortium Book Sales and
Distribution (www.cbsd.com) and internationally through Ingram
Publisher Services International (www.ingramcontent.com).

This book was published with the generous support of Lannan
Foundation, Wallace Action Fund, and the Marguerite Casey Foundation.

Special discounts are available for bulk purchases by organizations and
institutions. Please call 773-583-7884 or email info@haymarketbooks.org
for more information.

Cover design by David Mabb. Cover art is a detail from *Construct 69,
Morris, Daisy / Stepanova, Optical*, paint on paper (2019).

Printed in the United States.

Library of Congress Cataloging-in-Publication data is available.

Contents

Writing the History of France's Marxisms

Jean-Numa Ducange and Antony Burlaud

It was no foregone conclusion that a foreign product such as Marxism would take root on French soil. Rather, the work and thought of Karl Marx (1818–83) would have to surmount multiple obstacles in this country. At the end of the nineteenth century, anti-German prejudices were rife in France, including on the Left. Few of Marx's texts were available in French, and rarer still were the militants able to read German. In the early years of the Third Republic, the German thinker's work could count on only a handful of 'smugglers' to infiltrate it into French socialist ranks; they were, at first, a small minority, hit by a 'double exclusion' which both demoted them to the margins of politics and denied them legitimate standing in the intellectual arena.[1] Added to these conjunctural obstacles were handicaps specific to the theoretical character of Marxism, which developed outside of – and often in opposition to – France's own rich socialist tradition. Marxism seemed alien if not outright hostile to the republican institutions and, more broadly, the republican culture with which France was so deeply imbued. Lastly, being a product of German dialectical philosophy, Marxism had little prospect of making room for itself in an intellectual and academic climate where positivism and Kantianism largely predominated. 'Grafting' Marxism into this context looked like a difficult task – and this initial conclusion fed a whole literature on the supposed desert of French Marxist theory. In his 1965 preface to *Pour Marx*, Louis Althusser bemoaned the 'French misery' and the 'absence of a real theoretical culture in the history of the French workers' movement';[2] ten years later, Daniel Lindenberg reckoned that – confronted with 'French ideology' and the 'political antibodies' that it secreted (the radical university, spiritualism, Durkheimianism, and so on) – Marxism had arrived in France 'stillborn'.[3]

Nonetheless, this imported product has enjoyed remarkable fortune in France. Evidently, the notion of a French 'political civilisation' entirely 'defined by Jacobinism and Marxism';[4] of a Marx 'cooked in all manner of sauces' and

---

1 Ymonet 1984.
2 Althusser 2005a.
3 Lindenberg 1975.
4 Furet 1987.

'invading the great contemporary hodgepodge called the human sciences';[5] of French intellectuals who supposedly made Marxism the 'main theme of their debates' between 1945 and 1975;[6] or even of a France that remained 'under the command [of the Soviet] cadaver' many years after the fall of the USSR;[7] is the stuff of retrospective illusion and conservative fantasy. Yet, it cannot be denied that Marx and Marxism did, indeed, have an intensive presence in twentieth-century France, thanks to the political organisations that claimed inspiration from them, to the militants who appropriated them, and to the myriad intellectuals both major and minor who drew on them. France has a long and rich history together with Marx.

Yet no comprehensive approach to this history has ever been attempted. The works of Samuel Bernstein, Alexandre Zévaès, Maurice Dommanget and Thierry Paquot only cover up to the end of the nineteenth century.[8] Daniel Lindenberg's book does not go further than the 1920s, a decade which he treats with the incisiveness but also the briskness typical of the polemical essay as a genre. As for Tony Judt's volume on *Marxism and the French Left* from 1830 to 1981,[9] despite its title it is only a collection of disparate articles. So, apart from a few brief overviews, there is no comprehensive study of France's relationship with Marx and Marxism, and hardly any in-depth reflection on how Marxist ideas became such common points of reference in France. The rich research programme outlined by Georges Haupt[10] and applied in other national contexts by Eric Hobsbawm[11] – that is, the effort to produce a history of Marxism that spans its multiple dimensions beyond a simple doctrinal history (meaning, its theoretical, editorial, and militant dimensions) in order to understand its influence – has hardly stirred any response in France.

This absence is particularly surprising when we are considering a political tradition that is itself obsessed with the way in which 'ideas, taking hold of the masses, become material forces'. This is the gap that this volume, prepared through a series of seminars, seeks to cover, bringing together three generations of researchers from different disciplines (history, sociology, political science, philosophy). Although philosophy is not absent from its pages, this volume resolutely stands on the ground of intellectual history, of a history of political

---

5   Furet 1975.
6   Furet 1987.
7   Druon 2000.
8   Bernstein 1933, Zévaès 1947, Dommanger 1969, Paquot 1980.
9   Judt 1986.
10   Haupt 1980.
11   Hobsbawm 2012.

ideas attentive to the modalities of cultural transfers, to the multiple retranslations and appropriations to which a theory is subjected when it passes from one country, one environment, and one conjuncture to another. In its quest to place the march of ideas in its proper contexts – and careful not to cut it off from its practical stakes – this history is interested in the concrete conditions in which abstract notions can be disseminated.[12]

1   Which Marxisms?

This choice – to write the history of Marxisms, rather than to study Marxist thought per se – implies an approach to Marxism that does not define its contours too narrowly. The 'Marxism' being discussed here is a multifaceted and ever-changing object. Its very definition is a matter of dispute, and its content varies from one location to another: in one case, it may be a name ('Karl Marx'), a simple reference; and in another, a site of memory, an institution, which calls for reverence or blasphemy; elsewhere it will be a watchword, a collection of slogans; still elsewhere, a few concepts, a more or less coherent composite of ideas, a more or less conscious system of representation; in only a few places will it be a solidly constituted and mastered theoretical edifice. We make no *a priori* choice between these different avatars of Marxism, and nor do we seek to identify whether such and such a formulation of Marxism conforms more closely with the spirit and the letter of its founder than any other. If the contributions in this book do establish qualitative differences between Marxisms, the intention is not so much to pass judgement on their conceptual content as to distinguish between their bearers (the Marxism of intellectuals, Marxism for the masses, and so on) or to measure their deviation from a norm which is itself ever-changing ('orthodox' or 'heterodox' Marxism).

1.1   *Political Organisations' Marxism*

After a prologue recalling the relationship that Marx and Engels had with France during their own lifetimes, the book plunges into a study of the Marxism produced and disseminated in political organisations. It thus reminds us – if it were even necessary – that at the same time as being a theory, Marxism is also a political ideology, weapon and marker. And it reminds us that the demands of politics never cease to influence the fate of theory. The strength of Marxism in France – but perhaps also its tragedy – was that it was claimed,

---

12   Skornicki and Tournadre 2015.

upheld and promoted by two mass political organisations: the Socialist Party, in its various incarnations – the Guesdist Parti ouvrier français, the Section française de l'International ouvrière (SFIO), and then the Parti socialiste created at the Épinay Congress – and the Parti communiste français (PCF). The contributions devoted to these two parties show the role that these organisations played in the defence, popularisation and dissemination of Marxism, while paying particular attention to the various concrete means of this dissemination (celebrations, conferences, party schools, summaries and pamphlets, and so on). They also show the role that political leaderships had in regulating doctrinal production, concerned as they were to produce a Marxism adapted to the political conjuncture of the moment, attentive to controlling theoretical innovation, authorising (or even ordering) certain updates while forbidding others. As a counterpoint to these six contributions, another article examines some of the great postwar debates, inspired by Marx, among a (Trotskyist and Maoist) far left whose electoral weakness perhaps led it to over-invest in theoretical questions.

1.2   *Marxism through the Texts*

The second part of this volume is devoted to the textual and editorial dimensions of Marxism. The history of Marxism is, first and foremost, the concrete history of the gigantic body of written work bequeathed by Marx and Engels (the – non-exhaustive – *Marx-Engels-Werke* counts some 42 thick volumes). This corpus was taken in hand by different guardians (be they political or scholarly), and divulged slowly, subject as it was to the whims of archival mishaps, accidents of research, and the political needs of the moment. The control exercised over the availability of texts, and over their form and content, has always been an important battleground in the construction of Marxism, and the definition of the 'canon' offered to readers was in dispute throughout the twentieth century. After a contribution that examines some of the terminological, conceptual and political problems posed by the translation of Marx into French, three chapters track the editorial fate of Marx's works. These texts show the constant recompositions of the available Marxian corpus, which was subject to a series of constraints, be they political (only providing readers with what could speak to the 'masses' or serve the cause), practical (finding the texts, the translators, and the resources required to publish) or commercial (having a consistent editorial apparatus and an audience). There was, indeed, difficult and bumpy progress towards a more extensive (if not complete) and more scientific edition. By mapping the 'supply' provided by publishers, these contributions mark out the contours of the different Marxes that the French readership was able to encounter and appropriate.

1.3   *Some Scholarly Marxisms*

A third set of chapters examines the impact of Marxism in the social sciences and in certain scholarly discourses. It analyses the penetration of Marxist theses – or, at the very least, of references to Marx – into intellectual and (often academic) institutional universes which did not seem at all well-disposed to them, either because of their fundamental political conservatism, or because other alternative or opposed intellectual traditions were already occupying the field, or because some key Marxist ideas had already been integrated into them in non-Marxist forms. Here, we can get a sense of how far the penetration of Marxist theses and the formulation of research programmes inspired by Marx have been able to enrich these different disciplines – but also the very unequal spread of this Marxist influence across different domains, and the extent of the erasure (either in the form of exhaustion or repression) that Marxism has undergone in the social sciences in recent decades. Here we see that in some cases, Marxism has functioned less as a conceptual tool or as a research programme than as a marker which makes it possible to give a political twist to an essentially scholarly discourse. This has allowed some to draw on the prestige that comes with being radical, novel, avant-garde and scientific, and even to outcompete rivals in the intellectual space (generally to their Left).

1.4   *Intellectual Hybridisations*

Part Four looks back at the various 'intellectual hybridisations' which Marxism has undergone in France, which is to say, the association of the Marxist tradition with other theoretical traditions and other trends of ideas that took form elsewhere. These hybridisations have generally been attached to a few eminent figures but they have also been practiced by intellectual collectives or political organisations – and serve several functions. Through confrontation and friction, they have made it possible to enrich theory, to raise new questions, to deal more adequately with problems that Marxism alone did not suffice to solve. However, by combining Marxism with other more established traditions, they have also aided its acclimatisation within the French intellectual space. In addition, they often allow us to escape from Marxist monolingualism, to thwart doctrinaire mechanicism, and to develop a heterodox Marxism – often on the margins of the party, in the form of a contraband. As the chapter dedicated to the post-1968 period shows, this practice of hybridisation and search for an open Marxism did not disappear with the ideological reversal of the 1970s and 1980s: rather, it persisted, and to some extent even became the norm of a Marxism which, having lost its political effects and proxies, defined itself above all as a research endeavour.

1.5   *Marxism from Its Margins*

Finally, the fifth and last part of this volume sets out to approach French Marxism from the outside, or from its margins. This first means studying the view of Marx taken by individuals or groups who are not Marxists, or who at first sight do not seem to be Marxists – from the liberal economists of the late nineteenth century, to Raymond Aron and the galaxy of anti-totalitarian circles, or even Catholic ones. The interest in such unexpected engagement is that it highlights – beyond the (very real) antagonisms against Marxism, with the activism, attacks and trials directed against it – the possibility of an exchange, even if a conflictual one, through which Marxism also acts. In Part Five, these political and social 'margins' are also combined with geographical ones. In evoking the discovery of Marxism by Chinese students in Paris, or the dissemination of a French-language Marx on the African continent, it reminds us that in France, colonised people from all over the world were able to forge a Marx suited to their own struggles. In turn practising cultural transfer, they took this Marx back to their homelands and brought him to life there.

2   The Trajectory of French Marxism(s)

The chapters brought together in these five parts do not make up a uniform set. Some provide overviews while others are original case studies. They draw on different disciplinary and methodological traditions; each depends on how advanced the state of research is, with great variations from one subject to another. Moreover, the volume makes no claim to exhaustiveness and there are necessarily areas that have been left unexplored.

   It may be felt that this volume leaves out important authors, that it gives too little space to the constellation of far-left organisations, or that it gives too much prominence to the printed word – which is, after all, only one of the vehicles for Marxist ideas. As for more ordinary appropriations of Marxism, we have chosen to make only scant reference to them: there has undoubtedly been an everyday, essentially practical Marxism, which we may call the Marxism of militants. But its history – or its ethnography – exceeds our field of analysis.

   Nonetheless, we feel that this volume, conceived from the outset as a coherent whole, makes it possible to reconstitute the essential stages of Marxism's trajectory in France.

2.1   *Clearing the Ground and Acclimatising Marxism*

The three decades that followed Marx's death in 1883 were a time for laying the groundwork – a period of slow and difficult acclimatisation of Marxism. Marx's great texts remained little-known and found only a limited response in the intellectual world. While a few academics (economists, philosophers, and later sociologists) did discuss Marx, they generally did so in order to point out his limits and reject him. In the French socialist arena, Marxism penetrated little by little, thanks to the militant zeal of the Guesdists, and to a first series of translations, republications in serial or volume form, and its rendering in pedagogical formats (abridged editions, anthologies, and catechisms). This introduction of Marxism into the magma of French socialisms came at the cost of a certain simplification, as the Guesdists – concerned above all with political effectiveness – promoted an oft-impoverished Marxism. The creation of a unified socialist party in 1905 seemed to confirm the victory of this Guesdist propaganda effort: the SFIO was at least outwardly founded on Marxist bases. Yet, this political ratification of Marxism owed not only to Guesdist intransigence but equally to the diplomatic skills of Jean Jaurès, and to his tireless efforts to bring together the German social-democratic and French republican traditions.

2.2   *In the Wake of October*

Unquestionably, the revolution of October 1917 and the Communist/Socialist split at the Tours Congress in 1920 gave new vigour to French Marxism and brought it into a new phase. As against the SFIO, which continued to lay claim to Marxism – allowing the first great project for a complete works of Marx to develop on the margins of the party – the PCF endeavoured to present itself as the true heir to Marx. It strove, with the help of a constantly growing editorial apparatus, to offer Marx's texts to its militants. But this Marx was gradually subordinated, in Communist discourse and in its catalogues, to the Soviet leaders, meaning first Lenin and then Stalin. Thus a 'Marxism-Leninism' was invented which contributed both to popularising Marx and to obscuring him. But we must not have too simplistic an image of the Communist Marx. For alongside this 'Sovietised' and Stalinised Marx, there was also room, in the Communist space, for better elaborated Marxes: the PCF passed on, however, imperfectly, the progress of Soviet Marxology; it promoted, intermittently, and as the political situation required, a Marx reinscribed in the French rationalist and revolutionary tradition; it allowed some of its intellectuals to beat new paths. Outside the PCF's own ranks, this research intersected with other efforts at intellectual innovation: that of the second-generation Durkheimian sociologists, that of the founders of the Annales School, but also, in a different register, that of the Surrealists.

2.3   The Centrality of Marxism?

French Marxism would enter its most expansive phase in the post-World War II
period. The prestige of the USSR, the political and cultural power of the PCF,
and the influence of its counter-society played no little role in this expansion. Upon the Liberation of France, the omnipresence of the PCF compelled
intellectuals (even those most alien to Marxism) to get to grips with Marx.
Existentialism, which was then in vogue, crossed paths with Marxism. Literary
criticism, itself undergoing a process of renewal, also encountered Marxism,
via Bertolt Brecht and György Lukács. The Situationists also drew on it. Through
this engagement, a variety of Marxisms were developed – and they were rarely
orthodox. Marx had earned his place in the academy: in sociology, he became a
canonical author; in economics, he was hailed by a few eminent mandarins and
inspired new generations' research; in history, despite Braudel's reservations,
some of the great figures of the third generation of the Annales (Emmanuel
Le Roy Ladurie, Georges Duby, Michel Vovelle, and so on) were moulded by
their reading of Marx, and sometimes lay claim to him. While Marxism never
became hegemonic, for a few years it did acquire a certain centrality: the questions it posed were the subject of wide debate, its watchwords were taken up,
and its concepts circulated far beyond Marxist circles. This intellectual vigour,
embodied by some major figures of 'Western Marxism',[13] was supported by the
transformations of the academic field and by a real boom in Marx publishing. In
the PCF, party publisher Éditions sociales engaged in an increasingly demanding and systematic publication effort, calling on first-rate translators and making new texts available. This Communist publishing effort was complemented
by – and faced competition from – the work of a myriad of militant publishers, often 'oppositional' or 'gauchiste' in nature, such as Maspero or Anthropos,
which were joined by the large 'commercial' publishers, eager not to miss out
on this new market.

2.4   From the Ebbing of Marxism to the 'Winter Years'

In the 1970s, the climate changed, and Marxism lost its centrality. On the far left,
the dynamic of May '68 was exhausted and the gauchiste experiences fell into
decline. While the Parti socialiste founded at the Épinay Congress did oppor-
tunely 're-Marxify' its discourse in order to compete with its Communist ally
and give substance to the Common Programme, it also opened itself up to
various ideological currents and, after a long course of opposition, prepared to
liquidate its 'Marxist superego'. The PCF, for its part, struggled to manage the

---

13   Anderson 1979.

doctrinal *aggiornamento* begun in the 1960s, and oscillated between affirmation of 'Marxist-Leninist' orthodoxy, a controlled 'updating' process and an abandonment of its heritage. In the intellectual world, the Liberation generation was also fading away. Structuralism, which had at one time sealed an alliance with Marxism, moved away from it, before in turn itself being swept away. The anti-totalitarian offensive, embodied by the 'new philosophers' prominent in the media, found a wide echo even in the left-wing press, its attacks on Soviet state ideology also wounding Marxism itself. At a deeper level, the whole ecosystem of critical thought disintegrated: the university became more uniformised, disciplines tended to be reconfigured on less political bases, while some of the main militant publishers and the Marxist-inspired publications disappeared. The 1980s and 1990s, marked by the reorientation of the political and trade union Left, by the canonisation of liberal intellectuals (from Alexis de Tocqueville to François Furet, via Raymond Aron), and by the continuation of the trial of Marx on charges of promoting tyranny, were 'winter years' for Marxists in France. However, the intellectual ebb did not sweep everything away with it: a few places of refuge (for instance, journals like *Actuel Marx*, and certain seminars) remained, and intellectuals who refused to adopt the posture of the 'repentant' kept the Marxist flame burning, as best they could.

2.5   *A Revival?*

The period starting in the late 2000s and particularly with the economic crisis of 2008 saw a certain revival of interest in Marx, both in public discourse and on the shelves of bookshops. While a new French reference edition of the works of Marx and Engels – the *Grande Édition de Marx et d'Engels* (GEME), a project directed by Isabelle Garo – was being prepared, 'a thousand Marxisms' resurfaced.[14] This revival has uncertain bases, is limited in scope, and its connection with the political world is not obvious. But it is part of a more general rise in critical theory.[15] In October 2017, a survey carried out by Viavoice for the Fondation Gabriel Péri showed that one in four young people aged 18–24 had a positive view of Marx, and that almost half rejected the notion that communism is an outdated idea. Will this younger generation carry through a real reappropriation of Marxian thought? It would be foolhardy to make any such prediction. But these figures suggest, in any case, that the spectre of Marx has not finished haunting France.

---

14   Tosel 2009.
15   Keucheyan 2014.

Karl Marx's France

Antony Burlaud

According to a well-known thesis formulated by Karl Kautsky in his 1908 text *The Three Sources of Marxism*, which was then taken up a few years later by Lenin, Marx achieved the fusion of 'all that was great and fertile in English thought, French thought and German thought'.[1] In this schema, which quickly became a commonplace of the Second and Third Internationals, France represented – alongside the Germany of the philosophers and the England of the economists – the land of 'political thought', of radical practice and of 'revolutionary ardour'. In fact, France was, for Marx, the homeland of the Great Revolution, the wellspring of the explosion of 1848, and also the site of his own first encounter with a vigorous, organised workers' movement backed up by strong traditions. In short, for Marx, France was the country of *politics in action*. But Kautsky and Lenin's tripartite division (in large part taking up the intellectual schemas of early nineteenth-century German intellectuals) is also too convenient; for it provides a distorting mirror that uniformises and wrongly simplifies Marx's relationship with France. For the Trier thinker, this country was much more than a source of political inspiration: it was a place of asylum and pleasure, a mission country, a (theoretical and organisational) battlefield, a mooring point for his family, and also, on many occasions, a polemical foil. Above all, France, a land he examined for more than half a century, offered Marx more than a revolutionary past to ponder or working-class traditions to mimic: for a multiplicity of political formulas appeared on its soil – whether longlasting ones (Second Empire, Third Republic) or the ephemeral (the Paris Commune) – which surprised Marx, tested the limits of his thinking and compelled him to review and enrich his theories.

1   A Youth in the Shadow of the French Revolution

Marx was very nearly born on French soil. Trier, his birthplace, had been attached to the French Republic in 1797; under the Consulate, it received the

---

1   Kautsky 1947.

title of prefecture of the Saar department, which it retained until 1814. These twenty years of French presence had a profound effect on the region, bringing the 'language of universal rights'[2] and the legal modernity of the Code Napoléon.

For the very young Marx, France thus first appeared as the land of the Enlightenment, the Revolution and La Grande Nation, and enjoyed a certain aura. His father, Hirschel (Heinrich) Marx, had benefited from the French presence and the lifting of the restrictions faced by Jews. He had headed to Koblenz to attend the law school founded by the French and was preparing to become a jurist in the Empire when the Coalition armies drove the French out of Germany. Reclaimed for the Prussian authorities, Heinrich Marx remained, if not a Jacobin, at least an *Aufklärer*. His granddaughter Eleanor later described him as 'a true eighteenth-century Frenchman' who 'knew Voltaire and Rousseau by heart'. We also know that he belonged to a local literary society, the Casino, whose members sometimes sang *La Marseillaise*, waved the tricolour flag and eulogised the Revolution of 1830.[3]

While Heinrich Marx's Francophilia should not be overstated, it is certain that Karl was immersed in an environment where France was an important, indeed largely positive, point of reference. In school, after Latin and Greek, he was taught French (which he read, spoke and wrote throughout his life) rather than Hebrew. At the Gymnasium in Trier, and later at university in Berlin, his teachers included some outspoken admirers of the French Revolution.

This early French influence is undoubtedly the source of Marx's fascination with the conquering bourgeoisie of the Enlightenment, and of his fondness for authors such as Diderot and Voltaire. It is, in any case, at the origin of his interest in the French Revolution and its theoretical forerunners. These were the object of a first in-depth study in 1843, as can be seen from the notebooks that Marx produced in Bad Kreuznach in this period: composed of notes and extracts, they show that the young man had carefully read *On the Spirit of the Laws, The Social Contract*, as well as several works on the history of the Revolution.[4]

The French Revolution fascinated the young Marx, much as it had fascinated Hegel and many German intellectuals of his time. But Marx would always maintain an ambivalent relationship with the Revolution, in which praise always did battle with critique. For in demonstrating France's political superiority, the

---

2   Stedman Jones 2016.
3   Sperber 2014.
4   Rubel 1974.

Revolution also revealed the 'German misery' – that is, the political immaturity of a Germany swamped in an aristocratic and feudal system and reduced to thinking (admittedly at a superior level) about the great historical acts accomplished by others.

2   In the Parisian Cauldron

It was to escape this 'German misery' that Marx moved to Paris in October 1843. In the French capital, he wanted to work for an alliance between German philosophy and French political practice, a condition for a new revolution that would transcend the limits of the one that took place in 1789–93. This project for a theoretical-political alliance between two nations with complementary callings (thought for one, praxis for the other) was hardly unique to Marx: detectable in Hegel, explicit in Ludwig Börne, Heinrich Heine or Moses Hess, it was the common dream of all German intellectuals, liberals and radicals alike, burdened by the political backwardness of their homeland.[5]

But Marx had a particular crucible in which to work on bringing the two nations together: the *Deutsch–Französische Jahrbücher*, created together with Arnold Ruge. Unfortunately, this endeavour soon ran aground: the French politicians (Lamennais, Lamartine, Louis Blanc, Pierre Leroux) asked to contribute to the *Jahrebucher* refused or failed to answer promptly. A victim of the cultural gap between the German and French Left, it produced only one instalment – a brilliant issue, but one entirely written by Germans.

Despite this editorial failure, Marx had an exceptionally densely packed political experience during his first stay in Paris. For the French capital, which reached one million inhabitants in the 1840s, was the political centre of Europe, the 'great magic kettle in which the history of the world is boiling'. After the July Revolution, the memory of the Great Revolution resurfaced. A neo-Jacobin current took structured form, feeding on the testimonies of the revolutionaries of yesteryear. There was the emergence of working-class socialism, carried forth by a few great figures, and fuelled by an intense utopian ferment. Political activity was especially intense because Paris was one of the capitals of Europe's milieu of political exiles, under the July monarchy welcoming liberals and radicals from Poland, Russia and the German-speaking countries.[6] The German community alone is said to have counted some 60,000 members at the end

---

5   Bouglé, 1918; Calvié, 1989.
6   Aprile 2010, Diaz 2014.

of the 1840s.[7] The German communists had their own organisations, press and meeting places, generally meaning cafés, which were duly surveilled by police.[8]

Immersed in the Parisian cauldron, Marx evolved rapidly – a process accelerated, from late August 1844, by his association with Engels, with whom he shared, during his stay, a life that was both studious and dissolute, writing, drinking and entering into endless discussions in the cafés of the Palais-Royal or the Quai Voltaire.

Marx, who never hid his passion for bookworming, read, among other things, French socialist publications, but also novelists (Eugène Sue, George Sand), economists (Boisguilbert, the Physiocrats, Destutt de Tracy, Say), whom he discussed in his *1844 Manuscripts*, and perhaps also liberal historians (François Guizot and Augustin Thierry), whom he hailed as the discoverers of the class struggle.[9] He planned to write a history of the Convention, and to this end he absorbed a whole literature devoted to the Revolution, in particular the memoirs of René Levasseur de la Sarthe, the speeches of Robespierre and Saint-Just, and the voluminous works of Buchez and Roux, and of Cabet. This project did not come to fruition, but the knowledge Marx thus acquired would feed into certain passages of *The Holy Family*. Reading these French authors made enough of an impression on Marx and Engels that in 1845 they thought of creating a 'library of the best French socialist writers', in which Fourier, the Saint-Simonians, Morelly and others would be translated into German, with introductions by Marx. More generally, during this first stay in Paris, 'French' books began to take pride of place in Marx's personal library: of the 400 to 500 volumes that Marx entrusted to his friend Roland Daniels upon being driven out of Cologne in 1849, more than half were in French and a quarter were about France.[10]

In Paris, Marx and Engels did not settle for reading alone. For they also established contacts with certain figures of the French left and major newspapers such as *La Réforme*. They explored the young workers' movement. Marx later wrote in *Herr Vogt* that during his stay in Paris he had 'established personal contact with the leaders of the "League" living there as well as with the leaders of the majority of the secret French workers' associations, without however becoming a member of any of them'.[11] While it is not easy to determine exactly

7   Grandjonc 1973.
8   Condu 1962.
9   Ducange 2015.
10   *MEGA* 1999.
11   *MECW*, Vol. 17, p. 79.

what links Marx actually had with each of these 'leaders', he certainly was well-acquainted with the socialist workers' circles, and their meetings, of which he drew an admiring picture in the *1844 Manuscripts*.

This first stay in Paris ended in the winter of 1844–5. Under pressure from the Prussian authorities, Guizot's government expelled Marx, who left Paris for Brussels in February 1845. Engels, who had escaped proscription, only joined him later, regretfully abandoning the French capital, its charms and its 'very pretty grisettes'. The Parisian episode, which lasted less than a year and a half, nonetheless made a deep impression on Marx's life: as Auguste Cornu writes, it constituted 'a decisive turning point in the development of his thought and action'.[12]

3   Proudhon and the Deficiencies of French Socialism

One French figure would particularly occupy Marx's attention during his Brussels exile: Pierre-Joseph Proudhon. An admirer of *What Is Property*? – attracted by its polemical force and taste for concreteness – Marx had met the Besançon-born socialist at his home in the Rue Mazarine in October 1844, and kept in touch with him during his stay in Paris.[13] Although Proudhon does not seem to have attached much importance to this meeting at the time, Marx and Engels had clearly grasped the importance of Proudhon, 'the most consistent' and 'the most penetrating' of the French socialists, and had taken to his defence in *The Holy Family*. When, in 1846, the two friends tried, from Brussels, to set up a communist correspondence bureau in Paris, they wrote to Proudhon to offer that he take part, and also took the opportunity to warn him against one of his close friends, the German Karl Grün. Proudhon made a polite but circumspect reply, agreeing to receive the circulars, but not committing himself to contribute. An adept of the 'dubitative form', and a partisan of an 'almost absolute economic antidogmatism', he said he did not want to tie his hands. He also criticised Marx's radicalism ('I would rather ... burn property down than [make] a Saint Bartholomew's Day of the propertied') and cursed 'the petty divisions which, it seems, already exist in German socialism'.

This somewhat paternalistic response hastened the break between them. The publication, that same year, of *The System of Economic Contradictions or, The Philosophy of Poverty* – which even Proudhon's admirers agree is a rather

---

12   Cornu 1962.
13   Haubtmann 1981.

nebulous work – provided Marx's opportunity to publicly express his disagreement with the French theorist. He wrote a pamphlet directly in French, *Misère de la philosophie – The Poverty of Philosophy* – in which he spelled out his criticisms of Proudhon in his own both rigorous and scathing manner. In publishing this work – and it was self-published – Marx intended to make a strong intervention in the French debate. He even wanted to send copies of his work to the main figures of French socialism, and to 'sneak reviews into the main dailies'. But the book apparently did not reach its intended recipients and it made little impact.

Our concern here is not to detail the theoretical content of this 'Anti-Proudhon'. But the episode is worth mentioning, for several reasons. Firstly, because it is an exemplary case of the difficulties of sealing an 'Franco-German intellectual alliance' (Proudhon's distrust toward German socialism; theoretical and practical incompatibilities; Marx's inability to influence French socialism). Secondly, because it ignited a quarrel that would never be extinguished. And finally, because the criticisms levelled at Proudhon – his empiricism, theoretical weakness, charlatanism and bloatedness, his petty-bourgeois wiles and inability to really break with the established order... – would long be attached, in Marx's mind, to the whole French socialist movement, Proudhonian or otherwise.

4   1848: Revolution and Counter-Revolution in France

The February 1848 revolution, which Marx and Engels greeted with enthusiasm – to their eyes it appeared to herald the 'triumph of democracy throughout Europe' – caused consternation among the Belgian authorities. Marx, who had just published the *Communist Manifesto*, was expelled from Brussels in March, but the provisional government – in the person of Flocon, with whom Engels had established ties – offered him asylum in France. He arrived in Paris together with other leaders of the Communist League and saw the Second Republic take its first steps, before he left the following month for Cologne, where he took part in the German democratic movement as head of the *Neue Rheinische Zeitung*. Engels provided for him for a few months, before he was expelled by the authorities: expatriated, he made a long journey on foot from Paris to Bern in October–November 1848, which also provided the opportunity for direct, physical (and joyful) contact with rural France. The victory of the counter-revolution in Germany and the banning of the *Neue Rheinische Zeitung* brought Marx back to Paris in June 1849. He remained there for three months, until the government tried to place him under house arrest in Morbihan. Refusing this proscription in the 'marshes of Brittany', which he described as a 'camouflaged attempt at assassination', he left France for London.

If in this period in 1848–9 Marx and Engels devoted the bulk of their efforts to Germany, this did not mean turning their backs on French political reality. In their articles and correspondence, they commented extensively on the latest French developments, trying to make the historical process legible by distinguishing the forces at work and marking the moments of rupture. After the defeat for the people in June 1848, which they immediately saw as a turning point, they lucidly observed the consolidation of the bourgeois republic, then its decomposition under the effect of 'a royalist reaction … in full swing, more barefaced than under Guizot'.[14] But, as Raymond Huard notes, they did not cease, until summer 1850, 'to believe that a fresh surge in the revolutionary movement was possible, and even imminent'.

In 1850 Marx synthesised and systematised his vision of the Second Republic in a series of three articles published in the *Neue Rheinische Zeitung: Politsch-ökonomische Revue*, which later made up his work *The Class Struggles in France*. In this major text, Marx analysed the revolution and its aftermath in terms of classes, providing an account of the historical process by seeking to identify each major sequence with the social group ('workers', 'petty-bourgeois republicans', 'republican bourgeoisie', 'royalist bourgeoisie') which dominated the battlefield in that moment. With a wealth of detail and a pronounced taste for epigram, he outlined the various stages of the political process by which the Republic moved away from its origins: the popular revolution and the establishment of the provisional government, a compromise solution; the setting up of a bourgeois republic, 'surrounded by social institutions'; then, after the tug-of-war of spring 1848, the return to order in May's elections (where 'peasants and petty-bourgeois' voted 'under the leadership of the bourgeoisie') and the June days, the liquidation of the workers' movement; finally, the apparent triumph of a bourgeois republic, which was soon undermined by the election of Louis-Napoléon Bonaparte (a 'coup d'état of the peasants'), and then by the royalists' success in the elections of 1848. If certain points of Marx's analysis (such as his concept of the lumpenproletariat, or his aversion to the Montagne) have been debated or challenged, *Class Struggles* lays the foundations of modern political sociology, and even over a century and a half later, the best historians continue to acknowledge its merits.

---

14   Marx to Engels In Paris, 7 June 1849.

5   The Enigma of Bonapartism

During 1851, Marx and Engels continued to follow French political developments, and in their correspondence they speculated on the possible outcome
of the tug of war between Bonaparte and the Assembly. They only intermittently believed in Napoleon's chances, and they were surprised by the coup of
2 December. On the following day Engels expressed his astonishment, in a letter in which he already spoke of the coup d'état as a parody of Brumaire; Marx,
in his reply, said that he was 'quite bewildered by the tragi-comic sequence of
events in Paris'.[15]

Their theoretical reaction to the surprise of the coup d'état came in *The
Eighteenth Brumaire of Louis Bonaparte*. This text, written between January and
March 1852, was published in May in the journal *Die Revolution*, which Joseph
Weydemeyer published in New York. At first glance, *Eighteenth Brumaire* follows the same framework as *Class Struggles*, extending it chronologically, to
show 'how the class struggle in France created … a situation that enabled a
mediocre and grotesque character to play a hero's role'.

But it would be wrong to see this work as a mere rehash of *Class Struggles*,
or a simple caricature of the usurper Bonaparte, in the manner of Victor Hugo.
If in addressing the years 1848–50, Marx took up the already known account of
the progressive liquidation of the most left-wing elements (an evolution which,
as he points out, is the reverse of the revolutionary process from 1789 to 1794,
which radicalised and purged its right wing), here he also integrates two new
problems into his thinking.

First was the question of the state apparatus: for Marx, it was characteristic
of France that 'the executive power commands an army of officials number-
ing more than half a million individuals and therefore constantly maintains
an immense mass of interests and livelihoods'; that 'enmeshes, controls, reg-
ulates, superintends and tutors civil society'. The bourgeoisie so needed this
army of functionaries – both a reserve of sinecures and an instrument of repression – that it encouraged its growth, and 'render[ed] irresistible … the executive
power hostile to it'[16] – to the detriment of an Assembly already won to the
bourgeoisie's side. This criticism of a France locked into an overdeveloped state
apparatus was characteristic of Marx's thought up till the Commune, and subsequently fed into certain liberal readings of Marx.[17]

---

15   Marx to Engels, 9 December 1851, *MECW*, Vol. 38, p. 507.
16   *MECW*, Vol. 11, p. 139.
17   Furet 1988.

To this first mystery, Marx links another: the enigma of Bonapartism, its nature and its class function. What needed to be understood was how the reign of a figure so lacking in stature, an adventurer surrounded by adventurers, 'representative of the two series of heterogeneous social groups that were the peasants with their small plots and the parasites of all kinds'[18] came to appear, in a situation of political deadlock, as 'the only possible form of government'. And how, by finding a point of equilibrium between irreconcilable social groups, it would preserve the essential interests of the bourgeoisie, in opposition to the bourgeoisie itself.

6   The Empire as Seen from London

From the 1850s, France lost its centrality in Marx's thinking. There were many reasons for this development. With the end of the opening that began in 1848, Marx engaged in more theoretical work, examining new forms of social transformation distinct from the French revolutionary model. He turned his attention to other parts of the globe (the Ottoman Empire, Russia, the United States). He also tended to consider that the French proletariat had lost its historical preeminence.

This detachment was doubtless encouraged by the spectacle of the French exiles in London. Marx and Engels's correspondence over the 1850s and 1860s, is full of cutting and derisive comments on the pettiness of the 'great men of exile', their intrigues, their futile conflicts, and their theoretical confusion. In the course of these letters, the French émigrés even earned the recurrent nickname 'toads'.

Marx and Engels looked little more favourably on the French socialists who had joined the International Workingmen's Association (IWMA) from its foundation in 1864. The French troops of the International, led by Henri Tolain and Édouard Fribourg, were mostly of Proudhonian (and, to a lesser extent, Fourierist) sensibilities. Although Marx was able to show a certain diplomacy, he nonetheless considered the positions defended by the French First Internationalists – anti-statist mutualism, narrow workerism, a stress on trade-union action to the detriment of political action, rejection of collectivisation, rejection of women working, etc. – as archaic and harmful. He thus devoted his energies to gradually reducing the influence of the 'Paris imbeciles', 'those Proudhonian donkeys', within the IWMA. This was achieved by the end of the 1860s: the Basel

---

18   Agulhon 1973.

congress in 1869 confirmed the mutualists' defeat, and a new generation, closer to Marx's own ideas, took over the French component of the International.

Throughout the 1850s and 1860s, Marx and Engels followed the ups and downs of the Second Empire, either at a personal level or as journalists, especially for the *New York Daily Tribune*.[19] Their opinion of Napoleon III hardly changed: he was an 'adventurer' who was always on the verge of bankruptcy, a 'gambler' who 'dithered and, like all gamblers, totally lacked determination'. The two friends frequently prophesied the imminent fall of the man they called 'Krapülinski' or 'Boustrapa' in their letters. The Crimean War, the economic panic of 1857, the weaknesses of trade, diplomatic crises: time and again, Marx and Engels announced that 'catastrophe is going to strike', that Napoleon is 'in a strange mess', that he will 'hardly be able to get out of it', that he is 'wobbly', 'ruined'. We may find amusement in these diagnoses, constantly belied and then repeated across some two decades. But they are consistent with the Marxist representation of Bonapartism: as a default political solution, seeking a precarious balance between classes whose antagonism never ceases to sharpen; by definition unable to satisfy, all at the same time, the categories whose 'benefactor' it claims to be, such a regime is doomed to collapse. It could only hold on through mystifications, diversions (nationalism and war abroad), switching alliances, and by relying on the army and on corruption.

7   The Commune, a 'Sphinx'

When the 1870 war broke out, Marx and Engels sided with Prussia, deeming that the French 'need[ed] a thrashing'. This did not owe to chauvinism (even if this was also present, at least in a residual way, especially in 'General' Engels), but out of political calculation: 'If the Prussians win, the centralisation of *state power* will promote the centralisation of the German working class. Moreover, German predominance would shift the centre of gravity of the West European labour movement from France to Germany, and one only has to compare the French and German movements between 1866 and the present to see that the German working class is superior to the French, both theoretically and organisationally'.

Yet, when the Prussian war lost its defensive aspect, and Bismarck's troops invaded France, Marx and Engels grew alarmed. They had no illusions about the men who proclaimed a new Republic on 4 September, the 'miserable Jules

---

19   Rubel 1960.

Favre' or 'a government of the Left, which after some show of resistance will conclude peace.'[20] They feared, above all, that the people of Paris would rise up before peace was concluded, thus exposing themselves to being crushed by German troops. An address of the IWMA, written by Marx, warned the Parisian proletariat against such a 'desperate folly'.

The Commune, proclaimed on 28 March 1871, summoned Marx's attention. He kept informed about events in Paris and corresponded with Leo Frankel, to whom he also offered some advice. He perceived the limits and flaws of the movement – which, despite what the newspapers were peddling at the time, was neither 'Marxist' nor still even less controlled by Marx. But he hoped for its success and let his enthusiasm flow in a letter in April which termed the uprising 'the most glorious deed of our Party.'[21]

It was to defend the Commune – and to correct the various rumours which were then circulating – that the IWMA tasked Marx with writing an address on the Paris insurrection. Commissioned in April, the address was not finally completed and approved until the end of May – that is, after the Bloody Week. Known as *The Civil War in France*, it is one of Marx's most brilliant texts, part satire, part panegyric, part analysis. After having depicted with a vengeful pen Adolphe Thiers, this 'monstrous gnome' who had become a 'master in small state roguery', and the 'upstarts of September 4', Marx seeks to grasp what the Commune was: 'that sphinx so tantalising to the bourgeois mind'. Responding to *Eighteenth Brumaire*'s line of questioning about the state apparatus, he characterised it as the 'direct antithesis to the Empire', as the 'positive form of [the social] republic', committed to breaking the institutions of 'modern state power' (standing army, police, justice, Church) on which Bonaparte's regime rested.

8   Renowned in France?

It was with the Commune and *The Civil War in France* that Marx gained a certain notoriety in France. Until that point, he had remained little-known. *The Poverty of Philosophy* had a lowkey circulation, and his major texts on France had not been translated. In the 1860s, even such a well-informed reader as Sainte-Beuve could still refer to Marx, in a note in his *Proudhon*, as 'a writer of the young Hegelian school, who distinguished himself in the struggle against

20   Engels to Marx, 4 September 1870.
21   Marx to Kugelmann, 12 April 1871.

the Berlin school'. But his reputation as a leader of the International, and as the hidden inspiration behind the Commune, drew attention to him. He was mentioned in the newspapers and profiles were published even in the big dailies.[22] At the same time, the French police became interested in him. Jeannine Verdès counted no less than 165 notes and press cuttings covering the period 1871–83 in Marx's file at the Préfecture de police.[23] The information provided by finks was often fanciful, suggesting that Marx had tried to manipulate Freemasonry before creating the International, or that he was plotting the assassination of Thiers or the King of Spain. The rumour most often reported by spies – an accusation with a bright future ahead of it – was that he was an agent of Pan-Germanism, on a stipend from Bismarck.

The other event that contributed to Marx's renown in France was the publication in French of *Capital*. It was the result of a long process: Marx had envisaged a French translation as early as 1867, in order to 'rid of the French of the false notions that Proudhon has buried them in, with his idealisation of the petty bourgeoisie'. Nearly a dozen translators were considered, in turn, before Marx found a publisher in Maurice Lachâtre – a rather one-of-a-kind socialist – and a translator in Joseph Roy. The latter, who had already translated Feuerbach, seemed able to provide the necessary assurances. But both the author and the publisher were soon disappointed by the quality of his translation. Marx was forced to make extensive corrections to Roy's version of the text; he strove to make it more accessible to the French public, and to give it a more concrete and immediately political bent, sometimes to the detriment of its conceptual precision. *Le Capital* – as translated by Roy and rewritten by Marx – appeared in a series of instalments from 1872, then in a single volume in 1875. It was not a bestseller, indeed far from it: according to the information available, only a few hundred copies were sold, far below the initial aim of 10,000.[24] But this was the book around which Marx's scientific reputation began to take form, in the early days of the Third Republic.

9   Faced with the Third Republic

For Marx and Engels, the Third Republic was a problematic object.[25] This was a bourgeois regime, founded by men they despised; in its early years, it was in

---

22   Cordillot 2010.

23   Verdès 1966.

24   Gaudin 2014; Lefebvre 2016; Bouffard, Féron and Fondu, 2017.

25   Mainfroy 1983.

the grip of an ultra-reactionary majority. But, in comparison to the European monarchies, it was also a regime of civil liberties, allowing 'French socialists to act through the press, public meetings and associations'. As Engels put it, 'the modern republic is the consummate form of bourgeois rule, it is also the type of state that frees the class struggle from its last fetters and prepares the battleground for it'.[26] The two friends were not among those who lost interest in French affairs: they observed the consolidation of the regime, and criticised the German socialists who took 'history in France a little lightly', on the grounds that it 'was not the workers' primary concern'. They were especially well-informed about the French political situation because Marx's three daughters had each fallen in love with French socialists: Laura and Jenny had married Paul Lafargue (1868) and Charles Longuet (1872) respectively, while Eleanor was engaged, until 1880, to the Communard Lissagaray.

Marx and Engels initially set some hopes on the Radicals, and particularly on Georges Clemenceau; they did not rule out the possibility that he might evolve towards socialist positions (under the influence of Longuet, or after reading *Capital*). More seriously, they considered it 'difficult to move from a Gambetta-style republic to socialism without passing through a Clemenceau-style republic'.

But, more than the Radicals, it was of course the socialist movement that most benefited from the two men's support. In 1880, after the Marseilles congress, Marx met Jules Guesde and dictated to him the theoretical part of the Parti Ouvrier programme. While he lamented that the programme contained 'some incongruities which Guesde absolutely insisted upon' to please the French workers, he deemed it 'an enormous step to bring the French workers out of their phraseological fog onto the terrain of truth'.

Marx died in 1883, having made a final trip to France in 1882, which took him to Algiers, the Côte d'Azur, and Argenteuil, to see the Lafargues.[27] It was Engels who witnessed the slow rise of French socialism, which was one of the main subjects of his abundant correspondence with the Lafargues in the last years of his life. In 1885, he noted that 'scientific' socialism – Marxian socialism – was still weakly established in France: 'The mass in Paris is 'socialist' in the sense of an average and relatively neutral socialism, impregnated with Proudhon, Louis Blanc and Pierre Leroux. ... Even the French edition of *Capital* is Hebrew for them. ... The only thing they know is my Utopian Socialism and Scientific Socialism, which has indeed produced an unsuspected effect. None of

---

26   MECW, Vol. 23, p. 419.
27   Musto 2017.

the leaders ... know German. The leaders themselves have a still largely imperfect understanding of the theory.' But progress was rapidly made. A few months later, Engels could hail the 'constitution in the Chamber of a Workers' Party' and rejoice at seeing the 'old French socialism' crushed by the 'international socialism of today'. In April 1886, he noted with satisfaction: 'In short, there is again in France a remarkable movement which is working well, and the best thing is that it is led by our people, Guesde, Lafargue, Deville.'

In fact, it was mainly through the intermediary of this 'Guesdist' group, thanks to a first wave of translations (owing in particular to Paul and Laura Lafargue, and to Charles Longuet), to the writing of pedagogical summaries (such as Gabriel Deville's compendium of *Capital*), and to an intensive propaganda activity, that Marxism would in the final ten years of Engels's life penetrate French socialism, and begin the long journey we know today.[28]

---

28   Ducange 2014.

PART 1

The Political Uses of Marx

CHAPTER 1

The Socialists' Marx: The Guesde-Jaurès Moment

Jean-Numa Ducange

In a letter to his publisher Maurice Lachâtre dated 7 March 1872, Marx reasserted the importance of introducing *Capital* to a French audience. In this missive, he also expressed his acute awareness of the potential difficulties which they would have in reading his work:

> I do not take for my point of departure general ideas like equality etc., but on the contrary I begin from the objective analysis of economic relations such as they are. That is why the book's revolutionary spirit reveals itself only gradually. What I fear, however, is that the dryness of the first analyses may deter the French reader.[1]

In the years that followed, Marx repeatedly expressed his wish to see the publication of a popularising work that would offer French militants a way around this 'dryness'. His wish was granted a few weeks after his death. In 1883, Gabriel Deville, a socialist close to the conceptions of the Parti Ouvrier – whose fundamentals were largely inspired by Marx himself – published a compendium of *Capital* which was to remain a major reference point for many socialists for several decades. A militants' Marxism then took form, mainly within the current embodied by Jules Guesde, built around pamphlets and summaries of Marx.[2]

But this Marxism immediately had to confront two major challenges. The first was to give structured form to Marxism – a product of German origin – in a France that had other revolutionary and socialist traditions, and where Germanophobia had flourished in the period following the 1870 war. Both the republican and revolutionary heritage and the multitude of socialist currents from the early nineteenth century (Saint-Simon, Cabet and Proudhon) posed questions that were close to Marx's own concerns, at first glance making it easier to introduce him into the French context. But this proximity jarred with French intellectuals and activists, who sometimes saw Marx as an illegitimate 'German' competitor. What was to be said, for example, of the conception of the

---

1 Unpublished letter forwarded to the author by François Gaudin (Lachâtre papers, in the possession of François Gaudin).

2 Ducange 2020.

Republic that had resulted from the Revolution of 1789–94? Was the promise of republican emancipation compatible with Marxism, or instead a 'bourgeois' mystification that ought to be denounced? The second challenge related to the specific place that the reference to Marx would have within France's socialist currents: was he a critical theorist whose texts ought to be discussed (implying the need for translations, extending beyond the fundamental texts) or was he first and foremost an inspirer of immediate, programmatic political action – a tool for training up militants?

These two central issues – Marx's place with regard to 'national' traditions and the different uses of his work – will be here be addressed through the prism of three main moments: firstly, by studying Marx's place in the multiple pre-1900 socialist currents; secondly, by examining the heterodox revisions of Marxism by critical intellectuals close to the socialist movement at the turn of the century; and finally, by studying the place of Marx and Marxism in the Section française de l'Internationale ouvrière (SFIO) from its foundation in 1905 up till World War I.

1   Which Marxism for Which Socialism?

At the moment of Marx's death, the German Social-Democratic Party (SPD), which had united its forces back in 1875, was perplexed by the diversity of France's socialist currents. The SPD's theoretical and political leaders, including Wilhelm Liebknecht, August Bebel and, of course, Marx's faithful companion Friedrich Engels, despaired at any hope of seeing a solid current emerge, built on their foundations. Their most faithful French allies were those close to Jules Guesde and Paul Lafargue, the 'Guesdists' whom history has remembered as the introducers of Marxism in France. They transformed Marx's work into a 'socialist catechism' – as they called it – by borrowing some key concepts from him: the class struggle, the exploitation of workers by bosses, and internationalist solidarity between workers in different countries – all themes at the basis of an effective, action-oriented propaganda. The articles which they published in their press organs (the most important of which was the Parti Ouvrier's organ *L'Égalité* – *Le Socialiste*) or in short pamphlets took the form of small pedagogical treatises, intended to convince the reader to join the ranks of the Parti Ouvrier. The workers' almanacs, like the Guesdist press, regularly published short extracts from Marx's texts, sometimes meaning only brief quotations. They were Marxist in their own way, without really taking an interest in the letter of Marx's arguments. Guesde, for instance, was a defender of the iron law of wages, which had been theorised and defended by Ferdinand Lassalle, but which Marx had railed against. 'What I know is that I am not a Marxist', Marx is said to have told Engels. With these words, he distanced himself from those French socialists who lacked real interest in deepening their understanding of the mechanisms and developments of contemporary capitalism. But, despite Marx's own criticisms, we should draw a nuanced assessment of these 'Marxists': the relentless propaganda efforts at all levels of the party, particularly in the regions where it built up strong positions (such as on the periphery of Lille, at a time when Roubaix was seen the 'Mecca' of socialism, but also in the Aube, the Allier and a few other départements), did help familiarise a section of working-class France with Marx's ideas.

In these militant networks there was an – admittedly summary, but well identified – Marxism, which contributed to establishing Marx as an essential reference point for socialists. On the other hand, the Guesdists made little attempt to translate and systematically disseminate Marx's available works. Some figures close to Guesde were nevertheless among the rare introducers of Marx's texts: Édouard Fortin, Charles Bonnier and Alexandre Bracke-Desrousseaux instigated certain translations, with *The Eighteenth Brumaire of Louis Bonaparte* translated and published by Fortin in 1891, while Bonnier helped drive reviews such as *L'Ère nouvelle* or *Le Devenir social*, which published some of Marx's texts at the end of the nineteenth century. Paul Lafargue – husband to one of Marx's daughters, Laura, and a faithful comrade-in-arms of Guesde – also showed a certain mastery of Marx's body of work, which he intended above all to popularise among a militant audience. As Jacqueline Cahen has aptly explained, most of the real theoretical discussions about *Capital* took place outside of socialist circles.[3]

While Guesde's current was the one most influenced by German Social Democracy, Édouard Vaillant – a figure from the Paris Commune and heir to Blanquist thought – was also sensitive to Marx's writings and to the Marxist theoretical production coming from the SPD.[4] The main leader of Austrian socialism, Victor Adler, did not hesitate to define Vaillant 'half-German in his way of thinking'. Although Engels was suspicious of Vaillant, whom he described as a 'strict Blanquist', in Vaillant's current we do find references to Marx's texts, alongside other nineteenth-century socialists. Other influential currents, such as independent socialism and 'Broussism' (so named after Paul Brousse), showed a certain interest in Marx's work, though this was hardly exclusive and they quickly distanced themselves from the most revolutionary

---

3 Cahen 1994.
4 Robert 2016.

impulses in Marxist thought. It is important to understand that certain concepts associated with Marx and the Marxism of the time, such as class struggle,
owe a great deal – in the economy of Marx's own work – to his reading of
French thinkers (Augustin Thierry, Saint-Simon); this confirms a fundamental
affinity between socialism and Marxism, but for many in France it also put the
German thinker's originality in more relative terms. These latter were not very
sensitive to the theoretical and political effort represented by Volume I of *Capital*, and never considered Marx's work to be essential and central. To take just
one example, although *La Revue socialiste*, founded by Benoît Malon, did not
overlook Marx's work, many of its contributions distanced themselves from the
works of the master of 'scientific socialism'.[5]

Even in the case of the Guesdists, who did claim Marxism as the main theoretical matrix for their activity, this reference point remained relatively secondary in a context where the republican tradition weighed heavily. When Guesde
was elected an MP in the Roubaix-Wattrelos constituency in 1893, he did not
hesitate in stirring up patriotic reflexes, which it would be difficult to disen-
tangle from the heritage of the French Revolution. This did not mean rejecting
the internationalism of the *Communist Manifesto*, but the idea that 'the workers
have no fatherland' was never part of the alpha and omega of French socialism,
even among those who proclaimed themselves Marxists.

Jean Jaurès was emblematic of this complex link between republican tradition and Marxism. Initially close to Jules Ferry, he gradually moved towards
socialism in the late 1880s. Author of a dissertation on socialism in Germany,
he lay his hands on the work of Marx available at the time, while remaining firmly attached to the republican regime. The librarian at the École Normale Supérieure, Lucien Herr, introduced him to German thought, particularly
Marx and Marxist texts in German. From his reading of Marx, Jaurès grasped
the power of the concept of class struggle in explaining the dynamics of the
social world, and he admired the effort of *Capital* Volume I to understand
the complexity of the industrial revolution. But Jaurès was wary of that Marxism which he saw as incapable of integrating a humanist dimension into the
social struggle: at the time of the Dreyfus affair, which revealed the depth of
antisemitism at the end of the nineteenth century, Jaurès chose to ardently
defend – albeit after some hesitation – the French army captain accused of
treason. Conversely, in the name of implacable class independence, those close
to Guesde refused to defend an officer of the bourgeois state apparatus. There
was a clear break between a socialism concerned with establishing a strict

---

5   Lindenberg 1975.

delimitation between the workers' movement and the republican state, and another that was more sensitive to wider questions affecting all individuals. It should be noted that although Jaurès did not write any theoretical tomes on Marx, he did address his work in many articles. The target of his criticisms was not so much Marx, as Marxism as seen by the Guesdists, though he considered some texts by the German thinker either completely outdated or in need of major revision.[6] In particular, he chided the catastrophism of the *Communist Manifesto*: the French situation, with a republican regime, showed the possibility of partial and precious conquests, rendering obsolete formulations such as: 'The proletarians nothing to lose but their chain.' At the same time, Jaurès openly drew inspiration from Marx for his most important work, the *Histoire socialiste de la Révolution française* (in four volumes published between 1900 and 1904). Indeed, he claimed to be writing under the triple inspiration of Marx, Jules Michelet and Plutarch: Michelet for his writing style and a lyricism in defence of the people; Plutarch, when he offered portraits of the main revolutionary leaders; and finally Marx, when underlining the major role of economic and social factors in explaining the French Revolution – a very innovative thesis, this, at the beginning of the twentieth century. For Jaurès, the author of *Capital* had revealed the importance of these previously neglected factors and, as such, he could only acknowledge his considerable debt to him. However, Jaurès's appropriation of Marx in the *Histoire socialiste* – doubtless the work in which he refers to the Trier thinker most systematically and positively – dates to a time when the French socialist tribune crossed swords with the Guesdist Marxists and German Social Democrats. These latter each criticised his defence of a policy of alliances with the radical republicans. Here, there was a clear difference between, on the one hand, the 'official' Marxism of the SPD and of Guesde's supporters and, on the other, Jaurès own freer reference to Marx's work: he criticised the Marxists while accepting Marx. In other words, to draw strong inspiration from Marx did not necessarily imply siding politically with the dominant strand of Marxism.[7]

2   Revisionism and Heterodoxy

The example of Jaurès is illustrative of the French socialists' ambiguous relationship with Marx: his work was surely impossible to overlook, but many

---

6   Rebérioux 1977.
7   Candar and Duclert 2014.

integrated the author of the *Manifesto* and *Capital* into a larger whole, drawing their reference points from a republicanism of older vintage that, at least initially, owed nothing to Marx. During the 'revisionism' dispute, several intellectuals directed vigorous critiques against the founder of 'scientific socialism'. In 1899, Eduard Bernstein, one of the executors of Engels's will (upon his death four years earlier), compiled a series of articles in a volume first known, in its French version, as *Socialisme théorique et Socialisme pratique* and later as *Les Présupposés du socialisme* (in English, similarly, *The Preconditions of Socialism*). Bernstein summed up his approach to social-democratic politics in a phrase that would go down in history: 'Let it dare to appear what it is'. In other words, the labour movement should stop advocating an insurrectionary overthrow as if the situation had not changed since the glorious uprisings of 1789–1793 and 1848. In the 1890s, a form of parliamentary democracy asserted itself and workers experienced a relative improvement in their living standards; for Bernstein, the SPD should influence the political situation by supporting reforms whenever they moved in the right direction. What was to become known as 'reformism' provoked a lively debate within German social democracy, but also within all European socialist currents, which were compelled to take a position faced with this quarrel affecting 'the parent firm'.

In France, the theory immediately came up against a practical question: the problem of governmental participation. In 1899, amidst the Dreyfus affair, for the first time a socialist minister (Alexandre Millerand) took part in a broad unity government: many republicans and socialists such as Jaurès feared the overthrow of the Republic by the far right, and thus swung behind this union. The Guesdists radically rejected this alliance, thus thwarting a bid to unite France's socialists. In this context, Albert Thomas, who can be considered a founding father of reformism, was one figure to take positions highly critical of Marxism.[8]

Given that this debate concerned several of Marx's texts, it is no coincidence that there was a flurry of translations in France: the letter on the Gotha Programme, later known as the *Critique of the Gotha Programme*, was published, as well as Volumes II and III of *Capital*. However, to find a serious discussion of Marx's texts and books, we would have to look beyond the political organisations strictly speaking. Indeed, within the space of what has historically been termed as the 'workers' movement', a few journals and individuals contributed, at a completely different level from the Guesdists – who were mainly interested in reaffirming the validity of their propaganda – to introducing and challenging

---

8   Jousse 2017.

some of Marx's theses. *La Revue socialiste* (with Hubert Lagardelle a driving force) and *Le Mouvement socialiste* were much more the sites of this confrontation than the Guesdists' own press organs.

In this respect, one figure deserves particular attention: Georges Sorel (1847–1922). An alumnus of the École Polytechnique who worked as a civil engineer for the French state, Sorel resigned from his post at the age of forty-five and took a close interest in the evolution of the socialist movement. He frequented the Étudiants socialistes révolutionnaires internationalistes (ESRI), who from 1891 onwards discussed often still-unknown Marx texts. Sorel had an ambiguous relationship with Marx's thought, which he sometimes criticised in the sharpest tones. Susceptible to Proudhonian theories and an admirer of the revolutionary syndicalism influenced by them – himself becoming one of its main theorists – Sorel initially approved of Bernstein's theses against the Marxism of the SPD majority, which he considered narrow and rigid. But, committed to radical social upheaval – which he deemed possible thanks to the mobilising force of the general strike, which he saw as a 'myth' providing a call to arms – Sorel finally sided with a certain revolutionary radicalism. From this point of view, Sorel insisted that, so long as it renounced its scientistic and dogmatic perspective, 'Marxist theory is the idiom in which the proletariat has been able and will still be able to express its great refusal'.[9] Sorel's reading of Marx is illustrative of a particular relationship to his texts: since Sorel did not read German, he acquainted himself with certain texts not translated or not widely disseminated in French through the intermediary of Italian, thus showing how closely interwoven theoretical issues were with practical problems of translation and publishing.

Marx's theory of value, according to which the worker is not properly remunerated by the capitalist who steals part of his labour, was particularly challenged by the heterodox socialists. Charles Andler – a talented Germanist, who introduced Nietzsche to France and was also behind a new edition and translation of the *Communist Manifesto* – is an interesting case in point. After reading *Capital* and meeting Engels in 1891, Andler became increasingly critical of Marx's work. Although he had no influence in party organisations, he was an important actor in the debate on Marx's theses. In addition to points of confusion in his elaboration of the theory of value, the German thinker was said to have ignored two major elements of social organisation: the specificity of law and the question of morality. This thus echoed the disputes over the Dreyfus affair. Andler's commentary on the *Manifesto*, published in 1901, is cutting

---

9   Prochasson 2004.

in the extreme: angry at the Marxists of his time Andler sought to deny the unique importance of Marx's work by showing that his *Manifesto*, co-written with Engels, was merely a compilation of French socialist texts from the first half of the nineteenth century. From Auguste Blanqui to Constantin Pecqueur, from Saint-Amand Bazard to Pierre-Joseph Proudhon, it had all been done before. If Andler, carried away by his polemical tone, minimises the specificities of Marx and Engels, he did have the merit of highlighting one of the central issues of the use of Marx as a reference point in France: namely, that ultimately his reception was inseparable from the 'French' genesis of his thought.

It should be emphasised that the theoretical critiques levelled against Marx were in truth aimed at the real avatars of Marxism at the time, mainly meaning the Guesdists and German Social Democracy. Many of the criticisms of Marx were in fact directed against the simplifications and/or interpretations of those who claimed to be his heirs. This was the beginning of a long story: it is difficult to untangle relations with Marx from the Marxisms of each period. The opponents of these Marxisms have long oscillated between two attitudes. Some, with varying degrees of rigour and good faith, lump in Marx with the militants and/or theorists who claim to be Marxists, in order to reject the whole thing; conversely, others conduct a 'return to Marx' in order to detach him from his exegetes and disciples. From this point of view, even beyond its interest in terms of understanding the socialism of this period, the revisionist moment had an inaugural character: for these two attitudes could also be seen on numerous occasions throughout the twentieth century.

3   1905, a Marxist Compromise?

Officially, there was no doubt who had won the debate. Condemned in Germany in 1903, revisionism was apparently largely defeated. So, did this mean the triumph of Marx? It doubtless marked the victory of a certain kind of Marxism; but behind the radical ideology were concealed some less easily avowed practices. This meant that, while in theory the SPD was officially still a revolutionary party, in practice it was reluctant to prepare the slightest uprising or confrontation. Its 'revolutionary wait-and-see attitude'[10] made its relationship to Marx much more ambiguous than it wanted to admit: the Social-Democrats awaited the revolution, but without overly believing in it or preparing it. In this

---

10   Groh 1973.

context, in France, there was a strong aspiration to unity. In 1904, in Amsterdam, the congress of the Socialist International urged the French socialists to unite in a single organisation. With this impetus, and also thanks to pressure from below, a unified Socialist Party was finally founded.

What, then, was the nature of this SFIO (the unified Socialist Party)? Could the new party be described as 'Marxist'? The influence of Guesde and Vaillant was clear. The Socialist Party was defined as 'a class party ... while pursuing the realisation of the immediate reforms demanded by the working class, [it] is not a party of reform, but a party of class struggle and revolution'. On paper, it was largely Guesde who had won out against Jaurès. But what we have emphasised with regard to the SPD can also be applied, mutatis mutandis, to the French socialists: that is, there was the theory and the congress texts... and then there was the daily political practice. One of the major issues facing the new party was the question of its relationship with the rest of the Republican left. For example, when parliamentary elections headed to second round run-offs, those close to Guesde would always stress the 'class interest' in defeating conservatives, a vocabulary which differed from the republican discipline of the likes of Jaurès. But, if the ideological basis of the two positions was not the same, in practice it became increasingly common for advanced republicans and socialists to withdraw in each other's favour. Here again, the republican tradition still weighed with full force the new party, even if Marxist rhetoric remained paramount.[11]

But for all that, should we see the consolidation of a systematic alliance with the republicans as a betrayal of Marx's heritage? For many Marxists, notably for German theorists such as Karl Kautsky and SPD chairman August Bebel – and they crossed swords with Jaurès on this point – there could be no doubt that too much integration into the Republic was something suspicious, even dangerous, an analysis relayed in France by the Guesdists. The scathing remarks in the *Eighteenth Brumaire* and in many of Marx's other texts on France show how suspicious he was of republican unanimity and the 'great memories' of the Republic among the French. Yet, Marx, too, was confronted with questions of alliance policy, in 1848 and then within the First International. He did not himself witness the consolidation of the Third Republic, but it is difficult to imagine that he would not have been attentive to the specific roots that republicanism had sunk in France. Moreover, his faithful comrade in arms, Engels, who died twelve years after him in 1895, was both annoyed by these French peculiarities and keenly aware of how politically audacious certain republicans could be –

11   Bergounioux and Grunberg 1992.

even to the point that for a time Engels hoped that Clemenceau would rally to the socialist cause.

For practical purposes, it was difficult to set Marxism and republicanism in harmony. It would take the dexterity and the political genius of a Jaurès to create an original synthesis from these different elements. This would in turn enable him, from the Toulouse Congress of 1908 onwards, to establish his status as the main representative of French socialism. This socialism was thus above all republican, but also tinged with Marxism and various legacies of the utopias of the nineteenth century. Marx was both highly present within this socialism and relatively peripheral to it.

This is well illustrated by the reception of works building on Marx's own. Even if we look beyond strictly political matters, was his thought the subject of a theoretical debate? As far as publishing was concerned, structural weaknesses persisted, despite the efforts of certain editors. Hence, Jean Longuet – Marx's grandson and a member of the SFIO leadership – tried to initiate a French-language selection of his grandfather's works: the proposal was approved by the SFIO congress, but never saw the light of day. This would suggest that the interest in such an undertaking was only relative.[12] Between 1905 and 1914, Marx was often claimed as a reference point and his works were frequently cited. Yet no major debate on his fundamental theses really emerged within the SFIO, despite the commemorations, for instance, of the ninetieth anniversary of the German writer's birth in 1908. The journal of Guesde's allies, *Le Socialisme*, published numerous texts in homage to Marx, written by various figures from the left wing of the international socialist movement (including Rosa Luxemburg). Yet we can only be struck by the weak reception of Marxist works published in German – a weakness that cannot simply be explained by the lack of French translations (after all, figures like Jaurès did have a command of German). The reasons for this aversion to theoretical debate in the French workers' movement deserve further explanation (and this would have to include, among other things, the weight of Germanophobia and a certain anti-intellectualist workerism). Here, we shall merely note the weak echo of the major contributions analysing the mutations of capitalism at the time: Rudolf Hilferding's work on *Finance Capital* (1910) and Rosa Luxemburg's *The Accumulation of Capital* (1913) hardly received any attention, apart from a few sporadic references.

What can we conclude from this? The Marx of the pre-1914 socialists remained closely bound up with politics, and ultimately counted for little as an economist. For many militants he was less a theoretical resource from which to

---

12   Candar 2007.

draw cues for reflection than a 'mobilising myth' (to use Sorel's expression). For them, Marx was a point of identification, attaching them to a global perception of the social world in terms of class struggles.

4   1914: Marx Defeated?

The outbreak of World War I sounded the death-knell for the pacifist and internationalist hopes which had been raised by the socialist movement in the 1880s. At the Brest Congress of the SFIO in 1913, Édouard Vaillant still thundered that 'There is no socialist party with whom we march in greater union than the German socialist party'. However, a year later, on 4 August 1914, a few days after the assassination of Jean Jaurès, the SFIO's MPs rallied to the 'Union sacrée' and voted for war credits. Their German comrades did the same. The formula of Marx and Engels's *Communist Manifesto*, 'Proletarians of all countries, unite', proudly upheld by the Socialist congresses, had fizzled out: instead, it was the reflex in favour of patriotic defence that prevailed. For a man like Vaillant, the memory of the defence of France's borders in 1870–1 was still very much alive – not least since, in formal terms, Germany was the aggressor country. If Germany was the country of Marx and of social democracy, it was also – perhaps above all – the country of the Hohenzollern Empire. For many French socialists, even an imperfect and bourgeois Republic was preferable to a dynastic empire. Jules Guesde, the embodiment of a certain socialist radicalism, and a figure with a strong Marxist legitimacy, had no hesitation in taking sides in this counterposition between (French) republic and (German) autocracy. In late August 1914 he even became a minister; he had no particular function, but was included precisely to show a broad array of forces had rallied to France. The references to the French Revolution or to the glorious victory at Valmy, mobilised by official war propaganda, were no shock to the socialists, at least in the first months of the conflict. If the tradition of the French Revolution was fundamentally linked to the class struggle, it here served the definition of a French socialism whose national specificities were emphasised with ardour.

Did this mean Marx's posthumous defeat? Without doubt, it marked the temporary collapse of a certain idea of internationalism that had emerged with him and a few others in the mid-nineteenth century. The prevalent Germanophobia did not meaningfully spare socialist ranks. Albert Mathiez, a brilliant historian of the French Revolution with deep-seated socialist convictions, did not hesitate to assert, at the beginning of 1917, a radical opposition between the heritage of the French Revolution and the Prussian spirit:

The revolutionary tradition suffered an eclipse in France .... These so-called scientific socialists .... no longer knew the French Revolution, that incomparable source of examples and heroism, except through the abstruse books of the Prussian Karl Marx. Seeing as Marx had pronounced, from the height of his Germanic disdain, that the French Revolution was only a meagre, bourgeois affair, his docile pupils repeated this enormous nonsense.

Just a few weeks after these lines were published, the Russian Revolution began. This revolution was to change the course of world history, and it did so in the name of Marx and a completely rethought Marxism. In 1918, World War I came to an end. One hundred years after Marx's birth, and seventy years after the Spring of Nations of 1848, a revolutionary wave swept in from Moscow – and it was one that ardently identified with him. Soon in France, as in many other countries, the irreparable split between Communists and those who 'remained' Socialists had become apparent. A new period began for Marx's destiny in France: a period that would be difficult to understand without bearing in mind the conflicts within the early-twentieth-century socialist movement, which we have here briefly outlined.

CHAPTER 2

The Socialists' Marx: The Centenary of Marx's Birth, A Challenge for the SFIO

Raymond Huard

Karl Marx was born on 5 May 1818. In 1918, at a crucial moment of the war, could the Parti Socialiste commemorate the first centenary of the great German thinker's birth – and how? This was a question that cut through the Parti Socialiste: it answered its first part in the affirmative, though not without hesitation, and ultimately it opted for a rather modest celebration. However, the announcement that it would commemorate the centenary sparked a remarkably wide-ranging polemic across wide swathes of the French press. The primary objective of this offensive was, obviously, to back the Parti Socialiste into a corner. But beyond this tactical manoeuvre, the opponents of the celebration also tried to discredit Karl Marx himself, as a man and as a thinker.

1   An Unfavourable Context

As this centenary loomed, the Socialists faced extremely unfavourable circumstances. They had left the government in November 1917 and were thus the target of attacks from the ruling majority. Spring 1918 also saw the last great German offensive on the Somme, among the war's most deadly. The French nation was stretched in a last effort to cut down the might of the German forces. In this context, the CGT demurred from organising demonstrations to mark May Day. Hence, commemorating the birth of Marx – doubtless a great German thinker and internationalist socialist – in such a moment could appear at least inopportune and at worst as a kind of provocation, offending national sentiment.

The Socialists who supported this initiative included members of the SFIO minority hostile to the war, such as Jean Longuet – grandson of Karl Marx, deputy for the Seine since May 1914, a member of the party's Permanent Administrative Commission (CAP), and political director of the *Populaire de Paris* (which had become a daily on 10 April 1918); Paul Faure (originally from the Dordogne, editor-in-chief of this same newspaper); and Amédée Dunois, a journalist at *l'Humanité*. Yet supporters of the commemoration also included two important members of the pro-war SFIO majority, each belonging to the

Guesdist tradition: Alexandre Bracke, deputy for the Seine, and Jean Lebas, mayor of Roubaix, who were also both members of the party leadership. The centenary could also retrospectively make up for the missed commemoration of the fiftieth anniversary of the First International, which would have taken place in September 1914 had it not been for the outbreak of the war. In February 1918, a conference in London had brought together representatives of the socialist parties from Allied countries and seemed to herald the International's rebirth.

On 25 April 1918, *l'Humanité* reported the proceedings of the Permanent Administrative Commission of 23 April, including the following information: 'The Party's sections are ... invited to commemorate the first centenary of the birth of Karl Marx on 5 May. A declaration, the drafting of which is entrusted to Bracke and Longuet, will be published.'

This anodyne news prompted a gradually growing outcry in the press. On 27 April, a first series of articles protested against the announced decision. Once the Socialists' decision had been confirmed on 2 May, a second series of articles commented on it again. Further coverage from 5 May onwards mocked the 'failure' of the centenary. The main Paris newspapers took part in this campaign: *Le Temps*, *Le Figaro*, *L'Action française*, *La Croix*, *La Liberté*, *L'Écho de Paris*, *Le Journal des débats*, *La Victoire*, *L'Œuvre* and *La Lanterne*. Only *L'Humanité* and *Le Populaire* defended the principle of the commemoration, while *La Petite République*, at least initially, adopted a somewhat reticent position.

2   A Clutch of Hostile Arguments

If the words 'scandal', 'provocation', 'affrontery', 'madness', 'folly', 'indecency', and 'political error' – terms used widely on this occasion – were intended above all to arouse indignation, the arguments advanced by the opponents of the commemoration were much more varied. They were based on a few core themes: the accusation of pan-Germanism, the denunciation of Marx for hijacking French socialism, the questioning of what they termed the Marxist 'religion' and finally the stigmatisation of a commemoration that was alien to true working-class feelings. The accusation of pan-Germanism was exploited most. This old accusation had been renewed and spread before 1918 by two authors: the anarchist James Guillaume and the socialist dissident Edmond Laskine. In 1915, James Guillaume – a former member of the First International and Bakunin's lieutenant – had published *Karl Marx pangermaniste et l'Association internationale des travailleurs de 1864 à 1870* ('Karl Marx, the Pan-

Germanist and the International Workingmen's Association from 1864 to 1870'), a book which accused Marx and Engels of having betrayed the International from the outset in favour of German social democracy, the accomplice of Bismarck. A disciple of his, Edmond Laskine – a former pupil of the École Normale Supérieure who had passed through socialist ranks before the war – subsequently published several works highly critical of Marx and the socialists, including *L'Internationale et le Pangermanisme* in 1916.

If Marx's public stances were, taken as a whole, unambiguous, it was not impossible to find more questionable or more easily spun remarks in the correspondence which he exchanged with Engels or other Germans (such as Friedrich Sorge or Ludwig Kugelmann). Sometimes highly spontaneous, such comments could attest to a certain national pride, or even a contemptuous cynicism towards the French. This corpus of texts compiled by James Guillaume and completed by Laskine was tirelessly taken up by an adversarial press. It essentially contained five statements by Marx, taken from his correspondence recently published in Germany or from public statements of his, and quoted in many hostile articles.

The first was a letter from Marx to Kugelmann of 9 October 1866, about the Geneva congress, in which Marx sharply criticised the Proudhonians ('Proudhon has done enormous harm') and the 'ignorant, vain, gossipy, puffed-up French workers' delegates'.[1] The second was a short extract from a letter from Marx to Engels of 2 November 1867, at the time of the Luxembourg affairs, in which he had written: 'One good thing about our Bismarck is that he pushes things in France toward crisis.' The third, which was more explicit, was dated 20 July 1870: the day after France declared war on Prussia, Marx, reacting to an ultra-patriotic manifesto by the journalist Charles Delescluze, wrote to Engels that 'the French need to be thrashed' and he foresaw that Prussia's victory would 'moreover shift the centre of gravity of the West European workers' movement by transferring it from France to Germany', thus ensuring 'the supremacy of our theory over that of Proudhon'. Two other statements were also incriminated: an address of 23 July 1870 in the name of the General Council of the First International in which Marx specified that, 'on the German side, the war is a war of defence', and a piece of advice to the French workers on 9 September 1870, in the Second Address of the General Council: 'The French workers must not allow themselves to be carried away by the national memories of 1792' – a sentence which could be interpreted as incitement to desert the national defence. It was easy to conclude from these quotations – often

---

1 Guillaume 1905.

isolated from their context and cited with a certain spin – that Marx was a pan-Germanist, forgetting the equally sharp criticisms that he had levelled against Germany's rulers and their ideologues.

Le Temps opened fire on 28 April 1918 with an article entitled 'Karl Marx and France'. According to this daily, Karl Marx was 'the type of the pan-Germanist socialist, the initiator and educator of those *sozial-demokrats* who in 1914 betrayed the cause of right and freedom and who today ... persist in their felony'. *Le Temps* thus urged the French socialists to 'recover the generous strength of national feeling'. The attack on the socialists was even more virulent in the article entitled 'A scandalous centenary', published by E. Laskine in *La Liberté* on 29 April 1918; it saw in Marx 'the implacable sectator and constant auxiliary of German imperialism'. Drawing on the same stock-in-trade, *L'Action française* of 27 April pointed to 'the double favour which the Jewish doctrinaire showed toward German preponderance in Europe and to the centralisation of the powers of the German state'; the following day, Charles Maurras preferred to emphasise the more general dangers of 'Germanism', which could result 'in an immense barbarism'.

Karl Marx's supposed Germanism or pan-Germanism was not, however, the only angle of attack used by hostile press. Graver still, for Gustave Hervé – writing in his *La Victoire du 1er mai* – was the fact that Marx had turned French socialism away from its tradition of alliance with the bourgeoisie as represented by Saint-Simon, Fourier, Louis Blanc, Blanqui, and Proudhon; this latter especially was considered to be the very embodiment of French socialism, no doubt because of Marx's critiques of him. For want of such an alliance, Hervé insisted, France and indeed Germany and Russia condemned their countries to stagnation or disaster. Maurice Allard, another socialist who rallied to the Union sacrée, developed these ideas at greater length in two articles in *La Lanterne* (on 30 April and 3 May 1918): it was France which 'gave socialism to the world' with thinkers like Saint-Simon and Fourier, to whom Allard, with a certain erudition, added not only Proudhon but Considérant, Pecqueur, Louis Blanc and a few even lesser-known figures. A similar angle of attack was used not long afterward by Victor Augagneur writing in *La Petite République*: 'French socialism, flexible, ready for all adaptations, is a thousand times superior to Marxism' (*La Petite République*, 7 May). Maurice Allard, ardent in his anti-clericalism, added another more personal theme, holding that Marxism had become a new religion, and its works 'a sacred Bible that the common man does not read' (*La Lanterne*, 30 April).

Finally, on a slightly more trivial note, on May Day, *La Croix* tried to separate the socialists from their working-class base: 'The idea of celebrating the centenary of Karl Marx in France is not a thought in the minds of French workers.

It is the unified bourgeois like Sembat and Longuet who are trying in vain to make a home for it here'.

Did this campaign have an echo in the country? The right-wing press insisted that it did, pointing to a few protests, such as those by the Michelet Committee, in the name of the French teaching profession; by the Union of fathers and mothers whose sons had died for the fatherland (*La Croix*, 2 May); by 39 associations of various tendencies (*Le Journal des Débats*, 3 May); by Commandant Pilate, mayor of Sceaux, where Jean Longuet was an M P; and finally, those by the mayors of Alsace-Lorraine and by the Radical Party's federation in the Rhône region (*La Croix*, 5 May).

3   Shaken, the Socialists Hold Firm

It was faced with this 'frenzied outpouring of attacks and outrages', as Jean Longuet described it (*Le Populaire*, 30 April), that the Socialist CAP met on 29 April. Without abandoning the idea of the centenary celebrations altogether, it limited its initiatives to holding meetings on this subject in the local party sections. The reservations of certain members of the CAP, in particular Pierre Renaudel ('Let's not wound national feelings', he was quoted as saying) and Marcel Sembat, bore their effect on this decision. The final text on the commemoration of Marx was published by *L'Humanité* on 2 May. It did not respond to all the attacks, but rather concentrated on three points. Firstly, it insisted that 'even the hatreds built up by the war' did not forbid 'a large-scale commemoration'. It recalled all that Marx owed to French thought, 'a debt he always recognised'. It then quickly summarised the main achievements of Marx's thought; the theory of value, establishing the illegitimacy of individual ownership of the means of production and exchange; the need for proletarians to conquer political power with a class-based political party – a conquest which would guarantee an international existence which would cast aside the seeds of war between nations. Finally, a third part responded more specifically to the accusation of pan-Germanism by recalling that Marx had taken internationalist positions in favour of multiple oppressed nationalities around Europe, and had alerted the German working class against its government's aggressiveness and annexationist pretensions.

In the end, there was to be no central rally in Paris, and 5 May was celebrated mainly by *Le Populaire* and *L'Humanité* – albeit in slightly different ways.

The centenary issue of *L'Humanité* on 5 May consisted of three parts. A long article by Bracke justified the celebration of the anniversary, firstly in terms of the desire to show the peoples of Europe that the International was still alive. It was also necessary to remind the French 'how much the "German" Marx belongs to them, not only because of what is "French" in the origins of his thought, but also because of the place he has taken in the name of the International whenever France has found itself representing the cause of humanity'. This led Bracke to his retort to the somewhat embarrassing quotations highlighted by Laskine and reproduced by *Le Temps*, whose reality he here admitted. For the *L'Humanité* contributor, these quotations 'prove at most that Marx often found fault with the actions of certain Frenchmen ... It is very true .... that he often affected "cynicism" in his private remarks.' In support of Bracke's argument, the second *L'Humanité* article, 'Marx and the War of 1870', used the International's declarations during the war of 1870–1 to re-establish the facts as to the position that International and thus Marx himself had taken with regard to Germany. Finally, the last article was devoted to Marx's theory of value. Here it was Jaurès who was called on in support of Marx, using an extract from *L'Armée nouvelle* where the Tarn MP wrote: 'I believe that Marx's theory of value withstands all critique when it is understood in its true sense'.

Le Populaire, directed by Jean Longuet, handed yet greater importance to this event announcing, already on 1 May, a special centenary issue which was to be widely distributed. In the 5 May issue, bearing the full-page headline 'The centenary of Karl Marx', the main article 'Return to Marx' was entrusted to Amédée Dunois. He explained that Marx's thought had 'supplanted all the socialist doctrines which had preceded it, not only in France, but in England and Germany' simply because of its 'obvious scientific superiority', by its 'method of action' – for Dunois, encapsulated in the class struggle – and the fact that it had 'united the ideal of socialism and the class action of the workers'. Marxism was thus not 'Germanic' but 'international' and universal.

The rest of the issue contained a dozen or so miscellaneous contributions designed to refute the claims of Laskine and *Le Temps* as to Marx's positions in 1870 and regarding nationalities. Marx could not be held responsible for the failures and deviations of German social democracy. Finally, *To the "Master"*, a poem by CAP member Raoul Verfeuil, hailed him as a 'Great European', and a 'Citizen of the World'.

While *L'Humanité* and *Le Populaire* thus made substantial tributes to Marx, the response from ordinary activists seems to have been rather meagre. *L'Humanité* mentioned only one meeting, held by Bracke in the 14th arrondissement of Paris (*L'Humanité*, 3 May) and a motion of support for Longuet from the Union of Socialist Sections of Sceaux, where he was an MP (*L'Humanité*, 1 May). The manifesto of 2 May and the anniversary itself provoked a fresh wave of reactions from the right-wing and even the left-wing press, who preferred to more or less charitably mock the Socialists' 'retreat'. 'The celebration of Karl Marx's centenary,' said the *Journal des Débats* on 2 May, 'will be limited to a few vague branch meetings where the *common thought of the proletariat will* be commented upon privately'. In *Le Figaro* of 6 May, E. Grosclaude noted that 'the anniversary of the birth of Marxism has taken on the air of a burial'. Longuet's 'Grandpérialisme' was especially emphasised.[2] A cartoon in *La Victoire* of 5 May showed a civilian wearing a spiked helmet at the door of the socialist church of St Karl Marx and remarking, 'Mein Gott ... Nobody, not even the verger'. But if the authors of these articles or cartoons had no lack of wry tone, they also drove home the message that the centenary organised by reckless or perverse Socialists was truly a scandal.

4   The Académiciens Enter the Scene

New, often more subtle arguments were advanced, with new and more notable participants joining the debate – in particular two members of the Académie française (académiciens), Alfred Capus and Maurice Barrès. Alfred Capus wanted above all to see in the centenary celebrations a 'challenge to the thesis of fighting to the last'. He associated this with the Socialists' travestying of the figure of Marx, who was presented as 'sentimental and a friend of France' even though he would have 'ardently wished for Germany's victory' (*Le Figaro*, 5 May). Others sought more fundamental explanations. Pertinax (André Géraud), writing in *L'Écho de Paris* of 5 May, saw the success of Marxism as an effect of the prestige enjoyed in France by German philosophy, for instance that of Hegel and Schopenhauer, which insisted on inexorable laws of development, easing the path for the acceptance of the idea of 'integral socialist change'.

The highlight of the polemic, however, was provided by Maurice Barrès. He belatedly intervened in the debate with four major articles in *L'Echo de Paris* (7, 8, 9 and 11 May) published under the title 'Why the commemoration of Karl Marx failed'. He took up some of the themes mentioned above, even exalting the traditions of French socialism (indeed, in lyrical tones, a source of some amusement, coming from this man's pen). However, Barrès also tried to turn the debate to the very heart of the Marxism the Socialists defended, i.e. to *Capital*; he termed it 'this old book we don't read any more', though he could admit that it was sometimes 'erudite' and 'interesting' (8 May). But he disputed the theory of value and surplus value: 'Value is a judgment, and nothing else' (8 May). With the same assurance, he denied that the class struggle – an inven-

---

2   I.e. a compound of the words 'grandfather' and 'imperialism'.

tion, moreover, not of Marx, but of Saint-Simon and English trade-unionism – still had any relevance. For Barrès, 'Classes do exist, as an inheritance of the past, but under democracy they are dissolving. By this point, they mainly owe to differences in education' (8 May). Finally, he placed Marxism's adherence to pan-Germanism on a more historical and philosophical terrain. Haunted by the *imperium romanum* and then the *imperium germanicum*, the German social-ists envisaged universal revolution 'on the basis of the Roman Empire, estab-lished by arms and making possible the expansion of Christendom' through a kind of 'unity of opposites, à la Hegel'. For them, Barrès insisted, Germany was today the country best able to play the role of the Roman nation of old. Marxism thus found 'what is deepest in the psychology of its race'. But was it necessary to turn France into 'a province of an immense proletarian Ger-mania'?

5   A Half-Hearted Centenary

The first centenary of Karl Marx's birth was thus the source of a lively polemic that drew on a wide array of arguments. The socialists embarked on this adven-ture with a certain degree of courage despite the very difficult conjuncture they faced; overcoming their divisions, they succeeded in putting up a more or less united front. However, having already left the cabinet, they offered the govern-ment republicans, the right and the far right an opportunity to attack, and these latter took the opportunity, with the precious aid of defectors from socialist ranks such as Laskine, Hervé and Allard.

The Socialists' opponents used two tactics, either separately or in combin-ation. One targeted Karl Marx himself, described as an unoriginal, jingoist and pan-Germanist mind, a pure product of the 'Boches' and their culture. The other attacked the fundamental theses of Marxism, incompatible with the spirit of a truly French socialism. Paradoxically, while opponents of the com-memorations loudly denounced the failure of the centenary, the intensity of their reactions and the multiplicity of articles published at least gave it a certain visibility. In a book published a few months later, *La Politique internationale du marxisme* ('Marxism's International Policy'), Longuet replied point by point to the accusations levelled against his grandfather, though he also admitted that some of Marx's remarks could be 'very harsh' or take on a 'rough and familiar form'.[3]

---

3   Longuet 1918.

Doubtless, all eyes were fixed on the front, where a fierce battle was being waged; hence the debate does not seem to have affected public opinion in any great depth. But the vigour of the attacks on the Socialists reinforced them in the choice which they had just made to leave the government majority and seek new paths to peace. In this sense, the battle over the Socialists' use of Marx as a reference point was indicative of their relationship to the political conjuncture.

CHAPTER 3

The Socialists' Marx: The Blum Era

Thierry Hohl

'Without Marx as a constant reference, the Socialists would have become what each tendency wanted to make of them – meaning, in the political context of 1921, that without Marx, the French socialists would have been nothing at all. Following a disastrous split, this danger was far too real for it to be possible to abandon Marx'.[1]

This quote from Tony Judt well illustrates what Karl Marx was for the Socialists after the split with the Communists: an indispensable *viaticum* for retaining their ties to the past. Faced with Communist competition, keeping their moorings in this recent past was a necessity for the Socialists.

Seventeen years later, the Parti Socialiste, still known as the French Section of the Workers' International (SFIO), fractured over the Munich Agreement in 1938, before then dividing faced with the Nazi danger at the Nantes Congress of 1939. This chronological sequence was marked by the impact of the war and the divergence between pacifism and anti-fascism. But there were also other divisions, concerning the Socialists' relationship to governmental power, which some saw as a mere trap under a capitalist system and others saw as a necessary evil for the gradual move towards socialism. This set of polemics made French Socialism an arena of violent disputes, whether at party congresses, in the columns of Socialist daily *Le Populaire* or in the various tendencies' own reviews.

In this hubbub of speeches, articles and rebuttals, the reference to Marx remained central: it served to delimit what was legitimate in the party and in the parliamentary Republic. In this sense, examining the SFIO's Marxism in the 1920s and 1930s is less a matter of measuring its doctrinal adequacy, or the innovations and interpretations to which it subjected it, than of seeing how Marx functioned as an identity-marker within the workers' movement and the Left. The SFIO continually insisted that it was the Marxist centre of the workers' movement; this claim concealed many internal differences, both at the strategic and tactical levels, but it was also reflected in the training of party militants, which sought to transform the individual member into a conscious Marxist.

---

1 Judt 1976.

1   A Marxist Centre for the Workers' Movement?

The birth of the French Communist Party marked the beginning of a quarrel over the heritage of French socialism, between the new formation and the SFIO, which Léon Blum termed 'the old house' (*la vieille maison*). At the same time, many debated Marxism's capacity to analyse French society, which was deeply transformed during the interwar period.

1.1   *Debates: A Second(ary) Marxism*

At the Tours Congress in 1920, the speeches by Léon Blum and Marx's grandson Jean Longuet[2] echoed one another in inventing a common past based on Marx and the founding principles set out by the Parti Socialiste created in 1905. Most Socialists signed up to this narrative, which established a certain continuity with the prewar period and provided legitimacy to the minority at Tours even in the face of the Communist majority. Somewhat paradoxically, Marxism united the Socialists against the disciples of Bolshevism. But in 1921 this initial Marxist identification came up against a strong challenge from certain sectors of the SFIO, reviving the various debates that had developed before 1905. Indeed, under the nascent Third Republic, French socialism had experienced lively polemics between 'reformists'[3] and supporters of what was termed orthodox Marxism, around Jules Guesde.[4] The 1920s and 1930s saw this debate continue in new form, between a claim to the Marxist heritage and the challenge from the 'neo-socialists', who aimed to create a socialism detached from Marxist ideology.

Part of the SFIO remained determined to take part in governing the Republic, in order to implement reforms. In response to this repeated demand from the right wing of the party – soon to be embodied by the 'neosocialists' – the majority evoked Marx to demonstrate the futility of partial reforms and extolled the inevitability of social revolution based on the transformation of property relations. Léon Blum played an essential role, in this regard: his speeches in the Chamber and his articles in *Le Populaire* sought to hold the party close to the synthesis that had been reached in 1905. General secretary Paul Faure saw himself as the heir to the Guesdist Marxist tradition, and stressed the need not to change anything in the party's doctrinal foundations. He expressed this approach in vehement terms in a September 1932 editorial in *La Bataille*

---

2   Candar 2007.

3   Jousse 2017.

4   Ducange 2017.

socialiste, the organ of the socialist left. He emphasised that Jules Guesde 'was right' to found a party based on class struggle:

> Everything in the world cries out, everything screams that Guesde was right – right to the point of opening the eyes of the blindest and making himself heard by the deafest. To have sought, to have succeeded, in making the mass of militants understand, to have armed the workers for their class fight, to have willed that doctrine should escape the narrow circles of initiates and set them into life and action – this is something great, moving and fruitful, especially now that it has been more than demonstrated that the fate of the working class and of civilisation depends on the triumph of this doctrine.

Sometimes, a figure on the right wing of the party would lay claim to the Marxist tradition in order to justify this or that point of his programme. For instance, Pierre Renaudel evoked Kautsky to demonstrate the need for a coalition government combining Radicals and Socialists. But the – formal and purely tactical – reference to Marxists was increasingly neglected by the Socialist right, as the project of revising the tradition itself instead gained momentum. The indictment of Marxism, deemed incapable of understanding social and economic developments, was conducted on the basis of the writings of Henri de Man, a Belgian ex-Marxist who became a fervent defender of an idealist and plannerist socialism. His theses found an echo in France, notably among some socialist intellectuals gathered in a small group, 'Révolution constructive', and within the right wing of the party. One of its leaders, Marcel Déat, established a link between the French tradition and plannerist ideas in order to propose a different path for French Socialism than the one on which it had set out in 1905. Faced with this, the party majority – from Léon Blum to the left wing – mobilised Marxism to deny the innovative character of Henri De Man's ideas, which were presented as a simple rehash of pre-1914 revisionist theses. The departure of the pro-Déat 'neosocialists' in autumn 1933 brought this new revisionism dispute to a close. From that point, Marx seemed to fade into the background: the debates focused on anti-fascism and the 'exercise of power', to use the expression of Léon Blum, who became head of government in 1936.

In the 1930s debates among the Socialists, Marxism was certainly mobilised as an argument, but it remained secondary and never decisive. The exclusion of the neosocialists was justified in terms of their failure to comply with parliamentary discipline, rather than their growing detachment from Marxist doctrine. In the period of the Popular Front, Léon Blum's government based its activity on a social and political 'reformism' which drew on the experience of the World War I-era government, on the proposals of the International Labour Office, and on proposals from the camp of reforms, rather than on a strict Marxism. As for anti-fascism, it owed little to Marxism and, from 1935 onwards, above all reactivated republican energies centred on the nation.

1.2   *Against the Bolshevik Heresy*

The fight against communism did also involve an assertion of the SFIO's Marxism, as against Bolshevik 'heresy'. The Socialists denied the Communists the right to proclaim themselves Marxists, given how alien their practices seemed to pre-1914 socialism. Within this perspective there was a constant critique of the USSR, in particular from the moment when the Russian revolution was no longer threatened from abroad. Denying the USSR its status as a socialist country, presenting it as a land that had not reached the necessary stage for the realisation of the social revolution, and denouncing the oppression of the working class in Russia, the SFIO mounted a permanent rejection of the Soviet model. This opposition resulted in a discourse that denounced the totally anti-Marxist character of the Soviet Union – and therefore of the PCF. If the Communist Party and the International to which it belonged mounted a trial against the Socialists' Marxist legitimacy, these latter responded by evoking Russian Marxists like Georgi Plekhanov, but also others like the Menshevik Fyodor Dan, whose pamphlets denying that the USSR had any socialist character the SFIO published. Following this logic, one of the leaders of the left of the party, Jean Zyromski, produced a definition of communism, representative of the Socialists' feelings. In the August 1928 he wrote in *La Bataille socialiste* that 'Bolshevism here reveals its essential vice: an outdated neo-Blanquism, a puerile internationalism which manifests itself in the most complete disregard of material, moral and psychological conditions.'

The 'neo-Blanquism' denounced by Zyromski refers to a pre-Marxist conception, to a romantic insurrectionism, condemned by Marx himself. The appeal to authoritative figures in the pre-1914 International such as Karl Kautsky (his record distinguished by the fight against Bernsteinian revisionism and the rejection of the Burgfrieden in Germany during World War I), provided a guarantee of his Marxist credentials. This refusal to grant Marxist legitimacy to Soviet communism had, as its corollary, an interest in alternative models of Marxism abroad. For instance, for a time French Socialists turned toward Austria, under the sway of an 'Austro-Marxism' that was noted both for its electoral successes and the audacity of rigorous thinkers such as Max Adler and Otto Bauer. During the commemoration of the 109th anniversary of Karl Marx's birth, Paul Faure thus paid tribute to Austrian social democracy, whose successes, he said, owed to the 'Marxist propaganda of its leaders'; he ended his speech calling for a round of applause for Bauer and Adler (*Le Populaire*, 6 May 1927). But two events changed this situation. First, Austrian social democracy's inability to hold off Engelbert Dollfuss's coup d'état in February 1934 saw it lose its aura of prestige. Moreover, the turn toward Popular Frontism (from 1934 onwards) led the Socialists to tone down their criticism of the Communists. Only a minority fringe, around Marceau Pivert, still denied that 'Stalinism' had any Marxist character. But with the split/exclusion of Gauche révolutionnaire in 1938, the presence within SFIO ranks of this minority and its critical stance, influenced by the ideas of Rosa Luxemburg, came to an end.

2   The Leaders' Marxism and the Militants' Marxism

However, an understanding of the place of Marx and Marxism in the SFIO cannot stop at following the traces of how Marx was referenced as a marker of identity. For Marxism is also a political culture, whose degree of penetration among the world of French Socialism itself ought to be measured.

What role did Marxism play in drawing individuals toward socialism and a life of Socialist activism? The case of Léon Blum is well known. The many biographies of him[5] foreground his humanist socialism, destined to be fulfilled within the republican framework, and suggest that Marxism was only a façade of ideology used in order to maintain party unity. But can we understand the party's militants through just one man – even if he was the most important of the period – and deduce that for them Marxism was nothing but the mask for respectable republicanism? A pamphlet by Louis Lévy published in 1931, *Comment sont-ils devenus socialistes?* ('How Did They Become Socialists?') allows us to follow how several important cadres arrived at socialism.[6]

2.1   *How Did They Become Socialists?*

In his pamphlet, Lévy relates his interviews with such figures as Paul Faure, Léon Blum, Pierre Renaudel, Bracke (a Guesde-loyalist), Adéodat Compère-Morel (a Guesdist and expert on agricultural issues), Raoul Evrard (the miners' MP), Jean-Baptiste Lebas (a Guesdist and mayor of Roubaix), Arthur Groussier (an intellectual from the Seine Federation), Vincent Auriol (close to Léon Blum), Joseph Paul-Boncour (an independent socialist), Jean Longuet (grandson of Karl Marx), Jean Zyromski (at the head of *La Bataille socialiste*, on the

---

5   Berstein 2006, Monier 2016.

6   Lévy 1931.

left wing of the party), Marcel Déat (MP for the Marne, leader of the right wing of the party along with Pierre Renaudel), and Albert Bedouce (an MP for Toulouse). The list shows the author's concern for representativeness and his desire to respect a balance between Left and Right and between Paris and the provinces. When it comes to these militants' contact with Marxism, a few key themes emerge. First of all, we can observe the generally secondary character of reading Marx in their initial attraction to socialism. For many, it was current events that played the decisive role (in particular the Dreyfus affair); for others, it was reading French socialists (Benoît Malon, Proudhon, Blanqui); for yet others, it was the reading of popular pamphlets (in particular those by Guesde and Lafargue). In short: their initial contact with Marx's oeuvre was rather sparing. Only Bracke reports that his adherence to socialist activism and doctrine was a result of reading *Capital*. But this is an exceptional case, seeing as Bracke, a Germanist, was the SFIO's 'official Marxist' throughout this entire period.

In short, access to Marxism came through intermediaries and above all through pamphlets, in particular those of Gabriel Deville, author of an – at the time widely circulated – compendium of Marx's *Capital*. Marcel Déat is a significant case in point: he explains that he 'knew Marx at that time through Deville and through the flurry of pamphlets. Ah! the pamphlets! We used to buy them in college. I had a whole drawer full of them'. As for how Marx was read, let us listen to Jean Lebas:

> I first read Deville's compendium. Then, around 1895, I managed to get hold of the Roy edition (of Marx's *Capital*). I studied it as follows (I don't know if this is a valuable method, but in any case, here it is): I would first read a chapter by Deville, and then I would go back to the same chapter in the edition of *Capital*. Thanks to this approach, I understood perfectly.

Others, notably Léon Blum, emphasised the non-Marxist character of their intellectual formation. The fact remains that for most of them Marxism did constitute an important element of their culture. In each case (except Bracke), it was acquired by means other than specific study, though in most cases a grasp of Marxism was indeed necessary, justifying their socialist commitment over the long term.

However summary it may appear, this Marxism was not purely circumstantial, summoned up only to safeguard party unity on all occasions. It was, indeed, a choice, made at a time of controversy over the nature of socialism (in which Marxism was only one option among others), and maintained beyond World War I. Among this group of leaders, only few, like Pierre Renaudel or Joseph Paul-Boncour, overtly renounced Marxism.

2.2   *Talks and Educationals: The Socialist militants' Marxism*

These conclusions regarding figures at the top of the party have to be compared with the party 'down below' – its members and militants. Sadly, there are few pieces of testimony allowing us to measure the importance of ideology to these militants' political commitment. For the historian, it is difficult to make up for this absence, but it is at least possible to examine the party's internal training programmes, allowing us to discern the party's doctrinal priorities. Louis Lévy, secretary of the Jeunesses Socialistes (Socialist Youth), published a plan for socialist education in 1928 which is still a valuable source. We can also look at the educational lectures given by Socialist propagandists, which were regularly reported in *Le Populaire*.

In his plan, Louis Lévy proposed to begin the discussions designed for militants by establishing the then classic distinction between utopian socialism and scientific socialism, before then moving to the life and work of Marx and Engels. The study of some of the major themes of Marxism (historical materialism, the theory of value, etc.) was followed by a lesson on the Paris Commune, and a series on the history of Socialism. Then came the Jean Jaurès moment, the history of the International and a series on socialism and war, Russia and Bolshevism. Then came a disparate set of discussions around trade unionism and socialism, cooperatives, agriculture, the question of disarmament and, finally, feminism. The structure of this socialist education plan was backed up by a set of recommended pamphlets.

With regard to Marx and Engels's works, the proposed reading materials included the *Communist Manifesto*, the *Critique of the Gotha Programme*, an extract from *Capital* and, finally, Engels's *Socialism: Utopian and Scientific*. Historical materialism was to be grasped by reading lectures by Jaurès and Lafargue, and the Paris Commune by reading Marx's *Civil War in France*. 'For the theory of value,' wrote Lévy, 'the best thing is to have the good edition of Capital, published by Costes. Failing that, the short *Abrégé du Capital*, by Deville, which is very well documented and easily understood by all'.[7] This quotation says a lot about how party training was conceived. The reference to Marx was there, but his key work was not indicated as absolutely necessary reading. Deville's pamphlet was the possible alternative for whoever did not plan to read *Capital*. Marxism was necessary to become a socialist, but socialist educators addressed an audience unfamiliar with the doctrine, which they instead tried to educate them in through smaller-format works.

---

7   Ferreti 1928.

Reading the catalogue of the Librairie du Populaire (*Le Populaire*, 14 October 1926), the hierarchy among the different educational materials is clear. Two categories appear, here: the works of Marx, and pamphlets. A special insert was devoted to Marx, with *Capital* and *The History of Economic Doctrines* translated by Molitor. The high price of these volumes meant that they were more suited to an intellectual audience than to ordinary militants. Conversely, the section entitled 'educational pamphlets' was more specifically intended for militants. It contained all of Marx and Engels's shorter texts, from the *Manifesto* to *The Civil War in France*, as well as Deville's popularising compendium.

The seemingly disorderly promotion of books and pamphlets obeyed an editorial logic which foregrounded party publications above those issued by other publishers. Here, it is worth dwelling briefly on the editorial policy of the SFIO, since the selection of pamphlets which were published or republished point to the choices which the party made with regard to its written propaganda (*Rapports du Parti socialiste, 1923–1939*). Out of all of Karl Marx's works, only the *Communist Manifesto* was republished, for it appeared essential for militant consumption. A biography of Marx by Joseph Diner-Denès – a Hungarian socialist who enjoyed broad renown in the Socialist International – was also offered. But, not surprisingly, the pamphlets by Léon Blum, Jean Jaurès and Adéodat Compère-Morel were especially foregrounded. The SFIO's first concern was to popularise doctrine using second-hand texts. Marx's works seemed so dry and difficult to use to stir engagement that he could only play a secondary role. Acquiring a solid Marxist culture only seemed necessary in a second stage, once commitment to socialism had turned into commitment as a militant.

Lastly, written propaganda and the reading of texts were not the only means of gaining an apprenticeship in Marxism. The talks organised by local branches, federations, and the party, gave life to an 'oralised' Marxism, doubtless of key importance for the many socialists who were little-inclined to read. These conferences or talks could take place at various different levels. At the national level, they took the form of socialist schools, primarily aimed at students and experienced activists. In the talk which began the Seine Federation's winter series in November 1930, Jean Longuet emphasised its Marxist credentials (*Le Populaire*, 14 November 1930): 'All the teaching in the school will be largely inspired by the Marxist method. For us, Marxism is no dogma; it is a marvellous means of investigation, an incomparable tool which facilitates the study of the laws which govern societies'. In the provinces, socialist schools, which were often short-lived, set themselves the same programme of in-depth study of Marxism. Thus, when a socialist school opened in Marseilles in January 1923,

Le Populaire advertised three lectures, one of which was on 'Friedrich Engels and the Marxist school'.

But the socialist schools' lack of success, in the Seine as elsewhere, requires that we also look toward the lower level of party federations and sections. In the Seine Federation, a propagandists' school was set up in the 1920s, the better to train up speakers for public meetings. In an article on the internal organisation of propaganda in the Seine Federation and providing speakers, the editor wrote: 'Yesterday's workers followed Karl Marx because they understood him. They will follow us tomorrow if we know how to be the faithful interpreters of his thought and the informed continuators of the educational endeavour he undertook'. At a still lower level, the socialist sections did not hesitate to organise talks on Marx and Marxism – like the lecture on Marxism given in a Metz tavern by a member of the local section and reported by *Le Populaire* of 28 March 1929.

This educational impulse is also found across the various tendencies of the SFIO. The major tendency of the socialist left, *La Bataille socialiste*, was particularly concerned with promoting Marxist education. In January 1930, Jean Zyromski stressed the need 'to spread, in depth, Marxist education, which is essential for the development of members' class consciousness'. In December 1931, writing in another review, *Révolte*, he insisted on the benefits of an education in Marxism: 'A Marxist education provides advance protection against all utopianisms, falsifications of socialism.' In the 1930s, a small, essentially Parisian, group even made Marxist training the cornerstone of its activity, as publicised in its bulletin *Le Combat marxiste*. Its January 1934 issue helps us to understand the approach taken by the intellectuals behind this publication, Lucien Laurat foremost among them. The bulletin offered readers a 'Marxist Guide' to democracy and dictatorship. On the left were indicated the elements to be featured in the lecture; on the right, the reading – divided into basic and higher levels – necessary to develop an understanding of this subject.

2.3   A Marxist 'Superego'?

Familiarity with Marx and the main points of his doctrine was not central to the process of joining the SFIO, either among its leaders or among its ordinary militants – though we should not necessarily infer from this that they were ignorant of or disinterested toward Marxism. Among leadership circles, a relationship with Marxism was clearly one of the markers that distinguished the rest of the party (including Léon Blum) from its right wing. More than a 'superego',[8] this reference to Marx was a resource that was called upon as suited the

---

8   Bergounioux and Grunberg, 1992.

struggles waged within or outside the party. While this reference was regularly foregrounded in the 1920s to counter both Communist competition and the right wing of the Socialist Party itself, it became secondary in the 1930s, when the SFIO had to respond to the great challenge of the time – fascism – with a republican alliance, the Popular Front. But it remained an important component of socialist culture, transmitted and revived by pamphlets, debates and talks.

CHAPTER 4

The Socialists' Marx: From Guy Mollet to the Present

Mathieu Fulla

Marxism made a powerful contribution to shaping the political culture of French Socialism, even if this latter's relationship with this ideology remained problematic and ambiguous. For a long time, being a Socialist meant sharing a sentimental rather than rational adherence to a series of precepts forged in the time of the Second International (1889–1923), under the decisive influence of the mighty German Social Democratic Party (SPD). The British historian Donald Sassoon notes its three main pillars: the perception of capitalism as a fundamentally unjust system based on the exploitation of the worker; a materialist reading of history, considering capitalism as a stage that would be surpassed by the 'class struggle'; and the conception of the working class as a homogeneous class, united by common interests and forms of representation – this last idea being a legacy of the SPD rather than of Marx.[1]

In the interwar period, this vulgarised and highly politicised Marxism, of which Léon Blum elaborated the most subtle version, was a central political and cultural resource for the French Section of the Workers' International (SFIO), and it would remain so in the wake of World War II. Faced with the French Communist Party's (PCF) incessant accusations that the party was sinking into a reformist drift, this Marxism allowed Socialist leaders and propagandists to reaffirm the legitimacy of their own organisation as an embodiment of the working class. The Socialists' Marx should not, however, be reduced to a simple tool of legitimisation. The SFIO of Léon Blum and Guy Mollet, like the later Parti Socialiste Unifié (PSU) or François Mitterrand's Parti Socialiste, included intellectuals and experts with a refined knowledge of Marxist thought. These formations also tried – albeit with limited success – to inculcate in their militants the basics of Marxism through pamphlets, courses and educational sessions.[2]

Focused on the period stretching from the Liberation in 1944–45 to the present day, this brief overview examines the Socialist parties' relationship

---

1   Sassoon 2014.

2   Cépède, 2000.

with this vulgarised and politicised form of Marxism, understanding it less as 'a philosophical doctrine than as a set of convictions inseparable from a political commitment'.[3] It is important to note that the writings of Socialist theorists, who were often also political leaders, had no influence on the rich history of postwar critical Marxism. Indeed, with the notable exception of the 1970s, their sometimes lively disputes remained confined to party circles, and no Socialist Marxist enjoys a reputation comparable to that of Louis Althusser, Henri Lefebvre, Cornelius Castoriadis or Claude Lefort.

After World War II, the place of Marxism in these parties' intellectual life was, in any case, of little importance compared to its political role. For a Socialist leader to lay claim to Marx in his own writings or speeches was first – and perhaps foremost – to draw on a weapon whose effectiveness varied according to the period and the opponent being targeted. While such an identification was counter-productive in the fight against the Right, which readily conflated socialist Marxism with Marxism-Leninism, it was, conversely, a necessity in the fight against the PCF, though the Socialists struggled to assert themselves in the debate. Ultimately, the Marxist weapon only really came into its own in internal party debates. Within the postwar SFIO and the PS of the 1970s, speakers found in national congresses one of the rare theatres where they could deploy their rhetoric without fear of being baited either by the Right or by the Communists.

1   An Indelible and Unsurpassable Reference Point (1944–58)

Contrary to the legends fed by the PCF and the left-wing currents of the SFIO, the clandestine Socialist Party refounded by Daniel Mayer during the occupation did remain Marxist. No one within its ranks dreamt of questioning this identity. The occurrence of the terms 'Marx', 'Marxist' and 'Marxism' in the organisation's regular congresses underlines the importance of the reference to the 'master' in the period 1944–51 (Figure 4.1, p. 60). After the war years, which had been so painful for French Socialism – from (a minority engaged in) collaboration, to wait-and-see attitudes and resistance – quarrels over the doctrinal place reserved for Marx were part of the wider confrontation between two competing projects for the party. The first, as advanced by Léon Blum and Daniel Mayer, consisted of a broad opening of the party toward the 'fresh forces of the Resistance', in order to regenerate it. Promoting a humanist reading of

---

3   Furet 1987.

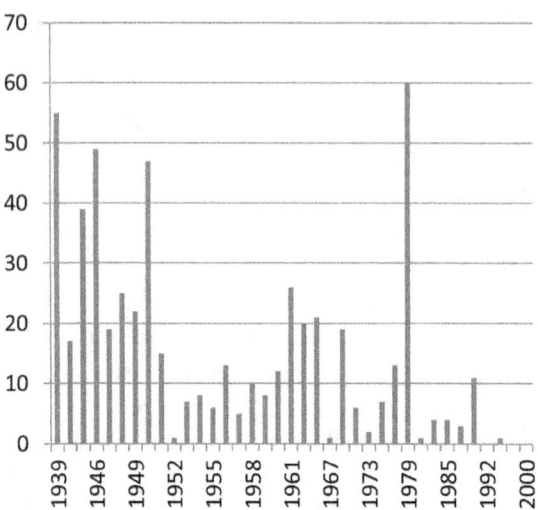

FIGURE 4.1   Instances of the terms 'Marx', 'Marxism' and
             Marxist at the Socialist Party's regular con-
             gresses (1939–2001)
             DATABASE ON THE DEBATES WITHIN THE
             SOCIALIST PARTY'S CENTRAL BODIES,
             FONDATION JEAN-JAURÈS, AVAILABLE
             ONLINE. (CONSULTED 20 SEPTEMBER 2017).

Marx, while also making this latter one among several doctrinal sources, would
encourage an opening to left-wing Christians and to the middle classes who
were sensitive to Socialism's key values but did not recognise themselves in
Marxism. This plea, however, came up against the intransigence of the SFIO's
left-wing currents, for which Guy Mollet acted as the spokesman at the 1946
congress. Hostile to this policy of reaching out to Christians – secularism being
at the time the strongest pillar of the party's political culture – the MP from
the Pas-de-Calais embodied that 'party patriotism without which the history
of socialism cannot be understood'.[4] To his eyes, removing Marx from his ped-
estal would be an act of self-betrayal for the SFIO.

So, in these early postwar years, there was no prospect of the Socialists
abandoning Marxism – but they did pose themselves questions about its form
and its place in their doctrine and propaganda. The fundamental disagreements between Léon Blum and Guy Mollet were only minor, and Daniel
Mayer's defeat at the 1946 congress mostly owed to his harsh policy of pur-

---

4   Lafon 1989.

ging party cadres as well as his desire to reduce the prerogatives of federation-level secretaries.[5] Under the Fourth Republic, Mollet's and Blum's distinct approaches fed into the SFIO with varying levels of intensity, though the balance of power was very much in the latter's favour. At a time when the PCF was asserting its domination over the Left, there was an urgent need to provide militants with weapons to counter accusations of crass ignorance of Marx's work. After the Communist ministers were thrown out of Paul Ramadier's government in May 1947, putting an end to *tripartisme* (the Gaullist-Socialist-Communist coalition) the conflicts between the two workers' parties became increasingly violent. Having been accused by PCF general secretary Maurice Thorez of deviating from Marxism by promoting a humanism that ran contrary to materialist principles, Blum retorted by casting Marxism-Leninism and its Stalinist avatar as themselves heretical.

Four years later, in one of his rare theoretical texts, Guy Mollet presented Bolshevism and fascism as two forms of state capitalism, representing the antithesis of the democratic socialism which his party promoted. The general-secretary's charge was in tune with party propaganda that pit Karl Marx in direct opposition to Joseph Stalin. Pamphlets as well as the arguments used by Socialists tirelessly insisted that Marxism-Leninism was a fundamental deviation from the work of the 'master', not its faithful exegesis.

The Socialists were constantly charged with doublespeak – an accusation levelled by the Communists, but also by the Right and figures close to Pierre Mendès France. This accusation was especially problematic in that many of Mollet's followers were reluctant to use any interpretative framework other than democratic Marxism for thinking about capitalism. The general secretary remained deaf to the pleas of his political opponents – Jules Moch, André Philip, Paul Ramadier – in favour of confronting the Marxist vulgate with the work of Keynesian-minded economists such as Jean Fourastié, Colin Clark and François Perroux.

The SFIO's hostility to any large-scale renovation of its doctrine, which also set it at odds with the Socialist International, contributed to its intellectual discredit, making its Marxism inaudible outside party circles. In the mid-1950s, as the left-wing electorate was seduced by the rival Mendesist and Communist projects, the SFIO was left 'stuck holding its Marxism' (Maurice Duverger), projecting the image of a party closed in on itself and incapable of thinking about modernity. In contrast to the interwar period, the party, which was losing electoral momentum, was no longer a pole of attraction for young experts and

---

5   Castagnez and Morin, 2000.

intellectuals tempted by Marxism, most of whom preferred to join the ranks of the PCF, the party of the 'metal worker' and the 'miner'.[6]

The weak appeal of the Socialists' version of Marx was accentuated by the reformist practices of the party's elites, both in the National Assembly and in government. When Guy Mollet came to power in 1956, he and his finance minister Ramadier did their best to pursue a Mendesist and Keynesian-inspired policy, in service of social reforms such as adding a third week of paid holidays and the creation of a welfare system providing greater provision for old age. Overshadowed by the bitter and painful failure in Algeria, this policy to some extent pointed toward the attempts at doctrinal revision that would come in the 1960s, seeking to break Socialism out of its Marxist ivory tower, or even to formalise its reformist metamorphosis.

2   The Impossibility of a 'Bad Godesberg' Moment (1958–68)

Hence, in the very moment that Sartre proclaimed Marxism an 'unsurpassable' horizon, the Socialists' attempts to distance themselves from it gained new momentum. This is only apparently a paradox, given the vigour of anticommunism within Socialist ranks. The SFIO was not, however, the main focus of this shift, given its delicate situation at the dawn of the Fifth Republic in 1958, which marked a real annus horribilis for the party. The Mollet leadership's support for General de Gaulle led a section of the party's troops, already hostile to the Republican Front's Algerian policy, to split away. Aware that the militants' attachment to the figures of Marx, Jaurès and Blum remained one of the party's few firm foundations, Guy Mollet tirelessly defended its fidelity to its original doctrine. Internal initiatives to confront Marx with other thinkers did not prove successful.

The questioning of Marx's centrality to Socialist doctrine thus took place around the margins of the SFIO. In the early 1960s, the socialist wing of the French Confederation of Christian Workers (CFTC), the PSU and the Jean Moulin Club defended a Keynesian and Mendesist-inspired socialism that took its distance from Marx without, however, banishing him from its texts in the manner of the SPD at the Bad Godesberg congress (November 1959). From 1963 onwards, Gaston Defferre conveyed this ideology within SFIO ranks. Mollet's main internal rival for the party leadership, the irremovable mayor of Marseille symbolically titled his programme for the 1965 presidential election 'A New Horizon'. Unabashed about his stance 'on the right of the party', he posed

---

6   Lazar 1990.

as 'the leader of the partisans of an *aggiornamento* of the doctrine, and the move to an openly-embraced reformism'.[7] But his candidacy, torpedoed by the People's Republican Movement (MRP) and by Mollet, proved abortive. At the doctrinal level, Marxism continued to reign supreme among the Molletists, not only out of routine, but also because the leadership – soon supported by Mitterrand's Federation of the Democratic and Socialist Left (FGDS) – was trying to strengthen ties with a PCF now emerging from the ghetto in which it had become stuck under the Fourth Republic. Negotiating with the communists required a mastery of the basic rudiments of Marxism. Mitterrand, who mounted a promising presidential bid in 1965, was a typical example of the uninitiated; after his campaign, he stepped up his efforts to learn Marxism's particular language.

Indeed, the PCF continued to dominate the battle among the Marxisms, dictating its agenda. At its conference at Choisy-le-Roi in 1966, it revived the theory of state monopoly capitalism (CME), rediscovered by the Communists at the beginning of the decade. The approach appealed to many engineers and economists – notably at the INSEE (National Institute of Statistics and Economic Studies) – as well as a few young graduates of the École Nationale de l'Administration committed to Socialism, of which Jean-Pierre Chevènement's Centre for Socialist Studies, Research and Education (CERES) formed the hard core.

French Socialism's intellectual contribution to the theoretical renewal of Marxism in the 1960s was therefore weak, if not non-existent. On the eve of 1968, only the CERES tried to revive some of the theorists of the Second International in its publications, such as the Austro-Marxist Otto Bauer. But the work of fashionable thinkers such as Nicos Poulantzas, Herbert Marcuse and Theodor Adorno remained unknown, even though it was passionately discussed in the intellectual circles of the militant radical left. Not until the social explosion of the '1968 years' did a strongly politicised Marx return to the forefront of the Socialist stage.

3   The Era of 'Re-Marxified' Socialism (1968–81)

The Socialist parties could hardly overlook Marx's return to prominence in the wake of May–June 1968. The only party to grasp the aspirations of the social movement, the PSU – which had now made a 'Left turn' – was the quickest to react. At the end of its Dijon congress in March 1969, it adopted seventeen

---

7   Ollivier 2011.

theses on self-management, a nod to the father of the October Revolution and a means of imposing on the political debate a concept of which it was the main promoter, along with the CFDT.[8] The PSU was able to mount this recovery of Marx because of the persistence of this political culture within its ranks, despite the 'Keynesian-Mendesist' thrust of senior functionaries such as Michel Rocard. The writings of Gilles Martinet on the 'Marxism of our time', of Serge Mallet and Pierre Belleville on the 'new working class' or the education dispensed by the Polish theorist Victor Fay and the former Trotskyist Pierre Naville fed into the thinking of PSU members engaged in the militant mobilisation of the '1968 years'.

The forces of the non-Communist institutional left proved less able to react to this moment. The FGDS, led by Mitterrand, did not survive the shock of May–June and disappeared in November 1968. In the 1969 presidential election, the managerial socialism championed by Gaston Defferre and Pierre Mendès France was unable to find an electorate. 'The air was coloured red' and the Socialist Party's survival depended on the re-Marxifying of its ideology, a step made all the more necessary by the priority placed on rapprochement with the PCF. This return to Marx was not unique to political parties alone; the CFDT, which officially committed to socialism in 1970, launched a programme of in-depth study of the different variants of Marxism, leading to the publication of an impressive 'Lexicon of the Main Marxist Terms'. The theory of state-monopoly capitalism was also examined with real attentiveness and the CFDT's study bureau did not hesitate to call on the services of experienced Marxists such as Nicos Poulantzas to hone its knowledge of 'social classes'. The main contribution of Marxist theory to the union's theoretical baggage came through its integration of the concept of alienation, central to Marx's *1844 Manuscripts*. Perfectly compatible with self-management (*autogestion*), this enabled the CFDT clearly to distinguish itself from the PCF and its intellectuals, who had banished it from their own interpretative framework.

The Socialist Party was not to be outdone. The choice of alliance with the communists and the 'great return of capital to the rich countries' (Thomas Piketty) pushed the party to defend economic positions very close to the Communist theory of state-monopoly capitalism. By making the 'rupture with capitalism' an essential marker of Socialist identity, Mitterrand eased the way for its rapprochement with the PCF. On 27 June 1972, the two formations – soon joined by the centre-left Mouvement des radicaux de gauche – approved a common programme for government stating that they wanted to 'break the domin-

---

8   Georgi 2003.

ation of big capital'. The document sparked many polemics; but it did put Marx back in the spotlight, alongside Keynes and self-managementist thinking. The analysis of the state apparatus as a 'class' instrument owed much to the Marxist interpretative framework, as did the document's economic aspects. The fact that the CERES – the main vector for the dissemination of the theory of state-monopoly capitalism in the party, and a great admirer of Poulantzas's analysis of ideological state apparatuses[9] – constitutes the main pool of internal expertise, was not unrelated to this surge of Marxism within the ranks of the Parti Socialiste.

The rallying of Socialist leaders such as Mitterrand, Defferre and Pierre Mauroy to a Marx not very far from the Communists' own – except on the major question of his relationship to democracy – was coupled with an attempt to disseminate his basic concepts. The educational department led by Pierre Joxe, who was also an expert on Marx, thus developed a *Socialist Economics Dictionary*. Intended for party militants, it focused on the concepts of surplus value, alienation, and the tendency of the rate of profit to fall. The positive electoral dynamic that set in motion after the signing of the Common Programme also encouraged specialists in Marxism, such as the economists Christian Goux and Jean Matouk, as well as Gérard Delfau, an *agrégé*[10] in literature. This latter – the main driving force behind the 'Démocratie et université' association, which had close ties to the Parti socialiste – organised a study series based on a return to reading what he considered Marx's greatest texts: the *Communist Manifesto*, but also extracts from *Capital*, the *German Ideology* and the *Critique of the Gotha Programme*. The political function of this return to the sources was openly admitted: the intention was to disseminate a 'limited and properly oriented' choice of texts and, even more, of proposing an interpretation of Marx which would allow the party to 'differentiate itself from the PCF'.

The 're-Marxification' process induced by the Common Programme also had an impact on the programmes published by the Parti Socialiste over the 1970s. Under the influence of Jacques Attali in particular, the party put forward proposals for a way out of the crisis that mixed the 'Marxist-Keynesian' thinking of regulation theorists (Robert Boyer, Michel Aglietta), the heterodox political economy of John Galbraith and the American neo-Marxist analyses developed over the previous decade by the likes of Paul Baran and Paul Sweezy. Despite the gnashing of teeth among the Rocardians – who joined the party in autumn 1974 – and personalities such as Jacques Delors, this regenerated Marx once

---

9   Merlin 2002.
10   An agrégation is a competitive examination for teaching in higher education.

again had a sanctified status and an undeniable power of seduction. Numerous left-wing Christians – some of them CFDT militants – fascinated by Marxism converged with the Socialist Party via CERES.[11] In the second half of the 1970s, even the Rocardians did not shy away from the debate, despite their pronounced dedication to self-management and anti-totalitarianism. While the main leaders and theorists of this current strongly criticised the Marxist exegeses promoted by both social democracy and communism, from 1974 onwards it benefited from the arrival of Christian Marxists and personalities such as Gilles Martinet, author of a standard work on international communism. These defectors from the CERES – disappointed by a current that confined them to subordinate political roles – brought Rocardism an in-depth knowledge of the 'master' and his texts. In the Socialist Party of the 1970s, the ability to deftly wield Marxist language was a political necessity, which none of the leaders of this current could do without. Rocard had a strong familiarity with its prose, having assiduously practised it in the 1950s under the tutelage of Victor Fay. In famous – and much-applauded – speech given on 18 June 1977 at the Nantes Congress, he did not hesitate to present self-management (*autogestion*) as the most authentic translation of Marx's thought.

More broadly, the Socialist Party's initiative to release eight luxuriant volumes with the publisher Martinsart in 1978, devoted to the 'great revolutionaries', attested to the dynamism of Marxism within its ranks. In his highly political preface to the volume devoted to Marx, Engels and Gramsci, Jean Pronteau – a member of the party's steering committee and head of the Socialist Institute for Studies and Research (ISER) – asserted that the synthesis of Marxist and Gramscian analyses on the questions of the state, ideology and intellectuals would 'provide the theoretical instruments capable of forging a strategy for the "Western road to socialism"'.

In perfect harmony with the official line of 'rupture with capitalism', the reflections of this former PCF cadre, who had long been chief editor of its journal *Économie et Politique*, illustrate the primarily strategic function of the Socialists' Marx. The Union of the Left did not put an end to Communist accusations of reformist drift and class collaboration. Still a mighty force, albeit on a downward slope, Georges Marchais's PCF continued to present itself as the only left-wing formation orienting 'its activity with the help of a living scientific theory, Marxism-Leninism'. This systematic trial of the Socialists' Marxism demanded a vigorous riposte, as symbolised – among many examples – by the report on PS-PCF relations which Lionel Jospin presented to the National Convention

---

11   Soulage 2012.

of May 1975, exhorting his comrades to assert their ideological autonomy from the Communists.

But in the 1970s, when the Socialist Party had set itself the objective of winning power, the Socialists' Marx was not only a pedagogical tool useful for reconstituting a party of militants, or a necessary instrument in a context of 'cold union' with the Communists.[12] It also served to settle internal rivalries between the Socialist currents. The table of references to Marx and Marxism presented at the beginning of this chapter highlights a surge of Marxist fever during the Metz congress of 1979, when Mitterrandists and Rocardians clashed for the party leadership and the nomination for the 1981 presidential election. On this occasion, François Mitterrand adopted a voluntarist and Marx-inflected discourse which helped to restore his authority. Posing as the heir to Jaurès and Blum and the sole guarantor of the 'Épinay line', the party's first secretary cast aspersions on Rocard and Mauroy, suspected of wanting to adapt capitalism rather than build socialism. He mentioned Marx's name fourteen times and paid unusually strong tribute to his analyses, while admitting that he was not himself a Marxist. His entourage was not to be outdone. In the short span of the congress, the Mitterrandists gave the Rocardians and Mauroy's supporters the same treatment which they suffered almost daily from the PCF: the accusation of a 'reformist drift', supported by all possible rhetorical devices. Less fond of this reference was Rocard, who mentioned it only three times throughout a lengthy speech. He challenged the essence of Marx's economic analyses – and nor did he hide this, especially when speaking before the Socialist International – and called on his comrades to 'absolutely reject Leninism' and slyly called on them to 'question Marx on the relationship of socialism to freedom'.

However, the Marxist and anti-capitalist postures of Mitterrand's hussars (Pierre Bérégovoy, Laurent Fabius, Lionel Jospin, Pierre Joxe and Paul Quilès, to mention only the most vehement) remained confined to the time of the congress itself. Having overcome the Rocardian obstacle, the majority current of the Socialist Party returned to its pragmatic reading of the Common Programme. The most embarrassing asperities of the Marxist, statist, neo-protectionist and anti-European discourse of CERES – an indispensable ally that had become cumbersome – were erased. During the 1981 presidential campaign, Marxism was muted, even if certain precepts continued to be hammered home: the reference to a class state in need of profound reform; a structural analysis of the crisis of capitalism; and the denunciation – shared by all currents –

---

12   Bergounioux and Grunberg 2005.

of the alienation of the worker on the shopfloor. The party's bid to maintain itself in power would rapidly undermine these certainties.

4   From Totem to Taboo

The decline of the Marxist reference in the Parti Socialiste was concomitant with Marx's waning fortunes in the wider Western intellectual landscape. More incremental than sudden[13] this rupture took place at different rates at the various levels of the party. In government and parliament, this point of reference was rapidly delegitimised; the choice of an economic policy of 'austerity' (*rigueur*) from late 1981 rendered suspect any specialisms of Marxist leanings. If at one point the Élysée had consulted economists from the regulation school, they were quickly banished from the decision-making process. The hardening of the 'austerity with a human face' (Eric Hobsbawm) decreed in March 1983 gave official form to the delegitimisation of anti-capitalist rhetoric, in favour of France's 'modernisation' and praise for business. In practice, however, this discourse was but an open and political embrace of a ideological and cultural shift that dated back at least to the second half of the 1970s. As soon as the Left came to power, Marxist economic experts were absent from the president's and prime minister's office and the ministries responsible for economic policy.[14] As in the case of the Auroux laws on collective bargaining, the public policies of this period reflected a cultural climate 'a world away from the Marxist flights of fancy at the Metz congress'.[15]

The abandonment of the Marxist reference point was, however, less clear-cut at the level of the party's own organisation. For a time, Marx remained a useful political resource and a subject of study which still aroused some interest. In 1983, the centenary of his death provided an opportunity to look back at his contributions. The publications of both CERES and the Office universitaire de recherche socialiste (OURS) founded by Mollet in 1969 opened their columns to Marxist philosophers and economists. However, as the decade progressed, CERES's penchant for the author of *Capital* faded in favour of a defence of a certain idea of the Republic and the nation. The split by Jean-Pierre Chevènement and his followers, who left the Parti Socialiste in 1993, formalised this shift, which had been latent for some years already. Jean Poperen's current was wedded to a similar path.

---

13   Yon 2011.
14   Fulla 2016.
15   Tracol 2015.

The attitude of the Socialists' internal currents reflected that of the party as a whole; Marx was increasingly seen as an object of historical interest and ever less as a guide to action. The 'Marx, Jaurès and Socialism Today' conference organised by the ISER in 1984, as part of the commemorations marking the centenary of Marx's death, was emblematic in this regard. While this event underlined the fact that a certain share of Socialist cadres and militants had an enduring sentimental attachment to the 'master', the exercise of responsibilities at the state level revealed the impossibility of relying on his analyses as a guide for how to govern. In the second half of the 1980s, only ultra-minority groups within the Socialist Party claimed a Marxist allegiance, such as Convergences socialistes, a dissident fraction of Pierre Lambert's Trotskyist Internationalist Communist Party (PCI). Its four hundred or so militants joined the party in the wake of the parliamentary elections of March 1986, which saw a defeat for the Left. Led by Jean-Christophe Cambadélis, they initially aspired to 'strengthen the left wing of the Socialist Party' by promoting a Marxist perspective. Two years later, following a both rapid and determined about-turn, the members of the group who remained loyal to Cambadélis participated in the 'erasure of Marxism' by marginalising those who, like Jean Poperen, did not (yet) accept the disappearance of this marker of identity.[16]

In the early 1990s, after the collapse of 'actually-existing communism', the Marxist reference tended to disappear from Socialist language. The declaration of principles adopted by the Parti Socialiste at the end of the contentious Rennes Congress renounced both the class struggle and the revolutionary end-goal. At family gatherings during the 'Jospin years', Marx was far more often by those who held him in contempt than by his devotees. After the painful defeat of 21 April 2002, Henri Weber decreed his fate, without any need for soul-searching: 'Socialism pre-existed Marx and will survive him'. The Parti Socialiste's leaders recognised, with some differences of nuance, that in the era of 'neoliberal' globalisation and the European Union, the (magical?) 1970s triad of 'nationalisation-planning-self-management' was now a matter of the past. The party's relationship with liberalism would now be an internal dividing line between the supporters of a modernised social democracy and those who openly embraced social liberalism.[17] In such a debate, there was no place for Marx. Symptomatic, in this sense, was the view of Léon Blum taken by Dominique Strauss-Kahn in 2006. Ignoring – or knowingly omitting – Blum's Marxist culture, this candidate for the party's nomination for the 2007 presidential elec-

---

16   Yon 2011.
17   Rioufreyt 2012.

tion held up Blum as the paragon of a reformism that had broken all ties with the author of the *Communist Manifesto*.

In the early twenty-first century, it very much seems that the Socialists' Marx is no longer with us; the reference to him is now the exclusive property of the radical Left. At the Socialist Congress in Poitiers, from 5 to 7 June 2015, none of the four motions in the running, including those on the party's furthest-left flank, mentioned his name. References to capitalism – including finance capitalism – to designate the current economic mode of production, were also reduced to a bare minimum. The credo, spelled out by Lionel Jospin in his day, according to which French Socialism rejects 'market society' but accepts the market economy, is now an established mainstay of its political culture, at the cost of any kind of anticapitalism. The relationship to Marx among the finalists in the party's primary for the 2017 presidential elections vividly confirmed how outdated this point of reference has become in Socialist circles. In Benoît Hamon's discourse, Marx was the object of a *damnatio memoriae*: for his analyses do not fit easily with the call for an ecological transition or with the loss of labour's centrality. As for former prime minister Manuel Valls, he had long since condemned the 'Marxist superego', unambiguously preferring Clemenceau to Jaurès and the liberal world order to the 'leftist verbiage of '68'.

CHAPTER 5

The Communists' Marx: Karl Marx, Marxism and Marxism-Leninism, 1920–55

Serge Wolikow

From its birth in 1920, the French Communist Party (PCF) asserted its desire to build upon the French revolutionary tradition. However, the reference to Marx was not at the heart of the debates that ran through the founding Tours Congress in December 1920; in this moment, he was not a central issue of dispute. During its first three decades of existence, the PCF was nevertheless an important protagonist in disseminating knowledge of Marx. Its editorial efforts were one of the indicators of this commitment, throughout this period. However, in order to understand the French Communists' version of Marx, it is also necessary to investigate the life of this organisation, its functioning and its ideology. Access to the archives of the French Section of the Communist International and the digitalisation of a significant part of its printed publications (journals, newspapers and pamphlets) allows us to reckon with Marx's place in the training and education of militants as well as in the regular functioning of Party organisms, including its leadership. Drawing on such sources, it is possible to complete the view that historical sociology and the history of publishing have hitherto taken of the relations between the PCF and Marxism.

To what extent did the Communist Party, from its creation in 1920, contribute to the dissemination of Marx's thought in France – and in what form? Did it do no more than introduce France to Marxism-Leninism, which is to say, Marxism as according to Stalin? The Stalinist interpretation of Marxism to which the PCF pledged allegiance from the 1930s certainly should be taken into account, because it designated a general orientation taken by this organisation. But in reality, the PCF's Marxism also encompassed much less standardised intellectual activities. Behind the simplifying formulations there was a real diversity, characterised by the coexistence, in the Communist space, of different uses of Marx, of more or less directly political, academic and popular variants.

The dissemination of Marxism in France, as identified here, depended on the PCF's various on-the-ground expressions – in working-class, urban and rural areas, as well as among the intellectual professions of education and research. Added to that, it also depended the on evolving political and ideological conditions from the 1920s to the early 1950s, from the Party's creation to its rise during the Popular Front era, and from its late-1920s retreat into sectarianism to its rise as a national force during the Resistance and the Liberation.

1   The Early PCF: Rediscovering Marx

The birth of the PCF marked the culmination of a crisis within the French Section of the Workers' International (SFIO) and a long period of debates that had agitated the Socialist Party since at least 1917.[1] There was a large majority in favour of joining the Third (Communist) International, bringing together both the early supporters of membership (around Fernand Loriot and Paul Vaillant-Couturier) and those in the centre of the party (with Marcel Cachin and Ludovic-Oscar Frossard) who expressed their agreement with the decisions of the International's recent congress.[2] Marx was not an essential issue in the Tours split – especially given that the 'rebuilders', who ultimately refused some of the twenty-one conditions for membership of the new International were grouped behind Jean Longuet, Marx's grandson, and themselves held up the author of *Capital* as a reference point. As for Léon Blum, who refused to join Communist ranks, he denounced the Bolsheviks' revolutionary practice, which he deemed 'Blanquist' and thus explicitly at odds with Marx's thought.

However, within the PCF (at least during the first two years of its existence) the reference to Marx rapidly became a marker of the Left, aligning itself behind the leaders and emissaries of the Communist International. Boris Souvarine, lead editor of the *Bulletin communiste*, took up arguments from Trotsky to rebuke Jean Longuet and his 'hollow assertions, unworthy of a man who claims to have a doctrine so rich in scientific observations' as Marx's.

Souvarine's comrades asserted the need to go 'back to the source' – meaning, to the writings and activity of Marx in his own time. The new International claimed to be reviving the International Workingmen's Association (IWMA), or First International, founded by Marx. Its leaders used commemorations, in particular the anniversaries of Marx's birth and death, to evoke his struggles and the continuity of his political commitment. This provided one way of insisting that the Communists were returning to a revolutionary Marxism which social democracy had forgotten.[3] Significantly, Marx was more often cited with reference to his historical and political works than his economic ones. References to the *Manifesto*, to his writings on the Paris Commune, and to his interventions

---

1   Ducoulombier 2010.
2   Wolikow 2017.
3   Wolikow 2010.

in the general council of the IWMA, gave a political framing to the Communists' activity, when they had to face the challenges of organisation and revolutionary activity in the French context. Writing in *Le Bulletin communiste* in May 1921, upon the 103rd anniversary of Marx's birth, Amédée Dunois spoke of militants' interest in commemorating Marx rather than... Napoleon, who died on Marx's third birthday: 'Let the decadent bourgeoisie celebrate Napoleon, the founder of bourgeois society. One anniversary against another! On 5 May, let all the thoughts of the working class be for Karl Marx, in whom scientific socialism – that is, the socialism of the proletariat – found its first artisan, its mightiest "animator".'

2   'A Work to Read, And Make Others Read'

Among the PCF leaders familiar enough with Marx's work to talk about it in detail, it is worth mentioning Charles Rappoport, whose personality and role as a populariser of Marx's thought especially stand out. During the early years of the PCF, he was in fact the main propagandist of Marx's work. Backed up by his political and intellectual career in the Russian émigré milieu in both France in Switzerland, his membership of various socialist groups and then his commitment to French socialism and his support for the supporters of membership of the Third International, he pursued an intense propagandist activity through his pamphlets and articles in *L'Humanité* and various journals. In March 1922, he waxed lyrical about the *Communist Manifesto* of 1848 and Marx's writing: 'The Communist Manifesto is the dynamite that will blow all the talkers into thin air ... That is why the *Communist Manifesto* is very much a work for the present, which we must read and have others read, meditate upon and have others meditate upon.' In the columns he penned for *L'Humanité*, republished in pamphlet form, he set out the history of revolutionary Marxism, which found its contemporary application in organised Communist activity. These 'communist précis' enjoyed real success. But Rappoport, considered an uncontrollable figure – especially as he knew most of the Russian leaders personally – was kept away from the PCF's leading circles from 1925 onward. Just before he was sidelined, he helped set up the first Communist schools, which gave an important place to Marx's work. In these schools, in 1922 and 1923, he devoted several courses to historical materialism, Marx's economic thought and his role in the history of the French and international workers' movement.

In 1925, the Communist International decided to organise a system of Leninist schools, which would also have their counterpart in France. With the invention of Leninism, immediately after Lenin's death, and the Communist International's proclamation of Bolshevisation, the PCF, like the Comintern's other national sections, set new training programmes on the agenda, to be handled by its agitprop section.[4] Leninist themes, the study of imperialism and finance capitalism, the critical theory of the state and the conception of the Party occupied pride of place therein. The international Leninist school in Moscow was based on the Marxist theoretical production under the direction of Nikolai Bukharin, who for a time headed the Communist International. In France, the development of educational programmes was all the more laborious because there was only scant Marxist culture among the PCF's young cadres – hence the strategic dimension of publishing popularising works, translated from Russian or German. In *Correspondance internationale* – the weekly organ of the Communist International – the activity of the Marx-Engels Institute in Moscow was presented by its director David Ryazanov. He tried to give the French reader an overview of Marx's oeuvre, which was little-known in its true proportions, apart from a few classics published before World War I. He emphasised the richness of Marx's work, while also announcing forthcoming translations.

For the time being – in particular in the *Cahiers du Bolchevisme*, the monthly theoretical journal of the PCF launched in 1925 – the responsibility for disseminating Marxism was entrusted to Marcel Ollivier (alias Aaron Goldberg), a close friend of Rappoport, who was engaged in Marx-related editorial work in Moscow. Ollivier undertook the translation of Max Beer's *Marx: His Life and Work*, placing this initiative in the context of a reflection on the 'necessity of a Marxist culture' in France. In October 1926, the *Cahiers du Bolchevisme* declared: 'It is an indisputable fact that, despite all the efforts that have been made up to now to spread Marxist ideas in France, Marx's work is still very little known to the French proletariat.' Subsequently, Ryazanov's lectures on Marx and Engels were translated and published in French by Éditions sociales internationales in 1927, in a bid to familiarise the French reader with Marx's texts by narrativising and presenting them in an accessible manner.

3   The Introduction of Marxism-Leninism

Beginning in the autumn of 1927, the turn in PCF policy resulted in a 'class against class' line, which echoed the changes taking place in the Communist International. The dismissal of Nikolai Bukharin coincided with the introduc-

---

4   Ducange and Wolikow, 2017.

tion of Marxism-Leninism, of which Stalin became the main protagonist with his *Foundations of Leninism*. Now, a specifically Stalinist ideology was born. In the French context, the agit-prop section was the key site for a turn in the party's way of envisaging Marxist educationals and the dissemination of Marxism. Young cadres such as Victor Fay took on the task of rapidly training up newly promoted cadres. Regional schools were organised, as well as a correspondence school for those cadres who could not drop their professional or militant activities for weeks at a time. To prepare for the training, a questionnaire was sent to the prospective students asking them to indicate their knowledge of the classics of Marxism. In most cases, their reading of Marx was limited to three texts: the *Manifesto*, *The Civil War in France* and Deville's compendium of *Capital*. Texts by Lenin and other Bolshevik leaders were better known than Marx's own. The Stalinist purge – marked in particular by the sidelining of Ryazanov, who was executed not long after – helped to push some of Marx's writings into the background, despite continued formal declarations as to the importance of knowing these texts.

4   A Research-Marxism: The Attempt to Build a Marxist Study Circle

At the end of the 1920s, the critical approach of young intellectuals close to the PCF, particularly among the students of the École normale supérieure, led to the creation of the *Revue marxiste*. Under the patronage of Charles Rappoport, the driving force behind this publication was Georges Friedmann.[5] Although short-lived, it nevertheless reflected the possibility for the PCF to find recruits for its ideological activity within the academic world. It was in this context that the PCF leadership proposed, in 1930, the creation of a Marxist study circle, reserved for party members and intended to draw in intellectuals. Different thematic sections were proposed as well as the production of texts for party reviews, particularly in the fields of economics and history. Maurice Thorez, from 1930 the PCF's new secretary, approved this – closely supervised – project, which would make it possible to involve intellectuals in political activity. But this ambitious plan, such as it was initially conceived, came to nothing. Some intellectuals came to work in the leadership, such as Georges Politzer, who took charge of economics and statistical analysis and wrote numerous articles in the *Cahiers du Bolchevisme* on the economic situation and on economic studies. But the PCF leadership proved incapable of directing or giving life to the

---

5   Racine and Trebitsch 1992.

planned structure. Ultimately, a different grouping of intellectuals, the Cercle de la Russie neuve ('New Russia Circle'),[6] constituted the breeding ground for these new Marxist studies whose growth Thorez so desired.

The dissemination of Marxism, as taken on by the PCF, took on distinct forms, aimed at different audiences. In the 1930s, we can identify a Marxism of the researchers (academic or otherwise), mainly in the humanities, largely to be found in a number of volumes entitled *À la lumière du marxisme* ('In Light of Marxism'), and then in the review *La Pensée*, launched in early 1939. Another Marxism was developed and disseminated in the PCF schools, both at the central level and in the local federations, around a programme geared towards organised political action, which took on structured form between 1933 and 1935. A variant of this popularised Marxism, aimed at a wider audience of militants, members or sympathisers, can be found in the PCF press and its pamphlets, and in the numerous public talks offered by structures on the model of the workers' (or people's) universities. In each case, the Communists' Marx bore the influence of the Comintern and the USSR, and indeed that of the French ideological and political situation. These latter thus made up an evolving context, which moulded the forms taken by the Communist reference to Marx. Three dates can be used as reference points for appreciating these evolutions and the play of influences: 1933 (the fiftieth anniversary of Marx's death); 1936, with the PCF's Eighth Congress, which celebrated Marxist research in France; and 1938–9, the years of the publication of the Stalinist textbook *The Short Course* and the creation of the review *La Pensée*.

4.1   *1933: 'Marx Belongs to Us'!*

The fiftieth anniversary of Marx's death, in spring 1933, was a moment for the PCF to affirm its attachment to the German author's thought and to the dissemination of his ideas and his works. This event did not go unnoticed. Various magazines and newspapers devoted articles to it: in *Europe* and *Monde*, close to the PCF; in *La Bataille socialiste* and *La Vie socialiste*, in the orbit of the SFIO; and in *Le Temps*, on the conservative wing of French politics. While they all observed that knowledge of Marx was progressing, his theoretical claims were the object of sharp clashes, in which the PCF tried to appear as the only legitimate heir to Marx's thought and as the political force that drew inspiration from it.

As early as September 1932, the preparation of this anniversary was the object of a decision by the Communist International. The Twelfth Plenum,

---

6   Gouarné 2013.

meeting in Moscow, called on the various national sections to commit themselves to a commemorative initiative, which would also be part of the Communists' dispute with social democracy. In France, it was Jacques Duclos who introduced the plans for these events, in a speech which he concluded with a stirring appeal not to leave Marx to the reformist social democrats. In response to the initiatives taken by the SFIO to commemorate Marx's death, he called on the PCF to react: 'No, Marx does not belong to social democracy. Marx belongs to us' (PCF Central Committee, February 1933). He insisted on the importance of Marx's ideas in the context of the crisis of the capitalist system, while also recognising the PCF's own weaknesses: 'Without doubt, our party has something of a shortfall in Marxist knowledge'. The party's various bodies mobilised to organise a series of events as well as the publication and translation of texts by Marx; all of these fitted into a very explicitly political framework. This was explained, for example, in the editorial of the special issue of the *Cahiers du Bolchevisme* on Marx – dated 14 March 1933, in the immediate wake of the Reichstag fire and the Nazis' campaign against Marxism in Germany. Party leaders and orators gave numerous speeches and published a series of articles in *L'Humanité* as well as the PCF's provincial newspapers. This campaign remained strongly dominated by the confrontation within the workers' movement and by the perspective of the imminent collapse of capitalism.

4.2   1936: 'Marxism's Growing Influence'

When we compare this 1933 campaign with the way in which the struggle for the dissemination and development of Marxism was seen three years later, the change of tone is striking. 1936, marked by the victory of the Popular Front, was also a year when new research appeared and established itself in France, referring to Marx's thought in the framework of academic studies based on scholarly practice.

The theme of 'Marxism's growing influence [*rayonnement*]' – a line that evoked the idea of an opening beyond a Marxism for militants alone – was introduced for the first time by René Maublanc in the January 1936 issue of the *Cahiers du Bolchevisme*. Maublanc drew an assessment which overlapped with the one advanced by Marcel Ollivier ten years earlier, noting the weak dissemination of Marxism in France. But he also emphasised the new factors favourable to increased Marxist influence, as he cited, in turn, the positive image of the USSR with 'its impressive progress'; the extent of the world economic crisis; the struggle against fascism, denounced as a 'return to obscurantism'; and the defence of culture and science. These provided so many foundations for arousing interest in Marxism. In this regard, he also referred to the role of the mobilisation led by the Association des écrivains et artistes révolution- naires

(Association of Revolutionary Writers and Artists; AEAR) and its journal *Commune*, with the staging of the International Writers' Congress in 1935.[7] The political terrain was thus prepared for widened familiarity with Marxism. Maublanc welcomed the proliferation of initiatives, talks and educational evenings in Paris and the provinces, at the instigation of various organisations such as Les Amis de la Commune, the Cercle de la Russie neuve and the workers' universities, which pursued their endeavours among different milieus: the working classes, of course, but also the world of students and teachers. At the end of this panorama, he mentioned the talks given to the Cercle de la Russie neuve, in particular by its scholarly commission directed by Paul Langevin and Henri Wallon. These lectures were grouped together and published under the common title *À la lumière du marxisme*.

At the beginning of 1936, the PCF congress was held in Villeurbanne under the banner of the Popular Front and anti-fascism. Marcel Cachin, a historic PCF leader, opened the congress by emphasising the progress that had been made and the political results already obtained by the new orientation. He illustrated his remarks with reference to the educational effort but also the new Marxist research, the significance of which he also stressed: 'I remember the difficulty we had in getting Marxism to penetrate our country and we should say that this fact, the fact of the publication of this work [*À la lumière du marxisme*], is a very important date in our country, at a time when Mr. Hitler is burning books on Marxism'. As for Thorez, throughout his speech devoted to explaining and justifying the PCF's policy, he constantly invoked the ideas of Marx, often associated with those of Lenin and Stalin, to shed light on the choices that had been taken and in particular the new popular-frontist line.

A dynamic was then set in motion: Marxist production in the fields of history, social sciences and natural sciences was constantly encouraged and reinforced by publishing efforts and the talks at workers' universities. These latter mixed purely political lectures, directly inspired by the Stalinist vulgate on the theory of the party and the history of the Russian revolution, with other courses based on the thought and experience of the PCF on the national question, the history of the French workers' movement and revolutionary traditions. The creation, in 1939, of a new review, *La Pensée. Revue du rationalisme moderne*, should be seen as a continuation of these endeavours.

These openings should also be set in contrast with the evolution of Marxist-Leninist doctrine. Just before the creation of *La Pensée*, the Communist International's official organ had transmitted to all Communist Parties the instruc-

---

7   Teroni and Klein 2005.

tions for the use of Stalin's latest work, a textbook entitled *History of the Communist Party of the Soviet Union (Bolsheviks)*. Known as the *Short Course*, it contained summaries of Marxist philosophy and the theory of the party, its structures and its activity. This Stalinist Marxism-Leninism was hitherto meant to permeate all their of propaganda and training activities.

The first 'battle for reading' waged by the PCF in spring 1939 allowed for the distribution of several tens of thousands of books. The orientation of *La Pensée* also stirred concerns in the Communist International leadership; in late 1939, it chided the French Communist review for not sufficiently linking critical analysis to the contemporary context, i.e. the knock-on effects of the German-Soviet Pact within the PCF, about which the journal maintained a total silence.

During the clandestine period (the PCF was banned in 1939), the party's theoretical publications, such as the *Cahiers du bolchevisme*, emphasised the reference to Marxism-Leninism, thus demoting Marx's own texts into the background. The curricula of the cadre schools integrated the recommendations of Stalin's textbook for the whole theoretical part of political teaching – this was the case, for example, in the schools organised in Algeria in early 1944 upon the authority of André Marty. In this programme, Marx's thought as such never appears, except occasionally and indirectly in Étienne Fajon's course on the Marxist-Leninist theory of revolution or in a commentary on Lenin's text on the three sources of Marxism, presented by Roger Garaudy in a course on the 'scientific bases of the Party's politics'.

5   'Militant Marxism' as a Party Doctrine after the War

In autumn 1944, when *La Pensée* re-emerged, the orientation which had prevailed upon its foundation was again confirmed. Alongside Paul Langevin, the editorial board included Frédéric Joliot-Curie and Henri Wallon. In the columns of the journal, there are quite a few articles on the formation of Marx's thought, his correspondence and the genesis of his best-known texts. The PCF provided a platform to the intellectuals and scientists who had joined it in large numbers during the war: they engaged in various projects that took up the theme of a Marxism fertilised by scientific practice and the heritage of the *Encyclopédistes*. For instance, Marcel Prenant, a professor of biology at the Sorbonne and a leader of the Francs-tireurs et partisans (FTP) during the war, extolled the links between the Marxist method and science in the January 1946 issue of *La Pensée*.

But when the PCF launched a new review for intellectuals in December 1948, as the Cold War was gaining momentum, it bore a conception which fitted into the tradition of Marxism-Leninism. In the Cold War confrontation, Marxism became first and foremost a tool of political combat. The title of the review, *La Nouvelle Critique*, and above all its subtitle, *Revue du marxisme militant*, were illustrative of this political-theoretical programme. The first issue of the journal outlined the contours and expectations of 'militant Marxism', which is 'a militant doctrine and not a material of disinterested speculation, a catalogue of dead references on which one can build the most gratuitous conceptual scaffolding'. The articles, which journalists were often tasked with writing, provided an intellectual underpinning for party policy.

Upon the death of Stalin in 1953, it was clear how much distance had been travelled since the days when the Communist International's leaders regretted the lack of knowledge of Marx in France. In the intervening period, the contribution of the PCF to the dissemination of knowledge of Marx had taken multiple forms. Alongside a revolutionary, immediately political Marx (the one presented in pamphlets and schools), the Communist milieu also got to grips with a more scholarly Marxism, in the 1920s based on the work of David Ryazanov and then, from the Popular Front years onwards, on the history of French materialism and of rational scientific thought more generally. But this Marxism, reborn in 1945–7, was periodically relegated to the background, as shown by the orientation taken in 1948. In short, thanks to its mass influence, its organisational and electoral weight, its press and the diversity of its cultural activities, the PCF contributed to making Marx more widely known. But the weight of Marxism-Leninism had the effect of putting Marx's own work at something of a distance (except for a few texts on French revolutionary history), such that his writings were known essentially only via the interpretations of those who presented themselves as his heirs. The return to Marx, which had been put on the agenda in 1920 and attempted at the end of the 1930s, did not take off. Nevertheless, it was a topic that would regain forceful relevance among Communist intellectuals after 1956, in the context of de-Stalinisation.

CHAPTER 6

The Communists' Marx: A (Now-)Problematic Reference Point, 1956–2017

Anthony Crézégut

In 1983, Marx's death was officially registered in the collective imagination. The slogan 'Marx is dead', proclaimed by the Nouveaux Philosophes, had become a commonplace in the French press. The poster put up by the Union of Communist Students (UEC) declaring 'Marx is dead? My eye!' appeared to be a provocation for a youth who, in the cinemas, jeered Charles Max, the teacher mocked for his fetishistic attachment to communist symbols in the film *Profs*. After the French Communist Party (PCF) abandoned the aim of the 'dictatorship of the proletariat' in 1976, Marxism-Leninism was dropped in 1979. The consequences remained uncertain – setting the party between the perspective of a return to Marx and breaking out of Marxism altogether. The crisis in the relations between the PCF and a major wing of its intellectuals led to the break-up of the review *La Nouvelle Critique*, the weekly *France nouvelle* and of the Centre d'études et de recherches marxistes (CERM). This identity crisis in the PCF in the 1980s brought a conclusion to a process which had begun in the 1960s, when the French variant of Stalinism from the immediate postwar period – this rigid but hybrid construction – was brought into question. The schematism of PCF thought – the dogmatism embodied, at least from 1947 to 1956, by the *Nouvelle Critique* team led by Jean Kanapa, or indeed Roger Garaudy, the party's official philosopher – contrasted with a sometimes more limited knowledge of Marx's whole oeuvre. At the beginning of the 1950s, a few academic Marxologists had a close knowledge of Marx, but the official conception among militants remained that of Georges Politzer's *Manuel de philosophie*, revised and corrected by Guy Besse and Maurice Caveing. The didactic nature and complex composition of this tome meant that it lagged far behind the most innovative writings of the 1930s, by Politzer himself, but also by Henri Lefebvre, Georges Friedmann and Henri Wallon, who rediscovered Marx's youthful philosophical work, while at the same time sketching out an original relationship between science and Marxism. In the second half of the twentieth century, 'vulgar Marxism' – drawn from Russian sources, from Plekhanov to Stalin, then grafted onto the trunk of French materialism and rationalism – became French intellectuals' main target. Brought up on a classical culture, ancient materialism and the philosophers of the Enlightenment – references acquired laboriously and lovingly – PCF general secretary Maurice Thorez, who imposed his writ on the party up till his death in 1964 – nevertheless remained strictly orthodox in the field of Marxism, marked by the canon set at the turn of the 1930s.[1] But how did this initially dogmatic postwar Marxism seek to transform itself to meet the challenges of its time, without calling into question its own theoretical foundations? In other words, how was it possible to maintain the equilibrium of the monumental edifice that was the PCF, avoid a split between its intellectuals and its generally working-class militants, and still guarantee the apparatus's control over the whole party structure?

1   Vulgarising Marxism: The 'Granite Masses' of French Communism (1945–60)

With the term 'vulgar Marxism', intellectuals like Jean-Paul Sartre, Henri Lefebvre and Lucien Goldmann castigated a conception of Marxism which was widely disseminated by the PCF, a mechanistic determinism that underestimated the subtleties of dialectics and subjective action in history. The philosophers' disdain for this vulgar Marxism should not blind us to another element of paramount importance: the unprecedented scale of the dissemination of Marx's texts in French society. The PCF had succeeded in making a vulgarised Marxism, partly taking up a schematic discourse of Guesdist mould, into indisputable horizon of its time and the central battleground for the French intelligentsia. The account given by the debonair mayor of a village in the Luberon, Bonnieux, interviewed by Michel Polac for ORTF in 1969, gives an idea of how solidly rooted this vulgarised Marxism had become: the mayor said that he read little, apart from the poetry of René Char, whom he had got to know during the Resistance, the bucolic novels of Jean Giono and ... Marx's *Capital*, which he displayed on his bedside table. This can be seen as a product of the web of PCF schools, a pyramid-shaped organisation structured across the entire national territory, where from the postwar period onward hundreds of thousands of militants, most of them of working-class origin, got in touch with a Marxist analytical framework which remained very widely operative at least until the 1980s.[2] The texts most regularly offered for militants to read in

1   Wieviorka 2010.
2   Mischi 2014.

elementary-level, federation-level and central party school courses at the end of the 1950s were the *Communist Manifesto* (the main text of reference), economic pamphlets such as *Wages, Price and Profits* or *Wage Labour and Capital*, and Engels's overviews, first and foremost meaning *Socialism: Utopian and Scientific*. The educational materials used were characterised by a very high degree of homogeneity and the repetition of one same discourse; this was gradually enriched as one progressed up the hierarchy of party schools, but it always retained a strong pedagogical dimension and a function of 'bringing into conformity' the political body constituting the communist 'counter-society'.[3] Critical investigation of Marx's work was limited, while the author of *Capital* – a work which was often cited, but little studied as such – was seamlessly fused with Engels. Marx in any case occupied only a secondary place in relation to Lenin, Stalin (at least before this particular reference point disappeared in the early 1960s), and especially Maurice Thorez. In addition to Party schools, militants could attend evening classes given by certain PCF federations, such as Paris's, and also by the Université nouvelle – not forgetting CERM's role as an alternative educational centre. In the 1960s, the PCF also offered popular editions of Marx and Engels, with bright orange covers; printed in large numbers, they gave privileged access to the pair's works, and especially to Marx's youthful texts, such as *The German Ideology* and the *1844 Manuscripts*.[4] The vulgar Marxism of the PCF meant these 'masses of granite', these ideas and formulas that the organisation engraved in the heads of each militant, giving an intellectual framework to the experiences they lived in the factory or the housing estate.

Marxism was not only inscribed in texts, but – from the interwar period onward – also on the walls of the streets governed by 'red' town halls. In the 1960s, nearly thirty streets and boulevards in France carried Karl Marx's name, as did a few schools, mainly in the 'red' banlieues. However, in this toponymy Marx lagged behind Lenin and far behind other Communist figures who represented the different phases of the PCF's history and the changes in the Party line: the martyrs of the resistance (Georges Politzer, Gabriel Péri), then the heroes of the renewed Soviet Union (Yuri Gagarin) and finally the figures of hope in Chile's Popular Unity (Pablo Neruda, Salvador Allende).

---

3 Kriegel 1985.
4 Bouju 2010.

2   The Theoretical *Aggiornamento*: Reconciling Continued Dogma with Adaptation to Social Change (1960–6)

God Is Dead. The title of Roger Garaudy's 1962 book on the relationship between Hegel and Marx could equally sum up the crisis that had broken out among French intellectuals, shaken by the death of Stalin, the revelations at the CPSU's Twentieth Congress and the desacralisation of Marxism-Leninism. All this makes it possible to question what the equivocal term 'Stalinism' might mean, in the French communist tradition.[5] Reviews close to the PCF, such as *La Pensée* and *La Nouvelle Critique*, rediscovered Marx. Émile Bottigelli, Gilbert Badia and Auguste Cornu historicised his work, identifying inflections, evolutions and ruptures. A number of Communist intellectuals laid their hands on Antonio Gramsci (dreaming of a more open and intellectual left, on the Italian model)[6] but also Georg Lukács and a whole French tradition of the history of mentalities, in particular that of the Annales school, in order to develop their Marxism at a distance from the canon. Marxism became problematic again. Sartre discussed 'questions of method' and completed Marx with Kierkegaard. Henri Lefebvre, with his *Problèmes actuels du marxisme*, envisaged the refoundation of a revolutionary romanticism, on the edges of Nietzsche and Goldmann, on the fringes of the PCF, and conceived of the choice for Marxism as a Pascalian wager. This research programme provided the possibility of questioning the formation of political ideologies, the relationship between the conception of the world and social classes, and to rethink the genesis of Marxism, in a humanist context. Jean-Pierre Vernant's 'open Marxism' studied the structure of Greek myth and the origins of scientific thought. In 1959, Louis Althusser developed a profound critique of Montesquieu's aristocratic worldview, linking his theory of history and political philosophy to both his class position and the time and place in which he thought. Before Althusser, as early as 1956 Jean-Toussaint Desanti had contextualised the originality of Spinoza's philosophy, a possible source of a scientific Marxism but also a dialogue with the demand for intellectual freedom (even if one emanating from a Jewish heretic in a bourgeois environment). Meanwhile the linguist Georges Mounin problematised the relationship between Machiavelli's thought, placed back in its own historical era, and the problems posed by Machiavellianism in 1958 – a thorny problem, this, in the aftermath of the CPSU's Twentieth Congress.

---

5   Martelli 1981.
6   Forlin 2006.

This opening up of the field of Marxist studies took place outside the PCF but also within it. However, the leadership was wary of overly critical lines of questioning and had a distaste for doctrinal hybridisations which broke down the conception of the world forged by Marxism-Leninism. It was all the more alarmed given that many of its critical intellectuals joined oppositional groups. *La Nouvelle Critique*, founded in 1948 by Jean Kanapa and subtitled *Revue du marxisme militant*, organised the ideological struggle on the basis of an intransigent political orthodoxy, against the problematic, tendentially eclectic openness of *Les Temps modernes* or *Esprit*. Having given the opposing positions a ruthless pounding up till 1956, several editors, including Henri Lefebvre, Annie Besse, Jean-Toussaint Desanti and Émile Bottigelli, began to have doubts. In 1957–8, the review was restructured and taken over by Guy Besse.

In 1959, Léo Figuères launched the CERM. In the 1960s, Roger Garaudy was its chairman, making it into the tool of a policy of intellectual openness, marked in particular by the first Semaines de la pensée marxiste ('Marxist Thought Weeks'). With Thorez's rather reserved support, Garaudy reopened the dossier on Marx, in the context of what was then called the 'critique of Stalin's philosophical errors'. He reintroduced Marx into the active and critical German idealism of Kant, Hegel and Fichte, as an alternative to the mechanistic eighteenth-century French materialism of Helvetius and Holbach, so cherished Guy Besse and Georges Cogniot. Another aspect of this revision was the rediscovery of the young Marx – the Marx of the *1844 Manuscripts*. His indignation against alienation and the spiritual impoverishment of man seems to open the way to a humanist Marxist refoundation and to allow a dialogue with the human sciences and other conceptions of the world, including religion. *La Nouvelle Critique* now welcomed a core group of philosophers – Michel Verret, Michel Simon, Lucien Sève, and André Gisselbrecht – who continued the movement of cultural openness begun by Garaudy, while distancing themselves from its philosophical foundations, which were considered weak (particularly in relation to religious ideology), sources of confusion and potentially submissive to the dominant ideology of the time.

For its part, *La Pensée*, the organ of 'modern rationalism', sought a refoundation of dialectical materialism in dialogue with the French epistemology of Gaston Bachelard, Georges Canguilhem and Alexandre Koyré. This programme partly coincided with that of Louis Althusser and his disciples Jacques Rancière, Étienne Balibar, Pierre Macherey and Roger Establet. Althusser, who was then an *agrégé-répétiteur* (a role similar to that of a teaching fellow) at the École normale supérieure in Rue d'Ulm, proposed to reconstruct dialectical materialism on the basis of Marx's mature work, of which he proposed a new, creative reading, and at the same time deconstructed the major categories of official

Marxism (history, subject, dialectic, praxis). Beyond his radical theses on the periodisation of Marx's work – a move deemed stimulating but philologically questionable by many Marxist philosophers in the PCF – Althusser had the merit of re-problematising Marx's work and of suggesting that readings of Marx were open to interpretation, outside the canon imposed by political authority. Althusser's endeavour was, more concretely, an intellectual engine directed at destroying the theoretical edifice built up by Garaudy, whom Althusser saw as a modern revisionist who had turned his back on the radicalism of Marx's enterprise. Doubtless, Garaudy, who was well-familiar with the classic texts, drew on often decontextualised citations from Marx in order to valorise the 'human foundation of religion' and insisted on the active side of *praxis* in the act of knowledge, even if this meant slipping into a 'philosophy of the act', closer to Fichtean activism than to a neo-Kantian criticism. It is also true that he drew on the Marxian concept of the 'collective worker' to theorise the displacement of the leading force of the revolutionary movement from the working class to the new intellectuals, thus bringing him toward the theses defended by the Parti socialiste unifié (PSU) and, at its margins, by André Gorz and Serge Mallet.

For the leaders of the PCF, the priority was that these intellectuals should remain within the limits imposed by the organisation, with each intellectual debate read by the yardstick of its immediate practical consequences. When Thorez died in 1964, the Communist leadership had to avoid both the retreat into a restricted base – the 'funereal solo' of the working class, as one established Marxian expression called it – to which Althusserian intransigence could lead, as well as dissolution into the transclassist new Left, towards which Garaudy's humanist reading seemed to be sliding. The conflicts which arose within Union of Communist Students (UEC) between 1961 and 1965 allowed the Thorezite leadership to measure the political consequences which the opening up of debate on Marx and Marxism could entail. Marx and Marxism were no longer obligatory references, a set of quotations to be endlessly repeated, but an open heritage, a place of confrontation between different interpretations, interwoven with different, even opposed, strategic options. A humanist and romantic young Marx, a quarrelsome wandering Jew who had broken from his bourgeois background, a critical intellectual – all this served as a model for the heralds of what became the Revolutionary Communist Youth (JCR; Trotskyist), Alain Krivine, Henri Weber and Daniel Bensaïd. They moreover associated this with such critics of bureaucracy as Leon Trotsky (naturally) but also Rosa Luxemburg. For the 'pro-Italian' leadership of the UEC (Alain Forner, Jean Schalit, Serge July, André Sénik or Bernard Kouchner), sympathetic to the Italian Communist Party, Marx was no longer necessarily a canonical reference but a method for action. For this current, it was primarily Marxism itself that needed to be renovated, rejuvenated, and brought up to speed with the evolution of society. This also meant connecting it to advanced research in the aesthetic field (from Louis Aragon's 'open realism' to Garaudy's 'realism without shores', which looked longingly toward the *nouveau roman*, the New Wave in cinema and contemporary art). As against this, the *Cahiers marxistes-léninistes* team (Alain Badiou, Étienne Balibar, Roger Establet, Benny Lévy, Robert Linhart ...) were concerned with the defense and re-establishment of a theoretical Marx; they partly rallied to the Chinese Cultural Revolution, taking up as their banner the well-known formula: 'the Marxist doctrine is omnipotent because it is true'.

The students in revolt, but also the rival philosophers Althusser and Garaudy, had in common the fact that they recognised the broad autonomy of the superstructural, and thus granted intellectuals a role that was anything but auxiliary. The PCF leadership responded by re-establishing an official interpretation, retrieving from the heritage of Marx and Engels all that allowed for the moderation of one-sided interpretations, and calming this youthful ardour. The Central Committee meeting in Argenteuil in 1966 – a real communist *aggiornamento*, two years after the Second Vatican Council – focused on ideological and cultural problems. It sought to reaffirm certain untouchable principles while also granting far-reaching freedom to intellectuals, so long as they remained within the limits set by the organisation. This was the conciliation achieved by the new general secretary, Waldeck Rochet, a conscientious leader lively and level-headed in his thinking and prudent as a politician, concerned with balance and progress.[7] Rochet's report summarising the meeting provides a complete doctrinal clarification, supported by methodically commented quotations from Marx, Engels and Lenin. Widely distributed under the title *Le Marxisme et les chemins de l'avenir* ('Marxism and the Paths of the Future'), this document was the theoretical basis of the fundamental political text of the years to come, the Champigny Manifesto of 1968. It laid the foundations of a pluralist and democratic socialism *à la française*, reaffirming the leading role of a working class in search of alliances with the new intellectual strata, of which the new Socialist Party (PS) was striving to become the party of reference.[8]

---

7 Vigreux 2000.
8 Burles 1981.

3   Marxism as a Battlefield, from Politics to the University (1966–78)

In May '68, Marx burst into the university, first through the portraits and graffiti that flourished on the walls ('The old mole of history truly seems to be gnawing away at the Sorbonne. Telegram from Marx, 13 May 1968'). Carried on the shoulders of a series of small groups breaking away from the PCF, this Marx was largely derived from the Situationists' light-hearted *détournement* or the seriousness – sometimes icy and sometimes boiling – of the various Maoist or Trotskyist groups. At the same time, intellectuals within PCF ranks entered the university, which had long remained closed to them, and indeed the Sciences Po, where the historian Jean Bruhat gave a course on Marxism every two years. Amidst this ferment, one of the symbols of this Marxism within the university was *Dialectiques*, a review founded by students at the ENS in Saint-Cloud. Situated at the crossroads between Gramsci and Althusser, it sought dialogue with the social sciences, especially anthropology and linguistics.

The leadership of the PCF watched this excitement closely, though it was divided between its interest in a politically advantageous opening and its concern about the centrifugal tendencies of such cultural operations.[9] Its first tactical objective was to seek alliances that would prevent its isolation, faced with the far-left *gauchistes* and a new Socialist Party that was extending its own antennae into the university. This approach was initiated by Aragon and *Les Lettres françaises*, which explored the formalism of the journal *Tel Quel*. For its part, Guy Besse's *La Pensée* tried to forge an alliance with critical epistemology. But in 1972–3, these alliances were already stillborn, or very much weakened. Only *La Nouvelle Critique* maintained a dialogue with a whole section of the social sciences: up till 1978–9 it kept alive the illusion of a potential autonomy for intellectuals within the PCF, which would make it possible to refound Communist discourse to adapt it to the challenges of the cultural crisis of the 1970s.[10]

The PCF leadership's second objective was strategic: to enrich its doctrine in dribs and drabs without calling into question its foundations, and to constitute a collective intellectual under the political apparatus's control.[11] Economic analysis remained the hard core, while the enrichment came from the works of Paul Boccara. Via the Economic Section, these latter directly influenced the line of Georges Marchais's PCF and played a role in the training of PCF militants and cadres.[12] A rereading of Volume III of *Capital* allowed Boccara's precious

---

9   Di Maggio 2013.
10   Matonti 2015.
11   Pudal 2008.
12   Ethuin 2006.

detection of a crisis of capital over-accumulation, in response to which came a search for counter-cyclical policies essentially taken up by the state, giving rise to a phase of state monopoly capitalism (SMC). This analysis, contested by the Trotskyist leader Ernest Mandel as well as certain regulationist theorists, allowed the PCF to identify a clear alternative: a left-wing Keynesianism that would revive production through the nationalisation of monopolies and stimulate demand through an expansionary monetary policy. The other social sciences made a far weaker contribution to the official PCF party line. Only urban geography – as embodied by figures like Félix Damette, François Ascher, Jacques Scheibling and Jacques Lévy in the journal *Espaces-Temps*, crossing geography with political science, sociology and economics, and drawing on Marx and Engels's scant writings on the spatial question – found a place. As for the political sociology sketched out by Marx and completed by Gramsci, it was taken into the PCF corpus through the publication of the volume *Les Communistes et l'État* in 1977. It gave the Eurocommunist line the concept of hegemony – a tactically opportune and strategically fruitful substitute for the concept of the dictatorship of the proletariat, which had largely fallen into disuse in the PCF's discursive practice. This line, theorised by *La Nouvelle Critique*'s driving force François Hincker, but also by the historian Jean Ellenstein, one of the leaders of the CERM, supported Jean Kanapa's efforts to draw Georges Marchais onto a Eurocommunist line.[13] In the context of quarrels in the media with a PS which tried to assert its democratic-socialist identity and presented the PCF as the heir to authoritarian socialism, the PCF general secretary buried the dictatorship of the proletariat in a 1976 TV appearance and then had his decision endorsed by the party's Twenty-Second Congress the same year.

The ephemeral Eurocommunist moment of 1977 – further visible in the pursuit of the policy of editorial openness begun by Lucien Sève at the head of Éditions sociales – was quickly thwarted by a general crisis in the organisation, at the heart of which was the relationship between the Party apparatus and its intellectuals. Panicked by the PS's advance, the Communist leadership was on the defensive, confronted with a virulent media offensive and undermined by stirrings of dissent from intellectuals, the bulk of them in the Paris PCF Federation, which experienced an acute crisis from 1978 onwards. The PCF, caught up in the contradictions arising from the will to openness displayed in previous years, stiffened around a narrowed, identitarian core – its working-class social base – and reaffirmed its rejection of social democracy. The PS then acquired a relative hegemony in the intellectual world, while a number

---

13   Streiff 2002.

of the Marxists of the 1970s abandoned the PCF and made their home in the university, repressing or subsuming their initial Marxist formation. The Communist intellectual world, now weakened in an enduring way, went through a recomposition process. The CERM, *La France Nouvelle*, *La Nouvelle Critique* and the Institut Maurice Thorez were each dissolved and d by the periodical *Révolution* and the Institut de recherches marxistes (IRM). In an unfavourable context, these latter to maintain a space for research in the historical and sociological fields, in step with academic production, and to pursue the ideological struggle on various levels.

4   The Farewell to Marxism-Leninism, the Return to Marx and the Flowering of 'A Thousand Marxisms' (1980–2017)

With the Communist 'home' now dilapidated, recomposition would proceed through the rediscovery of the materials from which it was built.[14] There were several possible paths to follow, in the bid to reconstruct a political and cultural alternative. One was taken by historic leader Pierre Juquin. Between 1983 and 1987, the former secretary of the PCF's Education Commission led a dissident grouping whose doctrinal coherence was all the less apparent given that it sought both to bring together Marxism with libertarian-inspired currents and build alliances with the PSU, the Revolutionary Communist League (LCR) and the Greens. He wanted the PCF to be refounded on the basis of a reinterpretation of Marx, ridded of the muck of Marxism, in order to revive the utopia of self-management and reconnect with the municipal, regional and European levels. Juquin's choice in favour of refoundation divided cadres in the PCF apparatus and was ultimately rejected by the party leadership, which marginalised him. Another, very different, path was the one proposed by Claude Mazauric and Roger Martelli, in dialogue with Michel Vovelle, as the bicentenary of the Revolution approached. It sought a re-actualisation of the political concept of the nation and of the radical-democratic Jacobin tradition – in turn requiring an engagement with the evolution of Marx's thought on the French Revolution. In this context of generalised crisis, what had been accepted as evident truths about Marx's work were themselves reconsidered, notably through Jean-Pierre Lefebvre's rich and thematised (re)translation of *Capital*, André Tosel's reappropriation of Italian Marxism – and of Gramsci, in particular – or indeed the search for the original philosophical foundations of Marxism

---

14   Lazar 1992.

and of Marx's own philosophy by philosophers such as Georges Labica and Étienne Balibar. This meant rediscovering that Marx is not thinker who theorised a complete system but a thinker of the possible, an analyst of the forms of a movement that always overflows all established frameworks. These plural readings, these 'thousand Marxisms', found their translation in intellectual circles often situated at some distance from the party, whose most notable expressions were the *Dictionnaire critique du marxisme* published by Presses Universitaires de France and the creation of *Actuel Marx* journal by Jacques Bidet and Jacques Texier, again during the 1980s.

After a period of decomposition in the international communist movement, Robert Hue took over from Georges Marchais as head of the PCF in 1994. He launched what he called the 'mutation', which was also an attempt to formalise tendencies that had already become manifest in the previous decade. Heir to a weakened organisation, deserted by its intellectuals and deprived of part of its editorial apparatus with the bankruptcy of Éditions sociales, he accelerated the shift by abandoning the centralisation of the educational apparatuses which had hitherto provided for the dissemination of Marx's texts at the various levels of the party. Refusing an Italian-style self-dissolution, Hue nevertheless declared himself in favour of abandoning part of the Communist heritage in favour of an ecumenical humanism, compatible with an alliance under the Socialist Party's hegemony. He did away with the insistent references to Marx and Marxist concepts in favour of less clearly defined categories such as 'people', 'the human' and 'citizenship', which the late Marchais era had already established in PCF discourse.

In the 2000s, as the PCF's membership collapsed, and with its electoral scores continuing to shrink, the party saw a confrontation among at least four lines, revealing how much the party had splintered. Each current had a specific relationship with Marx and Marxism – not excluding, in certain cases, syncretisms or assemblages which were less concerned with doctrinal or historical coherence than with identity construction. The first, 'pro-mutation', current was guided less by theoretical research than by the need to control the apparatus and political balances. It could celebrate both the humanist, indignant Marx of the *1844 Manuscripts* and Marx and Engels's late democratic writings reflecting on radical action within the parliamentary framework. On the whole, it sought to move away from the exclusive reference to Marx and Marxism and to open up to other contemporary or historical reference points from the French left's past. The second group were the 'innovators', structured around the economic section of the PCF, the Val-de-Marne federation and a leadership core in the CGT. Controlling what remained of its internal educational apparatus and journals like *Économie et Politique*, it continues to draw on and update

Boccara's theses on state monopoly capitalism, and found its basis in Marx's economic analyses in *Capital*. The third group were the 'refounders', bringing together part of the PCF's elected representatives (especially in the Paris region and in the Bouches-du-Rhône) and historical PCF intellectuals, among them Roger Martelli and Lucien Sève. They had a particular influence in *L'Human-ité*, in *Regards* magazine, and in the IRM, which became *Espaces Marx* in 1995. Theirs was a plural Marx with libertarian, sometimes utopian accents, the Marx of *The German Ideology* who – with Engels – revalorised the moment of cri-tique, as linked to activity that could transform reality. A formula drawn from this work written in 1845–6, 'Communism is not a goal, an ideal, but the real movement that abolishes the present state of things', taken up by Lucien Sève, became the motto of this current; it sought closer relations with alterglobalism, citizen forums and social movements. The fourth was the 'orthodox' current, which called for a return to an 'original' Marxism, or at least the one cultivated by the PCF before the 1990s. This current, rooted in a few working-class bastions in the Nord-Pas-de-Calais and Picardy, and built up from a dissident core in the Paris region, was enlivened by young militants active in the reconstitution of the Jeunesse communiste (JC) and the UEC; its message was also imparted by a smattering of municipalities in the Rhône-Alpes region. It distinguished itself less by its theoretical originality than by its work of popularising Marxism. This current regularly quoted the line 'The history of all hitherto existing societies is the history of class struggles', using it as the epigraph for their alternative text submitted to the Thirty-Fourth PCF congress in 2008.

Since the 1990s, there has visibly been a severe weakening of the PCF's organ-ised Marxist culture. This owes in particular to the abandonment of the party's schools and the loss of influence of its reviews. However, since 2008, with the crisis of financial capitalism and the cracks in the hegemony of neoliberal dis-course, the PCF's educational programmes, notably at the federation level or in the summer universities, have found a second wind, with young Communists showing a thirst for getting a Marxist training. In publishing, there is a revival of publishing houses which advance different facets of a neo-Marxist culture, whether it be the trusty 'Actuel Marx' collection with Presses universitaires de France, certain works by Éditions de la Découverte, following on from Mas-pero, or newcomers such as La Dispute, Le Temps des Cerises, Delga, Syllepse, Éditions critiques, or the refounded Éditions sociales. Marxist research spread again, overcoming old political divisions and generational chasms. As Nicolas Tertulian proposed to reread Lukács, and André Tosel did the same for Gram-sci – authors still relevant today, who have long been labelled 'Western Marx-ists' – Lucien Sève continued his patient work of philological reconstruction of the Marxian conceptual apparatus. Marx's work also found new fields of application in the social sciences, whether in linguistics with Jean-Jacques Lecercle, in anthropology with Maurice Godelier or in economics with Gérard Duménil. In philosophy, through the constancy of philosophers from the Althusserian tradition, Alain Badiou, Étienne Balibar or Jacques Bidet, Marx seems to have been installed as a legitimate author, including through his recent integration into the programme of the *agrégation de philosophie*. A younger generation is taking over the reins, providing seminars, university courses and research programmes, while also turning its hand to new translations of Marx. The French Communist Party also offers space to this Marx revival in its press, in debates or interviews in *L'Humanité* as well as in the in-depth studies in *La Revue du projet*. The Marx bicentenary was to be an opportunity to reaffirm what the party's relationship to Marx could be in the twenty-first century, between the discretion established in the 1990s and the multiple reappropriations that have taken place starting in the late 2010s. The craze around the film *The Young Karl Marx* by the Haitian director Raoul Peck – projected in many PCF sections, but also more widely in the circles of the Amis de *L'Humanité* and in the trade union sections of the CGT, offers a first sign of this renewal of a possible Communist reappropriation of Marx studies.

CHAPTER 7

The Far Left's Marx: The Politicisation of a Scholarly Marxism

Patrick Massa

One of the peculiarities of the French left is the relatively high and long-term influence of a far left critical of the Soviet model and of the French Communist Party (PCF), across a sequence running from the 1930s to the 1970s. Two major currents stand out in this regard. Trotskyism appeared in France at the end of the 1920s; the birth of Maoism came later, for its rise in the 1960s was prompted by China's 'Cultural Revolution'.[1] Both peaked around 1968 before falling victim to the discrediting of Marxism in the late 1970s.[2]

These two currents' contribution to the history of Marxism has often been noted. From the outset, it should be emphasised that their weak structural implantation relieved them of the concern of managing electoral clienteles, shaping a militant habitus that often lay high value on theoretical finesse. As they prepared their indictments of the PCF's lack of fidelity to Marxism, they were bound to rely on the foundational texts. Despite their outward workerism, these movements drew their strength from the student revolts: for instance, both the Trotskyist Ligue communiste révolutionnaire (LCR) and the Maoist Union des jeunesses communistes marxistes-léninistes (UJC-ml) arose as a result of the crisis in the PCF's own youth organisation, the Union des étudiants communistes (UEC). This anchoring in the student milieu reinforced their theoretical tropism, often inseparable from a long history of ruptures and splits provoking the birth of a multitude of small competing organisations, which each constantly sought to legitimise their existence in the name of Marxism. The presence of academics within their ranks has also allowed them to mobilise a scholarly knowledge of Marx, different from the vulgate that was usually transmitted in the big organisations' educational programmes. In this regard, we could cite the leaders of the Maoist group Gauche prolétarienne, who were often former students of Louis Althusser at the rue d'Ulm, which imbued them with dispositions conducive to an over-investment in theoretical jousting.

---

1   Chi et al., 2017.
2   Sommier 2008.

Yet, it would be reductive to see in the Marxism of the far left only a legitimising discourse or an erudite game. Militant intellectuals to the Left of the PCF have been able to make profitable use of Marx's work – and, far from practising a simple 'return to Marx', they have also aimed to provide an explanation of 'contemporary social processes'. Without any claim to exhaustiveness, here we will mention here some of the major debates conducted by the far left, in which the reference to Marx was of the highest importance.

1   Faced with the Soviet Sphinx: Marx against the USSR

One of the major points of division between the PCF and the Trotskyist minorities concerned the nature of the Soviet Union. Starting with the *New Course* in 1923, Trotsky diagnosed a worsening bureaucratism in the regime that had emerged from the 1917 revolution. This led him, in his major 1936 work *The Revolution Betrayed*, to define the Soviet state as a 'degenerated workers' state'. For him, the USSR remained a 'workers' state' because of the nationalisation and planning of the economy, but the political expropriation of the proletariat by the Stalinist bureaucracy demanded the conclusion that it had degenerated. At the end of his life, barely a year after the founding of the Fourth International in 1938, Trotsky had to battle *In Defense of Marxism* against a minority of the Socialist Workers' Party (SWP), the US American Trotskyist party, which judged that the USSR no longer had anything to do socialism and should thus no longer be accorded the status of a 'workers' state'.[3] After World War II, the continuation of this endless debate led to ever more layers of dissent within the dissent, in which reference to Marx was constantly mobilised. The position taken by Cornelius Castoriadis is one of the best-known examples of this. He published 'Les rapports de production en Russie' ('The Relations of Production in Russia') in *Socialisme ou Barbarie* in 1949, the year that this review was created, after his break with Trotskyism.[4] Here, he drew a number of quotations from *The Poverty of Philosophy* and Marx's *Contribution to the Critique of Political Economy* in order to refute the theory of the 'degenerated workers' state', which, he charged, mistakenly focused on 'juridical forms' (private or nationalised property) instead of concentrating on the real 'relations of production' in the factories. According to Castoriadis, Trotsky also made the mistake of counterposing 'production' that was socialist (because it was planned) to a 'mode of

---

3   Souyri 1970.
4   Castoriadis 1973.

income distribution' that was not yet socialist, whereas Marx had insisted on the inextricable connection between the two.

Marx's work – and *Capital* more particularly – was also used to condemn the collectivisation of agriculture in the USSR. Thus the Maoist anthropologist Pierre-Philippe Rey argued in *Les Alliances de classes*, in 1973, that the Soviet state had condensed into a short time period all the horrors described in the section of *Capital* devoted to 'primitive accumulation'.

Notable, among the Marxian concepts shelved in the USSR but particularly embraced by the far left, is the idea of an 'Asiatic mode of production', combining state despotism and the absence of private land ownership. This concept had been anathematised by Stalin, who feared that the similarities between his regime and these ancient societies would provide fodder for criticism. It is hardly surprising that his adversaries should have exhumed it in response. *Oriental Despotism* (1957) by Karl Wittfogel – a former Comintern cadre turned Cold Warrior anti-communist – was translated into French in 1964, and dissident Marxists were quick to seize on this idea. In 1965, *Socialisme ou Barbarie* published an article on Wittfogel with the unambiguous title 'Bureaucratie dominante et esclavage politique' ('Ruling bureaucracy and political slavery'). In 1967, the Fourth International leader Ernest Mandel devoted a chapter of his *Formation of the Economic Thought of Karl Marx* to the Asiatic mode. They each reproached the PCF's historians and anthropologists for avoiding the underlying political question. In 1982, Pierre Souyri, the leader of the current in *Socialisme ou Barbarie* that remained Marxist, returned to the whys and wherefores of this Stalinist falsification in *Révolution et contrerévolution en Chine*.[5]

Finally, the valorisation of the young Marx also contributed to the indictment of the Soviet regime. The *Critique of Hegel's Philosophy of Right*, in its day, caused trouble for the Prussian bureaucracy, its self-representation as a 'universal class' and its cult of secrecy: for Marxist critics Stalinism, the analogies between the USSR and Prussia seemed obvious. In his notes for a 1984 translation of Franz Mehring's *Karl Marx: The Story of His Life*, the 'Lambertist' Trotskyist Gérard Bloch (a member of the Organisation communiste internationaliste, OCI) thus explicitly drew a connection between the Soviet nomenklatura and the Prussian bureaucracy.[6] The passage from Engels's *Anti-Dühring* on the state, 'the ideal personification of the total national capital', is one of the other texts used to deny the USSR any socialist character.

---

5   Massa 2010.
6   Mehring 1981.

2   Faced with 'Late Capitalism'

The far left in all its diversity has advocated radical revolutionary overthrow, as against the social democrats and communists deemed too timid and integrated into the state apparatus. But after 1945, in Western Europe, the growth and strong development of capitalism seemed to invalidate revolutionary hopes, at least temporarily. The 'Trente Glorieuses' thus constituted a challenge for Marxists. Trotskyists, in particular, had reason to be thrown off course by this expansive long wave, since the Fourth International's 1938 *Transitional Programme* is premised on the thesis of the stagnation of the productive forces. In the 1960s, when the effects of prosperity had become noticeable to all, only the 'Lambertists' of the OCI remained faithful to this idea. The others considered it necessary to take stock of this new reality. Mandel returned to this problem in 1962 in his *Treatise on Marxist Economics*, starting from the *Grundrisse*. In these preparatory manuscripts for *Capital* he saw a brilliant anticipation of contemporary 'automation', which would create the possibility of liberating humanity from physical labour – an exciting prospect but one hindered by the logic of profit. For Mandel, the *Grundrisse* proved the absurdity of capitalism because 'the theft of other people's labour, on which today's wealth is based, seems a miserable basis, as compared to this newly developed basis'. Another way of combating the enchanted vision of postwar prosperity was to draw attention to the deskilling process which affected the proletariat, as reflected in the growing share of specialised workers (OS) within it. This meant showing that the increase in income was counterbalanced by a growing alienation in the workplace. Thus, starting from the unpublished *Chapitre inédit du Capital* (chapter six of *Capital* Volume I) which deals with the passage from 'formal subsumption' (the subordination inherent in the labour contract) to 'real subsumption' (the loss of autonomy in the organisation of one's work), thinkers influenced by the 'Cultural Revolution', such as the Sartrean André Gorz in his *The Division of Labour* (1974), denounced the de-intellectualisation of workers' labour caused by Taylorism.

Faced with the Trente Glorieuses, the far left also had to respond to the dominant ideology that claimed that growth and the absence of crisis were proof of capitalism's ability to overcome its contradictions. The 'disappearance' of crises led a revolutionary thinker like Castoriadis to abandon Marxism from the 1950s onward This shows how necessary it was to take up this challenge, by demonstrating, for example, that the 'tendency of the rate of profit to fall' evoked in Volume III of Capital remained the *memento mori* of this mode of production. As the council communist Paul Mattick noted in a review of Mandel's *Treatise*, what interests revolutionaries when they examine the functioning of capitalism are the 'historical limits of the system'.

In this context, dissident Marxists made a point of refuting the vision of capitalism's dynamics developed by the PCF. This party defended the idea of a 'scientific and technical revolution', a notion which turned the rollout of technology into an autonomous process that could itself explain postwar prosperity. Besides Mandel, this was the task undertaken by LCR economist Jacques Valier in his 1976 work *Le PCF et le capitalisme monopoliste d'État* and by the Maoist Benjamin Coriat in his *Science, technique et capital*. For these critical Marxists, the PCF's theses amounted to abandoning the Marxist method of explaining the incorporation of science into the process of production by starting from the logic of capital. The 'Stalinist' economists, they insisted, were in total contradiction with *Capital* when they maintained that monopolies escape the 'law of value'. The theory of the official PCF economist Paul Boccara (theorist of 'State monopoly capitalism', SMC) on the 'permanent devalorisation' of capital implies that 'over-accumulation' can be overcome, thus presupposing the possibility of a crisis-free capitalism.

From the mid-1970s onwards, the end of the postwar growth made it possible to reassert the relevance of the Marxian theory of crises. This is what Mandel did in *La Crise*, first published in 1978. The dispute with the PCF continued: both Valier and Mandel criticised the party for advancing a Keynesian reading of the crisis. But, paradoxically, this crisis, far from giving Marxism a mass audience, coincided with its decline. Gorz's about-turn is symptomatic in this respect. In 1980, in his *Farewell to the Working Class*, he claimed that the Marx of the *Grundrisse* believed that automation would give birth to a polyvalent worker capable of mastering the productive apparatus, and argued that contemporary unemployment proves, on the contrary, that it creates a 'non-class of non-producers', incapable of appropriating the capitalist 'great automaton'.

3   Which Working Class – and Which Allies?

Whatever the dynamics of capitalism, socialism only has a chance of succeeding it if its 'gravediggers' – those who make up the working class – remain faithful to their 'historical mission'. With prosperity came the idea that the proletariat was losing its revolutionary calling. In the 1960s, debate raged on the working class, its composition and alliances.[7] Serge Mallet in his 1963 work *La Nouvelle Classe ouvrière* and Gorz in his *Stratégie ouvrière et neo-capitalisme* the following year argued that the rise in purchasing power had 'integrated' the

---

7   Massa 1993.

proletariat. In *The Formation of the Economic Thought of Karl Marx*, Mandel underlines that the mature Marx had renounced the thesis of 'absolute immiseration' and based the historical role of the working class on two facts: its role in production and its capacity to organise, which have nothing in common with a metaphysical-type proletarian essence. In 1975, his comrade Henri Weber added in *Marxisme et conscience de classe* that Marx never established any mechanical link between impoverishment and the rise of class consciousness.

Supposing that he proletariat had indeed remained revolutionary, it needed allies. But in the 1960s and 1970s both Trotskyists and Maoists opposed the PCF's 'anti-monopolist alliance' strategy: they were particularly indignant about the hand extended to the bosses of small and medium-sized enterprises (SMEs). By isolating a handful of 'monopolists', the Communist theorists of state monopoly capitalism had, it was alleged, placed themselves utterly at odds with the method elaborated in *Capital*. Here, Marxological abstraction was placed in service of political struggle, for it was the electoralism of the PS-PCF Common Programme which was really being targeted.

So where to look for allies? If the *maos* of the Gauche prolétarienne were able to support the small shopkeepers in revolt, André Glucksmann, in an article in *Les Temps modernes* in 1974, entitled 'Nous ne sommes pas tous prolétaires' ('We are not all proletarians'), condemned a part of the middle classes as parasitic, citing Marx's *Theories of Surplus Value*. The same year, in *La Petite Bourgeoisie en France*, the Maoists Christian Baudelot, Roger Establet and Jacques Malemort calculated the difference between the value of 'simple' labour power and that of different 'complex' forms of labour power. This opposition between 'simple' and 'complex' labour came from *Capital*. The value of 'simple' labour power depends on the labour time needed to produce the worker's means of subsistence. But in the case of skilled labour, the value of this 'complex' labour-power also includes the costs of acquiring and maintaining this skill. According to the calculations of the authors of *La Petite Bourgeoisie en France*, the wages of the 'petty-bourgeois' are systematically higher than the objective value of their labour power. Those whom the PCF called the ITC (engineers, technicians and managers) thus seemed to benefit from a 'retrocession of surplus value'. In other words, it was claimed, they profited from the exploitation of the workers. The Maoists were also hostile to managerial personnel for a second reason. They accused them of being, through their role in the spread of Taylorism, the agents of a 'proletarianisation of the proletariat'. With this curious expression, Baudelot, Establet and Malemort denounced the de-skilling of workers, as reflected in the decrease in the number of professional workers (OP) and the rise of specialised workers (OS). Conversely, with his work on 'The absorption of agriculture into the capitalist mode of production', Claude Servolin –

driving force behind the bulletin *Paysans en lutte* ('Peasants in Struggle') and a researcher at the National Agronomic Research Institute (IN RA), gave a theoretical foundation to the Maoist policy of reaching out to small peasant proprietors.[8] The question was then being worked on by Bernard Lambert, leader of the 'peasant-worker' movement, who had just published *Les Paysans dans la lutte des classes* ('Peasants in the Class Struggle') in 1970.

The labour theory of value also served to affirm the centrality of the OS and to justify the alliance with the peasantry, by setting it within the Third Worldist perspective at the heart of Maoism. The anthropologist Claude Meillassoux explored this in depth in his *Femmes, greniers et capitaux* ('Women, Granaries, Capitals'), in which he observes that the Western proletariat benefiting from social security only constitutes a fraction of the class, alongside a superexploited 'peasant-proletariat'. This offered an opportunity to draw an accusatory parallel between the developed countries benefiting from the superexploitation of immigrant workers, Nazi Germany and the South Africa of the Bantustans. In 1979, he published *Les Derniers Blancs* ('The Last Whites'), which sought to demonstrate 'that by realising in full the repressive logic of the superexploitation of labour, nationalist South Africa places itself in the political vanguard of big capital'. Yet, when he defined 'imperialism as a mode of reproduction of a cheap workforce' operating through 'the exploitation of the domestic community', Meillassoux extended on and completed Marx. Reasoning within the framework of an 'integral' capitalism and forgetting that labour power is produced within the family, Marx assumed that once 'primitive accumulation' was complete, capital would no longer receive unpaid contributions from the outside. However, according to Meillassoux, *Capital* invites us to distinguish between three components of the value of labour power: its 'reconstitution', meaning the sustenance of the worker during his period of employment, its 'maintenance' in periods of inactivity (unemployment, sickness, and so on) and its 'reproduction', meaning the ment of the worker through the maintenance of his offspring. When the proletariat only receives a direct hourly wage, the cost of its maintenance and reproduction is instead taken on by the 'domestic mode of production' characterising many African or Asian countries. This reasoning in terms of the 'articulation of modes of production' provides grounds to argue that investments in the ex-colonies and the organisation of 'revolving-door migration' to the imperialist metropolises by working-age men sent back to their countries of origin in case of illness or old age are strategies aimed at paying below-value for immigrants' labour-power. It is hardly surprising that the

---

8   Tavernier et al. 1972.

Africanist P.-P. Rey, who, unlike Meillassoux, claimed to be a Maoist, engaged in similar analyses in 1976 with his *Capitalisme négrier* ('Slaver Capitalism'), which served not only to justify the alliance with the pauperised peasantry, but also to establish the hegemony of immigrant workers in the class struggle in France.

4   Against Structuralist Marxism

In the 1960s and 1970s, the questioning of structuralism, and in particular of its Marxist declension, was an important battlefront for a section of far-left theorists. Their critique was, naturally, focused on Althusser, whose positions ultimately seemed to provide justifications for the PCF leadership. Althusser's 'theoretical antihumanism' had nevertheless sometimes embarrassed a party which wanted to give itself an image of openness, and the conversion of a number of his disciples to Maoism had aggravated the apparatus's distrust towards him. Nevertheless, his loyalty to the PCF was a source of important symbolic capital for the party, as from the mid-1960s onward Althusser was perceived as *the* great French Marxist philosopher. The Trotskyists found themselves having to cross swords with Althusser, especially as his prestige was particularly strong in the student milieu which they sought to penetrate. Daniel Bensaïd, a leader of the LCR and editor of a volume *Contre Althusser* (*Against Althusser*) in 1974, said of Althusser that theory served to keep him 'out of reach of the empirical artillery of facts'. Several authors in this collective volume attacked the Rue d'Ulm philosopher, claiming their own inspiration from Marx's 'revolutionary humanism' and arguing, with reference to the 'heroism' of the Tupamaros, that only the 'energy' and 'initiative' of men 'in flesh and blood' would allow for victory – something which, they claimed, the structuralism of the author of *For Marx* had obscured. The second of Marx's *Theses on Feuerbach* ('Man must prove the truth – i.e. the reality and power, the this-sidedness of his thinking in practice') also served the LCR intellectuals who contributed to *Contre Althusser* to pillory his 'pulpit' Marxism.

Pierre Fougeyrollas, close to Pierre Lambert, also violently attacked the Communist philosopher in his 1976 work *Contre Lévi-Strauss, Lacan et Althusser* ('Against Lévi Strauss, Lacan and Althusser'). But here, the line of attack was rather different. The fight was not waged in defence of humanism, but in the name of the Marx who wrote in *The German Ideology* that 'philosophy is to the study of the real world what onanism is to sexual love'. Althusser, conversely, purported to read Marx from his own position as a philosopher, arguing that Marx's scientific discovery of the 'continent of history' should be followed by the elaboration of a new philosophy, which, he asserted, was implicitly contained in *Capital*. Fougeyrollas, a philosopher who had turned to sociology, saw in this a revisionism that broke with Marx's idea of the 'end of philosophy'. His approach was thus much more positivist than that of the LCR's philosophers. He was also attached to a historicism which led him to castigate contamination by a structuralism infatuated with 'invariants' and permanence. In this spirit, he took up Henri Lefebvre's condemnation: Althusser's Marx was 'Heraclitus seen, revised and corrected by an Eleatic'.

5   Class Viewpoint and Revolutionary Praxis: Marxism against
         Academic Sociology

The 1973 work *Dialectique et Révolution* by Michael Löwy, another LCR theorist, expressed this same anti-Althusserian inspiration. But here, the target was not just the 'master' at the ENS, but academic science as a whole. The book ended with a chapter entitled 'Science and Revolution: Objectivity and Class Viewpoint in the Social Sciences'. In it, Löwy insisted on Marx's originality, claiming that his scientific work expressed the viewpoint of a class, and he counterposed it to sociological 'positivism' which claims to separate factual and value judgements. Durkheim had claimed that the use of rigorous methods would allow the scholar to set aside 'prenotions'. This is to forget that these prejudices 'are, like strabismus and colour blindness, an integral part of the gaze', for 'it is the class point of view (involving normative elements) which defines, to a large extent, the field of visibility of a social theory ... its myopia and hypermetropia'. But, if any approach to the social is socially conditioned, how can we 'find a way out of the sidetracks of relativism'? If the 'perspective' of the proletariat is 'epistemologically privileged' in deciphering the 'hieroglyphs' of capitalism, this is, Löwy explains, because as the 'last revolutionary class' it is a universal class which has no need to create illusions for itself.

     Fougeyrollas arrived at comparable conclusions, albeit not drawing on the same Marx texts.[9] He started out from *The German Ideology* and the theory of ideology as an inverted representation of fundamental social relations, as illustrated by the double metaphor of the camera obscura and the retina. But if Marxism presents itself as a critique of ideology, the social sciences treat it as one ideology among others. For this OCI militant, this debate could not be settled on a theoretical level. He drew on Marx's second thesis on Feuerbach to argue that 'knowledge is an integral part of the human practice of transform-

---

9   Fougeyrollas 1979.

ing reality'. This consecrated the centrality of the Marxian thesis of 'the unity of theory and practice on the basis of practice' as 'the criterion of scientific truth'. For Fougeyrollas, the source of Marxism's heuristic fertility is not the 'proletarian point of view' but rather participation in the class struggle, which is the only way to dispel the opacity of the social. Since the ideological inversion is a necessary consequence of exploitation, only the destruction of exploitation will make a clear view accessible. Academic scholarship is thus unable to escape its grip.

While Löwy wrote that the proletariat is 'the first revolutionary class whose ideology has the objective possibility of being transparent', the Lambertist sociologist Fougeyrollas seems to be more rigorous in observing that the term 'ideology' always has pejorative connotations in Marx. But this rigour could also secrete a certain sectarianism, which becomes visible when he addresses what he calls the 'quarrel among interpretations'. Faced with the multiplicity of Marxisms, how would it be possible to separate the wheat from the chaff? The author of *Processus sociaux contemporains* (1980) answered that this was not a matter of choosing between bodies of doctrine, but rather of getting stuck into the struggle, since organisation and consciousness go hand in hand. This suggested that only the OCI itself embodied Marxism as 'the conscious expression of the unconscious historical process' (Trotsky).

6   A 'Chamber Marxism'?

We have to conclude that knowledge of Marx was real in this 'chamber Marxism' pilloried by the philosopher Lucien Sève, then a member of the PCF leadership. The economists, sociologists, anthropologists and philosophers of the far left thought *En partant du Capital* ('Starting from Capital') – to use the title of a book published in 1967. Enriching the heritage, they drew on recently translated works or on passages of Marx's work that had been overlooked up to that point.

Unlike much of 'Western Marxism' – which, according to Perry Anderson, was primarily concerned with aesthetics or the philosophical genealogies of Marxism[10] – their thinking was focused on problems of political strategy. Although much of their argument now dated, how can we not welcome the prophetic insight of a Souyri or a Rey who stressed that employers would react

---

10   Anderson 1977.

to the fall in their profits by offshoring to the Third World?[11] Or the pertinence of Mandel's 1967 observation that, far from the totalitarian holism with which he was associated during the Cold War, Marx had favoured a growing 'individualisation of man'?

However, it would be naïf to believe that the quality of this intellectual work was the source of the influence that Trotskyism and Maoism were able to exert. Indeed, such a judgement would itself undoubtedly belong to the realm of scholastic illusion. The matrixes of political commitment are multiple and complex. The daily experience of struggle doubtless stirred as many, if not more, militants into being than did the contemplation of Marxist texts.[12] This is especially true given that these analyses were characterised by a high level of sophistication, which constituted an obstacle to their broad dissemination. What did considerations on the Asiatic mode of production count for, compared with the belief that the USSR had gone 'from the muzhik to Sputnik'?[13] If the theoretical virtuosity of Trotskyist or Maoist academics was able to provide their organisation with symbolic capital, especially among students, it also offered a hook for the accusation of 'intellectualism' that Stalinism has always levelled against 'ultra-leftists',[14] helping to explain their weak influence in French society.

The tradition examined here has maintained itself across a long stretch of time, even if it no longer enjoyed the same audience once revolution had faded from the horizon of expectations.[15] While Maoism disappeared from the scene at the end of the 1970s, Trotskyist intellectuals continued to combine detailed references to Marx and applications of his thought to the most burning questions of the present. Among the figures who pushed on throughout the 1980s–90s, Daniel Bensaïd embodied his continuity until his dying breath, alongside other protagonists such as Michael Löwy.[16] Still in 2007, in his *Les Dépossédés. Karl Marx, les voleurs de bois et le droit des pauvres* ('The Dispossessed. Karl Marx, the Wood Thieves and the Right of the Poor'), Bensaïd studied the problems of intellectual property and the 'new enclosures', on the basis of Marx's youthful writings on wood theft. At the beginning of the twenty-first century, what philosopher André Tosel called the 'thousand Marxisms', owed much to the heritage of these far-left currents.

11   Souyri 1983.
12   Yon 2005.
13   Aunoble 2016.
14   Boulland et al. 2008.
15   Lindenberg 2004.
16   Bensaïd 2015.

PART 2

Translating, Editing, and Publishing Marx

∵

CHAPTER 8

How to Translate Marx into French?

Guillaume Fondu and Jean Quétier

The history of the translation of Marx's texts into French is punctuated by a number of distinct episodes, each corresponding to its own historical logic. However, there are also shared theoretical stakes and questions. The majority of these translations, at least until the turn of the millennium, had a militant dimension, and their authors therefore often had to arbitrate between two contradictory demands. On the one hand was the concern to provide an accurate rendering of Marx's language – marked by certain evolutions due to the various polemics through which it was forged – even if it meant producing a French text that was sometimes difficult to access for the general public. On the other was the concern to construct a unitary language that would allow for the widest possible dissemination of Marx as well as his systematisation. Stalinist diamat (the 'dialectical materialism' forged by Stalin) constituted the paradigmatic example of this. The tension between these two demands ran through all the French translations of Marx's body of work, beginning even during his own lifetime with Joseph Roy's translation of Volume I of *Capital* (1872–5), which was reread by the author and widely revised by him. In the letters between Marx, Joseph Roy and Maurice Lachâtre (the publisher) on this subject we can detect many of the debates that would later trouble Marx's translators. The main problem was how to render in French the German terms' underlying systematic character, be it in a strictly linguistic sense (as in *Mehrarbeit*, *Mehrwert*, *Mehrprodukt*, and so on) or in terms of their inscription within the philosophical systems that constitute the matrix of Marxian thought – most decisively, the Hegelian system. In the following text, we will try to bring out some of the specificities of Marx's language which explain the need for an exacting translation, before we then review some specific translation debates that have marked the French reception of Marx's work.

1   An Inherited, Philosophically Informed Language

If the translation of Marx's writings is a matter of theoretical dispute, this firstly owes to the fact that these texts are literally saturated with concepts inherited from classical German philosophy. From the 1960s onwards, the debates between French translators would especially focus on the visibility of this philosophical vocabulary in the target language. Let us look at three examples.

The first concerns Marx's use of the term *Subsumtion* (subsumption; in French, *subsomption*), borrowed from Kant. In the *Critique of Pure Reason*, subsumption is presented as the activity of the faculty of judgement which consists of placing an object under a concept. It allows us to know the particular by setting it under the universal. While the concept of *Subsumtion* is present on numerous occasions in *The German Ideology*, its presence is somewhat obscured in Gilbert Badia's translation, which uses the French term *subordination*. *Subsumtion* is then considered as a simple synonym of *Unterordnung*, a much more common and less conceptually connoted term. However, when Marx and Engels speak of the subsumption of the individual under the division of labour, they are not simply saying that the individual is subjected or subordinated to it: they add to the perspective of domination the idea that the division of labour becomes the truth of the individual, which is to say that this individual himself becomes a partial and mutilated individual.

The second example, which also concerns Marx's relation to Fichte, is the conceptual couple *Selbsttätigkeit/Selbstbetätigung* (self-activity/self-activation). For Fichte, self-activity designates the original freedom of the self-posing ego. For Marx, self-activation designates the mastery of the conditions of one's own activity – primarily meaning the activity of production, of labour. No longer a primordial fact, as in Fichte, but a real stakes of history, self-activation may exist in degrees and even progress, reaching its highest stage through the proletarian revolution which transforms labour into self-activation. In his translation of the *1844 Manuscripts*, Franck Fischbach was one of the first to draw attention to Marx's use of this term, whereas most French editions of the text simply make this concept disappear, using various expressions that do not highlight the link between *Selbstbetätigung* and productive activity.[1] Jacques-Pierre Gougeon's translation, in particular, proposes a somewhat unfortunate solution; he uses the notion of 'manifestation of the self', which may suggest that this has to do with the proletariat expressing its subjective interiority, whereas it is rather more a matter of it becoming the principle of its own activity.

The third example concerns a concept that Marx borrows from Hegel: *bürgerliche Gesellschaft* (civil society/bourgeois-civil society). The central concept of *Elements of the Philosophy of Right*, for Hegel *bürgerliche Gesellschaft* designates the social sphere, understood as distinct from the political sphere, which

---

1   Fischbach 2007.

is that of the state. *Bürgerliche Gesellschaft* is the site of the satisfaction of ego-istic ends. One of the issues raised – but also one of the difficulties of translating the term *bürgerliche Gesellschaft* into French – has to do with the duality of the bourgeois and the citizen. This is why in his translation of the *Kreuznach Manuscript*, Albert Baraquin proposes the use of the term 'bourgeois-civil soci-ety'. Moreover, it may be observed that Marx uses the term in two different ways, at least in *The German Ideology*. Firstly, it refers to the totality of the material intercourse among individuals within a given stage of the productive forces – in this case it does not refer specifically to bourgeois society, but more gener-ally to what we call civil society. Secondly, it refers to the particular form that civil society takes under bourgeois rule, which Marx and Engels call *bürgerliche Gesellschaft als solche*, 'bourgeois civil society as such'. The tension to which we referred in the introduction is evident here, since the earliest translations, pro-duced in a context of strong politicisation, use the term 'bourgeois society' – thus choosing to reduce the notion to its solely political and thus axiological dimension, to the detriment of its more descriptive conceptual aspect.

In most cases, this importing of concepts from classical German philosophy went hand-in-hand with their re-elaboration. This only added to the trans-lator's tasks, since the terms thereby acquired a very different meaning and scope.

This is especially true of one of Marx's most hotly contested terms – ali-enation – which corresponds to several German words: *die Entfremdung, die Entäußerung, die Veräußerung*. In nineteenth-century German philosophy, the term refers to the way in which the subject produces an object that comes to confront the subject in an autonomous way. In these authors, there is an oscil-lation between a descriptive (Hegel) and a critical (Feuerbach) meaning. After having used the term abundantly in a critical sense in the *1844 Manuscripts*, Marx quickly dropped it, seeing it as a paradigm of philosophical jargon with which he intended to break. Yet we find it throughout the elaboration of his project for the 'critique of political economy', right up to *Capital*. This raises the question of its status: is it a merely evanescent survival of earlier writ-ing of his, or a genuine concept which ought to be identified as such? Given the plurality of German terms, it is left up to the translator to decide. From the 1960s, the debate on Marx's humanism crystallised around this question: this opposed those who insisted on the continued presence of the concept of alienation (Roger Garaudy) in Marx's mature texts, those who spoke of its disappearance (Louis Althusser) and those who spoke of its transformation (Lucien Sève). In any case, from a purely terminological point of view, the term did remain present, albeit discreetly, and now bearing on very diverse realities: Marx speaks of alienated phenomenal forms, of alienated configurations, alienated social power, and so on. Whatever position one takes in the theoretical debates linked to this term, it seems obvious that it was the focus of a theoretical re-elaboration. This, in turn, makes it possible to measure the evolutions of the schema by which Marx strove to think the relations between the social activity of production and the figures in which it is objectified: the commodity, money and – finally and above all – capital. The whole issue for the translator is to give the Francophone reader the possibility of following the trail of this concept while also respecting the evolutions of its meaning.

In addition to such central terms, there are also many more local concepts subject to such re-elaborations, and which pose similar problems of translation. For example, in *The German Ideology*, Marx and Engels take up Hegel's notion of *Weltgeschichte* – global history or the history of the world – and subject it to critique. Indeed, they do not consider this latter as the history of a world that somehow pre-existed historical development, but as a historically situated phenomenon that begins with the extension of the market and the transformation of human activities into global ones. This explains the need to translate the term not as 'history *of the world*', as is the case with Hegel, but as '*global* history', in order to avoid the translation filling it with greater substance than the German does. This is especially true given that the term is closely correlated with *Weltmarkt*, which must be translated in French as 'marché mondiale' ['global market']. The same problem arises with many compound words, which allow German a middle ground between the use of an adjective and the addition of a noun complement. This has led many translators to use the hyphen in order to signal the relative looseness of the German way of bringing two terms together: *Wertform* is thus usually rendered as 'value-form', *Geldform* as 'money-form', and so on. On this point, the fate of Marx's translators is similar to that of most translators of German philosophy, at times forced to resort to neologisms, most often meaning compound terms which are inelegant but sometimes indispensable.

Rooted in classical German philosophy, Marx's language is also permeated with terms drawn from English political economy, which Marx helped to introduce into German at a time when the German-language economic literature was very poorly developed. Here again, faced with the multiple senses of the German terms, the French translator is forced to choose between maintaining a certain technical rigour and the need to go beyond the pure and simple economic domain, in order to render the full dimensions of Marx's writing. The case of the German term *Geld*, equivalent to the English money, offers a telling example: there is a change of tone depending on whether it is translated into French as *monnaie* ('money', 'currency', 'coins') or *argent* ('money', 'cash', 'silver'). In the first case, Marx is integrated into the scholarly landscape of monetary debates as an economist – which he most certainly is – while leaving out a whole aspect of what is more commonly called *argent* in French. But Marx was writing at a time when economics was not separated from the other fields of social science, and he himself theorised this non-separation. This is why the term *argent*, which places him on the same footing as Georg Simmel (*Sociologie de l'argent*) and even Charles Péguy and Émile Zola (*L'Argent*), doubtless makes it possible to better account for both the anthropological dimension of his texts and the fact that he saw money not as a simple technical notion belonging to economic science but rather as a multi-dimensional social phenomenon.

The awareness of this philosophical heritage developed as the German philosophers in question were introduced into the French intellectual landscape. Up till the 1950s, Fichte, Hegel and Feuerbach were practically inaccessible to a French readership: the few translations that existed had a relatively lowkey circulation and they were absent from most philosophy curriculums. To take the example of Hegel, he did not really become known until after Alexandre Kojève's lectures at the École pratique des hautes études (between 1933 and 1939) and the publication, in 1941, of Jean Hyppolite's translation of the *Phenomenology of Spirit*. Paradoxically, Lenin's *Conspectus of Hegel's book 'The Science of Logic'* was published by Gallimard in 1938, at a time when Hegel's works were virtually absent from the publishing market, if not from libraries, as the existing translations dated from the mid-nineteenth century. It is thus understandable that the first translators of Marx had to grope around for solutions, since they were faced with texts based on a philosophical language – the language of German idealism – of which there was no French equivalent.

From the 1950s onwards, the evolution of the translation of Marx's works was closely parallel to that of the German philosophers, and each new instalment of Marx in French took advantage of the progress made in the translation and knowledge of other philosophers. This is notably the case of the first complete French translation of the *1844 Manuscripts*, by Émile Bottigelli; it was based on Jean Hyppolite's translation of the *Phenomenology of Spirit*, but also on the translation of Feuerbach's texts collected by Louis Althusser in 1960 under the title *Manifestes philosophiques*. Conversely, Émile Bottigelli's translation was commented upon by Louis Althusser and would serve him when he wrote the articles that were to make up *For Marx* in 1965. More generally, this trend toward more sophisticated translations and an enrichment of their language went hand-in-hand with a reflection on the nature of Marx's intellectual enterprise, which – it was increasingly clear – could not be reduced to Stalin's theses on the dialectic or to a linear scheme of capitalist development. After the Liberation in 1944–45, at a time when the French social sciences were questioning their method and the specificity of their object, the restitution of philosophical language was thus a means of asserting what Marx's point of view could be and of proposing a non-positivist theoretical path. Up till the present (for instance, with the recent translation of the *1844 Manuscripts* by Franck Fischbach, or the work carried out within the framework of the *Grande édition Marx Engels* [GEME]), this is the path that the translation of Marx into French has taken – with the exception of undertakings such as those of Maximilien Rubel or Roger Dangeville, which place greater emphasis on the directly ethical or political points of Marxian discourse. However, this restitution has not been conflict-free, and translators and commentators have repeatedly clashed in debates that would have an enduring impact on the French reception of Marx's work.

2   The Theoretical and Political Stakes of Marx Translations in France

In addition to the technical problems posed by the accurate rendition of Marx's philosophical language, there are a number of more directly theoretical debates, often linked to political issues, in which questions of translation have taken on an essential significance.

The first and most famous example is Louis Althusser's re-translation of an entire passage from the Postface to the second German edition of *Capital*. This re-translation serves as the starting point for his article 'Contradiction and Overdetermination' (1962, reprinted in *For Marx*) and is thus placed in the service of the conceptual elaboration of a new notion of contradiction, ridded of the muck of idealism. In this text, Althusser critiques the metaphor of 'overturning' which is usually used to summarize Marx's relationship with Hegel, that is, re-establishing the empire of the material over the ideal. But this critique first of all concerns Joseph Roy's translation, which Althusser substitutes with his own translation of the fourth German edition of *Capital*. In Joseph Roy's text, we read: 'In [Hegel, the dialectic] is standing on its head; it suffices to put it back on to its feet, to find its entirely reasonable physiognomy'. Althusser, on the other hand, translates in a much more literal way: 'With [Hegel, the dialectic] is standing on its head. It must be turned right side up again, if you would discover the rational kernel within the mystical shell'.

The overturning is thus only a preliminary to the work of extraction, itself being, according to Althusser, only a first approximation of the real treatment that Marx gives to the Hegelian dialectic. And 'in other passages [Marx] puts it clearly enough, though Roy has half spirited them away'.[2] In the rest of his

---

2   Althusser 2005b, p. 91.

article, Althusser elaborates, from a commentary on Lenin, what he thinks he has found in Marx, namely a new notion of contradiction that breaks with the simplicity with which this concept appears in Hegel and makes it possible to acknowledge the overdetermined character of any situation, always marked by multiple contradictions taking place within heterogeneous instances (super-structures and diverse infrastructures) whose 'specific effectivity' must be thought through.

Throughout his rereading of Marx, Althusser was thus driven firstly to re-translate the texts he studied. This is also what his disciples would do in their expositions collected in *Reading Capital*, extending this work of retranslation to passages from Volumes II and III of Capital, as well as *Theories on Surplus Value*. In each case, this means going back to the German text to find the con-cepts that allow us to go beyond a simplistic and often scientistic reading of Marx, but also to criticise any reduction of Marx to one of his predecessors, Hegel or Feuerbach first among them. Lucien Sève could therefore rightly credit Louis Althusser, despite all of their disagreements, with having introduced into French Marxism reading practices that respected the letter of Marx, based on a prior work of retranslation. It was also in the wake of the new theoretical ques-tions raised by Althusserism that a polemic between Adam Schaff and Lucien Sève took place in the journal *L'Homme et la sociét*, at the very beginning of the 1970s; it concerned the translation of the concept *menschliches Wesen* ('human essence'/'human being') in Marx's sixth thesis on Feuerbach, which affirms that 'the human essence is no abstraction inherent in each single individual. In its reality it is the ensemble of the social relations'. In many respects, this richly argued debate makes visible both the theoretical and political stakes of Marx translation, in a period when the PCF was exploring new ways to overcome Sta-linism's misadventures. The Twentieth Congress of the Soviet Communist Party foregrounded the critique of the cult of personality, which led many Marxist philosophers to look for the root of this critique in an original Marxist 'human-ism' that had been perverted by Stalinism.

Taking his cue from a passage in Sève's *Marxisme et théorie de la personnal-ité* critical of Roger Garaudy – who had chosen to translate the term *Wesen* as 'being' rather than 'essence' – Adam Schaff found fault with the author for rein-troducing a metaphysical perspective into Marxism, where Marx had instead simply sought to say that it is the individual who is 'the ensemble of the social relations'. For Schaff, the sixth thesis on Feuerbach contained only the 'ellipt-ical and metaphorical'[3] formulation of an idea that while certainly brilliant,

---

3   Schaff 1971.

had become banal: the individual is determined by social relations. For Sève, on the contrary, if there is one meaning that the word *Wesen* cannot have in the context of the sixth thesis on Feuerbach, it is to refer to an individual. Insisting on the need to translate the term *Wesen* by 'essence' rather than by 'being', he maintained that the relation of essence to being is not a matter of opposition but rather of specification: essence is essential being, as distinct from empirical being. For Sève, the heart of the question was clear: Schaff, like Garaudy, wanted to revise the Marxist conception of man in the direction of a humanist primacy of the individual. To say that it is the individual and not the human essence is the ensemble of social relations is, Sève insists, a deformation of historical materialism in two ways: in the direction of a psychologisation of social relations and in that of an absolutisation of the individual. For Sève, Shaff was ultimately reverting to a pre-Marxist sociologism and humanism because he ignored the radically new meaning that the concept of essence takes on in the sixth thesis on Feuerbach. Translated into political terms, the question posed was how valid it was take up the concept of the individual from liberal thought in order to oppose it to Stalinism.

The argumentative strategies developed by the two authors deserve to be examined in detail, as they always combine philological, theoretical and political considerations. Both authors took recourse to arguments from authority, albeit in what were certainly different ways. For example, Sève sought to back up his reading of the sixth thesis on Feuerbach by citing the Russian translation of the term *Wesen*, as proposed by the researchers at the Institute of Marxism-Leninism in Moscow. This itself was a way of posing as a guarantor of Communist orthodoxy faced with Adam Schaff's 'revisionism'.[4] By choosing to translate Wesen as 'sushchnost' rather than 'sushchestvo', the Russian translators chose to cut through the ambiguity of the German term in the same way as Sève had. However, even as he criticised Sève for replacing some of his arguments with appeals to authoritative figures, Schaff played the same game, including in the final article of the polemic a letter from Auguste Cornu backing up his viewpoint.[5]

The first act of another inseparably both theoretical and political debate came at the end of the 1970s: namely, in the controversy over the translation of the term *Mehrwert*. In issue 197 of *La Pensée*, Étienne Balibar and Jean-Pierre Lefebvre co-authored an article entitled 'Plus-value ou survaleur?'. Written the context of the preparation of the publication, a few years later, of the

---

4   Sève 1971.
5   Cornu and Schaff 1972.

Grundrisse and a new translation of *Capital* Volume I, this articule aimed to justify the choice of the term *'survaleur'*. The article gave rise a few months later
to a response by Gilbert Badia, entitled 'Défense et illustration de [la] "plus-
value"'.

If the idea of a new translation of the term *Mehrwert* may have seemed
surprising at the time, this firstly owed to the fact that there was a French translation of *Capital* Volume I which had been revised by Marx himself, which
rendered the term *Mehrwert* as 'plus-value'. As a sign of an era when, within
PCF ranks, voices were being raised in favour of a relationship to Marx that was
both freer and more rigorous, Balibar and Lefebvre did not see this as a suffi-
cient grounds to refute their proposal. They spoke of Marx's 'disappointment'[6]
at Joseph Roy's translation, but also the evolution of the norms of translation
over the course of the twentieth century, demanding a level of precision that
had not been common in the late nineteenth century. Balibar and Lefebvre
firsted highlight the unfortunate connotation of the term 'plus-value' in French:
it is above all an accounting concept that designates the difference in price
between two operations affecting the same object. The link between *Mehrwert*
and production is therefore lost with 'plus-value'. Conversely, there is a gain
in intelligibility if the semantic inter-relation between *Mehrwert*, *Mehrarbeit*
and *Mehrprodukt* is foregrounded. Balibar and Lefebvre thus proposed a solution which consisted in harmonising the series by translating these terms as
survaleur, *surtravail* and *surproduit* respectively. In a context marked by the
rejection of a purely economistic reading of Marx, the retranslation of the term
Mehrwert thus served to point out that this is not simply an immediately meas-
urable notion, drawn from the domain of accounting, but rather a complex
concept useful for thinking about the specificity of capitalism and its dynamics.

For Gilbert Badia, on the other hand, translating Mehrwert as *survaleur* is
to confuse surplus with excess. For Badia, the term *survaleur* does not indicate
'more', but 'too much', which would not accurately render the concept elaborated by Marx. For Badia, something that is 'overvalued' is something that has
less real value than it is attributed[7] – and this is far from corresponding to the
idea of an increment of value provided to the capitalist by unpaid labour. More
recently, this argument has been further developed by Paul Boccara in issue
658–659 of the journal *Économie et Politique*: for Boccara, Mehr- is not Über-
and the difference between the two prefixes is far from secondary. Boccara –
who, like Badia, defends the choice of the translation *plus-value* – considers
that the term *survaleur* introduces a harmful confusion with overproduction

---

6   Balibar and Lefebvre 1978.
7   Badia 1978.

(*Überproduktion*) and overaccumulation (*Überakkumulation*), both of which designate an excess and not a simple surplus.[8] However, the appendix 'Sur la traduction du mot Mehrwert' ('On the Translation of the Word Surplus-Value') in the volume published by GEME with chapter VI of *Capital* Volume I foregrounds the idea that there are a number of terms in French beginning with the prefix '*sur-*' that indicate surplus without indicating excess. Such is the case of *surcroît* ('extra', 'additional') but also of the term *surplus*.[9]

3   A Still-Open Question

The French translation of Marx has never been simply the stakes of philology, and nor will it ever be. Even during his own lifetime, it took the form of an inseparably both theoretical and political question. It is unsurprising, therefore, that it has given rise to bold innovations as well as intense polemics. In the twentieth century, its evolution followed that of the norms of philosophical translation and the internal debates of the workers' movement. At the beginning of the twenty-first century, through the intermediary of the GEME in particular, it also seems to be gradually finding its place in the academic field. If we are now beginning to know 'How not to Translate Marx', to use the title of an article by Engels published in 1885 in the journal *The Commonweal*, how we should translate him remains an open question.

---

8   Boccara 2009.
9   Cornillet, Prost and Sève 2010.

CHAPTER 9

PCF Publishing Houses and Marx in France, 1920–60: From Politics to Scholarship?

Marie-Cécile Bouju

The leadership of the French Communist Party (PCF) long hesitated over the Party's role in the domain of propaganda. Was it a populariser of political thought, with a view to mobilising the masses, or an educator using science for the sake of human progress? It especially dithered over the place that the publication of Marx's works should occupy in its activity. It was, without question, necessary to disseminate the doctrine. But the PCF, which wanted to be a 'party of a new type', with different forms of militancy, ruled out any 'intellectualist' approach to politics. Marx, the canonical author, was first and foremost to be used in political combat. As a political issue, the publication of his works by the Communists did not escape Soviet controls and injunctions, and was, at first, dependent on a poorly stabilised translation and publishing apparatus. It was only gradually, under the influence of certain Communist leaders and intellectuals, that the PCF came to offer readers an extensive, reliable and less immediately political edition of Marx's oeuvre.

1 Early Publishers: Between Politics and Academia

The militant publishers who issued writings by Marx at the end of the nineteenth and start of the twentieth centuries wanted to disseminate texts for narrowly political purposes, and sometimes had no hestitation in vulgarising his thought. The most famous of these was undoubtedly Maurice Lachâtre (1814–1900), the first French publisher of *Capital*. The more 'classic' publishers who took an interest in Marxism belonged to the world of medical, legal and economic publishing, such as Schleicher, Giard & Brière and Guillaumin. If Marx appeared in their catalogues, he did so as an author proposing an analysis of the contemporary society and economy through their ongoing change. He was relatively well known to economists during his lifetime, and his work entered the French university through the law faculties and the political-economy courses taught there.[1]

---

1 Cahen 1994.

But one of the main obstacles to access to Marx's work in France was a linguistic one. At the end of the nineteenth century, translations represented only about 5 percent of publishers' output, and even that largely meant novels. Translators' work did not enjoy recognition and the level of quality demanded of translations was very low.[2] In Marx's case, militant publishers often relied on those close to him, whether politically (Gabriel Deville) and/or in terms of family ties (Laura and Paul Lafargue). In the interwar years, the academic and militant registers still coexisted, with publishers such as Alfred Costes (who took over the Schleicher collection in 1910 and undertook the publication of Marx's complete works in 1927 and 1947), Frédéric Rieder (who took over the Édouard Cornely bookshop in 1913) or Marcel Rivière (who created his own publishing house in 1906).[3] But then new and rather particular actor appeared: the publishing houses of the French Communist Party.

1.1   *The Communist Publishing Apparatus and Marx*

In December 1920, upon the conclusion of the Tours Congress, the young French Section of the Communist International (SFIC), the future French Communist Party, inherited one of the editorial structures of the SFIO, the Librairie de l'Humanité. Responsibility for it was entrusted to Boris Souvarine, who had supported membership of the Communist International, along with Amédée Dunois.

The Librairie de l'Humanité was not a 'publishing house' in the strict sense of the word: it was a department of a political party, which published and distributed books, brochures and magazines, but also sold various objects aimed at militants, such as busts and pins. For a few years, it was also a library. The Librairie de l'Humanité (1913–25) and its successors – the Bureau d'édition, de diffusion et de publicité (BEDP, then BE) in 1925, and the Éditions sociales internationales (ESI) in 1927 – contributed to the transformation of the SFIC into a PCF based on the Bolshevik model of the Russian Communist Party. The political literature of the day had two main functions: to disseminate Marxist-Leninist thought, and then Stalinism, in France, and to disseminate the PCF's chosen themes of agitprop. The Communist publishers thus came to centralise publishing operations: in principle under the control of the Central Committee, but in reality at the behest of the PCF leadership and the Comintern's own publishing department. The catalogue of PCF publications grew consid-

---

2   Wilfert 2003.
3   Bouju 2010.

erably during this period, even if, in terms of print runs, there is no indication of spectacular growth. Qualitatively, the new catalogue gave pride of place to translations from Russian.

With 18 titles in 37 editions published between 1920 and 1939, the PCF offered the French readership a substantial list of Karl Marx's works. It published an average of two titles per year, but at an uneven pace: half of these titles were published between 1935 and 1939. The most reprinted texts were *Communist Manifesto* (eight editions), *Wage-Labour and Capital* and *Wages, Price and Profits* (four each), *The Civil War in France* and the *Inaugural Address* (three each). Of these eighteen titles, ten had apparently not been published in pamphlet or book form before 1920. The others were already present in the Schleicher and especially Giard & Brière catalogues. The PCF's editorial contribution was thus far from negligible. But unlike the catalogues of Costes or the *Revue philosophique*, it did not leave a mark on the memory, including militants' memories.

The editorial work done by the PCF was of limited quality. Indeed, its editions drew above all on the available 'stock' of French translations of Marx, dating from before World War I, and which came (when the translator was indicated) from Laura Lafargue or Charles Longuet. The only new translator publicly referenced was Marcel Ollivier – real name Aron Godelberg – to whom ESI entrusted the translation of *The Eighteenth Brumaire*. But why so few new translations? Like all contemporary publishers, the PCF's leaders attached little importance or care to translations and do not seek out experienced translators. It was then commonplace for the translators' names not to be mentioned on books' title pages.

1.2   *Publishing Under Soviet Influence*

Yet, translations were politically important to the Comintern. Translators were 'engineers' essential to the organisation's agit-prop, and it was through them that the international revolution could be made known. But it seems that the Comintern had the greatest difficulty in finding competent men and women, especially from the late 1920s onwards. Translators could occupy three functions in the international organisation: translator, editor and consultant, the work of the first being controlled by the second, and the second by the third. This editorial chain had two objectives: to achieve a readable and politically reliable translation, though in archival sources the ambiguous meaning of 'good translation' is never resolved (*politically* good translation and *linguistically* good translation are often confused). But this scientific-ideological control led to a bottleneck in working through texts, and thus to tensions between Moscow and Paris.

In addition, from 1927 onwards, the PCF leadership was under strong pressure to publish Lenin's works first and foremost, a project which was at the origin of the ESI. For the edition of Marx, it had to submit to Soviet supervision, which did not make its task any easier. In fact, the Soviets had founded the Marx-Engels Institute (MEI) in 1921, under the direction of David Ryazanov. All works by Marx published in the USSR and by sections of the Communist International had to be authorised by the MEI. Its main task was the German edition of the first complete works of Marx and Engels (*Marx-Engels-Gesamtausgabe*, or *MEGA*), launched in 1924. In November 1929, the Comintern expressed its desire to see an 'international edition' of these works and 'to publish selected pieces by Marx and Engels'. A timetable was even set: these editions were to be produced within two years, by the Publishing Service of the International and the national sections. Since the MEI had access to the original texts and was the actor best able to guarantee good translations, the national sections were totally dependent on it to have access to the reference texts. But this supervision slowed down the French edition of the works, especially as the MEI (which became the Marx-Engels-Lenin Institute, MELI, in 1931) was going through a series of crises: its management was affected by the first Stalinist purges (Ryazanov was sent to a labour camp in 1930); and the Nazis' arrival in power in 1933 dismantled a large part of the Institute's intellectual and scholarly network.

Lastly, this relative lack of interest in publishing Marx's works can also be explained by the attitude of the French cadres responsible for it, who showed little ambition. Doctrinal works were not considered central to everyday party-political activity. For sure, the orders from Moscow were answered, but the PCF leadership was mainly interested in pamphlets that disseminated political speeches in large numbers, republished important articles and popularised doctrine. It was fond of such 'digests', an editorial object halfway between a textbook and a political popularisation.

1.3   *A Desire to Return to the Texts*

This highly pragmatic and anti-intellectual posture among PCF leaders contrasted with the publishing personnel's own; they all took their role as publishers seriously and wanted to offer the public a coherent catalogue. This ambition was only fuelled by the competition from publishers such as Costes and Rieder, whose literary director, Jacques Robertfrance, welcomed with open arms the Philosophies group (Politzer, Lefebvre, Guterman, and such like), who threw themselves into an innovative work of new Marx translations.[4] In other circles

---

4   Trebitsch 1987.

close to the PCF, this desire to return to the text was also strongly felt. As Isabelle Gouarné has shown in her study of philo-Soviet milieux during the interwar period, intellectuals in the New Russia Circle (which in 1934 became the Society for the Study of Soviet Culture, and in 1936 the Association for the Study of Soviet Culture) made the reading of Marx a philosophical and political imperative, and a means of responding to the crisis of reason which would allow for the construction of a modern rationalism. Much like the Philosophies group, the New Russia Circle helped to construct a new approach to Marx, which left the fold of political economy in favour of philosophy.

1.4   *The Contradictions of the Fiftieth Anniversary*

In 1933, the Comintern decided to celebrate the fiftieth anniversary of Marx's death. It therefore planned the publication of texts from the Marx-Engels-Lenin Institute. Jacques Duclos declared at the Central Committee of February 1933: 'Without doubt, our party has something of a shortfall in familiarity with Marxism'. This was followed by a 'jump' in editorial output in France; in 1933 the BE and the ESI published six texts, as compared to three the previous year. Party publishing was visibly trying to make up for earlier slowness. The *Inaugural Address*, published in 1921, was reprinted in 1933; the translation of the *Critique of the Gotha Programme* produced in 1922 by Amédée Dunois was foresaken for a second edition in 1933; the *Genesis of Capital* was reprinted in 1934, ten years after its first edition.

But MELI also made sure that these translations conformed to its expectations. *The Civil War in France*, translated by Dunois in 1924, was republished in another (anonymous) translation in 1933, but the MELI ultimately requested that it be pulped, since it had just prepared a new edition. But it was above all the edition of *Capital* that provoked the Moscow-based institute's ire. On 4 June 1933, it wrote to M.E. Krebs, the Comintern's director of publications: 'The Publications Bureau is indeed issuing *Capital* without our authorisation. We have no objection to the La Châtre edition which was revised by Marx being used for this purpose, but it seems desirable to us to review the French text, cross-checked with the original German in order to correct certain misprints and inaccuracies'. Indeed, the Institute asked for the Publications Bureau to suspend the project and remind the French that 'anything that concerns Marx-Engels-Lenin can only be published with the authorisation of the Institute and after its verification'. The French Communists abandoned the project to publish this edition of *Capital*; Costes was thus left as the only publisher able to supply this book in Paris.

1.5   *The Rise of the Popular Front*

During the Popular Front, these various obstacles were partly cast aside. Two publications especially symbolise this passing from one era to another.

Léon Moussinac, head of the French Communists' publishing apparatus, and René Hilsum, like him a PCF militant, were also recruited for their professional skills and their ability to mobilise the intellectual world. For these two men, the fact that the PCF did not offer its own edition of *Capital* to the public bordered on the absurd. They fought, successfully, for the party to take over the rights to the Lachâtre edition of 1872; this was, admittedly, limited to Volume I, but the translation by Joseph Roy had after all been checked by Marx himself. Volume I was finally published starting in 1938 (it came in three instalments, the third of which appeared in 1939) by the PCF Publications Bureau. At the same time, the lectures given by the intellectuals of the New Russia Circle were published in *À la lumière du marxisme* (1937). This emblematic publication embodied the recognition of Marx as a philosopher and the (precarious) legitimisation of Communist intellectuals within PCF ranks.

These two publications were not only symbolic, however. In the second half of the 1930s, Marx's books probably sold much better. The information we have allows us to say that the print runs of the PCF editions were close to those of the commercial edition: 6,000 copies on average between 1921 and 1934, and 17,000 between 1935 and 1939.

1.6   *Collections and Small-Format Publications*

However, the Marx-Engels-Lenin Institute remained reticent. The translation circuit still required that the party publishers go via Moscow. Moreover, the anti-intellectualism of the PCF leadership remained a brake on any policy of systematic translation of Marx's works.

The leadership's attachment to the most popular forms of political literature, as embodied by the pamphlet, remained strong. This explains why Marx's works were mainly published in an emblematic collection, 'Les Éléments du communisme'. During the interwar period, 31 of the 37 editions were published in collections: 'Grands textes du marxisme' (1 edition), 'Pages socialistes' (2), 'Bibliothèque marxiste' (5) and above all 'Les Éléments du communisme' (23). The collection, a publishing practice born in the nineteenth century, has both educational and commercial aims: it is a means of effectively directing the customer towards a type of text/product that corresponds to his or her intellectual, cultural or commercial expectations. The labour movement has thus widely used the form of the collection to guide militants in their purchases.

The 'Eléments du communisme' collection, created in 1928, was devoted to Marx, Engels, Lenin and Stalin, and offered at affordable prices (3 francs maximum, €1.84 per volume in today's money). However, the print run remained average (5,000 copies). In 1933, the PCF presented the collection in the following terms: 'To get a good grasp of the fundamental ideas of Marxism, read the works in the "Eléments du communisme" collection. Nicely printed and moderately priced, the short pamphlets which make up this collection will provide you with the best pages of the masters of scientific socialism.' In 1937, the description changed: 'The purpose of the "Eléments du communisme" collection is to popularise the teachings of Scientific Communism as formulated by its founders Marx and Engels …' So, from the one statement to the next, from 1933 to 1937, there was a shift that made Marx and Engels the authors of a political and scientific oeuvre, and no longer just barely distinguished elements of a wider corpus. But between these two dates, the popular form remained a selling point of paramount importance.

2   Éditions sociales' Postwar Hegemony

From the Liberation to the beginning of the 1950s, 70 percent of editions and reprints of Marx's works came from the PCF publishing house responsible for ideological questions, the Éditions sociales. But despite its established dominant position in terms of sheer quantity, publishing Marx's works remained a thorny issue for the Communists.

Between 1944 and 1960, the PCF publishing house published 39 titles with works by Marx: an average of two and a half titles per year. Another difference with bibliometric findings regarding the interwar period is that the publication rate was extremely regular. The explanation is simple: from 1944 onwards, there was only one publishing house that published Marx's works on behalf of the PCF, Éditions sociales, founded in autumn 1944. It was run by a former publishing technician, Joseph Ducroux, until 1955, then by Guy Besse from 1955 to 1969.

At first, this new structure republished earlier texts, based on old translations: for example, its catalogue incorporated Roy's translation of Volume I of *Capital*, by definition a legitimate translation, seeing as it was 'entirely revised' by Marx. In 1947, Georges Cogniot – an *agrégé* in philosophy, MP, member of the PCF since 1924 and member of its Central Committee – launched the Éditions sociales into a new adventure: publishing the complete works of Marx and Engels in an *original and rigorous* translation. To this end, in the late 1940s he gathered together a small group of translators: Émile Bottigelli (an *agrégé* in German at the ENS in Saint-Cloud), Pierre Angrand (an *agrégé* in history), Erna Cogniot (his wife), Paul Meier, Renée Cartelle, and Catherine Cohen-Solal.

This group was replenished ten years later with the arrival of Maurice Husson (an *agrégé* in German), Henri Auger (a qualified German teacher), Lucienne Netter and Gilbert Badia (an *agrégé* in literature and experienced Germanist).

The creation of this group marked a break with the past. On the one hand, at Cogniot's initiative, these politically significant texts were now treated in a scholarly manner, in accordance with new academic practices, particularly with regard to translation. On the other hand, the works published under the brand name of Éditions sociales were now books in their own right, and no longer pamphlets intended primarily for the political education of Communist militants. But this was a long-term undertaking. In the 1940s and 1950s, readers of Marx still had to make do with old translations or original-language editions. Thus, the complete works of Marx (1927–47) by Costes, translated by Molitor, were still widely used by all 'Marxists' into the 1960s.

Although still-present in law-school courses and cited in debates, Marx's works had little weight in French commercial publishing. There were few publishers specialising in philosophy, and few of them were interested in Marx: the PUF (which publishes the works of Henri Lefebvre, Auguste Cornu and Pierre Bigo), Vrin and, more occasionally, Le Seuil, Minuit and Albin-Michel. The university publishing world was itself not so innovative, for a simple reason: the university syllabus, particularly that for *agrégation* exams, remained the backbone of their editorial strategies. Marx was an author to whom a part of the intellectual world referred, without reading him.

3   Marxism: A Competitive Publishing Market

The end of the 1950s saw an important shift. Marx became a major intellectual reference (both politically and for scholarship). After 1958, a year in which no texts by Marx were published, the publication of his texts resumed at an average rate of three titles per year. Publications of studies on Marx (a field in which Éditions sociales were near-absent) multiplied from 1959 onwards. In the Éditions sociales catalogue, the texts of Marx and Engels published from 1952 onwards had frequent reprints. Out of 63 titles written by Marx or Engels, 13 were reprinted at least once. The second print run was two or three times larger than the initial one. For example, the *Communist Manifesto* was printed in 6,000 copies in 1956, 8,400 in 1961, 10,000 in 1962, 12,000 in 1963, 10,000 in 1965, 15,000 in 1966 and 1967.

This growth is explained by the emergence of a new readership. The world of education (high school students, students and teachers) was going through a real boom. In addition to this demographic shock, there was the force of the political experiences common to the younger generations (the crises of 1956, the Algerian war, Maoist China, Third Worldism, and feminism). Marx gradually left the world of law faculties (25 percent of the student body) for literature departments (30 percent). If the teaching of philosophy was dominated by the history of philosophy, the rise of the human sciences brought new authors into the bibliographies, especially meaning Freud and Marx. At the end of the 1960s, these two authors appeared in publishers' catalogues for high school philosophy classes, in the humanities. This new 'introduction' of Marxism into the intellectual field, after that of the Belle Époque and the 1920s, was distinguished by the place that Marx now occupied in the academic world, and no longer only in politics.

Louis Althusser's approach symbolised this decisive shift. His research enabled this work to move from the status of a political reference to an intellectual one. His seminar on the 'young Marx' in 1961–2 and on *Capital* in 1964–5 led him to several publication projects starting in autumn 1963: a collection of articles (*For Marx*) and the texts from his seminar on *Capital* (*Reading Capital*), which appeared in 1965. The Communist Althusser chose Maspero as the publisher. He informed Besse, director of Éditions sociales since 1955, of his intentions, and on 2 June 1965 he wrote to Henri Krasucki, a member of the PCF Politburo, to inform him of his project and to explain it to him. Althusser told him that he was going with Maspero in order to respond to the demands of an increasingly wide audience interested in Marxism and to ensure that this thought would have 'a very wide dissemination in academic, scientific, artistic and other circles'. Moreover, Maspero 'already has a public and a large audience in the academic and student world'. Meaning, that to his eyes the same could not be said of Éditions sociales. On 15 June, the PCF Secretariat was officially informed of comrade Althusser's initiative, but did not show any great deal of emotion or concern. However, the cadres in charge of the Éditions sociales were disturbed by this reversal in the French publishing world, which seemed to want to capture their own 'commercial niche'. The threat was real. In 1956, Maximilien Rubel sent Dionys Mascolo, a reader at Gallimard, a project to publish the complete works of Marx.

As Rubel embarked on his project to retranslate Marx, the PCF had no monopoly position. It had laid claim to Marx but so, too, other authors (Lenin, Stalin, Thorez, and so on); since the Popular Front it had revived its relationship with the socialist authors of the nineteenth century and gave an important place to popular forms of political expression. PCF leaders could have settled for this situation, had it not been for Communist intellectuals' demand for quality editorial work, from the 1930s onwards, and had Marx not been taken over by the intellectual field, particularly in the 1960s. But this slow conversion to a 'modern' editorial treatment of Marx was not without its tensions: the sale of Marxist books, from 1956 onward, was both a public valorisation of the work of Communist intellectuals and of party publishing, and at the same time a political instrumentalisation of their work.

CHAPTER 10

Marx's Works in the 'Bibliothèque de la Pléiade': A Paradoxical Legitimation

Aude Le Moullec-Rieu

Unlike Russian, German, English or Italian speaking countries, the Francophone countries do not have a reference edition of Marx and Engels's writings. Although unfinished, it is the *Œuvres de Marx* in the 'Bibliothèque de la Pléiade' that offers the richest French-language corpus of Marx's writings to be published according to homogeneous rules of translation and edition. This version has one undeniable advantage over its competitors: it is still available, as it is backed by a major publisher, Gallimard, and it has recently been reissued in paperback format. However, this edition, put together by Maximilien Rubel and published from 1963 to 1994, is not considered as a reference edition in French, in the manner of the *Marx-Engels-Werke* (MEW) in German, published from 1956 to 1968 by Dietz Verlag (East Berlin), or the *Marx & Engels Collected Works* in English, produced on the same model as the MEW.

The Rubel edition is an original editorial object, which sheds essential light on the dissemination and reception of Marx and Engels's writings in France since the 1960s. It combines the militant objective of a scientific editor, Maximilien Rubel – a devotee of Marx's teaching and yet an anti-Marxist, who sought to get Marx out of the ideological sidetracks to which, as he saw it, the Communists had confined him – with the principally commercial objectives of Gallimard as a publisher. The discourse surrounding its publication, amplified by its inclusion in a collection with a strong power of legitimation, allow for a better understanding of the criteria of a reference edition and translation, as applied to writings whose publication constantly touches on political issues.

1 The Genesis of an Editorial Project

The edition of Marx's writings in the 'Bibliothèque de la Pléiade' is strongly marked by the imprint of its master builder. Maximilian Rubel was born in 1905 in Czernowitz, in the Austro-Hungarian Empire. His mother tongue was German, but his parents also spoke Yiddish. In 1919, his native region became part of Romania and he was forced to continue his studies in Romanian. He discovered French in high school and had the opportunity to learn English, which he mastered, although he still had some discomfort writing in it. According to his own admission, Latin and Greek were missing from his culture.

Rubel emigrated to Paris in 1931. During his formative years, his taste for philosophy grew stronger. Spinoza, Nietzsche and Kierkegaard became his favoured authors. Initially attracted by the study of Karl Kraus's aphorisms, he only discovered Marx during World War II. He read Marx in the first scholarly edition of his writings, the MEGA, undertaken in the USSR in the 1920s by David Ryazanov (1870–1938), of whom he was a great admirer. He went to the CNRS as a research associate in 1948, defended his thesis – an intellectual biography of Marx – at the Sorbonne in 1954, and presented a bibliography of Marx's works as a complementary thesis. In it he asserted his central idea, which he would develop in his subsequent writings: Marx had inherited his ethics from the utopian socialists, before then grounding it in a sociological theory. This work explicitly prepared the production of a French-language edition of Marx's works, which would not be in hock to 'Marxism', or undertaken by a party or a state for ideological reasons. To Rubel's eyes, a complete edition of Marx's works was the only way to denounce the 'greatest mystification of this century': Marxism. This fight was also a chance to put across his taste for controversy, in which he saw the means to widen the audience for his ideas. Indeed, his article 'Karl Marx auteur maudit en URSS?' ('Karl Marx, An Author Damned In the USSR?') had international repercussions. But it was above all the subject of an sharp debate with the communists, in particular Émile Bottigelli, himself a translator of Marx for the Éditions sociales, who replied to him in *La Nouvelle Critique*.

Rubel was attached to the Institute of Applied Economic Sciences (ISEA), directed by François Perroux. This latter's benevolence towards Rubel's work was real: from 1959 onwards, a series of *Cahiers de l'ISEA* was devoted to the work that Rubel had done or otherwise inspired on Marx: these were the *Études de marxologie*, which Rubel gladly sent to his international correspondents. Rubel defined the neologism 'Marxology', modelled on Ryazanov's *Marksovedenie* and proposed in 1946 as a translation of *Marxforschung*, as the 'scientific, historical-critical study of the work of Marx and Engels'.[1]

After the war, Rubel mixed among the Communist Left in France, which laid claim to the ideas of the Italian Marxist Amadeo Bordiga (1889–1970). Hostile to the party form, Rubel was won to council communism, which promoted organisation in workers' councils and opposed Leninist conceptions of the party.

---

1   Ragona 2003.

From 1963 to 1968, he led a group around the *Cahiers de discussion pour le socialisme des conseils*. The relative isolation he suffered on the French intellectual scene did not prevent him from maintaining a correspondence with theorists of council communism around the world, such as the Dutchman Anton Pannekoek (1873–1960) and the American Paul Mattick (1904–1981).[2]

Rubel took the initiative of making a proposal to Gallimard, for an edition of Marx's texts to be published in the 'Bibliothèque de la Pléiade'. In June 1955, Rubel gave Dionys Mascolo (1916–97) – a reader at Gallimard, but also author of a critical book on *Le Communisme*, and a PCF expellee – a first plan for an edition of Marx in this collection. Not only did Mascolo not follow up on the proposal, but Rubel learned in 1957 that Gallimard had tasked Lucien Goldmann (1913–70) with a Pléiade edition of Marx. Rubel was concerned that Goldmann, who had never been a member of the PCF, instead identified with the Hungarian philosopher György Lukács, who attributed to Marx the idea of a mediating party, the embodiment of the historical totality. A dispute soon arose between the two men in *Les Temps modernes*, after Goldmann sharply criticised Rubel's thesis, published by Marcel Rivière in 1957.

However, Goldmann's project, of which nothing is known, came to nothing, and Rubel made a new proposal in 1960 to Brice Parain (1897–1971), a member of the reading committee who had already taken the opportunity to tell Rubel of his admiration for his great erudition. Michel Gallimard then asked Rubel for a plan for an edition of the three volumes of Capital, and Robert Gallimard (1925–2013) – who succeeded his cousin Michel as head of the collection after the latter's death – decided to entrust Rubel with the Pléiade edition of Marx. Several indicators would suggest Brice Parain had a decisive role in this choice, although this role cannot be clearly established. Subsequent events show that Robert Gallimard was hardly averse to consulting Parain, still an influential member of Gallimard's reading committee despite his retirement in 1961; this may well confirm his pre-eminent role in the choice in favour of Rubel.

Although Michel Gallimard's views are not directly known, what can be supposed is the publisher had some reticence about publishing Marx in the 'Bibliothèque de la Pléiade' before 1960. Marx was, certainly, not absent from its catalogue: since 1934 it had offered *Morceaux choisis de Karl Marx*, with an introduction by Henri Lefebvre and Norbert Guterman. Intellectuals such as Albert Camus and Althusser had their first contact with Marx through these selected texts, which were republished in 1950.

---

2 Bourrinet 1987.

Rubel's doggedness in not offering his project to another publisher shows how much importance he attached to publishing *his* Marx in this already prestigious collection. The collection founded by Jacques Schiffrin, where nonliterary works have always had their place, was first born of the desire to gather a large number of writings by one author in a single volume. The shift towards academic-quality critical editions only became systematic in the 1960s.[3]

2   The Principles of Rubel's Edition

How did Rubel prepare this edition? The example of the first two volumes, *Économie* I and II, allows us to understand Rubel's editing choices and what was at stake therein. They contain the three volumes of *Capital*, as well as other emblematic texts, such as the *Communist Manifesto*, the *1844 Manuscripts* and the *Grundrisse*. Rubel opted for an edition that did not respect the chronology of Marx's writings. His plan was organised around two decisions. The first was the thematic tripartition, between economic, philosophical and political writings. One of the ambitions of Rubel's editorial endeavour was to render Marx's work, particularly his great project on *Economy* – which gives its name to the first two Pléiade volumes – in its incompleteness, that is to say, only to offer *Capital* as framed by its preparatory materials. Correspondence with Gallimard shows that Rubel first conceived these first two volumes long before he set out the subsequent volumes, perhaps on the grounds that the publisher was more likely to be persuaded of the merits of an edition of *Capital*. This explains the difficulties Rubel later faced, especially when he had to come to terms with the absence from *Politique* I of the *Communist Manifesto*, which had already been published in *Économie* I, because Marx had said that the *Manifesto* was a good introduction to reading *Capital*. The second editorial principle was the separation between writings published during the author's lifetime and posthumous texts, although Rubel did allow himself some exceptions. His insistence on setting apart Marx's posthumously published writings must be understood in the light of his categorical rejection of the entire Marxist tradition.

In the format imposed on him, Rubel could only propose a selection of writings. He thus had to decide which texts should feature in the 'Bibliothèque de la Pléiade' volumes. In his work of selection, Rubel openly excluded the contributions of Engels – both in his own writings and in his role as Marx's editor –

---

3   Gleize and Roussin 2009.

whom he considered to be the founder of Marxism. This also politically motiv-
ated challenge to the dogma of the unity of Marx and Engels continued a tradition in Western Marxism that was started by Georg Lukács and Karl Korsch,
and which developed in the 1970s in the Federal Republic of Germany (FRG)
under the name *neue Marx-Lektüre*.[4]

As Marx's major work – and the one at the heart of *Économie* – *Capital*
posed many problems of edition and translation. There are several different
established texts for Volume I, with two editions and a French translation during Marx's lifetime, followed by two further editions prepared by Engels. Rubel
chose to use Roy's translation, which has the legitimacy of having been revised
by the author. Although Marx made some additions of great theoretical interest
(which Engels nevertheless neglected for his German editions), the Roy translation is nonetheless questionable.[5] Rubel himself agreed on this score, when
he compared the translation with the original text, and was careful to point this
out in the notes and with the variations included. He remained greatly respectful of Roy's translation, even if he did allow himself a little retouching of the
text, which was not systematic in character. This makes all the more surprising
the changes that he did make – the reversal of the order of the last two chapters
and the removal of certain passages from the appendix, out of 'concern for clar-
ity' as he put it. The other two volumes present a quite different case, since they
were edited by Engels. Rubel claims greater fidelity to Marx's project and proposes a restructuring of the sections and chapters proposed by Engels. Rubel
especially relies on the manuscripts discarded by Engels, which Rubel consulted during multiple spells at the International Institute of Social History (IISG)
in Amsterdam.

As for the other writings in *Économie* I and II, Rubel was always more
inclined to rely on the texts prepared for Ryazanov's MEGA, even if he kept a
critical distance from it; as an alternative, he willingly drew on the *Marx-Engels-
Werke*. Rubel always preferred editions, even Soviet ones, that could boast of
having been able to consult the original texts. He himself does not neglect to
indicate when he was able to consult the manuscripts at the IISG in Amsterdam; such was the case of the *Grundrisse*, which the Pléiade edition did not
publish in their entirety.

Rubel attached great importance to the abundant and meticulously updated
critical apparatus that he provided, believing this to be the foundation for the
originality and scientific character of his edition. François Perroux opened the

---

4   Elbe 2008.
5   Lefebvre 1982.

first volume with a preface celebrating social dialogue. It seems that the initiative to ask the influential economist for this preface was Rubel's own, although he was not satisfied with it – to the point that he considered deleting it, given the opportunity to produce a second edition. The very exacting notes illustrate the interest, already present in Rubel's bibliography, in the details of the original editions and the existing French translations. While Rubel uses the notes in the traditional way – to aid in the understanding of the text or to inform on variants of translation and among editions – they are also an opportunity for him to assert his own ideas, basing himself on the text. The introduction to the second volume is thus a real exposition of Rubel's theses concerning the incompleteness of Marx's work on *Economy*, of which *Capital* was only one part, against the idea – as sustained since Henryk Grossman in 1929 – of a 'change in the plan' for a study of *Economy*, which would thus make *Capital* itself a finished work. Rubel also asserts that Marx's planned book on the state would have theorised its disappearance. This was a thesis that he would develop further in his 1983 collection of articles *Marx, théoricien de l'anarchisme* (*'Marx, Theorist of Anarchism'*).

The *Œuvres* of Marx were issued by a publisher whose interests were primarily commercial. If the logics of the main protagonists were not in outright contradiction, Rubel's critical and militant project did not correspond to Gallimard's own strategy. Robert Gallimard, who was in charge of the 'Bibliothèque de la Pléiade', was Rubel's main contact within the publisher. As far as the first two books were concerned, his respect for Rubel's editorial decisions was total, even if he did venture suggestions to ensure the volumes commercial success. Rubel's financial demands, which were present from the beginning, gradually took precedence over the rest, and became more pronounced when he was pensioned off from the CNRS in 1970. Discussions for the preparation of the subsequent volumes began in 1965; Rubel wanted Gallimard to provide him with qualified translators so that he could devote himself to the critical apparatus.

3   Rubel's Collaborators

Rubel drew on other collaborators mainly for the translations. Louis Évrard (1926–95) was literary director of Éditions du Rocher in Monaco until 1966, when he became a regular contributor to Gallimard; Pierre Nora hired him on account of his erudition and his qualities as a translator. In 1977, Louis and his wife Nicole, who still lived in Peymeinade, near Nice, came to work with Nora in Paris for financial reasons. Here, Louis Évrard played an essential role in the creation of the 'Bibliothèque des sciences sociales' collection and the journal *Le Débat*, while Nicole Évrard was Nora's secretary.[6] For the first volume of Marx's *Œuvres*, Louis Évrard produced the translations from English into French and reread all the other translations, a task he also fulfilled for the following two volumes. Rubel generally submitted his texts to Louis Évrard for rereading; they enjoyed a great intellectual bond. The highly respected collaborator Louis Évrard contributed to the later volumes at a greater remove. Yet, he played an important role as an intermediary with Robert Gallimard during the difficult preparation of the third volume, *Philosophie*, when the publisher rejected Rubel's translations, which were checked and deemed to be of insufficient quality.

The writer Jean Malaquais (1908–98), author of *Les Javanais* and *Planète sans visa*, is listed as the second translator for several texts by Marx in the second volume of the *Œuvres*: according to Rubel, he was responsible for 'honing them stylistically'. Rubel was so pleased with this that he proposed the writer as coeditor of the third volume; but Malaquais, who had worked with Rubel mainly for financial reasons, did contribute to the next volume.

It had been intended that Serge Bricianer (1923–97) would collaborate on the second volume, and indeed Rubel included him in the acknowledgments in the first, but then the two men fell out in 1964. Also mentioned were Claude Orsoni, with reference to the *1844 Manuscripts*, and Michel Jacob and Suzanne Voute (1922–2001), for *Capital* Volume III: their role is more difficult to define since their correspondence with Rubel is absent from the archives. The same difficulty arises with Roger Dangeville (1925–2006), who was Rubel's assistant, at least in 1963. Dangeville gathered documentation for *Économie* I, and Rubel planned to task him with the translation of chapter six of Capital Volume I, for *Économie* II. But the two men drifted apart, and in 1967–8 Dangeville instead published the first French translation of the *Grundrisse* with the young publishing house Anthropos, under the title *Fondements de la critique de l'économie politique*. Rubel was sharply critical of the translation.

These various collaborators belonged to the same political circles as Rubel. Jean Malaquais was initiated in politics by Marc Chirik, leader of France's Left Communist circle, with which Rubel had mingled after the war, but also by Louis Évrard and Serge Bricianer. Malaquais received Suzanne Voute, a major figure of the French Bordigist current, who would oppose Roger Dangeville, whom she had herself trained. Serge Bricianer was, among other things, the translator of Paul Mattick, with whom he had developed a political corres-

---

6 Dosse 2011.

pondence through Louis Évrard, and whom he met in 1981. All of these contributors were experienced as translators, often on a militant (rather than paid-
professional) basis.

The two figures who remained, Louis Évrard and, to a lesser extent, Jean
Malaquais, were nevertheless what might be called professional translators.
Rubel enlisted the help of others for some of the translations of the last volume:
he recruited these translators on the basis of their mastery of the language, as
assessed by an essay, and less on the basis of militant connections.

From the second volume onwards, there also appeared the man who was
to become Rubel's closest collaborator: Louis Janover (born in 1937). In 1964,
the dissident surrealist journal *Front noir*, which he edited, devoted an issue to
council-socialism, to which end Janover first entered contacts with Rubel. For
the last three volumes of the *Œuvres*, Janover produced the indexes with the
help of his wife, Monique, and also gladly took on proofreading the texts and
revising the translations.

4   A Successful Effort

The edition of Marx's *Œuvres* in the 'Bibliothèque de la Pléiade' was a commercial success: the first volume had six printings, four of them between 1963 and
1972, and the second had three between 1968 and 1979. Given Marx's importance to the French intellectual and political life of the 1960s, it is hardly surprising that the publication of Marx's works in the 'Bibliothèque de la Pléiade'
aroused interest in 1963, and even more so in 1968: Marx's entry into the Bibliothèque de la Pléiade was, moreover, seen as a sign of the times. The singular place that the collection occupies in the French publishing landscape
means that the edition reached a wide audience. Its publication was commented on in the daily and weekly newspapers, by renowned intellectuals such as
Raymond Aron and François Châtelet. But the collection was also attributed
a scholarly calling – not belied by Rubel's own ambitions – and it was also
received in more specialised journals, whose requirements were of a different
order.

The erudition of the edition proposed by Rubel was readily recognised
and celebrated. However, several authors mentioned one same regret: that
the theses of Louis Althusser (1918–90) were not discussed. Rubel's approach,
which consists in mocking Althusser's language in a note in his introduction
to the second volume, drew sharp criticism. The question of the quality of the
translations remained secondary. The key point in the reception of the 'Bibliothèque de la Pléiade' edition of Marx's *Œuvres* was the discussion of its

scientific character. The revision of Engels's edition of Volumes II and III of *Capital*, on the basis of Marx's manuscripts preserved in Amsterdam, did raise questions. Yet, this issue emerged right from the publication of *Économie I*, given Rubel's choice to reverse the last two chapters of Volume I. The editors of Marx and Engels for Éditions Sociales, Gilbert Badia in the lead, were unsurprisingly the first to criticise the edition proposed by Rubel. Without disputing the political antagonism between the protagonists, it must be stressed that they were careful to set their criticism on a scholarly level, where they often overlapped with critics to whom Rubel's project was convincing, such as Aron. The responses from Rubel and his collaborators allow us to understand that to their eyes the scientific character of this edition resided first and foremost in its critical apparatus, whereas critics concentrated on establishing a reliable version of the text.

5   A Singular Edition

Since his first works on Marx, Rubel had constantly asserted the need for a historical and critical edition of Marx's writings, in line with the first MEGA undertaken by Ryazanov in the USSR in the 1920s. Rubel's insistence led Gallimard to see him as the right editor for Marx in the 'Bibliothèque de la Pléiade'. Rubel made no secret of the fact that he wanted to produce the French reference edition, which could even be a reference among all the editions of Marx. Could the 'Bibliothèque de la Pléiade' fulfil this ambition? Originally, the collection was intended to bring together a given author's writings in a single volume, without any further treatment of the text. But by the time that *Économie I* appeared in 1963, the 'Bibliothèque de la Pléiade' already had the legitimating power for which it is known; many observers took the publication of this volume for confirmation that Marx had, indeed, become a classic. The fact remained that Gallimard's interests were commercial in nature. Its reluctance to include Marx in the 'Bibliothèque de la Pléiade' at the time of Rubel's first initiatives, in 1955 and again in 1957, clearly showed this. Only in 1960 did Michel and then Robert Gallimard give in, at a moment when interest in Marx and Engels was growing and their works were penetrating the academic field, becoming an intellectual and no longer merely political reference point. Moreover, the edition of Marx's works in the 'Bibliothèque de la Pléiade' was a success. This no doubt explains the indulgence Rubel enjoyed, particularly from Robert Gallimard, notwithstanding the build-up of delays on his part – he produced four volumes in thirty years, for an edition which would be left unfinished – and the sharp criticism which he attracted. Rubel was perhaps aware of the limits of the 'Bibliothèque de la Pléiade' project; as 1983 approached, he proposed a twenty-three-volume centenary edition to another publisher, Slatkine.

Rubel, who claimed Marxian inspiration for his anti-communism and anti-Marxism, could well point out that these criticisms often came from his political opponents, first among them the PCF editors of Marx and Engels. However, these critics challenged the scholarly character of the Gallimard edition, while taking care to avoid the direct terrain of political confrontation. The theoretical aspect of certain points, such as Engels's role, should not conceal their also political significance. Yet it should be noted that there was also a divergence over the criterion (or criteria) for judging what made an edition scholarly. For Rubel, the highly erudite 'historical-critical apparatus' that he proposed – which, as he never tired of repeating, made for the originality of his edition – counted for more than fidelity to the original... This would, in any case, have required the existence of such an 'original', insofar as Marx wrote and rewrote the same texts, even after having published them.

CHAPTER 11

A Golden Age for Marxist Publishing? The 1960s and 1970s

Julien Hage

In the political context of the thawing of the Cold War, the deep crisis of the international communist movement, the hopes raised by decolonisation, the May '68 movements and the dynamism of the different forces of the Left, there was a period of profound renewal in the publishing of Marx and Marxism in France. These years saw the rise of new collections of political and philosophical theory, the translation of numerous unpublished works and the production of multiple anthologies in paperback format. Even as the PCF's publishing house began its 'mutation',[1] the endeavours of new actors in the far-left publishing world energised these editorial efforts, instigated debate and fuelled dissident thinking within the Communist Party and on its margins. Meanwhile, the dozens of Communist and far left bookshops, the 'alternative bookstores', which sprang up all over France in the aftermath of May '68, filled their shelves with 'Marxism' and 'Theory' sections. In turn, university presses and some of the big generalist publishers hastened to invest in the now-emerging market for Marxian and Marxist texts.[2]

From the nineteenth century to the interwar period, the publication of Marx had been taken up by militant and party presses – and, more often than not, disseminated en masse in the form of pamphlets. However, in the 1968 years Marx found right of place in book form, in both commercial and academic publishing. Marx's work was included in optional secondary school curricula (*The Communist Manifesto* and *The German Ideology* were now among the texts for the baccalaureate-level oral examination in philosophy) and even more widely in higher-education courses and debates, having long being confined to law faculties. The most eloquent symbol of the changing place granted Marx's *oeuvre*, and the recognition it now enjoyed, was doubtless its introduction into Gallimard's 'Bibliothèque de la Pléiade' collection, in Maximilien Rubel's edition.

---

1   Bouju 2010.
2   Mollier 2014.

Driven both by the development of the human and social sciences after World War II and by the 1968 movements, Marx's work experienced a golden age of publications and met with academic, commercial and public success. This would, however, be a brief spell of success. After these 'ten glorious years', the publication of Marx declined at the turn of the 1980s, against the backdrop of the saturation of the political book market and the ideological retreat of progressive ideas faced with the neoliberal counter-offensive.[3] If the one-hundred-and-fiftieth anniversary of Karl Marx's birth in 1968, was marked by a great editorial dynamism – with the release of hitherto unpublished works, reissues and critical editions – the centenary of his death, in 1983, appears as the beginning of a long journey across the publishing desert, with the disappearance of most theoretical collections and the growing scarcity of paperback editions of Marx and Marxism. This decline was aggravated by the disappearance of the Communist publisher Messidor at the end of the 1990s, before the relaunching of the new Éditions sociales and a new complete edition of Marx's works at the turn of the 2010s.

1   The Thawing Cold War and the Revival of Marxism

After World War II, which had brought a halt to the development of Hegelianism and Marxism in France, and the constraints of the Cold War, which hardened ideological positions and encouraged a retreat to a corpus that was often Engelsian (Engels's *Anti-Dühring* being one of the main points of reference), there began a new period of returning to the texts. This movement was enabled by the reconstitution of the Marxian archives and libraries which had been dispersed by the conflict, both nationally and internationally; this owed to the efforts of the Marx-Engels-Lenin Institute (MELI) in Moscow and the Institute of Social History in Amsterdam, as well as newcomers such as the Fondazione Feltrinelli in Milan, created by the publisher Giangiacomo Feltrinelli. Raising the prospect of a second push to prepare a complete works of Marx, these initiatives at exhuming texts and recovering documentation considerably revived reflection and publications on Marx and Marxism, as well as the political uses of Marxist theory. There was a strong desire to return to the texts of Marx and Engels, which had been drowned in glosses during the Stalinist period. This meant calling on sources both old and new, and sometimes even constructing a 'Marxological' scientific approach, emancipated from its milit-

---

3   Pouch 2001.

ant uses and ideological readings. The need, now, was to put together critical editions based on more reliable translations.

The new editions of Marx thus found themselves at the crossroads of a renewal of the uses of theory,[4] a revival of speculative and academic research on the subject, and a growing interest among the general public, especially among students and the activists in left-wing movements. This interest was stimulated by the multiple Russian, Chinese and soon Albanian editions in the French language, sold at the price of pamphlets, which circulated in this country thanks to their distribution by sympathetic organisations. For the Marxist sociologist and philosopher Nicos Poulantzas, it was with May '68 that perspectives for Marx and for work on Marxism were flung wide open: 'A whole crowd of new ideas emerged at the time. But what 1968 first produced was the hegemony of Marxism. The books on desire, on anti-authoritarian discourse, came out later, after 1971. It was the reaction of disappointed people who had not digested the fact that May had been Marxism's victory rather than their own ...'

2   Flourishing Availability

In the mid-1960s, students looking for editions of Marx's works, and in particular of *Capital*, were still obliged to consult the old Costes editions, which certain bookshops, such as La Vieille Taupe (then on the ultra-left), profitably put into circulation in May '68 and the years that followed. But there was soon a complete overhaul in the supply of Marx's works coming from publishing houses. Many of them began to publish, republish and translate his works. This emulation led to a diversification in the range of titles available, and sometimes even to strong competition between editions of the same text issued by different publishers.

In the 1970s, the *Communist Manifesto* was available in French from more than ten different publishers: Éditions sociales (ES), in a single edition in the 'Classiques du marxisme' (1966), as well as in a bilingual edition (1972); Union générale d'éditions (UGE) 10/18, in an edition prefaced by the historian Robert Mandrou (1962); the Fondazione Feltrinelli, in a scientific edition prepared by Bert Andreas (1963); Beijing's Foreign Languages Press (1970); Aubier Montaigne (1971), in the new collection 'Connaissance de Marx'; Livre de Poche, in a new translation by Corinne Lyotard, including also the *Critique of the Gotha*

---

4   Ducange and Garo 2015.

Programme and a preface by François Châtelet (1973); the Italian publisher Savelli, in an illustrated edition in comic strips, prefaced by Les Cahiers du Forum-Histoire directed by Jean Chesneaux (1977); Nathan, in Laura Lafargue's translation and with an introduction by Gérard Noiriel (1981); the Éditions de la pédagogie moderne, which reprinted the Châtelet edition (1981); and finally Champ libre, in the form of a reproduction (1983). This competition did nothing to hurt sales of the *Manifesto*: tens of thousands of copies were sold every year in the 1970s. According to Lucien Sève, Éditions sociales alone sold 600,000 copies between 1945 and 1983.[5]

3   New Texts for 'New Readings' of Marx?

The questioning of and debate around a 'Communist canon', often identified with the vulgate, fed the arrival of competing, 'heterodox' Marxisms. These were disputed and enriched in the context of an international debate which proceeded both within the labour movement, student organisations, and political parties – even including within the PCF[6] – and the intellectual world. Marx's contributions to a critical apprehension of the lands of 'actually-existing socialism' and to the understanding of the Third World were particularly examined. Marx's texts were, moreover, put into perspective and compared with the 'pre-Marxian socialists', the thought of his own time, but also with contemporary philosophies, which in turn considerably reinvigorated the publication of his texts. Especially pushed into the foreground were the texts of the young Marx, a large part of his hitherto unpublished correspondence on the questions of value and the commodity, or his reflection on the nationalities question and imperialism, published in the newspapers of his own day.

The publication of and interest in Marx's work thus shifted from the canonical works and toward texts that had hitherto mainly been taken up by left-wing and far-left oppositionists, who looked therein for an alternative to the Soviet readings and the courses dispensed by PCF party schools. They were particularly interested in *The German Ideology*, which was first made available by Costes, and then from 1953 by Éditions sociales. The Éditions sociales edition, conveyed in numerous reprints devised by Gilbert Badia, enjoyed great success over the 1960s and 1970s. Even more significant is the story of the publication of the preparatory manuscripts for the writing of *Capital*, the *Grundrisse* (or

---

5   Labica 1985.
6   Di Maggio 2013.

Foundations of the Critique of Political Economy). Belatedly translated by Roger Dangeville in two volumes published by Anthropos in 1967–8 – although the German text had been fully available since the immediate postwar period – the volumes were then reprinted by Éditions La Découverte in 1972–5. They were especially put to use by the Trotskyist *Critiques de l'économie politique* (Maspero) school, which also translated and published the works by Isaac I. Rubin and Roman Rosdolsky inspired by the *Grundrisse*. Stung by this, at Lucien Sève's instigation Éditions sociales formed a working group under the direction of Jean-Pierre Lefebvre, so that the PCF press could produce its own translation. This project finally resulted in a publication only in 1980, in a version prepared by Gilbert Badia, Étienne Balibar, Jacques Bidet and Yves Duroux. In these same years, the *1844 Manuscripts*, published in 1962 by Éditions sociales, then in 1974 in Kostas Papaioannou's edition for 10/18 under the title *La Première Critique de l'économie politique*, were read within the Catholic movement, in the quest for a Marxist humanism with an ethical calling, far-removed from the Althusserian anti-humanist reading. With decolonisation, the contributions of Marx and Marxism began to be used for reflection on the Third World and the critique of economic imperialism, by interrogating 'The Pillage of the Third World' (*Le Pillage du Tiers-Monde*, Pierre Jalée) or 'Unequal Exchange' (*L'Échange inégal* by Arghiri Emmanuel). In 1962, the anti-colonialist activist and journalist Patrick Kessel, who was the first editor of the 'Bibliothèque socialiste' collection at Maspero before the arrival of the Romanian historian Georges Haupt, published *Seven Interpretative Essays on Peruvian Reality* by José Carlos Mariátegui, the inventor of Latin American Marxism. In 1969, Éditions sociales published *Sur le "mode de production asiatique"*, while Beijing's Foreign Languages Press – anxious to present China as a leader of the non-aligned movement, faithful to the Marxist-Leninist doctrine as against the Soviet model – delivered a collection of texts by Marx and Engels entitled *Sur le colonialisme* ('On Colonialism', 1970).

4   Emulation among Publishers

In the first half of the 1960s, a new generation of political presses, stemming from decolonisation and the new far left, made their way into the French publishing field: in 1965, Maspero launched the 'Théorie' collection, while from its creation in 1965–6 Anthropos provided a whole series of works on Marx This meant that Éditions sociales – which in 1965 published Volume III of *Capital*, dedicated to the critique of political economy – faced increasingly stiff competition in a field that had hitherto been something of its own preserve, without, however, ever being able to speak of editorial hegemony over the texts. Ever more important to Maspero's catalogue was the Maoist and above all Trotsky-ist school of intellectuals of the Ligue Communiste – the 'Cahiers rouges' with their 'Marx ou crève' ('Marx or Bust') series and the journal *Critiques de l'éco-nomie politique* (1970–82).

The arrival of philosopher Lucien Sève at the head of Éditions sociales in 1971, after the serious crisis that had hit the publisher in 1967–8, brought about a complete renewal of the Communist press.[7] The new director assigned it the intellectual task of methodically translating Marx's work, by consolidating the bureau of translators created by his predecessor Georges Cogniot, and by enga-ging in a profound epistemological reflection on the order and conditions in which Marx should be translated. One of the indirect outcomes of this was the *Dictionnaire critique du marxisme* published by Presses universitaires de France in 1982, ahead of the centenary of Marx's death. In addition to the new translations, Éditions sociales also gradually undertook major revisions of the translations inherited from the 1930s, and especially of the critical apparatus of a large number of texts, which was often determined by the Cold War con-text. These new editions gave order to a hitherto rather empirical programme of Marx publishing, for they distinguished between philosophical works, eco-nomic works, correspondence and writings published in periodicals: the first two volumes of the new edition of the *Correspondance* of Marx and Engels, edited by Jean Mortier and Gilbert Badia, appeared in 1971, the same year as the first three volumes of the *Rheinische Zeitung*. At the turn of the 1980s, at a time of great reduction in its editorial output, the Communist presses, united in the Messidor group, nonetheless issued new revised and explained editions of Marx in the 'Essentiel' paperback collection, alongside anthologies of texts by Trotsky and Stalin.

Not to be outdone were university presses, taking advantage of the arrival of Marx's texts in the secondary school curriculum. Presses universitaires de France had a strong tradition of Marxist research, with its 1956 edition of *Cap-ital*, complemented in the mid-1960s by a collection of texts with comment-ary by Henri Lefebvre. In 1977, it published the Marx-Lassalle correspondence (*Correspondence entre Marx et Lassalle, 1848–1864*, introduced, translated and annotated by Sonia Dayan-Herzbrun), and in 1985 the collective work *L'Œuvre de Marx un siècle après*. In 1970, the publisher Aubier-Montaigne began a col-lection entitled 'Connaissance de Marx', which was designed to host texts by Marx, often in both bilingual and critical editions: Thus it published the *Com-*

---

7   Ducange, Hage and Mollier 2014.

munist Manifesto, introduced and translated by Émile Bottigelli (1971), *On the Jewish Question*, in a translation by Marianna Simon introduced by François Châtelet (1971), the *Contribution to the Critique of Hegel's Philosophy of Right*, in a bilingual edition, translated and prefaced by the same authors (1971), *Les Documents constitutifs de la Ligue des communistes* ('Foundational Documents of the Communist League'), published by Bert Andreas, with translation and notes by Jacques Grandjonc (1972). During this same period, especially thanks to Maximilien Rubel, another publisher, Payot, was also strengthening its 'Petite Bibliothèque' with texts by Marx: the anthology *Pages pour une éthique socialiste*, published in 1970, was followed by a collection of articles by Rubel, *Marx, critique du marxisme* (published in English as *Marx, Critic of Marxism*) in 1974.

5   The Rise of Theory Collections: Louis Althusser's 'Théorie', Published by Maspero

If there is one publishing venture that symbolises the intellectual ferment around Marx's work in the 1960s and 1970s, it is the 'Théorie' collection, founded and directed by Louis Althusser. When François Maspero planned to launch 'Théorie', Althusser insisted to Communist Party leaders that no 'bourgeois' publisher was ready to make such an investment.[8] In the Rue d'Ulm philosopher's first draft outlines, 'Théorie' was conceived as a structuralist collection, before it became the collection of the Althusserian school, and indeed one with a double vocation: it corresponded to the demands of both academic-scientific research and political intervention. A preparatory document reveals his plans for it: a collection of articles by Georges Canguilhem (edited and unpublished articles), a book by Michel Foucault on the theory of the history of ideas, a translation of the *Essence of Christianity* prefaced by Jean-Pierre Osier, *A Theory of Literary Production* by Pierre Macherey, *Le Concept de roman* by Alain Badiou, and the texts of Marx's *Grundrisse* introduced by Maurice Godelier. According to a later presentation, written by Althusser, the collection – cast as a 'collection of Marxist theory' – intended 'to take note of the de facto encounter, which is taking place before our eyes, between the conceptual elaboration of the philosophical principles contained in the discovery of Marx, and, on the other hand, certain works of epistemology, the history of ideologies and knowledge, and of research. It would like to make this encounter clear and useful to all those, theorists and practitioners, whom it may interest, and to offer a com-

---

8   Hage 2010.

mon place of examination, exchange and confrontation for works of research that are now indispensable to each other'.

Louis Althusser had extensive power as the collection's director, as well as a percentage on sales. The collection began with his book *For Marx* in 1965 (30,000 copies sold by 1981), followed the next year by *Reading Capital* (a product of the work of the seminar run together with Étienne Balibar, Roger Establet, Pierre Macherey and Jacques Rancière). It would publish no less than twenty-eight titles, counting its various series, before Althusser left for Hachette and the collection died out in 1981. It sold 92 percent of its print runs in 1972, by which point one-third of all its titles had been published (a remarkable figure for works of this type, with first print runs ranging from 1,000 to 3,000 copies). Some of his works, such as *Reading Capital* in two volumes (1965), were then included in the 'Petite Collection Maspero' in 1968, with a cumulative print run of over 70,000 copies (including the new 'entirely revised' edition of 1971, which removed the texts by Rancière, Macherey and Establet and left in only the ones by Althusser and Balibar).

6   The Fulsome Success of Anthologies and Paperbacks

The texts and anthologies of Marx and Engels in paperback were a great success: they were undoubtedly the main vehicle for the dissemination of their oeuvre during this period. The paperback took over the role of the pamphlet of the interwar years, but less for militants' use and with students making up the bulk of the readership. Far from necessarily constituting critical editions, anthological works are the easiest and most pedagogical way for most people to gain access texts, thanks to their thematic treatment and translations designed to be as readable as possible. But they also provide a way out of the difficulties and delays which the translation undergoes as it is being prepared for a complete works. They further play on the unpublished nature of the texts to intervene in the political, intellectual and philosophical debate. In 1971, Roger Dangeville published *Un chapitre inédit du Capital* (*Premier livre, chapitre 6*) ('An unpublished chapter from *Capital*: Volume I, chapter six') with UGE 10/18. In the introduction, quoting Karol Kosik and Roman Rosdolsky, he rejects any distinction between Marx's early and mature works, here taking aim at Althusser. After *Marx et les marxistes*, published by Gallimard in 1965, Kostas Papaioannou used the translation of the *Critique of Hegel's Philosophy of Right* (1976) to take up the 'endless debate' on the question of the relationship between Marx and Hegel. In the 'Petite Collection Maspero' (PCM), launched in 1967, but also published by 10/18, Roger Dangeville produced, between 1970 and 1978, numerous thematic anthologies, conceiving introductions and notes in a very hybrid format. Moreover, the translation was often not very rigorous, indistinctly (and without even using quote marks) mixing in Marx's texts with Bordigist formulas (drawn from Communist Party of Italy founder Amadeo Bordiga). Thus, Maspero published *Le Mouvement ouvrier français* (1973, four volumes), *Le Parti de classe* (1973, two volumes), *Critique de Malthus* (1978), *Critique de l'éducation et de l'enseignement* (1978), *Traduire et éditer Marx* (1976), *Utopisme et communauté de l'avenir* (1976), *Les Utopistes* (1976), and *Le Syndicalisme* (1972, two volumes). Under the direction of Christian Bourgois at the Union générale d'éditions, the 10/18 paperback editions were not to be outdone. They offered numerous thematic collections which 'decentred' Marx's thinking: *La Guerre civile aux États-Unis, 1861–1865* (1970), *La Chine* (1972), *Russie* (1975), again by Dangeville, *Marx et les Marxists* (1970) by Kostas Papaioannou, and *Marx, marxisme et Algérie* by René Galissot and Gilbert Badia (1976). In this field of thematic anthologies, Éditions sociales, a pioneer in the field, was for a time supplanted by its rivals' dynamism. But it was not slow to pick up the gauntlet, basing itself on collective intellectual structures such as the *Centre d'études et de recherches matérialistes* (CERM). Notable volumes it published included Marx and Engels's letters on the natural sciences and mathematics (*Lettres sur les sciences de la nature et les mathématiques*, 1974) in an edition devised by Jean-Pierre Lefebvre; *Sur les sociétés précapitalistes*, a collection of Marx, Engels and Lenin on precapitalist societies (1976) compiled by Maurice Godelier in collaboration with the CERM, and *Marx, Engels et la IIIe République* by Claude Mainfroy (1984), on the pair's reading of the French Third Republic.

7   The Late 1970s Decline in Editions of Marx's Writings

Fuelled by the exhumation of texts, editorial dynamism and the research undertaken over decades past, the new collective histories of Marxism, launched during the 1970s, came to an abrupt halt at the end of the decade, at the same time as most of the new Marx editions in commercial and academic publishing ran out of steam; from this point onward, Éditions sociales was going it alone. In 1979, Christian Bourgois at UGE 10/18 interrupted the publication, with the fifth book, of the translation of *The History of Contemporary Marxism* which had been published in Italy on the initiative of the Fondazione Giangiacomo Feltrinelli and adapted in France under Dominique Grisoni's direction. The French publishers also stopped their participation in the co-edition of the *Storia del Marxismo* instigated by Einaudi, which remained unpublished in French despite the many contributions by French researchers.

After a rich decade of publications, editions of Marx remained highly incomplete and fragmentary, with a large part of his oeuvre still not available in French. Among these publications, the presence of critical editions remained highly relative, hotly debated and shrouded in misunderstanding. Many of the translations conceived by Éditions sociales in this period were still received as 'ideological' in nature, even though they were often, if not the most reliable translations, at least the most cogent, the work of seasoned translators, and sometimes – as with the *Grundrisse* translated by Jean-Pierre Lefebvre – the most philosophically rigorous ones. At the turn of the 1970s, the use and reception of Marx's work remained highly politicised and disputed among organisations. The growing involvement of public and academic institutions, although sometimes resented, was without precedent in the previous period and undoubtedly heralded the future conditions of Marxian publishing in a world where party presses had completely collapsed.

8   A 'Living Marxism'

The intensity of the clashes in debates and in publishers' catalogues also reveals the reality and combativeness of 'living Marxism' in these years. Even at Maspero alone – a publishing house that was the crossroads of different left-wing currents in 1968 – there was a powerful confrontation between Althusserian, Communist, Trotskyist and Maoist readings, both in the text and in the paratext.[9] In Marx's case, political publishing had a decisive role in stimulating debate, ordering this thinker's oeuvre and interrogating it in depth through its militant, intellectual and institutional uses. It, just like the structures of militant reflection and academic institutions, played its part in bringing together booklovers, activists, archivists, researchers, thinkers and translators, around the effort to publish Marx. All this provided for the crystallisation of a critical knowledge which was both shared and disputed.

9   Guichard, Hage and Léger 2009.

PART 3

Marx and the Social Sciences

∵

CHAPTER 12

Marxism and Rationalism in the French Social Sciences (1930–60)

Isabelle Gouarné

Long ignored by the academic world, in the 1930s Marx became established as a pivotal figure of French rationalist thought – a legacy which, starting from the Comtian inheritance, provided a point of reference and of aggregation for republican philosophy and the academic social sciences. With this, Marx emerged from the 'situation of double exclusion' which had resulted from the struggles for 'hegemony within the workers' movement' in the late nineteenth century. This had meant exclusion in the political field, where – with the uses that the Guesdists made of Marx's texts, in order to distinguish themselves from other intellectuals purporting to embody the 'proletarian' cause – Marxism had been reduced to a doctrinal corpus which endlessly repeated canonised formulas. Alongside this was an exclusion in the intellectual field, where Marxism had been locked into a fatalistic vision of history, based on a one-dimensional economic determinism.[1]

This is the turn of events that we shall study in this chapter. We will show how Marxism was able to appear as a renewal of the French rationalist matrix which, since the beginning of the Third Republic, had associated social sciences and the philosophy of science with a form of civically engaged knowledges and reflection on progress.[2] Marx's status changed in the span of a few years: he became a legitimate reference in the social sciences, which had in the interwar period still been deeply marked by Durkheimianism, and where previously only intellectuals marginal to the academic world such as Jean Jaurès or Lucien Herr had taken up his work. After being rejected by the first Durkheimian generations, Marx was now presented as one of the 'founding fathers' of the French social sciences, alongside Émile Durkheim.[3]

---

1   Ymonet 1984.
2   Fabiani 2010.
3   Gouarné 2013.

1   The Invention of a 'French-Style Marxism', and the Surrounding
        Tensions

Such a revision was only possible thanks to a strong politicisation of the French
intellectual field, from which the Communist Party especially benefited. In
the 1920s, with its 'Bolshevisation' and the adoption of the 'class against class'
strategy, professional intellectuals had been sidelined and marginalised from
the Communist Party that emerged from the Tours Congress. But Maurice
Thorez's arrival at the head of the party in 1930 ushered in a period of intellectual and political openness, culminating in the Popular Front, with the implementation of a real cultural policy.[4] Young intellectuals from the post-World
War I generations, marked by an anti-institutional mood – for instance Georges
Friedmann, Paul Nizan and Georges Politzer – had, certainly, drawn closer to
the Communist Party at the end of the 1920s, after being involved in the circles
of the cultural avant-garde. However, it was not until the early 1930s that they
became ever-more closely associated with PCF structures, whether in connection to its press, propaganda, militant education or culture.[5] Communist organisations linked to Soviet cultural diplomacy (such as the New Russia Circle)
or to the Communist Party (such as its journals and cultural associations),
also managed to mobilise a wider galaxy of intellectuals, with eminent figures
from the academic-scientific field now defining themselves as 'sympathisers' or
'fellow travellers'. The physicist Paul Langevin, the psychologists Jean-Maurice
Lahy and Henri Wallon, the biologist Marcel Prenant, and the linguist Marcel Cohen, were among the best-known such cases. After their Dreyfusard and
socialist commitments, in the 1930s these academics showed the same concern
about the rise of fascism. They were anxious to defend Reason and to rethink
Progress, as against those who proclaimed its 'failure' and 'crisis'. Soviet communism now appeared to them as a possible response to the decline of the
idea of progress in the West.

    Associated with the Communist cultural initiatives of the 1930s, these pro-
fessional intellectuals helped to legitimise the Communist Party as the guarantor of the philosophical rationalism born of the Enlightenment, of the political rationalism born of France's revolutionary traditions, and of a scholarly
rationalism confronted with an erudite (literary) anti-modernism. The writings
which they published in cultural journals and in the PCF press attested to the
doctrinal work that they pursued in order to inscribe communism and Marx-

---

4   Pudal 2004.
5   Pudal and Pennetier 2017.

ism in the political and intellectual traditions of French republicanism. As the Communist Party sought to anchor itself in the republican political field and to develop a 'Marxism à la française', these intellectuals were invited to rethink Marx's relationship with the great French thinkers (Descartes, Comte, Fourier, Proudhon, Diderot, and so on), no longer in the form of an irreducible opposition, but rather that of a line of descent. This was illustrated by the 'Socialisme et culture' series published by Éditions sociales internationales (one of the main French Communist publishing houses). The sociologist Georges Friedmann was tasked with directing this collection, in which various academic intellectuals were involved (for example, Armand Cuvillier, Valentin Feldman, Paul Labérenne, René Maublanc, Lucy Prenant, Edmond Vermeil, as well as Lucien Febvre, Alexandre Kojève and Paul Bénichou, although this latter's publication projects were not successful). The aim of this collection was to 'provide a survey of humanist forces'; to do this, it had to study the 'historical role' of this or that thinker, by situating them 'in the current of ideas which, through rationalist criticism, leads to the *Encyclopédie*, the critique of the Church and of religion among the Philosophes, up to the French Revolution', and 'to draw out the main lines of the movements of ideas which enabled the formation of socialist thought'.

Even so, the meeting between Marxism, communism and the rationalist tradition of the French academic-scientific field was not without tensions. It was only after hard-fought negotiations with the PCF leadership and the Communist International that the creation of *La Pensée*, subtitled *Revue du Rationalisme Moderne*, was achieved in 1939, giving institutional expression to this encounter. It was then up to philosopher Georges Politzer, a PCF member since 1930, to give doctrinal form to this 'modern rationalism', by presenting Marxism as the 'most modern form' of 'French thought' – characterised, according to Politzer, by the 'consequential, merciless struggle against superstition and prejudice', the 'faith in reason enlightened by science' and the 'use of science to advance the material and moral civilisation of humanity'.[6]

Such a (re)definition of Marxism was flexible enough to allow for a gathering of major sections of the academic-scientific field. However, the status of 'modern rationalism' always remained ambivalent and politically suspect, because of the implicit critical distance from the ecclesiastical mode of doctrinal production characteristic of the Stalinist-Communist world.[7] At the end of the 1930s, the Georges Friedmann affair exposed these contradictions: while Friedmann had been one of the academics most committed to the Popular-

---

6 Politzer 1938.
7 Pudal and Pennetier 2017.

Front-era Communist cultural enterprise (without, however, joining the PCF as a member), his politico-intellectual stance became untenable with the Stalin-isation of the party and the imposition of the Stalinist vulgate which denied professional intellectuals any historical role. In 1938, Gallimard's publication of his book *De la Sainte Russie à l'URSS* ('From Holy Rus to the USSR') in which he reaffirmed his sympathy for communism but also proposed a critical assessment of the Soviet situation, was violently denounced in the Communist world; and he was then unable to regain the 'place of friend, of fighter' that he still wished to occupy with the PCF. This affair provoked a real controversy between PCF leadership bodies and Communist or Communist-sympathiser French intellectuals, who were anxious to defend their autonomy. Several publications proposed to Éditions sociales internationales by 'fellow-traveller' intellectuals were thus unable to proceed. During this period of great tension, the relations that these PCF-adjacent intellectuals had established with their Soviet counterparts were also broken off; indeed, these latter were particularly targeted during the Stalinist repressions of the late 1930s, with their research agendas condemned as 'bourgeois science'.

2   A Marxist Way of Renewing Durkheimian Rationalism?

In the mid-1930s, during this moment of Communist openness also marked by tensions, a new reading of the relationship between Marx and Durkheim emerged. This was especially the work of 'sympathiser' intellectuals who had been trained in sociology in the Durkheimian world before World War I, at a time when Durkheimianism was the very embodiment of a social science in tune with the issues of the day (Marcel Cohen, Jean-Maurice Lahy, René Maublanc, André Varagnac), or in the postwar years, when the Durkheimian paradigm had become 'one of the symbols of all that was rejected as old-fashioned and corrupt'[8] and seemed to call for theoretical and methodological renewal (especially in the cases of Georges Friedmann, André-Georges Haudricourt, Henri Mougin, and Jacques Soustelle). All these intellectuals had, in the interwar period, joined the Communist movement (often, as communist symathisers or fellow-travellers) and started to make reference to Marx. Their political-intellectual stance thus placed them at odds with commonly accepted interpretations of the relationship between Marx and Durkheim. Both in the Communist world and in the French social sciences, where the

---

8   Heilbron 2015.

Durkheimian school had condemned historical materialism, there instead prevailed the thesis of a radical opposition between the two. Making Marxism and Durkheimism compatible was thus a way of justifying and giving a certain coherence to the path that had led them to communism and Marxism.

René Maublanc (1891–1960), a 'fellow traveller' of the Communist Party before joining its ranks in the Resistance, was one of the main architects of this doctrinal development. He defined himself as an heir to Durkheim and as a 'Marxist' philosopher in the mid-1930s and strove to undo the initial oppositions between Marxism and Durkheimianism. He instead underlined the convergences between these two conceptions of the social world: their affirmation of a non-mechanistic social determinism, the definition of society as a 'creative synthesis', rejection of introspection as a method of analysis, their 'materialist' stance and recognition of the role of ideas.[9] This Durkheimian-Marxist reading soon received academic endorsement thanks to Armand Cuvillier (1887–1973), who during these same Popular Front years grew closer to Communist-leaning intellectual circles and shared their interest in a sociological reading of Marxism. In his 1936 textbook *Introduction à la sociologie*, Cuvillier hailed the 'lasting glory of Marx's genius' and his 'role as a precursor'; he contributed to legitimising 'Marxist sociology' at the scholarly level, as a 'knowledge of synthesis', affirming 'sociological determinism' 'without falling into a theoretically and practically unacceptable fatalism'.

This new interpretation of the relations between Marxism and Durkheimianism had a real echo in the French humanities in the second half of the 1930s, giving rise to an innovative research programme centred on the study of technology and work. Its guiding hypothesis was that the fundamental social bond was not, as Durkheim thought, social morphology (the volume and density of populations), but work and technologies – meaning, the ensemble of the activities of production and of the transformation of nature. Such a postulate made it possible to define a unitary social science, the aim of which was to question the links between scientific and technical development and social evolution, and thus to propose a response to the 'crisis of progress', to use the title of a work by Georges Friedmann (1936). This politico-intellectual ambition undergirded much of the research carried out during the 1930s by Communist or Communist-leaning intellectuals: in sociology first of all, with the research of Friedmann[10] or Feldman and Mougin, but also in ethnology (Soustelle), in the study of folklore (Haudricourt, Parain, Varagnac), in psychology (Lahy, Wallon), and in the history of science (Langevin, Mineur), and so on.

---

9   Maublanc 2011.
10   Vatin 2004.

From the mid-1930s onwards, a Marxist research collective thus took form, sharing – beyond common political struggles – the same 'style of thought'. This first generation of Marxist intellectuals was inserted within the academic networks of the time and was able to establish an open dialogue with the most innovative poles of the social sciences, the Annales historian group first among them. Despite their initial reticence about the ecclesiastical relationship that these militant intellectuals might have had with Marxism, Marc Bloch and especially Lucien Febvre gave them their support. Several of them contributed regularly to the *Annales* review, Friedmann, Soustelle and Varagnac even joining its editorial board at the end of the 1930s, while Bloch and Febvre agreed to collaborate on the review *Europe*, linked to Communist cultural efforts.

From the mid-1930s, in the book reviews that Lucien Febvre wrote for the Annales, he repeatedly emphasised the communion of ideas that, he claimed, united the Annales' 'total history' programme and the Marxism developed by Communist-sympathising intellectuals around one same project – that of a social science which went beyond disciplinary divisions and focused on social groups, their living and working conditions and their 'mental equipment'. In March 1936, for example, Lucien Febvre agreed to take part in a public conference organised by Communist or sympathisers intellectuals (notably by his friend Henri Wallon and Georges Friedmann), upon the publication of their first collective volume entitled *À la lumière du marxisme*. Published in 1936 (by Editions sociales internationales), this was the fruit of their reflections on the history of science and technology and Marxism. He reported on it to Marc Bloch: 'Your ears must have been ringing on Saturday night. I was chairing for the second time a public meeting devoted to the discussion of *À la lumière du marxisme*. ... I gailed this "living Marxism" which comes to us from Russia, taking us away from the "fossil Marxism" of the old Guesdists, those unreal living catechists. My feeling is clear. In ten years' time, everything that counts in history will be "Marxist", a very flexible, very broad Marxism, perhaps a heretical one (I don't know! and I don't care to find out!), in any case, a very comprehensive one, against which neither you nor I can raise any fundamental objections. It was quite moving to see'.[11] Seeing as in the interwar years networks in the humanities and in social sciences were being restructured around history, such support from the Annales group had a strong legitimising effect. This 'open Marxism', oriented toward a renovation of Durkheimian social science, became a pole of attraction in relation to which all others now positioned themselves.

No doubt the politicisation of intellectual circles favoured such convergences. Such was the case of Georges Canguilhem who, after having gradually

---

11   Bloch and Febvre 2004.

distanced himself from intransigent pacifism, drew closer to fellow-traveller intellectual circles in the anti-fascist struggle. He hailed the efforts to reread Marx that they undertook in 1935 by launching a 'Chronique marxiste' in Alain's review, the *Feuilles libres de la quinzaine*. A similar shift can be observed in the itinerary of Alexandre Kojève. This Moscow-born philosopher established himself as one of the main introducers of Hegel's thought in France. His militancy led him, in the mid-1930s, to adopt a Marxist perspective, in particular in the (unfinished) project for a book on Pierre Bayle and Fontenelle that he proposed to Éditions sociales internationales (in the collection 'Socialisme et culture'). Another sign of this success was the reflection developed by left-wing Christian intellectuals (for instance Paul Vignaux) in the Catholic cultural reviews that flourished in those years. Such intellectuals were driven adopt a position on Marxism on account of the Communist Party's own so-called 'policy of reaching out' to Catholics. Finally, the first-generation Durkheimians themselves had to revise their positions regarding Marxism. Perhaps the most significant change was that of Célestin Bouglé, who had adopted a resolutely critical position towards Marxism and Bolshevik Russia in the 1920s and 1930s. However, in 1938, in the newspaper *Marianne*, he published a review of Georges Friedmann's recent book, *De la Sainte Russie à l'URSS*, under the title 'Variations sur le marxisme', in which he observed: 'In the end, we find ourselves faced with a Marxism, not watered down, but enriched and flexibilised, ready to tolerate, to welcome, to seek out shades of explanation which would have made a Lafargue shudder with horror in our student days. The most curious thing is that Russia itself, the Russia of the Soviets, is collaborating in this enrichment, in this intellectual flexibilisation.'

3   The Self-Evidence and Marginalisation of a Tradition of Thinking

Marxism was now part of the intellectual horizon of the French social sciences, which had been built since the end of the nineteenth century on the basis of the Durkheimian reference point. However, after World War II it did not regain either the same impetus or its initial coherence: the intellectuals who had rallied to this new social science in the 1930s thus continued their research in a dispersed manner. It is true that the strengthening of disciplinary logics may have weakened this programme, which had instead sought to unify the various human and social sciences. Nevertheless, this splintering mainly owed to political tensions: whereas the political issues underlying social-sciences debates had, during the anti-fascist struggle, been able to encourage dynamics of rapprochement between intellectuals from different backgrounds, during the Cold

War they contributed greatly to their dispersion, especially since the zeitgeist had changed. For with the 'Trente Glorieuses', a technological optimism had d the anti-modern mood which had so preoccupied republican academic-scientific circles in the 1930s.

'Marxist social science' was henceforth doubly marginalised. On the one hand, in the Communist world Stalinisation, in denying all autonomy to cultural production, from the end of the 1930s led to a series of sharp tensions between professional intellectuals and Communist leadership bodies. The journal La Pensée experienced difficult times with the establishment of cultural Zhdanovism: many scientists who had come to Communism on rationalist and anti-fascist grounds now pulled back. Within the French social sciences, on the other hand, even though the double reference to Marx and Durkheim was now self-evident, Marxist Communist intellectuals became increasingly isolated. The ideological and political campaigns orchestrated by the Communist Party led to the de-legitimisation of their position, especially among academics (for instance Febvre and Canguilhem) who had in the Popular Front years shown a keen interest in their re-readings of Marxism.

In such a conjuncture, even the Communist intellectuals who stood for a more open Marxism found themselves forced into strategies of evasiveness or smuggling the message across. This was evident in the political and intellectual trajectory followed by Ignace Meyerson and Jean-Pierre Vernant after World War II. They developed a Marxist programme of 'historical psychology', whose ambition was to study 'psychological functions' (the person, work, action, memory, space, and time, for example) through the great works of humanity (languages, social institutions, religions, techniques, sciences, arts, and so on). With its totalising and interdisciplinary ambition, its interest in techniques and labour and the questions it raised over Progress, this research programme followed the Durkheimian-Marxist perspective that had emerged in the 1930s. Meyerson and Vernant belonged to the intellectual generations that came to communism through the anti-fascist struggles of the 1930s and the Resistance and to Marxism through Durkheimianism. Both of them intended to use their research to offer a different perspective on the social and political concerns of the time, but they also tried to guard against any party interference in intellectual affairs. Jean-Pierre Vernant later explained how his research on ancient Greece had been a way of avoiding any confrontation with PCF leadership bodies on immediate political issues and of preserving his intellectual autonomy. However, in the Cold War-era Communist Party, their efforts to seek recognition of the political legitimacy and usefulness of their research programme recognised were in vain: for example, Georges Cogniot, who played the role of political director at La Pensée, criticised them for not taking into account the 'class struggle in the development and in the transformations of psychological functions' and, still more so, for not addressing the 'problem of differentiation according to the classes in struggle'.[12] Similarly, within the French social sciences, the interest aroused by this research programme was initially limited to a restricted circle of intellectuals, most of whom were Communists, before it was given a wider echo in the 1960s, thanks in particular to the work of Jean-Pierre Vernant on Greek reason, myth and religion. In 1958, he was appointed director of studies at the sixth section of the EPHE (which later became the EHESS), and there he brought together intellectuals similarly committed to the Left (Maxime Rodinson, Maurice Godelier, André-Georges Haudricourt, Pierre Vidal-Naquet and others) for a common reflection on Marxism. In 1964 he created the Centre des recherches comparées sur les sociétés anciennes (Centre for Comparative Research on Ancient Societies). Jean-Pierre Vernant thus paid tribute to this Durkheimian intellectual who, alongside Ignace Meyerson, had been his 'master' and also signified the Durkheimian line of descent that he, in turn, intended to pursue as a Marxist.

As we can see, the Marxist reflection in the social sciences of the 1930s, committed to a renewed conception of Enlightenment and Progress, continued to nourish the thinking of left-wing intellectuals confined to marginal positions during the Cold War years. It was not until the 1960s, with the symbolic crisis of Communism prompted by the Twentieth Congress of the Communist Party of the Soviet Union, that this Marxist rationalism acquired new topicality. The number of Marxist renewal projects multiplied; starting from a critique of Stalinism, they sought to position themselves within the social science debates of the time, dominated by the question of structuralism.

For instance, such an approach undergirded the work of Jean-Pierre Vernant in the 1950s and 1960s. In his first work, published in 1962, *The Origins of Greek Thought*, he proposed a comprehensive study of the intellectual and political revolution that had led to the evolution from Mycenaean royalty to the democratic and egalitarian polis, 'the decline of myth and the advent of rational knowledge'. He concluded with this now famous formula: 'In its limitations as in its innovations, [Greek reason] is a creature of the city'. This analysis was not without political intentions, as he later made clear: by bringing to light the political conditions for the emergence of rational thought, he intended to reaffirm, within the Communist world, that the confrontation of ideas is constitutive of rational thought, and thus show the need to open up the debate in order to break communism out of a mythical way of thinking.

---

12   Letter from Cogniot to Meyerson, 20 March 1952.

This rationalist critique of Stalinism was pursued collectively in the Communist Party. The Union rationaliste, for example, founded in 1930 by the big names of French republican science, had passed into the Communist sphere of influence and, during the Cold War, constituted a haven for Communist scientists who thus managed, albeit with difficulty, to maintain a dialogue with other 'rationalist' fractions of the academic-scientific field. In the period of renewal of Marxism that accompanied de-Stalinisation, the Union rationaliste became a site of exchange on the relations between Marxism, social sciences and the history of science. This is well-illustrated by the journal *Raison présente*, launched in 1966 by Communist intellectuals critical of their party's leadership (Émile Bottigelli, Maurice Caveing, Yves Galifret, Maurice Godelier, Ernest Kahane, Victor Leduc, Jacqueline Marchand, Jean-Pierre Vernant ...).[13] Their aim was to redefine Marxist rationalism by distinguishing themselves in two ways: in relation to the 'alienated' stance of the party philosopher embodied by Roger Garaudy, as they demanded autonomy for intellectuals within the party; and also in relation to Althusserian structuralism, as they reaffirmed the humanist scope of Marxism and the social sciences – in Jean-Pierre Vernant's words, its ambition was to understand how 'man is determined and determining', how 'man is made at the same time as he is made'.

4   Marxist Rationalism in History

With the various attempts to renew Marxism, the dialogue with the social sciences and the history of science and technology was resumed in the 1960s. But it was now part of a reflection on the errors that rationalist thought had seen in the twentieth century, first and foremost in the Stalinist Communist world, which had once appeared as the camp of science and reason in the face of the excesses of capitalist machinism and fascism. Built up since the 1930s as a refuge for rationalist thought, academic Marxism did not constitute a homogeneous research programme with well-defined contours. But it did embody one of the possible responses to the political and intellectual attacks on the idea of Progress. This Marxist rationalism was, however, permanently affected by the negotiations and tensions, both covert and explicit, underlying the relationship between intellectuals and Communist leadership bodies. It was able to stimulate major innovations in the French social sciences inherited from Durkheimiansm and to reformulate their articulation with a project of social

---

13   Laurens 2019.

and political emancipation, without escaping twentieth-century illusions on the 'sense of history' and the 'powers of reason'. In one of his last writings, Georges Canguilhem questioned 'the conditions in which the idea of Progress had lost its prestige and its role'. He thus pointed out the impasses into which Marxist thought had run; by maintaining the idea of Progress in 'its cultural function of millenarian anticipation', it had been caught up in the contradictions of this century. And here, he concluded by quoting Freud, 'we find with astonishment that progress has sealed a pact with barbarism'.[14]

14   Canguilhem 1998.

CHAPTER 13

Marx's Peculiar Fate in French Economic Scholarship

Thierry Pouch

A large majority of – mainstream – French economists did not celebrate the bicentenary of Karl Marx's birth in 2018. To do so would be to abandon their stigmatisation of a thinker whose work is, in their eyes, unscientific, and who, moreover, has been defeated by history, as the collapse of the Soviet bloc seems to demonstrate. For heterodox economists, on the other hand, the 'spectral emergence' (as Derrida put it) of Marx upon this anniversary provides an opportunity to recall that Marx was and remains a fundamental source of inspiration for understanding the workings of capitalism, and for criticising both its mode of operation and its social consequences. For these heterodox economists, Marx untangled the logic and dynamics of capitalism, exposing its contradictions while outlining revolutionary perspectives. The great capitalist crisis that began in 2007 with the bursting of the real estate bubble in the United States did not allow Marx to be restored to the economics curricula of France's universities, and still less so to scholarly journals dealing with economics. In the field of economics, Marx remains marginal. But, as we shall see, this was not always the case. Marxism had managed to establish itself in the universities from the 1950s onwards, and to gain an audience there, before leaving them again some thirty years later.

1 The Social Conditions for Marxism's Place in the Economic Field

1.1 Law Schools in the 1950s: A Hostile Setting Becomes More Open to Marx

At the end of the 1940s, there was nothing to predispose the scholarly field of economics to open up to Marx and Marxism. The borders of the university were not easily penetrated by a thinker as inflammatory and subversive as Marx. And law schools, where economics was taught, had a reputation for being particularly conservative. Connoisseurs and disseminators of Marx's thought, such as Jean Duret, were thus located outside of the university field in this era.

A turning point came in the 1950s: several professors at the Paris law faculty brought Marxism into their courses and publications. Jean Lhomme, Jean Marchal and André Piettre were among the academics most receptive to the Marxist message. They deemed it impossible to teach economics without making a detour via Marx's economic work. Students could not approach the economic and social problems of their time without knowing everything about this author.[1] Motivations both internal and external to the university explain this intellectual stance. For these economists, this was a question of counterbalancing the rise of neoclassical theory, which accompanied the decline of the US institutionalist school. They thought it necessary to learn the lessons of the disaster caused by the 1930 crisis – and the pretence of the neoclassical school to dominate the field of economic science by producing a pure economics without institutions or history had to be fought. The recourse to Marx provided a weapon in this fight. The creation in 1950 of the *Revue économique* – which was meant to be called the *Revue économique et sociale* – by these economics professors was a strong sign of the ambition to make economics a discipline open to other fields, such as sociology and history.[2] This school of thought, called 'sociological realist', became dominant in scholarly production. It established its pre-eminent position in the universities, and especially in the Paris law faculty.

The roots of such a position in the field of economic scholarship can be found in social Catholicism, of which these professors mostly saw themselves as custodians. This is why they tended to emphasise a humanist rather than a revolutionary Marx. But there was a more directly biographical reason for these economists' adherence to Marxism. Indeed, in this we should see a way for them to erase their direct or indirect involvement in the corporatist ideology of the collaboration years. All the economists mentioned published texts during the 1940s on the virtues of corporatism and stressing the importance of artisans and the peasantry in the renewal of France. This was also the case of a professor at first glance little suspect of having compromised himself, since his work would several years later constitute one of the main vehicles for the establishment of Marxism in French economics departments. Namely, Henri Denis. The publication in 1941 of his book La Corporation in the 'Que sais-je?' series provides a good illustration of the ideological commitments and reversals of this cohort of economics professors. In another work, *Introduction aux problèmes économiques*, published in 1942 in the 'Bibliothèque du peuple' collection

---

1 Marchal 1955.
2 Steiner 2000.

published by Presses universitaires de France (PUF), Denis put forward the idea that 'the advent of socialism would consecrate the ruin of all human civilisation'.

The only exception to this picture was Henri Bartoli's position. This son of a Resistance fighter, a Catholic intellectual, close to the personalist current headed by Emmanuel Mounier, professor of economics at the Grenoble faculty, then in Paris, tried, unlike his colleagues, to reconcile humanism and communism, without in any way converting to Marxian thought. In several works that contributed to the dissemination of Marx's thought on economic matters, Bartoli indicates that it 'restored the dignity of man', by refusing to make him a commodity.[3]

Marxist economics' arrival in the universities was greeted with a measure of wry irony by the French Communist Party (PCF). But the creation in 1954 of the Marxist journal *Économie et Politique* at the party's initiative allowed the constitution of a platform where debates could be held between humanist economists and those who identified with Marx as the bearer of the communist idea. Henri Denis, freshly interested in Marx, played a decisive role in Économie et Politique: a figure of French Marxism, an associate professor at the law faculty in Rennes, he was the journal's editor-in-chief. In several of his articles, as well as in his book *La Valeur*, published by Éditions sociales in 1950, Denis criticised the interpretation of Marx's economic work by his colleagues in Paris, but also by the Jesuit Pierre-Yves Calvez. A true 'Marxist science' had to be opposed to 'Catholic science', and the revolutionary project must be substituted for the project of liberating man through God.[4] A whole space of ideological confrontation emerged in this era, allowing Marxists to contradict the vision of economists whose allegiance was to Catholicism.

1.2 *Making Marxism a Science, or the Apogee of Marxism in the Universities*

In the 1960s, three poles took form that would spread discussion of Marxism even more widely through France's economics departments. The first of these was built on the current of ideas known as State Monopoly Capitalism (SMC). This intellectual construct, which emanated from economists in PCF ranks, had arisen at the International Conference at Choisy-le-Roi (26 to 29 May 1966). It was to constitute a fundamentally important anchoring point for many heterodox economists who claimed to be more or less Marxian and who set

---

3   Bartoli 1950; Pouch 2001.
4   Denis 1950, 1957.

themselves the perspective of the transition to socialism. Gravitating around Paul Boccara, a lecturer-researcher at the University of Amiens, this current of thought pointed to the new form that capitalism had taken as it reached the third stage of its development (after the primitive-manufacturing and classical-competitive stages): namely, the imperialist-monopolist stage, taking the form of the SMC, which must necessarily lead to socialism, seeing as the concentration and over-accumulation of capital called for the nationalisation of monopolies.[5]

A second pole, more academic than the previous one, emerged more or less simultaneously, namely development economics. This pole took form in the context of decolonisation and the French economists who instigated it argued that the way out of underdevelopment was through socialism. These economists' ambition was to counterbalance the model of Rostow, whose famous work, *The Stages of Economic Growth*, translated into French in 1963, was subtitled 'A Non-Communist Manifesto'. But these debates quickly radicalised with the creation, in 1960, of the journal *Tiers-Monde*. There were two figures leading the chorus: Gérard Destanne de Bernis, professor at the University of Grenoble, and Charles Bettelheim, director of studies at the sixth section of the École pratique des hautes études (EPHE). Destanne de Bernis produced analyses on socialism, accompanied by recommendations to the Algerian government; he also published – notably in *Tiers-Monde*, but also in François Perroux's journal, *Économie appliquée* – numerous articles devoted to the theory of 'industrialising industries' and 'import substitution'. Bettelheim, who joined the Jeunesses Communistes at age twenty and was director of the 'Économie et Socialisme' collection published by Maspero, intended to show that underdevelopment was not a form of backwardness to be made up for according to a capitalist logic, but should instead be combated by means of socialist planning. He strove to elaborate a genuine political economy of socialism.[6] Bettelheim would leave a real mark on the younger generation of economists; Gérard Duménil, who followed Bettelheim's seminars at the EPHE, provides one illustration of this. A few years later, he and Dominique Lévy formed a pair of economists whose analyses of capitalism and understanding of the genesis and stakes of neoliberalism have, to this day, greatly contributed to keeping Marx's thought alive.[7]

The fact remains that the implantation of Marx and Marxism in France universities owed, last but not least, to the teaching of Henri Denis, who taught

---

5   Various authors 1971.
6   Bettelheim 1964; De Bernis 1966; Denord and Zunigo 2005.
7   Duménil and Lévy 2014.

the History of Economic Thought course at the Paris law faculty. It is worth noting the decisive impact that this economics professor, transferred from Rennes
to Paris, had on a whole generation of students. The publication of his textbook *Histoire de la pensée économique* in 1966, alongside the great academic
textbooks (in PUF's 'Thémis' collection) was a crucial moment for Marxism's
penetration into the universities. More than a third of the book is devoted to
Marx and Marxism, with Denis also making digs at all of the other currents
of economic thought (the neoclassicists, of course, but also – more surprising
from today's perspective – the Keynesians and the institutionalists); a sharply
critical stance that would be toned down in subsequent editions.

The second half of the 1960s thus confirmed the vitality of Marx and Marxism in an academic field – economics – which had previously kept them at a
distance. A generation of talented economists with a fine knowledge of economic theory and all the attributes of academic capital (theses d'État,[8] articles
in what are now called 'peer-reviewed' journals, books and, for some of them,
a higher education *agrégation* in economics) would then, in the 1970s, pro-
pel Marx and Marxism to the forefront of the academic scene. Two currents
each made a no less decisive contribution. The first was the group of economists who published in the *Cahiers d'économie politique*, a journal founded in
1974, and whose work was published in the collection 'Interventions en économie politique' by Presses universitaires de Grenoble. Carlo Benetti, Suzanne
de Brunhoff and Jean Cartelier were among their leading figures. This entire
undertaking was geared towards the study of the logical structure of political
economy and producing a critique. This meant summoning Marx, no longer
to make him a support for any kind of political conquest, but rather to confront his economic work *qua* scientific discourse (essentially Volume I of *Capital*, in their view the only accomplished theoretical work), with classical and
neoclassical political economy, whose supposedly natural categories they challenged.[9]

The second group formed around another journal, *Critiques de l'économie
politique*, published by Maspero. Pierre Salama, a university professor, was one
of the key figures. His articles and books were also oriented to contributing
to a fierce but scholarly critique of political economy. However, he was dif-
ferentiated from his 'comrades' in the *Cahiers d'économie politique* by both
their interpretation of Marx and their positioning in the field of political activism. The economists grouped around *Critiques de l'économie politique* did not

---

8   An advanced thesis, following the doctorate and habilitation.
9   Benetti 1976.

want to limit themselves to *Volume* I of Capital, that is, to the critique of polit-ical economy alone. While this dimension remained central, to their eyes it had to be completed through the elaboration of a political economy of social-ism. That was why they attached so much importance to readings of *Capital* Volume III, and in particular to the problem of the transformation of values into production prices. These economists, for the most part members or sym-pathisers of the Ligue communiste révolutionnaire (LCR), were concerned not to dissociate theoretical analysis from political action, and they set both their reflection and their militant activity within the framework of the Fourth Inter-national. Jean-Luc Dallemagne and Jacques Valier should also be mentioned, here, two economists who contributed to the formation and dissemination of this review.

1.3   *The Diversity of Marxisms*

On the periphery of the university, among the economist-engineers, two other currents of critical thought based on Marx and Marxist authors developed. At INRA, economists launched a debate on the status of agriculture in con-temporary capitalism, updating the debate initiated by Marx in *Capital* and continued in 1900 by Kautsky (with his *The Agrarian Question*), Rosa Luxem-burg and Lenin. These authors sought to verify whether small-scale market production (in this case, on the small family farm) would be absorbed, as Marx and Kautsky had predicted, by and into the capitalist mode of production, or whether the very evolution of capitalism would lead to the maintenance of these forms of production.[10] During the same period, the French regulation school was established, with Michel Aglietta, Robert Boyer and Alain Lipietz among its leading figures. These economists were distinguished by their train-ing (at the École Polytechnique) and by their institutional affiliation with the economic administration (INSEE, Direction de la prévision, CEPREMAP, and so on), where they each had varying degrees of involvement in France's version of economic planning and in the construction of macro-econometric models. They drew their vision of capitalism and their methodological tools from the work of the 'sociological- realist' school mentioned above, and produced an analysis of the regimes of accumulation and modes of regulation (state/eco-nomy relations, monetary regime, wage relations, forms of competition, forms of insertion in the international division of labour) that have punctuated the history of capitalism. For regulationists, a 'big capitalist crisis' reflects the sys-tem's inability to maintain the pace of capital accumulation and the previ-

---

10   Cavailhès 1979.

ous mode of regulation.[11] Present in academic journals because of their symbolic capital (mathematics, statistics, economic theory, and so on), the regulationists enjoyed a considerable academic audience and international visibility.

Journals, books, theses, seminars, courses and textbooks: the Marxist reference was an obligatory crossing point for young economists and for enthusiastic cohorts of students in the 1960s and 1970s, who were also involved in the maze of political activism and the anti-imperialist struggle. The Left's arrival in power in May 1981, after nearly a quarter of a century of opposition, doubtless sounded like a culmination, the political reward for the intellectual energies that had been deployed.

2   The Ebb of Marx and Marxism: Irreversible or Temporary?

The visibility of Marxism in economics at the turn of the 1970s and 1980s appears deceptive. For at the very moment when this current of thought appeared triumphant, conservative forces were setting in motion. The entire 1980s ideological cycle was structured around the issue of human rights, the critique of the state and utopianism, and the celebration of the liberalised economy and the globalised market. In this ideological context, the visibility of Marxism in the field of economics was eroded. It coincided with the affirmation of what was quickly called 'neoliberalism'. The emblematic figure of this 'conservative revolution' was Friedrich von Hayek, winner of the 1974 Bank of Sweden Prize for Economic Science (wrongly called the Nobel Prize for Economics). A fierce battle was waged against any form of state interventionism in the mechanisms of the economy and, by consequence, against the previously triumphant Keynesianism. Marx did not escape this struggle to impose liberal ideas and practices, in economics as in politics.

2.1   Economics Declines from within

In this new conjuncture, economists who had in the past worked on and disseminated Marx's economic ideas, and even associated them with their own political perspectives, now came to discredit Marxism from within. Two fundamental works made a decisive and, could it be said, irreversible contribution to the process of the decline in critical Marxist thought. First of all, Henri Denis, who, in L'Économie de Marx. Histoire d'un échec ['Marx's Economics. History of

---

11   Aglietta 1976.

a Failure'], published in 1980, continued his dissection of Marx's economic writings, and revealed the contradictions and limits of the German philosopher's work. According to Denis, these were rooted in Marx's hesitations with regard to the Hegelian dialectic, leading him ultimately to opt for Ricardo's labour theory of value. This reading, which amounts to categorising Marx among the classical economists, at the same time disqualified his critical charge.[12]

This effort to make Marx into the direct heir of the classical economists, and to eliminate value and surplus-value, proceeded in a second book: Carlo Benetti and Jean Cartelier's *Marchands, salariat et capitalistes*, published in 1981 by Presses universitaires de Grenoble, in the collection 'Interventions critiques en économie politique' (which came to an end two years later). Benetti and Cartelier saw in Marx's economics a transposition of the classical economists' categories which, moreover, he never ceased to critique. A few years later, Cartelier, in an article on regulation theory co-authored with Michel de Vroey, indicated that it was necessary to abandon the emphasis on the ideological critique of neoclassical theory and that it was necessary to rub along with this latter.[13] The regulation school followed a largely similar trajectory. In their *La Violence de la monnaie*, published in 1982, Michel Aglietta and André Orléan sought to get past the theory of value. The limits of value led them to construct a theory of money based not on social relations of production, but on an approach to violence which these two authors had found in the work of the anthropologist René Girard.[14]

These about-turns were also part of a vast process of professionalisation of the field of economics, with 'the desire to do science' having ever more of a role in structuring economists' research.[15] This field effect translated into the formation of a common knowledge and language among economists worldwide; this gave them ever-more control over the political justification of economic choices, and the opportunity no longer to be confined to the university, instead penetrating the market of expertise. This left no, or only very marginal, room for Marx's message.[16] From this further ensued procedures for recruiting teaching staff and criteria for publication which hindered the visibility of Marx and his vision of the economic world. These procedures were in turn challenged by heterodox currents, which called for more pluralism in the field of economics.

---

12   Denis 1980.
13   Benetti and Cartelier 1981 and Cartelier and de Vroey, 1989.
14   Aglietta and Orléan 1982; Orléan 2011.
15   Arena 2000.
16   Lordon 1997; Fourcade 2009; Heredia 2014.

3   The End of a History?

This brief overview of the relationship between French economists and Marx, from the 1950s to the present, has shown that the presence of the author of *Capital* in higher education institutions where economics courses are taught was only a relatively short episode. The Marxist chapter in economics seems to have closed starting in the late 1970s, under the effect of exogenous political and social phenomena as well as under the influence of academic actors themselves.

What can be expected of Marx's presence in this field, in future? The very dynamics of capitalism, its human impacts and the impasse in which mainstream economic thought finds itself, encourage heterodox thinkers to persist in their struggle to ensure the visibility of this extraordinary thinker. But it must be admitted that Marx is unlikely to regain a strong position in the teaching of economics, in a context where far from all heterodox (minority) economists claim to be Marxians.

CHAPTER 14

Sociology and Marxism

Gérard Mauger

The analysis of the relationship between Marxism and sociology comes up against a whole set of obstacles. Firstly, because in the different stages of their history, Marxism and sociology have appeared as configurations of producers competing for intellectual authority (a 'field'). That is, no matter which period of their history we look at, there is not one Marxism or one sociology, but Marxisms and sociologies. Secondly, because by limiting our inquiries to France's own borders, we neglect the effects of the international intercourse of ideas (be it, for example, the reception in France of the work of Max Weber, or of Soviet 'Marxism-Leninism'). Moreover, we cannot ignore all that the relationship between Marxism and sociology owes to the relations they entertain with the political field, and to the 'effects of theory' that they exert there (hence the mobilisation of political arguments from various directions, for the purposes of scientific disqualification). Finally, because the study of this relationship, even apart from presupposing the existence of 'tangled' readings, must above all take into account what ideas owe to the social and intellectual conditions of their production.

Without ignoring these difficulties, here we will sketch out an analysis of the relationship between sociology and Marxism, which is probably closer to a classical history of ideas than to a social history of the social sciences, and an initial periodisation (obviously a debatable one) which successively addresses the relationship to Marxism of the 'Durkheimians', of postwar French sociology, of the French sociology of the 1970s and 1980s, and finally that of Pierre Bourdieu. We will see that, unlike not only philosophy, but also history, economics or anthropology, the existence of a Marxist sociology in France was, all in all, ephemeral and limited to a few choice subjects, even if Marxism has never ceased to be a reference point for French sociology, whether seeking to borrow from it or to distance itself from it.

1 The Durkheimians, 'University Socialism' and Marxism

Developers of a major epistemological innovation, the Durkheimians constituted, through their recruitment, a component of the dominant fraction of the academic establishment. Their leader's foundation of a new discipline, claiming to be the successor of philosophy, was based on a strategy of both scientific and institutional legitimisation which rigorously excluded from their work, as from L'Année sociologique, any reference to current socio-political events. But the Durkheimians were also, for the most part, activists of the Dreyfusist generation and, as such, 'committed' intellectuals. And although Émile Durkheim himself was often perceived – not without some reason – as a 'conservative' sociologist, Marcel Mauss, François Simiand, Célestin Bouglé, Maurice Halbwachs and Robert Hertz were active contributors to the Socialist L'Humanité and the Revue socialiste.

Sticking to Durkheim specifically, an epistemological convergence with Marxism emerges on the terrain of the 'rationalist mindset', on the claimed political utility of social science, on the very possibility of a social science, and on the criticism of 'subjective explanations' of social facts. 'We regard as fruitful,' wrote Durkheim, 'this idea that social life must be explained, not by the conception of those who participate in it, but by profound causes that escape consciousness'.[1] But Durkheim refused to see Capital as an entirely scientific work, and rejected the idea that 'the causes of social phenomena ... are ultimately reducible to the state of industrial technique and that the economic factor is the mainspring of progress'. He insisted that, given the state of available knowledge, religion was 'the most primitive of social facts' and that 'the economy depended on religion much more than the latter on the former', even if he did grant the economic factor 'an effectiveness of its own'. However, without seeing in Durkheimian sociology an instrument for the repression of Marxism,[2] some of Durkheim's criticisms seem to be more 'political' than strictly scientific (although it is sometimes difficult to distinguish between the two). Apart from the fact that he was undoubtedly closer to Freud's pessimism than to Marxist messianism,[3] Durkheim, 'inhabited by the spirit of national unity',[4] refused to grant a decisive role to the 'baleful conflict among classes' and to see violence as a necessary means for the transformation of society. According to Mauss, Durkheim 'was reluctant to adhere to socialism proper only because of certain features of its activity: its violent character, its class character, more or less open workerism, and also its political and even politicking character. Durkheim was deeply opposed to any war of classes or nations'.[5]

---

1 Durkheim 1970.
2 Lindenberg 1979.
3 Filloux 1970.
4 Lacroix 1976.
5 Mauss 2011.

This table of convergences and divergences between Marxism and Durkheimian sociology can be complemented by the one established by Célestin
Bouglé, who in 1908 published one of the few even somewhat developed analyses of Marxism by a Durkheimian. Among the convergences, he agrees that
the materialism of Marx and Engels does not deny that social life presupposes a
psychic life: 'men make their own history', even if, for Marx as for most sociologists, 'the reasons that man gives himself to explain his conduct rarely express
the true causes of institutions'. As for the disagreements with Marxism, they
have to do with the 'materialist explanation' of ideology, of which 'technological automatism' constitutes 'the kernel'.[6] According to Bouglé, it is necessary
to 'broaden' or 'rectify' the Marxist conceptions in this matter: 'the social phenomenon [is not] a sort of double of the material phenomenon', 'inventions
alone cannot create institutions' and 'social forms do not derive from material
forms'. Furthermore, he criticises 'the traces of teleology' in Marx and Engels. It
is instead necessary, he explains, 'to show how a class comes into existence not
only in itself, but for itself; in other words, how the individuals who compose it
become aware of their unity, and pose their collective self'. In this perspective, it
is necessary not only to critique Marxist 'economism' by avoiding 'lending class
consciousness too clear a vision of class interest', but also to recall 'the necessity of "ideological cross-dressing"'. Well-rooted illusions, beliefs and doctrines
have a power of their own: this is, moreover, the case of 'the force of propaganda' exercised by 'Marxist formulas themselves'. Distinct from the Marxist
perspective, the study of 'ideology' or 'collective representations' from a sociological perspective does not approach them as 'epiphenomena', but as *sui
generis* syntheses': 'prisms, not just reflections'.

2   Postwar Sociologists and Marxism: 'Theories without Facts' and
       'Facts without Theory'

If Durkheim remained an 'obligatory reference' in French sociology, there were
other factors limiting its importance. The weakness of academic sociology, 'the
almost exclusive preserve of philosophers',[7] the internal divisions within the
Durkheimian group, a 'primary' anti-Durkheimianism holding that 'social facts
are not things', the emergence of a new 'social demand' linked to the crisis
of economic liberalism and the spread of different forms of 'plannerism'; all
led to the gradual abandonment of Durkheimian sociology, which Paul Nizan

---

6   Bouglé 1908.
7   Karady 1976.

described as 'a "doctrine of obedience" and social conformism for the use of schoolteachers'.[8] As Durkheimianism declined, the '1930s generation' asserted itself; it was politically committed, 'allergic' to Durkheim's sociology, and imported works discovered in Germany or the United States.

After the war, French sociology was a marginal activity, both in the intellectual field and in the world of applied research (in institutes like INSEE, INED, and such like). Marked by the Resistance, the postwar generation of sociologists was distributed between 'the opposing poles of "commitment" and "expertise"'.[9] The researchers of the Centre d'études sociologiques (CES) founded by Georges Gurvitch on his return from the United States can be characterised both by their commitment (five out of twelve were members of the PCF, while the others were linked to far left-wing groups or to th eleft-wing Catholics), their 'fascination for Marxism' and their 'interest in the working class': 'for some, there wasn't much difference between research and militant activity', Johan Heilbron explains. Thus the thesis on the *Problèmes du machinisme industriel* by Georges Friedmann, who succeeded Gurvitch as CES's director, was unique in that it drew inspiration from both Marxism and US sociology in focusing on the working class.

On top of the opposition between commitment and expertise there was also one between 'theoretical' work (reserved for professors) and 'empirical research', in between 'academic sociology' and research. On the research side of things, the paradigm of 'survey research' established itself, it was defined by the valorisation of fieldwork, the standardisation of research procedures, the promotion of quantitative techniques and the rejection of theory, whether of Durkheimian or Marxist tradition. Insofar as no one contested the need for investigation per se, the political positions taken by sociologists, their commitment, and their 'Marxism' were reflected in the choice of subject (the working classes), their approach ('going to see on the ground'), and the assertion of the usefulness of the surveys carried out, albeit without escaping, according to Alain Touraine, a rudimentary empiricism.[10]

On the 'theory' side, the academic field of the time was subject to 'the party's' power of attraction over intellectuals. Several of the central figures in the institutional refoundation of sociology after 1945 – Gurvitch, Friedmann, Pierre Naville, Henri Lefebvre, Armand Cuvillier – remained marked by their reading of Marx. Gurvitch was part of the scholarly and philosophical tradition of sociology, 'very much influenced by Marxism and German phenomenology',

---

8   Heilbron 1985.
9   Heilbron 1991.
10   Heilbron 1991.

and imported an American sociology which he deemed too lacking in theoretical grounding. In an intellectual field dominated by existentialism, he strove to invent 'a French Durkheimian tradition revisited and reconciled with Marxism', making the 'young Marx' a central reference and 'attempting a kind of synthesis between Mauss and Marx'.[11] Thus he posed afresh the problem, inherited from Durkheim's disciples, of the relationship between 'individual psyche' and 'collective psyche'. Friedmann, a graduate of the École Normale Supérieure and a philosopher, was a member of the Philosophies group and a critical supporter of the USSR, actively involved in the Resistance. He has been described as a 'convinced Marxist in the 1930s', a 'nuanced Marxist after his third visit to the USSR', and a 'psychologising Marxist at the end of his life', but also as the 'founding father of a "different" sociology', characterised by the interest devoted not only to the 'producing worker' but also to the consuming worker and (as a precursor to 'Freudo-Marxism') by the search for a path between 'Marxist optimism' and 'Freudian pessimism'.[12] Stressing how far the Durkheimian critique of Marxism owes to Antonio Labriola's version of this latter rather than to 'authentic Marxism', and highlighting 'ignored or misunderstood' texts by Marx and Engels, Armand Cuvillier showed that the double antithesis 'conservative sociology/revolutionary sociology', 'idealist sociology/materialist sociology' abusively caricatures Durkheimism and Marxism and that 'Durkheim himself was much closer to Marxism than he supposed'. As against the imputation to Marxism of a 'pure economic determinism', Cuvillier cited Friedrich Engels's letter to Joseph Bloch of 21 September 1890, in which Engels reaffirms that, '[a]ccording to the materialist conception of history, the ultimately determining element in history is the production and reproduction of real life'; and his letter to Conrad Schmidt of 27 October 1890, in which he insists on the relative autonomy of the law as well as of the other 'realms of ideology' (religion, philosophy, and so on) which 'react back as an influence upon the whole development of society'; and, indeed, a passage from *Capital* where Marx 'shows, before Max Weber, the affinities of the spirit of the Reformation with the development of capitalism'.[13] Thus, according to Cuvillier, in Durkheimism as in this 'rectified' vision of Marxism we can see the beginnings of the sociology of knowledge. As for Henri Lefebvre, who dismissively bound Émile Durkheim to Gabriel Tarde because of their common 'idealism', he calls for an investigation of the 'current sociological concreteness' and for 'saving French sociology', by resorting to the 'Marxist

---

11   Marcel 2001.
12   Bolle de Bal 2004.
13   Cuvillier 1948.

method', defined as a 'dialectical' analysis and synthesis of a contradictory real-ity in movement. This method does not exclude any investigative technique: 'statistics, surveys, questionnaires, interviews, descriptions – all these informa-tional processes can be used'. But if thus sociologists agreed on the importance of investigation, it is nevertheless necessary to note, at least until the end of the 1960s, 'the rather speculative character of many Marxist studies'.[14] So much so that, as Simiand said, 'theories without facts' rubbed shoulders with 'studies of facts without theory'.

3   The Ephemeral Marxist Sociology of the 1960s–70s

Despite or perhaps because of the Cold War, Marxism occupied a central place in the French intellectual field in the 1960s. On the 150th anniversary of Marx's birth, Raymond Aron asked 'If we measure Marx's grandeur by the scale of the quarrels he provoked or aroused, who over the last two centuries could even compare?'. In fact, the conceptual schemes of Marxism (in its vari-ous forms) – bourgeoisie/proletariat, base/superstructures, science/ideology, idealism/materialism, reform/revolution, capitalism/communism, and so on – defined the intellectual doxa of the era.

Although most sociologists were particularly receptive to Marx, the future 'big names' of French sociology were – could not but be – subject to Aron's appeal. Appointed at the Sorbonne in 1955, he was for a time the true patron of French sociology, encouraging the marriage of philosophy and fieldwork. Aron was also the introducer of Max Weber in France, often used later (espe-cially by the promoters of 'methodological individualism') as an 'antidote to Marxist orthodoxy'.[15] But those who saw (and still see) it as an 'antibody' have generally underestimated the fact that Weber was also one of the first schol-ars to make Marxism an object of academic dispute,[16] and have mostly ignored the deep kinship between Weber's and Marx's perspectives, as evidenced by the existence of a 'Weberian Marxist' current.[17] Weber denied that he claimed to 'substitute a one-sided "materialist" causal interpretation with an equally one-sided spiritualist interpretation of civilisation and history'. Yet for many of those who, even today, draw on Weber's rejection of the 'so-called "mater-

---

14   Bottomore 1968.
15   Pollak 1988.
16   Kalinowski 2005.
17   Löwy 1992.

ialist conception of history"', *The Protestant Ethic and the Spirit of Capitalism* reverses the places of the 'determinant' and the 'determined' as compared to the Marxist vulgate.[18] This dissemination of Weber's work contributed to the transformation of French sociology, of which Aron was the 'initiator and mediator'.

Marxist hegemony and the disputes it prompted, on the one hand, and the repeated injunctions to empirical research, on the other, meant that the 1970s were the years in which a 'Marxist sociology' developed in several choice domains. Responding to research programmes launched by the Délégation générale à la recherche scientifique et technique (DGRST), the Ministry of Public Works, the Commissariat au Plan, Manuel Castells and Jean Lojkine – affiliated to the Centre d'études des mouvements sociaux (CEMS) founded by Alain Touraine, Christian Topalov and Edmond Préteceille, and researchers at the Centre de Sociologie Urbaine (CSU) founded by Paul-Henri Chombart de Lauwe – were the inventors of a Marxist-inspired urban sociology, more or less close to Henri Lefebvre, Louis Althusser and the problematic of State Monopoly Capitalism.[19] At the same time, other researchers were renewing Marxist studies of social classes: in a perspective inspired by both Gramsci and Althusser, Nicos Poulantzas studied the state, political power and social classes. The Laboratoire d'études et de recherches sociologiques sur la classe ouvrière (LERSCO) founded by Jean-Claude Passeron and Michel Verret, carried out large numbers of socio-ethnographic studies on workers. Meanwhile, Christian Baudelot, Roger Establet and Jacques Malemort,[20] using the available statistical data, tried to give empirical content to the Marxist concept of the 'petty bourgeoisie' in contemporary French society (by introducing the criterion of 'retrocession of surplus value' and distinguishing among three distinct fractions). Earlier, Christian Baudelot and Roger Establet[21] had tried to give an empirical content to the Althusserian concept of 'state ideological apparatus' by highlighting the division of the capitalist school in France into two ('what appears as an orientation of schooling is in reality a division of social classes'). This outline inventory of Marxist sociology in France in the 1960s and 1970s is obviously not exhaustive. Firstly, because it would be necessary to mention those who contributed in other fields of inquiry (such as Michel Freyssenet in the sociology of work or the Marxist theorists of feminism). But, moreover, because the drawing of disciplinary boundaries (institutionally justified but

---

18   Colliot-Thélène 1990.
19   Préteceille 1989; Topalov 2013.
20   Baudelot, Establet and Malemort 1974.
21   Baudelot and Establet 1971.

epistemologically questionable) that separate sociology from the other social sciences, leads to the – artificial – isolation of historians, economists, anthropologists, and, of course, the 'Marxist' philosophers of the time.

4   Bourdieu and Marxism

The ebb, then the dissipation, of the course upon which Marxism had begun in the social sciences in the second half of the 1970s, obviously owes less to theoretical criticism than to the reversal of the political conjuncture, which concluded in the collapse of the Soviet regime and the rise of neoliberal hegemony. References to Marx's work became very marginal until a more recent revival of interest, itself likely rooted in the effects of neoliberal policies (a dizzying rise in inequalities, financial crises, destruction of the ecosystem) that led to a renewed interest in the critique of capitalism. If critical thinking did not disappear from the social sciences – and, more specifically, from sociology – it is undoubtedly embodied in Bourdieu's work (which is not without its links to Marxism).

Bourdieu's relationship with Marxism in the 1950s reflected his ambivalent move to get to grips with the state of both the intellectual field and the political field. Marxism was then 'on the agenda': 'I did a scholastic reading of Marx at that time', 'I was especially interested in the young Marx and had been fascinated by the *Theses on Feuerbach*', writes Bourdieu.[22] But he was also one of those exasperated by Stalinism. Although he was separated by a few years from the 'structuralist generation' (that of Althusser and Foucault, whose lectures he attended), Bourdieu shared many of its characteristic intellectual dispositions, which, he averred, could explained in terms of 'the determination to react against ... the soft "humanism" that was in the air'. However, Bourdieu quickly distanced himself from 'structuralism' – a habitus effect and/or a generational effect – and distanced himself from the Althusserian philosophers, criticising their 'philosophical aristocratism'[23] and reduction of agents to the status of simple epiphenomena of the structure.

This had the effect that, in the symbolic struggles that traverse the French intellectual field, where the position one adopts with regard to Marxism has always had a particularly strong 'classifying' effect, Bourdieu could be perceived as both anti-Marxist by Marxists and Marxist by anti-Marxists. The imputation

---

22   Bourdieu 1987.
23   Bourdieu 1975.

of 'Marxism' has indeed become a commonplace tactic of academic disqualification. After the 'nouveaux philosophes' made their breakthrough, this tactic has consisted in establishing the family relationship between Marx and the targeted author, who is disqualified by the equation 'Marx = collectivist materialism = Gulag'. This is, in essence, the procedure used, for example, by Jeffrey C. Alexander[24] with regard to Bourdieu's work. 'In an age marked by the death of communism,' Alexander writes, 'his oeuvre can be seen as the most impressive living embodiment of a neo-Marxist tradition that, triumphant only a decade ago, currently is struggling to survive.'

If, apart from this kind of anathema – which targets the very project of a scientific knowledge of the social world – one wonders about the uses that Bourdieu may have made of Marx's work, it is undoubtedly necessary to recall first of all the 'very pragmatic relations' that he had with the canonical authors, whoever they may be. Thus, most of Bourdieu's uses of Marx's work – beyond a related terminology (capital, reproduction, classes, and so on) – combine borrowing with critique. We will give some examples here: the theory of practice, economic sociology, the theory of symbolic production, the theory of domination and the vision of social space.[25]

Bourdieu's theory of practice was constructed in opposition to Lévi-Strauss and the Marxism of the Althusserians, who made the agent a mere 'auxiliary to the structure'. Yet he did this borrowing from Marx. Against Feuerbach and, in general, against scholastic thought (that which mistakes, as Marx put it, 'the things of logic for the logic of things') and with Marx (but rejecting both humanist and structuralist readings of his work), Bourdieu's theory of practice aims to grasp the perceptible world, 'as concrete human activity', 'as practice'.

Studying Kabyle society, Bourdieu drew explicit inspiration from Marx. But he also sought to break with economism and understand the decisive contribution that ethical and mythical representations can make to the reproduction of the economic order of which they are the product. In so doing, Bourdieu founded both a '"radically sociological" economics',[26] and – against 'the dichotomy of the economic and the non-economic' – a *general science of the economy of practices*, capable of treating all practices, including those purporting to be disinterested or gratuitous, and hence non-economic, as economic practices directed towards the maximizing of material or symbolic profit'.[27]

---

24   Alexander 1995.
25   Mauger 2012.
26   Lebaron 2001.
27   Bourdieu 2010.

An original synthesis of Marxist and Weberian approaches, field theory appears as a way out of the dead ends of the reduction of symbolic structures to economic structures, as well as those of 'reflection theory'. It appears as a solution to the 'short-circuit' that directly relates the relevant features of such symbolic production to the characteristics of the class fraction of their producer, and also as a response to 'the worst kind of functionalism' associated with Althusser's 'ideological state apparatuses'. Assuming a relative autonomy of the production of symbolic goods from external constraints, it challenges both the claim that symbolic productions have absolute autonomy and their direct reduction to the most general conditions of their production. In the case of religion, for example, Bourdieu finds in Weber the means of escaping 'the opposition between the illusion of absolute autonomy which leads one to conceive of the religious message as an inspired emergence and that reductive theory which makes it the direct reflection of economic and social conditions'.[28]

As for the vision of social space that Bourdieu proposes, it makes a double break with the Marxist theory of social classes. It breaks with economism by defining the structure of the social space through the distribution of different kinds of capital: 'economic capital', 'cultural capital' and 'social capital', which can be converted into 'symbolic capital'. Moreover, it breaks with 'the intellectualist illusion that leads one to consider the theoretical class, constructed by the sociologist, as a real class' and 'leads one to ignore the symbolic struggles of which the different fields are the site, where what is at stake is the very representation of the social world'.[29] In order to account for the passage from the 'probable class' ('logical' class, class 'on paper') to the 'mobilised class', or, in Lukács's terminology, from the 'class in itself' to the 'class for itself', it is necessary to analyse the symbolic and political work that manages to produce, if not the mobilised class, at least the belief in the existence of class.

It is clear that with and against Marx, Bourdieu is no more 'Marxist' than he is 'Weberian' or 'Durkheimian': claiming a 'relaxed eclecticism',[30] he is none of these things, or all of them at once. He inherits from Marx, Weber and Durkheim, appropriating them for himself. Starting from them (and others), he advances by solving the problems raised by the confrontation between them and their testing through empirical research, himself discovering new difficulties.[31]

---

28   Ibid.
29   Bourdieu 1985, p. 723.
30   Bourdieu, Chamboredon and Passeron 1991.
31   Mauger 2015.

5   The Disappearance of Marxism?

French sociology in the age of the mass university is predominantly 'ethno-graphic', but often reduces scientific practice to 'recording' and thus ignoring the fact that any observation, whether 'qualitative' or 'quantitative', involves hypotheses. As in the days of 'survey research', it is abdicating 'the right and duty of theoretical construction in favour of spontaneous sociology', sacrificing this need to what Nietzsche called 'the dogma of immaculate perception'.[32]

What remains of Marxism in the discipline today? Taking refuge in a few none-too-demanding allusions to interactionism, venturing to foreground an 'intersectionality' perceived as 'avant-garde', and most of the time avoiding any 'claim to be part of the discipline',[33] it displays a cautious circumspection (if not outright hostility) towards Bourdieu's work (often perceived as 'Marxist'). It goes without saying that it dismisses any reference to Marx. So, if there is, indeed, a 'return to Marx', it is probably not so much among sociologists as elsewhere, for instance among philosophers.

32   Bourdieu, Chamboredon and Passeron 1968.
33   Chenu 2002.

CHAPTER 15

Marx and French Historians

François Dosse

French historians' relationship with the work of Marx is particularly ambivalent. It is all the more difficult to pin down given that one may well wonder how to define 'Marxist history'. Should it be identified with a teleological form of history writing, based on the theory of the stages of evolution in the mode of production? Should it be understood from the angle of the historians' openness to the contributions of the social sciences, particularly economics? Whatever the definition used, it is important to historicise this phenomenon, as Marxism's echo in the French historical discipline has varied greatly over time. From a phase in which it had next to no influence to a moment in which it enjoyed a wide audience, Marxism was to explain historical phenomena, often from a deterministic perspective (inspired by reflection theory). The 1960s saw real theoretical enrichment, with historians striving to make their causal schemes more complex (especially under the influence of Althusser). Finally, it can be seen that historians have distanced themselves from, and even rejected, Marxism, which no longer exerts more than a diffuse influence on this discipline.

1   The Nineteenth Century: Historians without Marx?

1.1   *The German Historical School, Rather than Marx*
If we look back at the nineteenth century, which was the century of the professionalisation of the historian's craft, we can say that Marx did not have an echo among French historians. On the contrary, it can be said that it was the French historical school that had an influence on Marx, as he himself recognised. At the beginning of the century, the romantic and liberal historian Augustin Thierry saw in what he described as the 'race war' the motor that explained history's upheavals. It was from this notion that Marx drew his major concept of 'class struggle' as the driving force behind the transition from one mode of production to another, leading to a classless society. Acknowledging his debt to Thierry, Marx would call him the 'father of the class struggle' in historiography.[1]

---

1   Marx 1854.

Unlike Marx, however, Thierry conceived of this agonistic reality only in the context of the national melting pot, and not as a universal key to analysing Humanity's onward march.

When the historical discipline became professionalised in France, following the disastrous defeat at Sedan in 1870, French historians went to Germany to find the keys to success. They made the journey, immersing themselves in the reality of German universities in order to better understand the national vitality of this country and to prepare for the *revanche*. They returned to France convinced the need for a scientific historical discourse, as close to the empirical as possible, cut off from literature and fiction and giving proper value to fact and contingency. They came back with a true methodological discourse, drawing on the effectiveness of German historicism and its leading light, Leopold von Ranke, for whom the historian's ambition was reduced to showing 'the past as it actually happened'. This German school built itself at a critical remove from all forms of philosophy of history, and thus it kept its distance from Marxism as from Hegelianism and Kantianism. This break between history and philosophy was accentuated by the long-term marriage contract that historians entered into with geographers (particularly the Vidalian school), which enjoyed very great influence at the time.

1.2   The History of the French Revolution, a Bridgehead of Marxism?

If there is one historiographical field that has divided historians throughout the nineteenth and twentieth centuries, it is the history of the French Revolution. It was on this fundamentally important battleground that Marxism penetrated the historian's gaze, providing weapons to the defenders of the Revolution's ideals. Between 1898 and 1903, Jean Jaurès devoted himself to writing a *Socialist History of the French Revolution*. In its pages, Marx's influence is palpable, insofar as the French socialist leader strongly links political struggles to the economic interests of the contending social forces: 'The essence of history does not consist in the external development of political forms. It is quite certain that it is the interplay of economic interests, of social forces, that gives them a sense'.[2] The same thrust can be found among those who devoted their careers as historians to the study of the French Revolution, whether Alphonse Aulard, a zealous partisan of Danton, or Albert Mathiez, a great admirer of Robespierre. If the Sorbonne chair in the history of the French Revolution escaped Mathiez's clutches, it was instead successively occupied by Georges Lefebvre, Albert Soboul, and then Michel Vovelle, providing a haven for a whole historiographic tradition marked by Marxism.[3]

---

2 Jaurès 1983.
3 Lefebvre 1937, Soboul 1967, Vovelle 1982.

2   The Annales: In the Vicinity of Marxism

2.1   *A Critical Kinship*

Through its virulent criticism of the methodical school, disparagingly described as *histoire historisant* (a merely chronological telling of facts) the journal *Annales d'histoire économique et sociale*, founded in 1929 by Lucien Febvre
and Marc Bloch, seemed to stand close to Marxism. This closeness was favoured
by the fact that the journal, which was soon to become a school of thought,
had a priority interest, as the title suggests, in the economic and social domain.
However, even if the kinship is undeniable, the founders of the Annales school
maintained a critical distance from Marx. Thus, in 1922, in the context of his
dispute with the sociologists, Lucien Febvre presented Marxism as a form of
'economic spiritualism'. And when the translation of Engels's *The Peasant War
in Germany* was published in 1930, Febvre firmly denied that this work had any
historical significance. Under the title 'Un livre périmé' ('An obsolete book') he
wrote: 'To get to know Engels, yes. To get to know the peasants' war, it is a joke'.[4]
After World War II, in a review of Daniel Guérin's thesis on the French Revolution, this same Febvre was denunciatory 'This collusion of Michelet and Marx
is an incest ... The historian is not a judge'.[5] He criticised Marxism for having a
conception of history that was as obsessed with the event as that of traditional
history, which he opposed, and which lay too much emphasis on political ruptures.

However, at the same time, Marx was greatly admired by the founders of
the *Annales*. Lucien Febvre also highlighted Marx's attributes in a 1934 piece
in the Catholic review *Foi et Vie*: 'The vast, powerful problem of the relationship between capitalism and the Reformation ... who posed it first? Let us not
hesitate to answer: it was Karl Marx'.[6] However, Febvre did not share Marx's
prophetism – his causalism. Faced with the overly direct link which Marx estab-
lishes between capitalism and the Reformation, Febvre opposes to this the idea
of an imbrication of heterogeneous elements: 'The Reformation as daughter
of capitalism or, conversely, capitalism as fruit of the Reformation: no, a thousand times no. Let us the dogmatism of such a simple interpretation with the
fresh notion of the interdependence of phenomena'. As for Marc Bloch, he also
expressed the importance that Marx had for him, and at the same time the
distance that he kept from him as a historian: 'I personally have the greatest

---

4   Febvre 1930.
5   Febvre 1948.
6   Febvre 1962.

admiration for Karl Marx. ... Is it enough, however, for his lessons to serve eternally as a template for any doctrine?'.[7] If we look at the table of intellectual attachments that Lucien Febvre himself drew up, in order to highlight the thinking that had influenced his positions, Marx is conspicuous by his absence.[8] The German historian Peter Schöttler performed the same exercise with regard to Marc Bloch: here again, Marx is absent.

2.2   *A Labroussean Marxism?*

The economic and social history that triumphed in the postwar years has been overly identified with just one current – the Annales – and its leader Fernand Braudel. Braudel's economistic orientation did bring him closer to Marxism, but this proximity does not mean that he embraced it outright. In his studies on the dynamics of capitalism, in his work on the market and material civilisation, the influence of Marx's thought is more than noticeable: it is an essential resource.

But the doubtless masterful qualities of the man sometimes described as the 'Pope of history' should not make us forget the figure of another researcher, reader and continuator of Marx, Ernest Labrousse. He had an orchestrating role at the Sorbonne, allowing him to direct the great social-history studies pursued by an entire generation. In addition to his position as chair of the Institut d'histoire économique et sociale at the Sorbonne, which Labrousse held for a quarter of a century between 1945 and 1967, he was director of studies at the sixth section of the École pratique des hautes études (EPHE) and played an eminent role in the recruitment committees at the Centre national de la recherche scientifique (CNRS). Labrousse's model of economic and social history is conceived as a hierarchy of three moments: the economic, the social and the mental, with the interlocking and sequential delays in between them. The order of dependencies is articulated around the primary historical fact of economic evolution. The other levels simply graft themselves onto this main level, with an inertia of their own: 'The historian distinguishes between the different speeds by which phenomena are propagated. The economic phenomenon is probably most often the antecedent; social change is already relatively belated; and the change in mentalities wins the race to come slowest'.[9]

From 1955 onwards, upon the International Congress of Historical Sciences held in Rome, Labrousse reoriented his field of investigation towards social

---

7   Bloch 2015.
8   Dosse 2010.
9   Labrousse 1980.

history, albeit without abandoning the economic dimension which remained the fundamental basis of his model. He thus came together, in an even more marked way, with the initial orientations of the Annales school.

At the beginning of the 1970s, Pierre Chaunu judged that 'the entire French historical school is Labroussean .... Labrousse's thought is so much incorporated into our practice of history, the treatment of material and the conceptualisation of discourse, that we sometimes forget its origin: by dint of its triumph, it has become indistinguishable'.[10] In fact, Labrousse contributed to the formation of a whole generation of historians – the generation that reached maturity in the 1960s and 1970s – even if some of his thesis students, conscious of the limits of the Labroussean model, broke away to follow their own paths (as in the cases of Maurice Agulhon, Michel Vovelle and Michelle Perrot).

3   A Generation of Communist Historians

In the 1950s, many historians identified their fate with that of the French Communist Party (PCF), and it was through the party, at least as much as the Annales, that Marxism penetrated history as discipline. In 1952, the group of history graduates who were PCF members was particularly rich in personalities. It included Claude Mesliand, Pierre Deyon, Jean Dautry, Jean Nicolas, François Furet, Robert Bonnaud, Jacques Chambaz, Denis Richet and Emmanuel Le Roy Ladurie. Communist historians had such force of numbers that upon the publication of the results of the *agrégation*, François Furet and Jean Chesneaux, counting the successful candidates, wryly commented in the courtyard of the Sorbonne that it was only right to leave a few places for the bourgeois ...

Up till the 1960s, Marxism influenced history as a discipline essentially through economic history. It conjugated a dual reference to both the Annales and to an open Marxism, as attested by the theses of communist historians such as Jean Bouvier on the Crédit Lyonnais (1961) or Pierre Vilar on Catalonia in the modern era (1962). Following the general evolution of historiography, from the 1960s onwards this Marxist history no longer limited its field of investigation to the economic dimension, and explored what it described as 'superstructures', meaning, the vast domain of mentalities.

---

10   Chaunu 1974.

4   Enriching the Model, Articulating Different Dimensions

4.1   *Althusser's Lessons*

In the 1960s and 1970s, the presence of Marxist theses in the practice and discourse of historians especially owed to the influence of Louis Althusser at the École normale on the rue d'Ulm. In identifying an 'epistemological break' in Marx, Althusser advanced the consideration that Marx had achieved a scientific analysis with *Capital*, breaking with the bourgeois idealism still conveyed by his early work. Althusser's analytical scheme broke with reflection theory and the linear determination of the superstructure by the base. He distanced himself from a certain form of economic determinism by making the interplay of different dimensions more complex, which could lead to a dominance of the political in Antiquity or a dominance of the religious in the Middle Ages – it being understood that the economic remained the determining factor 'in the last instance'.

4.2   *From the Cellar to the Attic*

Many historians shifted their gaze from the economic to the other dimensions of the social whole and questioned the articulation between them. If we look at Georges Duby's career, we can see that his path – symptomatic of that of his generation – led him through three successive stages: starting with the economic, he ends up with the imaginary, passing through the study of the social. For him, these three levels remained inseparable in his approach to the feudal era: 'A society forms a whole. I do not think it is possible to dissociate politics from economics or culture. It is this combination that obliges us to draw on all kinds of information'.[11] Duby had discovered Marxism in philosophy class in 1937; he always considered it an essential contribution, to which he never ceased to compare his own work. His reading of Louis Althusser's and Étienne Balibar's texts in the 1960s also bore strong influence on him, and he long considered the notion of 'determination in the last instance' most effective. This led him to begin his work starting with economic phenomena, not in an arbitrary manner, but because for it is these phenomena that make access to other levels of a society possible.

The concern to analyse the different dimensions of the social whole *in combination*, without abandoning the achievements of Marxism, also inspired other great historians. One was the medievalist like Guy Bois, whose thesis[12]

---

11   *Magazine littéraire* 1982.

12   Bois 1984.

analysed the crisis of feudalism not as the outcome of a simple contradiction between resources and population, but as a general crisis of society. But there were also modernists like Robert Mandrou, pioneer of the history of mentalities, Michel Vovelle, who sought to situate the concept of mentality in relation to that of ideology, or Pierre Vilar, who worked ceaselessly to enhance the Marxist conceptual system through the study of Catalonia. When Vilar worked on the Spanish theologians of the seventeenth century, he did so in order to seek therein the first elements of a macroeconomic theory in the making. He wanted to show how much history is a totality, the only possible synthesis of the other human sciences. The essential reference for Vilar was Marx who, he credited with realising this historicisation of all the data of human life. 'To think everything historically is Marxism's very calling'.[13]

4.3   The Renewal of Ancient History

The scholars of ancient history who added most to methodological renewal – from Jean-Pierre Vernant to Pierre Vidal-Naquet via Marcel Detienne, Pierre Lévêque and Claude Mossé – also asserted the need for a global approach to history and identified with an open Marxism. As the driving forces behind the Gernet Centre founded by Vernant, they constituted what has been called the Paris School, which radically renovated classical Hellenists' approach to Greece. Taking the example of religion in ancient Greece, Vernant criticised its traditional conception as a separate domain, where to understand it properly it is necessary to 'think together' politics, religion, ethics and everyday life. This is the only way to understand the essential articulations of a society in its dialectical development. Vernant thus showed how politics, which took root in Greece, encompasses all the relations of production. Like most historians of his generation, Vidal-Naquet's itinerary led him to focus primarily on the study of economic and social phenomena, in an essential partnership with Moses Finley. It was in this spirit that he published *Economic and Social History of Ancient Greece* with Michel Austin in 1972. He examined the status of slaves – which could not be thought in isolation from the development of citizenship – in categories that could not be the same as those of our modern society. In particular, he noted the absence of economic autonomy in the ancient world. His historical exploration therefore gradually led him to question the effectiveness of the myths and values of Greek society: 'It was increasingly the history of representations and the imaginary that, along with historiography, was to take pride of

---

13   Vilar 1982.

place in his work as a historian of ancient Greece'.[14] He then extended the scope of his studies to include Greek tragedy, conceived not only as fictional text, but as a revelation of the fundamental forms of the Greek world.

4.4   Writing the History of Ideology

Around 1968, at the University of Nanterre, a junction took place between Marxism and a socio-linguistics based on the discourse analysis inspired by the Althusserian linguist Michel Pêcheux. This new research programme focused on lexicology, in interdisciplinary research bringing together, among others, linguists and historians: Jean Dubois, Jean-Baptiste Marcellesi, Denise Maldidier, Françoise Gadet, Régine Robin, Jacques Guilhaumou and Antoine Prost. This lexicological orientation aimed at continuing Althusser's enterprise of elaborating a critique of the dominant ideology, and it thus adopted a both theoretical and political perspective. Jean-Baptiste Marcellesi's thesis on the Tours congress was to serve as a model for numerous case studies.[15] Just before the May movement, in April 1968, a conference on political lexicology was held in Saint-Cloud, during which Annie Kriegel analysed the Communists' 'unitary' vocabulary during the Popular Front. Denise Maldidier studied political vocabulary during the Algerian war, based on six daily newspapers. Antoine Prost compared the vocabulary of France's political families at the end of the nineteenth century, by studying the 1881 elections. This whole lexicological project was to develop around Nanterre after May 1968. These discourse analyses did not stop at quantitative lexical studies on the frequency of word use; rather, they sought to establish a relationship between behaviour and its verbal manifestations. Such was the case of Denise Maldidier's analysis of the political discourse of the Algerian War. The historian Régine Robin, marked by her reading of Althusser, tried to make historians aware of the contributions coming from linguistics.[16]

4.5   English Marxism Makes Its Mark

Those French Marxist historians who found themselves too constrained by Althusserian schemas tended to turn to English Marxist historians, who more closely studied concrete cases and made more room for representations. They drew their inspiration from Christopher Hill, Rodney Hilton, Eric Hobsbawm and EP Thompson, re-evaluating the fruitfulness of Marxist concepts in the light of historical analyses of specific objects. Eric Hobsbawm warned as early as 1965 against over-simplifying approaches to industrial labour, highlighting

---

14   Mossé 1998.
15   Marcellesi 1971.
16   Robin 1973.

the importance of rural and domestic industries in the establishment of a manufacturing industry.[17] EP Thompson quickly became a major reference point, radically renewing Marxist social history despite the only belated translation of his work into French.[18] In a break with the Labroussean schema, Thompson no longer defined the working class by its objective components (economic function, level of wealth, and so on): the working class is not a thing, a reification, but rather is embodied in individuals, in a context, by an active process set to work by 'agents'.

5   Two Great Disputes

5.1   *The Labrousse/Mousnier debate*

The 1965 conference at the ENS in Saint-Cloud was the occasion for a key joust between two approaches to the social history of the modern era: on the one hand, the economic and Marxist approach defended in particular by Labrousse, Albert Soboul and Adeline Daumard, and on the other, the institutional approach advocated by Roland Mousnier. A specialist of the seventeenth century, Mousnier had authored an authoritative dissertation, defended in 1945, on *La Vénalité des offices sous Henri IV et Louis XIII*,[19] based on the consultation of the very rich Séguier collection. Roland contradicts analysis in terms of social classes, which privileges the economic dimension, with the fact that the social hierarchy in the seventeenth century cannot be deduced from its professional anchorage, nor from the levels of wealth, but is fundamentally based on the social esteem attached to such and such function. He concludes that the seventeenth century was still based on a system of orders, not classes. While advocating a social history, Mousnier favoured its political dimension, against the current of the dominant economic-focused view, and asserted the importance of representations. The analytical criteria he puts forward to understand seventeenth-century society are based on the place given to honour, dignity and social esteem. According to Mousnier, the practice of arms and the service rendered to princes are more relevant factors of classification than one's place in the mode of production. This vision of society leads Mousnier to take a completely different view of the popular movements that marked the seventeenth century than did the Marxist current. The Soviet historian Boris Porshnev, who also worked on the Séguier collection, analysed

---

17   Hobsbawm 1968.
18   Thompson 1963.
19   'Venality' refers to the sale of public offices to raise funds for the crown.

such movements as precursors of the French Revolution to come: 'We want to oppose a radically different point of view, centred on the question of the evolution of capitalism within feudal and absolutist France'.[20]

5.2   *The Question of the Asiatic Mode of Production*

In 1959, Pierre Vidal-Naquet, then a professor at the University of Caen, discovered *Oriental Despotism*, a study by Karl Wittfogel, a German Communist exiled in the United States. Vidal-Naquet devoted his course to it in 1959–60 and recommended its publication to his friend, the publisher Jérôme Lindon. The book was published in French by Minuit in 1964, with a preface by Vidal-Naquet. He was convinced by Wittfogel's thesis and saw in it an extension and enrichment of Marxist thought. Relying on an intuition of Marx's, Wittfogel perceived the existence in the East of a peculiar Asiatic mode of production, characterised by an omnipotent state which alone possessed all the means of production in 'hydraulic societies' in which the control of irrigation systems is essential and can only be ensured by the state. Vidal-Naquet nevertheless distanced himself from the book's political theses, which suggest that despotism and torture were the distinctive features of Asian societies until the contemporary era, and thus may have served to challenge the Stalinist system or, in the context of tension between the Soviet Union and People's China, the Maoist regime.

6   A Farewell to Marx?

The collapse of communism also had its impact on a certain Marxist teleology, which assumed history's march towards an ineluctable emancipation of humanity, a society without social classes and freed from all blockages and contradictions, achieving transparency and the realisation of the dream of equality. The USSR's disastrous fate and the fall of the Berlin Wall in 1989 plunged the world into a new regime of historicity. This was marked by the opacity and crisis of the future, undermining a model in which the direction of history seemed to be drawn, even if with phases of ebb and flow and possible regression. The result of this, more than the abandonment of Marxist teleology, was the abandonment of all forms of chronosophy, of heteronomous explanations of the historical process, and a shift in the attention of historians and social scientists in general towards the actors themselves. In the words of the former secret-

---

20   Porshnev 1972.

ary of the *Annales*, Bernard Lepetit, who initiated the journal's 'critical turn' in 1988–9, they began to 'take the actors seriously'. The result was a turn that can be described as pragmatic. For the major question that historians would henceforth ask is what action meant, for historical actors past and present. This turning point would affect the very practice of writing history, the profession of the historian, which would no longer be conceived as the expression of a scientificity set outside of contingent time. Rather, it would now be considered in its internalised relationship to the present, as the construction of a historiographical operation situated in a particular place and giving rise to a specific way of writing. Hence the increased importance, among historians, of historiography and ego-histories which relativise historical discourse; this latter was no longer posed as judgement from above in the name of a transcendental truth, but as so many sedimented layers of meaning, building up to our own present.

The second reason why historical studies grew distant from Marx and Marxism lay in the challenge to explanatory determinisms. One of the effects of the practice of 'the history of present time' (which has developed over the last few decades, even beyond the specific influence of the Institut d'histoire du temps présent, IHTP) has been to remove the fatalism from what historians had earlier tended to fatalise, with Marx, through the use of causal schemas that encapsulated the enigma of the new, of the event, in explanations that proved too rigid. On the contrary, the experience of the history of present time refers to the indeterminacy of the future, to the plurality of possibilities, to the inability to forecast.

The third reason why historians distanced themselves from Marx was the re-evaluation of singular phenomena, with a greater attention to the contingent. In this spirit, from the 1980s onwards, there was an astonishing vogue for the biographical genre, which had previously been particularly discredited because of its 'unscientific' character, too close to fiction, and carefully avoided by professional historians, who preferred collective, mass and anonymous phenomena.

These few dominant features of current historical research show the extent to which we have moved away from the Marxist horizon – which does not necessarily mean, as was once said, that we should throw the baby out with the bathwater. Marx undoubtedly remains a more widely disseminated and less exclusive resource for historians, especially in certain fields of research such as the history of the workers' movement or economic and social history.

CHAPTER 16

Marxism and Literary Criticism

Lucile Dumont, Quentin Fondu and Laélia Veron

Neither Marx nor Engels, nor Paul Lafargue, Lenin or Trotsky, proposed a theory of literature. Their literary analyses took the form of occasional writings, without any in-depth reflection on the specificity of literature or its ideological status. The absence, among communism's classic texts, of a body of work on literature, long prevented the emergence of a Marxist literary critique relatively independent of political issues.

From Liberation onwards, however, Marxist approaches to literature developed, addressing the social determinations of literary production from a materialist angle, as against the dominant idealist traditions. The initial control of the French Communist Party (PCF) over the Marxist corpus and then over its dissemination was relaxed from the mid-1950s, thanks to the international crisis prompted by the Soviet Communist Party's Twentieth Congress, which began the process of de-Stalinisation. At the same time, references to Marxism multiplied in the cultural and intellectual fields. Literary critics identifying as heterodox Marxists, many of them members of the anti-Stalinist left, delved back into the question of form, as against the idea that artistic productions were merely a 'reflection' of their material conditions of production. For some authors, this also meant making visible the mechanisms of power conveyed by discourses, through the practice of ideology critique. In the context of the transformations of French literary criticism, the appropriations of Marxism diversified, gradually coming to encompass heterogeneous intellectual practices and political positions. From the 1970s onwards, although some academics who continued to construct Marxist approaches still found a place in the university, the explicit claim to Marxism declined in literary studies.

1 The Introduction of Marxism into Literary Criticism in the 1950s

1.1 *The PCF and the Literary Question*

The PCF's interest in literature certainly did not begin in 1945, as shown by the existence of Communist literary criticism in several newspapers (in particular *L'Humanité*) during the interwar period, and indeed by the role given to writers and artists in the anti-fascist struggle. In those years, PCF oscillated between promoting (mostly French) authors considered progressive and the political use of literary issues.

It was only after Liberation that the party developed a specific approach to literature. Socialist realism – the USSR's cultural doctrine promoting a figurative and heroic representation of the people – had been imposed against the artistic avant-garde by Andrei Zhdanov as early as 1934. Yet it was not until 1947 that the PCF adopted this creed, in line with the ideological hardening which, as in the USSR, marked the beginning of the Cold War. But the principles of socialist realism are multiple and its definition was a subject of constant conflict. The debate between two members of the PCF, the painter Francis Jourdain and the writer André Wurmser, in the pages of *La Pensée* in 1950, provides a good example of this uncertainty and points to the opposition between an orthodox conception (to the detriment of aesthetic freedom in art) and a more flexible one (to the detriment of the political conception of art). Concluding his exchange with Jourdain, Wurmser illustrated these two positions by writing: 'I am therefore pleased that you congratulate me for having spoken out against this "crude Marxism that would allow itself to be reduced to a table of logarithms". Allow me, however, not to prefer to it that excessively modest Marxism which, knocking on the door of the studio, would apologise to His Majesty the artist: "Oh, sorry, I was on the wrong floor ..." and go back down to the cobbler's shop, determined never to go higher than the shoe'.[1] Roger Garaudy, for his part, successively embodied both positions: initially faithful to the principles of Zhdanovism, which demanded that politics be a 'guide', he then abandoned them in his book *D'un réalisme sans rivages* ('For a Realism Without Shores', 1963).

In this same period, the PCF's policy of publishing Marxist authors became increasingly important, consistent with its strategy of investing in intellectual spaces. Éditions sociales thus offered translations or re-editions of works by Marxist authors devoted to literature, accompanied by long introductions signed by the writer and critic Jean Fréville, a close ally of Maurice Thorez. Such was the case of the reissuing of an anthology of texts by Marx and Engels on literature and art (1954), of *Art and Social Life* by Georgi Plekhanov (1950) and of a selection of texts by Lenin, *Sur la littérature et l'art* (1957). For the PCF, it was necessary to build up a Marxist canon of interpretation of literary and artistic subjects, but also to set socialist realism within both the history of Marxism and the French national tradition.

---

1   Wurmser 1950.

1.2   *The End of a Monopoly?*

If the PCF increasingly took over intellectual spaces and particularly the field of literary criticism in the years following the Liberation, this also owed to the competition it faced on this terrain from intellectuals who, while not party members, were increasingly moving towards Marxism. In *What Is Literature?* (1948), Sartre opposed traditional literary criticism, emphasised the responsibility of the writer and theorised a new form of intellectual and artistic commitment that was not subordinated to party-political issues (Sartre only became a PCF fellow traveller in 1952, and only for a few years). He gradually moved closer to Marxism, promoting a materialist critique of literature which he later put to work in *The Family Idiot* (1971–2).

The postwar years were also marked by the import of György Lukács's early works into France, notably by left-wing intellectuals critical of Stalinism gathered around the journal *Arguments* (1956–62). The circulation of his writings owed much to Lucien Goldmann, who devoted a long text to the Hungarian theorist, published in *Les Temps modernes* in 1962. As against what he called the Marxist 'reflection' theorists (Georgi Plekhanov and Franz Mehring in particular) and Robert Escarpit's empirical sociology of literature, Goldmann built up a singular epistemology and methodology which was attentive to social structures and their transformations. This 'genetic structuralism' provided the foundation for his sociology of literature: it opposed both the reduction of the work to the context of its production – which, Goldmann claimed, was promoted by mechanistic Marxism – and its reduction to the author's biography, practised in literary education. In *Le Dieu caché* (1955) Goldmann showed that the proper understanding of Pascal's works, like Racine's, demands that they be linked to a 'world view': 'that set of aspirations, feelings and ideas which unites the members of a group (usually a social class), and opposed them to other groups'. This tragic conception – that of the nobility of the robe, brutally demoted by royal authority – is a paradoxical vision of the world, without the possibility of transformation, indeed, without history, that we find both in Jansenist theology and in the structures of the works of Racine and Pascal, where God is at once omnipresent and absent. Goldmann's reference to the young Lukács, the choice of a prestigious corpus and the open assertion of a Marxist textual analysis thus outline a doubly heterodox positioning – in relation to the political line of the PCF and in relation to the dominant literary criticism.

1.3   *The Promotion of a Heterodox Marxism: The Case of Brecht*

In the period of discredit for the PCF that followed the Soviet intervention in Hungary in 1956, the reception of Bertolt Brecht in France also contributed to the promotion of a heterodox Marxism. Little-known before the war, it was only in the 1950s that Brecht triumphed on French stages. While the PCF deemed him too formalist and far from the canons of socialist realism, for young intellectuals such as Bernard Dort he represented the possibility of 'Marxist reflection but through Brechtian channels'. By recommending a combination of the pleasure of theatrical performance and the educational role of the theatre, and by formulating his theory of 'distancing', which rejects theatrical illusion and the identification of spectators with the characters ('the spectator should not experience what the characters experience, but rather question them'), Brecht consequently proposed a new theory of artistic engagement, the aim of which was to deconstruct the dominant ideology rather than to act as propaganda. The Brechtian aesthetic-political project was introduced and supported in France by the team at *Théâtre Populaire* magazine, and in particular by Roland Barthes who, in *Mythologies* (1957), set out to hunt down expressions of ideology by observing, in everyday objects and discourses, 'the way in which a lexicon and a grammar can be politically engaged'. Both theorist and artist, Brecht could thus represent both an aesthetic and political 'model' during this period, while Lukács, through his accommodation to Stalinism, acted as 'foil'.[2]

These two forms of heterodoxy towards communist orthodoxy – the first refusing, in the tradition of the work of the young Lukács, to sacrifice works on the altar of social determinations, and the second opting, following Brecht, for a non-ideological critique of ideology – shared a common opposition to the 'reflection theory', a negative label attached to the criticism practised in the PCF's orbit.

2   From Marxist Theory to Literary Theories: The 1960s–70s

2.1   *The PCF and the End of Zhdanovism*
De-Stalination was accompanied by a gradual shifting of the balances within the PCF. This provided the context in which the party's literary doctrine and policy evolved. The beginning of the 1960s was marked by the PCF's desire to win over the intellectual professions, through reflection on their role and by the decision to give them an important place in the *aggiornamento* process. The public debate organised by the Union des étudiants communistes (UEC) and its journal *Clarté* in February 1965 was one of the emblematic moments of

---

2   Matonti 2005a.

this policy of openness. Entitled 'What can literature do?', this debate brought together Jorge Semprún, a former member of the Spanish Communist Party who called on literature to rediscover its rebellious power rather than get lost in formal research; Simone de Beauvoir and Jean-Paul Sartre, advocates of a 'committed literature' that allowed the author and the reader to experience their own freedom; but also Jean-Pierre Faye, Jean Ricardou and Yves Berger, who defended the *nouveau roman* and emphasised the self-referential character of literature.[3]

The party's journey towards greater freedom of creation and expression culminated in 1966 in the Argenteuil central committee meeting on culture, at which socialist realism and Lysenkoism were officially abandoned. The resolution adopted by the party congress changed the status of intellectuals: creatives could exercise 'their taste and their originality in the free deployment of their imagination', provided that they supported the 'ideological and political positions of the working class'.[4] Philosophy, theory, and the humanities and social sciences remained subject to tighter party control, which maintained an ambiguity about the situation of literary criticism and theory, as André Stil pointed out in his speech. Louis Aragon, who had an enormous reputation both inside and outside the PCF, played a leading role in the turn enacted at Argenteuil. A member of the Central Committee since 1950 and chief editor of *Lettres françaises* since 1953, Aragon was the central actor in a 'de-Stalinisation of realism' that 'contributed to the de-Stalinisation of everything'.[5] His eminent position in the party and in literary life enabled him to become the protector of novelty, and in his journal he welcomed the literary and theoretical avant-gardes of the 1960s, in particular the group attached to the *Tel Quel* review, of which Philippe Sollers was the driving force.

2.2 A Marxist-Structuralist Hybridisation?

In the 1960s, the rising number of journals devoted to literature and the transformations of university spaces (the rise of the social sciences, the progressive overhaul of literary studies) contributed to the Sartrean model losing influence, to the spread of structuralism and to the expansion of formal research in literature. It was around this research that various attempts at Marxist-Structuralist hybridisation were developed, both in the orbit of the PCF and in the academic world.

---

3 Beauvoir et al., 1965.
4 Martelli 2017.
5 Olivera 1996.

The import into France of the Russian formalists, crucial for the constitution of structuralism, took place in Communist publications (with the support of the couple made up by Louis Aragon and Elsa Triolet) and around *Tel Quel*, a hub of avant-gardism. Created in 1960, this latter publication was initially apolitical and promoted the *nouveau roman*, but became more politicised toward the end of the decade as it drew closer to the Communist journal *La Nouvelle Critique*. Aimed at an intellectual readership, *La Nouvelle Critique* was one of the tools of the Communist *aggiornamento*. Several of its members delved into literary questions and constructed their 'own theory of literature, a middle way between reflection theory and *Tel Quel's* formalism'.[6] The rapprochement between *Tel Quel* and *La Nouvelle Critique* allowed the latter to indirectly support and disseminate Althusser's thought, and to make literary theory a privileged critical instrument, notably through the importation of the works of Mikhail Bakhtin and Brecht. By bringing the political aura of the PCF to the *Tel Quel* group, *La Nouvelle Critique* enabled it to forge an avant-garde stance, as a bearer of aesthetic and political radicalism. From Marxism, *Tel Quel* took above all the idea of revolution, constitutive of all avant-gardes. The collection *Théorie d'ensemble* (1968), placed under the patronage of Stéphane Mallarmé and Karl Marx, thus aimed to think of writing and theory as instruments of revolution. However, *Tel Quel's* use of the alliance with the PCF was mainly strategic: Sollers spoke of 'a rather pragmatic desire to take advantage of the disarray of the party press' and Julia Kristeva, also a member of the group, saw the PCF of the 1960s as the 'best loudspeaker'.[7] This alliance broke down at the end of the 1960s. The organisation of the first Cluny conference on 'Literature and Linguistics' in April 1968, marked the end of the joint venture between *Tel Quel* and *La Nouvelle Critique*. In May–June 1968, the 'orthodox' positions of the *Tel Quel* group put it at odds with the movement, which borrowed instead, 'against communist orthodoxy, from the anarchist tradition, from the "artistic critique" of capitalism and from heterodox Marxism'.[8] All this prompted the group to reorient itself towards Maoism, and then textualism.

The revival of literary criticism, built in particular on structuralism and the importation of Russian formalists, did not wait for *Tel Quel* to anchor itself to the left and engage in dialogue with Marxism. Roland Barthes, the main representative of this revival, only belatedly claimed – with some exaggeration – to be a Marxist. However, it was through the intermediary of 'Trotskyite microcosms'

---

6 Matonti 2005a.
7 Ibid.
8 Gobille 2005.

(notably Maurice Nadeau) that he entered Parisian intellectual life, around the journals *Combat, Les Lettres nouvelles* and then *Arguments*.[9] An 'adept of the Marxist "grand system" from which he drew a impulse for writing', Barthes was not, however, familiar with Marx's texts and never joined the PCF, whose organic intellectuals, Garaudy and Stil, he did not hesitate to attack in *Writing Degree Zero*. Only occasionally, mainly in the 1950s, did Barthes places himself under the banner of Marxism – a dissident Marxism, marked by his reading of Brecht and conceived above all as a tool of ideological contestation. But Marxist concepts do not seem to constitute privileged elements of Barthes's theoretical development. Barthes's participation in the *Tel Quel* group's 1974 visit to China did not lead to a renewal of his thinking on Marxism, although the 'dialectical-materialist reference (Marx, Engels, Lenin, Mao)' is invoked in his 1975 article on the theory of text.[10]

The emphasis on the notions of 'materialism' (the materiality of language) and 'production' in that literary criticism which lays claim a form of Marxist-structuralist hybridisation is one of the main points of contact between the literary and the political, the theoretical and the revolutionary. Althusser's work offered literary scholars a structuralist alternative to structural linguistics. Above all, in a context where they manifested a radical opposition to the model of chronological and national literary teaching, the Althusserian perspective provided at least three elements. First of all, the scientific argument, which, by making theorisation the correlate of scientificity, makes it possible to claim a scientific status while rejecting the positivism of literary history. Secondly, the break with history, which allows for analysis to focus on the internal coherence of the objects of study and to distance itself from the historicist model of the study of literature. Finally, politicisation, which gives the structuralist enterprise in literature all its revolutionary force, insofar as the 'epistemological break' that Althusser identifies in Marx 'gives the theoretical in general maximum political legitimacy, and all the more so because it elevates it to the rank of a practice'.[11]

Althusserian theoretical practice found an application in the first book by Althusser's pupil Pierre Macherey, *A Theory of Literary Production*. Published in 1966 in Maspero's 'Théorie' collection, it called for the transformation of literary criticism into a science of the literary. In its pages, Macherey proposes an approach to literature in which the latter is no longer creation but *literary*

---

9   Roger 1996.
10   Barthes 1975.
11   Kaufmann 2011.

production, and the writer is no longer a creator but the *worker* producing his text. This meant denaturalising literature in order to understand the laws of literary production and to shed light on the ideological projects implicit in literary works. At the same time, the *Cahiers marxistes-léninistes*, created in 1964 on the initiative of the Union des étudiants communistes (UEC) group at the rue d'Ulm, promoted similar conceptions, notably in the issue 'Pouvoirs de la littérature' ('Powers of Literature', 1965–6).

Close to *Tel Quel* and a student of Goldmann and Barthes, Julia Kristeva proposed an alliance of Marxism, semiology, structuralism and psychoanalysis. Based on Bakhtin's research, in the 1960s she developed the notion of intertextuality, which aims to identify the combination of texts set in relation within a given text. The attention paid to intertextuality is intended to situate literary structures in their historical and social dimensions and is presented as an adaptation and linguistic specialisation of the critique of ideology.[12] In *Revolution in Poetic Language*, Kristeva envisages literature as a practice of 'positive violence', which functions in a similar way to 'political revolution'. In Kristeva's theoretical compound, the part played by Marxism gradually diminished until disappearing outright – following a shift that affected the whole of literary studies.

3   The Mutations and Decline of Marxism in Approaches to
       Literature

The claim that Marxism embodied an all-encompassing doctrine gradually faded from the mid-1970s onwards. The PCF's loss of influence in the academic world was not compensated by new forms of institutionalisation of Marxist approaches to literature. Pierre Macherey and Étienne Balibar's 1975 article 'Literature as an Ideological Form: Some Marxist Propositions', which claimed to establish a theory of literary effects, appeared more like a swansong of Althusserianism than an index of theoretical revival. The favourable but occasional reception of certain Marxist figures at the university (Pierre Barbéris, Roger Fayolle); the birth of a discipline, sociocriticism (originally marked by a Marxist sensibility, but which was developed on the basis of new concepts); and the rise of the sociology of literature; show both an often eclectic interest in Marxist-inspired methods and an abandonment of Marxist theory *qua* system.

----

12   Kristeva 1969.

3.1   *Barbéris, a Marxism from the Academic Chair*

A teacher, researcher, but also a militant, Pierre Barbéris is one of the major figures of Marxist criticism within literary studies. Author of a considerable body
of work, he became a recognised figure in the academic world (teacher at the
ENS in the 1960s, then professor at the University of Caen from 1972 onwards),
despite clashes with the Sorbonne or with critics who accused him of taking
an overly doctrinaire approach. While many literary scholars have expressed
a Marxist sensibility, Barbéris is one of the few to have proclaimed himself,
throughout his career, a Marxist critic. In his major works, which are mainly
readings of classical texts (Balzac, Stendhal), he seeks to inject a refined Marxist conception of history into the approach to literary texts and to place the
authors studied in relation to the horizon of the class struggle. To do this, he also
rids himself of a certain Marxist orthodoxy (the overly philosophical Lukács,
Althusser as too much of a theoretician) as well as the positivist or idealist
visions dominant in literary studies. Barbéris's institutional position allowed
him – through training disciples who were in turn called upon to teach – somewhat to extend the Marxist influence over this the discipline. But Barbéris
lacked the resources to really set the tone, and his work of the 1980s and 1990s
appears more like a resilient but residual outlier, a persistent trace of an era
when Marxism and literary research had been closely linked.

3.2   *The Development of a Non-Marxist Sociology of the Literary Field:*
The Example of Bourdieu

The sociology of literature has gradually detached itself from the Marxist approach promoted by Lucien Goldmann in the late 1960s. Goldmannian sociology was undermined both by the success of immanentist critics and by Goldmann's own difficulty in evolving his critical approach while remaining faithful
to Marxist theoretical principles (the substitution of the notion of 'social group'
for that of 'social class', for example, earned him the charge of anti-Marxist devi-
ationism). After Goldmann's sudden death in 1970, this sociology had no strong
institutional anchor and did not succeed in perpetuating itself either among
literary scholars or among sociologists.

    Among the new sociological approaches to literature that supplanted Gold-
mann's was that of Pierre Bourdieu, who took up certain Marxist concepts
(class, capital), but within a different theoretical and methodological perspective. On the one hand, by establishing the specificity of a literary field governed
by its own constraints, Bourdieu outlined a complex and fragmented social
space far from the traditional Marxist philosophy of history (some Marxists
reproach him for not specifying the way in which these fields fit together,
and thus for not proposing a general theory of society). He rejected the idea

of a direct relationship between the work and the social whole. On the other hand, Bourdieu's method of analyising the literary field (the situation of the literary field within the field of power, internal analysis of the literary field, analysis of the writer's habitus) aims to understand authors' trajectories, but in the same way as Goldmann, without attaching them to the expression of a transindividual existential situation: 'The homology between the two types of structures – novelistic and social – is conditioned by the writer's socialisation and by the resulting habitus (and not, as with Goldmann, by the worldview of his social group)'.[13]

3.3   The Ambiguity of Sociocriticism

In the ideological and political context of the post-May '68 period, sociocriticism, a 'theoretical dissidence from the traditional Marxist approach', was introduced by Claude Duchet at the University of Vincennes in 1971. In his manifesto-article, Duchet challenged both poetic readings that excluded the social from the text and the treatment of the social by Marxist literary analysis, which, he alleged, was fixed by 'reflection theory, the concept of the typical ... and an insufficient exploration of ideologies and the nature of the literary signified'.[14] He thus sought to delimit a new approach, not to the literary text as a social fact (which is the object of the sociology of literature), but to the social in the literary text. A new disciplinary space was opening up, the contours of which were not clearly defined. This became the object of symbolic struggles and theoretical debates, from which Marxism emerged as the loser at the end of the millennium.

Indeed, the word 'sociocriticism' soon fell victim to its success: claimed from very different perspectives, it struggled to designate a precise approach. This embarrassment, expressed by Henri Mitterrand at the closing of the Toronto conference in 1972 ('We have not succeeded ... in coming up with a definition of sociocriticism, nor even a clear awareness of its objectives, perspectives and languages'), was also visible in Duchet's preface to *Sociocritique*.[15] Here, he sought both to pay homage to Marxist materialist criticism (embodied notably by Goldmann) and to distinguish himself from it, by advocating a 'reorientation of socio-historical investigation from the outside in, that is to say, the internal organisation of texts, their systems of functioning, their webs of meaning, their tensions'. This ambiguous relationship between sociocriticism and Marxism was illustrated in the field of literary studies by the opposition between Duchet

---

13   Dirkx 2015.
14   Duchet 1971.
15   Duchet 1979.

and Barbéris. Over the years, Duchet increasingly asserted his distance from Marxism and established new methodological concepts (*sociotext*, *sociogram*, *cotext*, and the triptych *information*, *index*, and *value*). On the other hand, Barbéris,[16] while recognising the interest of sociocriticism as a factor for the renewal of Marxism, did not adopt these concepts and refused to dissociate Marxism and sociocriticism.

Despite a certain theoretical ferment (notably at the University of Vincennes around the journal Littérature), sociocriticism, caught between poststructuralist approaches and the sociology of literature inspired by Bourdieu, has really gained an institutional base in France. As Claude Duchet and Isabelle Tournier write, higher-education institutions have preferred approaches inherited from structuralism, that is, 'unifying linguistic-based schemes based on works of diverse origin, construction, history and values'.[17] The meeting of sociocriticism and discourse analysis has certainly made it possible to overcome the unfortunate opposition between 'right-wing' stylistics (Sorbonne) and 'left-wing' sociocriticism (Vincennes). Yet this has come at the cost of a certain methodological watering-down of sociocriticism. This overlapping of sociocriticism with another, more fashionable discipline completed its detachment from Marxism.

16   Barbéris 1990.
17   Duchet and Tournier 1994.

PART 4

Theoretical Hybridisations

∵

CHAPTER 17

Marx and the Marxists, Children of France's Eighteenth Century?

Stéphanie Roza

In France itself, Marx's relationship with the French Enlightenment and the French Revolution has mainly been of interest to historians.[1] Among philosophers, Stathis Kouvelakis seems to be the exception that proves the rule. However, the study of the legacy of the eighteenth-century in Marx's thought presents an important theoretical challenge, both for understanding his approach and that of some of his epigones. We will begin by noting the role that the Enlightenment legacy had as a catalyst for the formation of Marxian theory in the 1840s. Without dwelling for too long on the question of Marx's relationship to French political traditions in the second half of the nineteenth century, we will then turn to the question of the French Marxists' relationship to the Enlightenment and the Revolution, albeit here limiting ourselves to citing a few important figures: Paul Lafargue, Jules Guesde, Louis Althusser and Albert Soboul.

1 Marx, the Enlightenment and the French Revolution in the 1840s

In Germany, the period from the fall of Napoleon in 1815 to the outbreak of the 1848 revolution throughout Europe is known as the *Vormärz*. Such a name indicates that it was seen in retrospect as a time of ferment which prepared future revolutionary events, similar to what had happened in France a few decades earlier. Engels explicitly wrote in 1886 that 'just as in France in the eighteenth century, so in Germany in the nineteenth, a philosophical revolution also ushered in the political collapse'.[2] However, the term *Vormärz* also refers to the conception that some of its actors already had of their own political and philosophical activity and in particular of the mission to which they attached it.

---

1 Bruhat 1966; Mainfroy 1985; Furet 1988; Calvié 1989.
2 Engels 1941, p. 9.

Among the oppositional intellectuals of the time, the most critical of the social and political order were to be found among the Young Hegelians, a milieu to which Marx and Engels belonged up till the mid-1840s. In this decade, the movement as a whole underwent a political radicalisation, assuming an ever-more clearly revolutionary perspective. At the same time, the Young Hegelians made increasingly frequent references to the Enlightenment and the French Revolution. They distanced themselves from their teacher's ambiguous appreciation of the French philosophers of the eighteenth century, as they laid claim to these figures' legacy as against political romanticism. For these young thinkers, the Enlightenment embodied, in a most timeless way, the principle of the autonomy of individual reason and freedom of criticism against all forms of traditional authority: hence why the term was not necessarily reserved for the eighteenth century. Thus, the young Marx, in his 1841 thesis, saw Epicurus as '*der grösste grieschiche Aufklärer*' [the greatest enlightened thinker of Greek antiquity]. Nevertheless, the members of this group continued to be committed to a dialectical perspective: if the French Enlightenment initiated the modern drive towards freedom, it must now be supplanted by new theoretical-political productions that would preserve its spirit, if not its letter.

It was thus necessary, at the very least, to deepen and extend the Enlightenment. Yet, opinions within the Young Hegelian current on the art and the manner of doing so increasingly diverged. Marx's point of view, which asserted itself from 1843–4 onwards, bore the mark of his several-month-long spell in Paris during this same period. It was probably there that he discovered Buchez and Cabet's overviews of the French Revolution, as well as the critical edition of Robespierre's works published by Laponneraye and Carrel in 1840. It was probably also through contact with French neo-Babouvist militants, whose ideas considerably influenced the Paris-based associations of German émigrés, that Marx took up the communist project, which was to remain his lifetime political goal. In a famous line in *The Holy Family*, published in 1845, Marx and Engels presented communism as 'the idea of the new world order', as the result of the 'revolutionary movement': 'the French Revolution gave rise to ideas which led beyond the *ideas* of the entire old world order'.[3] After Marx's death, Engels even considered that 'in its theoretical form, modern socialism originally appears ostensibly as a more logical extension of the principles laid down by the great French philosophers of the eighteenth century'.[4] From this point of view, the Enlightenment and the French Revolution must be considered as

---

3   *MECW*, Vol. 4, p. 119.
4   *MECW*, Vol. 25, p. 16.

a major source of Marxian communism. In any case, they make up the undeniable background to Marx's thinking in these decisive years.

However, in Marx, the idea of the necessary transcendence of the Enlightenment and the Revolution often takes the form of a severe critique, even an indictment, of their legacy. The critique of bourgeois civilisation in all its dimensions (economic, social, legal, political, ideological) often redounds against the thinkers and actors of eighteenth-century France, reduced to the sad role of midwives of a new world characterised by a 'naked, shameless, direct, brutal exploitation' of labour.[5] In the famous *Communist Manifesto* of 1848, we find this highly disparaging statement: 'The ideas of religious liberty and freedom of conscience [proclaimed in the eighteenth century] merely gave expression to the sway of free competition within the domain of knowledge'. The possible progressive and emancipatory aspect of these new freedoms is totally hidden, here. Even more strikingly, the 1844 text *On the Jewish Question* mounts a scathing critique of the *Declaration of the Rights of Man*, a condensed version of the political thought of the French Enlightenment. The Marxian critique is even more remarkable in that it does not focus on the 'bourgeois' *Declaration* of 1789, but rather on the Montagnard Constitution of 1793. Yet even in the 1840s many French socialist and communist militants continued to lay claim to this legacy.

The specificity of Marx's analysis in the *1844 Manuscripts* owed to the radicalism of his determination to *do away with politics*, as an illusory form of emancipation. While recognising – briefly – that political emancipation marks a great step forward, his line of argument proposes such a radical critique of this emancipation that many commentators have overlooked its nuances. Marx was responding to Bruno Bauer, who had argued in an article in the *Deutsche Annalen* of November 1842 that the political emancipation of the Jews, their integration into the constitutional state, would require that they abandon their religious beliefs and practices. In other words, they had to first accomplish a private work of religious disalienation, of internal emancipation, before they could claim political emancipation through access to citizenship. According to Bauer, the state, on the other hand, only offers true political emancipation if it has completely rid itself of any connection with any religion. In Marx's view, this position betrays a profound misunderstanding of the nature of human emancipation, which is reduced to its spiritual dimension alone and is ultimately a matter of individual responsibility. It reveals the illusion that real political emancipation is equivalent to universal human emancipation. *Con-*

---

5   *MECW*, Vol. 6, p. 487.

tra Bauer, Marx opposed the promises of political emancipation to the reality of the modern state. He shared with Bauer the observation that the state is far from living up to expectations, even in France. Nevertheless, he considered these shortcomings insurmountable by politics as such.

The Marxian critique of the modern state and its right is based neither on the legacy of the past nor on an alternative conception of the state. Where Bauer opposed an ideal state to its reality, Marx challenged both the political and the law that emanates from it, in their very principle. This is why 'what Marx criticises in the rights of man is not that they are formal rights, but that they are rights':[6] his entire exposition aimed to show that right, in its principle, is not liberating, and nor can it be. In so doing, the young philosopher sought to go beyond the legacy of Hegel. This latter, it should be remembered, had based himself on an attentive (and well-inclined) reading of the French revolutionary process and its philosophical sources, with Rousseau in the forefront, such as to see in the state the very principle of individual emancipation.

The heart of Marx's 1844 argument is well-known: the modern state cannot put an end to economic warfare (for it is itself the direct product of this warfare), any more than its right can overcome the social defects which result from the unequal property relations of which it is the fundamental guarantor. The rights of man are, like religion before them, only an ideology that provides an idealistic consolation to the members of civil society. Behind the charming appearance of universalism, meant to benefit all, they in fact contribute to the consolidation of the bourgeois organisation of society. By enshrining equality as an equal right to protection by the law, they ultimately reduce it to the equal right to enjoy one's property without fear; by enshrining liberty as the right to separate one's private life and aspirations from those of one's fellow man, they reduce it to the freedom to possess personally what others will not have.

If natural law is a sham, and if political liberty and equality prove powerless to seriously limit oppression, one may wonder what of the French eighteenth-century heritage does survive in Marx, at least on a political level. It is striking how far Marx and Engels's 1845 text *The Holy Family* represented – if not an about-turn – at least a rebalancing in their appreciation of this heritage. This, even to the point that it risks undermining the coherence of their perspetive. Indeed, in their assessment that the Revolution had given rise to the communist idea, Marx and Engels attributed the French revolutionary process a political fertility that had hitherto been absent from their writings, especially Marx's. Here, we find Marx and Engels doffing their hats to the French communist

---

6   Binoche 1989.

movement, acknowledging a debt to it, as against the spirit of Marx's 1844 text *On the Jewish Question*, which seemed partly directed against nostalgists for the Constitution of 1793.

Other texts from this same period do not lessen this ambiguity but accentuate it. While Marx never abandoned the idea that the French Revolution had essentially brought the bourgeoisie to power, he was much more ambivalent in his appreciation of the Terror and of Jacobinism. *The Holy Family* still presented the Jacobins as leaders who made an *illusory* claim to represent the interests of society as a whole, while *in reality* with their *Declaration of the Rights of Man* they represented the interests of the bourgeoisie. On the other hand, certain passages in another manuscript written shortly afterward, *The German Ideology*, provide a significantly different interpretation of the Jacobins' historical role: as compared to the Girondins and Thermidorians, Robespierre and Saint-Just are presented as 'the real representatives of revolutionary power, i.e., of the class which alone was truly revolutionary, the "innumerable" masses',[7] on the grounds that, in the eyes of their adversaries, their political approach violated '*sainte propriété*' – holy property. For Marx and Engels, the *terroristic* measures requisitioning grain and redistributing émigrés' assets among needy republican soldiers or their families thus did temporarily place the Jacobin state at the service of the entire population. Was the Terror thus the path that the bourgeoisie had, paradoxically, taken to impose its interests and its power over the whole of society against the old established order? Or was it, on the contrary, a moment which escaped its control, in which the interests of the 'innumerable mass' temporarily prevailed? Clearly, Marx and Engels's view oscillates between these two poles.

At a philosophical level, the reading of French-Enlightenment materialism which they offered in *The Holy Family* poses the same kind of problems. French socialism and communism are presented as the expression of a 'humanist materialism' rooted in the doctrines of Enlightenment philosophers like Helvétius. Indeed, the materialist idea that education and external circumstances are directly responsible for human behaviour leads to socialism, as it is based on the belief that the key to human emancipation lies in the overhaul of the material conditions of existence. Again, such a development greatly adds to eighteenth-century France's contribution to the genealogy of communism, but does not sit well with some of the more terse formulas in the *Manifesto*. For example, in the 1848 text we find the idea that '[t]he ideas of religious liberty and freedom of conscience [proclaimed in the eighteenth century] merely gave

---

7   *MECW*, Vol. 5, p. 178.

expression to the sway of free competition within the domain of knowledge'.[8] Apparently, according to this quote from the *Communist Manifesto*, this proclamation did not lead to any liberatory consequences.

Hence, two images stand in opposition to each other: on the one hand, the Enlightenment and the Revolution seem to be essentially bourgeois, moreover carrying a dangerous *illusion in the political* which ought to be denounced as a false emancipation. But, on the other hand, they carry within them the theoretical and even political seeds of true human emancipation: both in their (materialist and humanist) theory and in their (revolutionary and terroristic) practice, they bore an audacity and radicalism that were transmitted to the socialist and communist movement of the nineteenth century.

The rest of Marx's theoretical and political evolution does not really offer a synthesis, even in outline, of these two aspects, or a resolution of the paradox. If his allusions to the Enlightenment and the Revolution became rarer after 1848, they remained in the same indeterminacy and oscillated from one pole to the other. They seem illustrative of a difficulty in passing firm judgement on a heritage that was both undeniable and cumbersome. From the 1840s, Marx planned to write a history of the (Jacobin) National Convention: a project he would never complete. This silence seems related to a perplexity that was never overcome, leaving the Marxist tradition with a thorny theoretical and political problem.

2   The French Marxists Faced with the Enlightenment and the Revolution: Paul Lafargue and Jules Guesde

Marx's son-in-law Paul Lafargue was one of the first introducers of Marxism in France. At the beginning of 1879, he began his correspondence with Jules Guesde, a former anarchist who had converted to Marxism: the two men soon initiated an ideological collaboration aimed at creating a workers' party distinct from the traditional bourgeois and republican formations. This undertaking led to the creation of the Parti Ouvrier at the end of September 1882, more than twenty years before the founding of the French Section of the Workers' International (SFIO) in 1905, in which the so-called 'Guesdist' current, inspired by Marxism, rubbed shoulders with more republican socialists such as Jean Jaurès. Lafargue's relationship with the Enlightenment was political and militant, rather than theoretical, in character: he was above all a pamphleteer.

---

8   *MECW*, Vol. 6, p. 503.

In 1880, his *Right to Be Lazy* was serialised in the newspaper *L'Égalité*. This famous pamphlet contains a few allusions to the Enlightenment and the Revolution, showing that Lafargue followed in Marx's footsteps – and inherited his ambiguities. In his dedication to his comrades in at *L'Égalité*, Lafargue writes: 'Let us raise the flag of the materialists of the Renaissance and the eighteenth century, let us proclaim in the face of all the cockroaches ... that the earth must no longer be a valley of tears for the working class'.[9] Here, eighteenth-century materialism is praised as a theory that rehabilitates human passions, as against the reactionary and Christian mortification of the flesh.

On the other hand, a few pages further on, we can read this comment about the situation of French workers in the 1840s: 'There existed in France, which had made the Revolution of '89, which had proclaimed the pompous Rights of Man, "factories where the day was sixteen hours long ..." – oh, miserable abortion of the revolutionary principles of the bourgeoisie!' Here, Lafargue seems to enter into a non-Marxian critique of the rights of man: here, it is less a matter of criticising them in principle, as rights, than of denouncing – as was more classically the case in the French socialist movement of the nineteenth century – their hypocrisy, their obsolescence in a bourgeois society which does not hesitate to trample on them in order to preserve its profit rates. In such a situation, it was still possible to demand that they genuinely be applied, as most French socialists and communists did at the time.

This is no longer the case, however, towards the end of the text, when the author urges the working class to rise up 'not to claim the *Rights of Man*, which are only the rights of capitalist exploitation, not to claim the *Right to Work*, which is only the right to misery, but to forge an iron law, forbidding every man to work more than three hours a day'. The characterisation of the Rights of Man as 'capitalist' rights runs closer to Marx's analysis. Unlike most other socialists, Lafargue refused to call for their real implementation. Moreover, the condemnation of these rights is accompanied by the condemnation of the right to work, which had been one of the major demands of the republican socialist movement since Babeuf. It seems that Lafargue was here trying to distance himself from the entire galaxy of French republicanism, including its socialist fringe.

In 1883, the Marxist activist, at that time imprisoned for his propaganda activities, planned to write a history of the French Revolution, though he like his father-in-law before him would abandon this project. Did he do so for the same reasons? In any case, the result of this initial project was an article, co-

---

9 Lafargue 2009.

written with Guesde and entitled 'Essai critique sur la Révolution française du xviiie siècle' ('Critical Essay on the French Revolution of the 18th Century', which was not published until twenty years later, in 1903, in Georges Sorel's *Études socialistes*). Written in the Republic's jails, at a time when the regime was still being consolidated, it even more clearly bears the mark of a desire for ideological distinction from the Republican camp.

For this reason, its viewpoint on the Revolution and its historiography is eminently critical. Lafargue and Guesde began by repudiating almost all the writings on the French Revolution produced up till then, to their eyes incapable of giving an account of its most characteristic feature: the multi-front class struggle that played out between the bourgeoisie, the aristocracy and the 'common people'. According to the authors, the bourgeoisie only 'abused' the populace through the exasperating 'phraseology of freedom, equality and brotherhood' aimed at gaining its support in its own selfish struggle against the power of the old nobility. This one-sided reading of the process tended to present the whole of revolutionary politics as a Machiavellian plot to first harness and channel popular energy and then violently repress it afterwards. Within this radical perspective, excessive claims are peppered throughout this short text, for instance stating that the rights of man 'have resulted in a new slavery of mankind, man, woman and child, worse than the old one'. Once again, it would be risky to see this as the result of a long meditation on the Revolution, as in the case of Jaurès, or as a point of view based on an in-depth knowledge of events. In these terse statements, we see above all the needs of a strategic positioning in which historical truth is far from the main concern.

3   The French Marxists, the Enlightenment and the Revolution: Louis
       Althusser and Albert Soboul

From the 1930s onwards, the internal ideological evolution of the French Communist Party (PCF) led to a reconciliation between Marxism and the Enlightenment tradition. Thus, with a view to popular education, from 1950 to 1981 Éditions sociales pursued a project of republishing classics of world literature, political and scientific thought, including many texts from eighteenth-century France. In the 'Les Classiques du peuple' collection, the substantial introductions to these texts – written by Communist intellectuals or others close to the party – most often express a deep attachment to this heritage, manifesting itself in more or less successful attempts to develop and illustrate the rather terse remarks on Diderot, Rousseau, Robespierre, Babeuf, and so on to be found in Marx and Engels's writings. The relationship to the Enlightenment was less polemical, here, than it had been in Lafargue and Guesde, and more concerned with philological accuracy. The authors sought to flesh out Marxist theory by giving greater substance to their analyses of the French eighteenth century. The postwar intellectuals Althusser and Soboul, professor of philosophy at the École Normale Supérieure and professor of the history of the Revolution at the Sorbonne respectively, in their own way embodied this new Marxist view of the eighteenth century. The philosopher and the historian took two very different approaches to the question, and ultimately focused on quite distinct objects of study, for one addressed the Enlightenment and the other of the Revolution. But it was Soboul who contributed most elements for resolving the paradoxes Marx had bequeathed.

With the notable exception of Rousseau, and to a lesser extent Montesquieu, French authors from the Enlightenment tradition did not feature among the philosophers studied by Althusser, who attributed them a much less important place than Spinoza or Machiavelli, let alone Marx. Particularly strikingly, Althusser never wrote anything specifically about Diderot, and devoted little more than a radio interview to Helvetius. Moreover, the French Revolution is conspicuous by its near-total absence from his field of reflection. The low importance of the eighteenth century in his work is especially surprising given that at the same time many intellectuals who were PCF members, like Althusser, or at least fellow travellers, attached such great significance to this heritage: for instance, Jean Varloot, Anne Ubersfeld, and Claude Mazauric among others. This relative silence on Althusser's part should probably be seen as a field effect, as philosophical studies in France have for a long time respected a radical division between 'prominent authors' and 'minores', preventing them from taking an interest in those classified in the second category. Among the authors of eighteenth-century France, only Rousseau, followed by Montesquieu, escaped such an academic downgrading, because they were considered great philosophers: it is thus no accident that only these two really held Althusser's attention.

But it seems that, in the field of Marxist interpretation of the Enlightenment, Althusser's analyses were not the most innovative. Ultimately, when he addresses Rousseau, Montesquieu and a few others, he only develops – albeit often in a finegrained and convincing way – the intuitions and hypotheses more summarily formulated by Marx a century earlier. In his interview devoted to the question of education in Helvetius, for example, Althusser shows that the philosopher's profound originality lies above all in the idea of an absolute 'plasticity' of man, who is born without any determination and who is therefore entirely produced by the environment in which chance would have him be born and grow up. This is exactly the idea that inspired Marx and Engels's positive appreciation of the humanist materialism of Helvetius, who for this very reason is considered an inspiration for modern socialism.

In the same way, Althusser's study of Montesquieu *in La Politique et l'Histoire* appears to be a way of proving and illustrating one of the fundamental hypotheses of historical materialism: namely, the explanation of ideologies in terms of the social interests and positions of their sycophants. The author shows how the views expounded in *De l'esprit des lois* reveal the class interests of the former *président à mortier* of the Bordeaux Parliament, a prominent member of the nobility of the robe. In particular, the famous theory of the balance among the legislative, the executive and judiciary is analysed through the prism of how it in fact favours the nobility in the distribution of political powers.

Althusser's 1965–6 lectures on the 'discrepancies' in Rousseau's *Social Contract*, later turned into an article, fit in line with the same theoretical perspective, although his analyses here are not limited to it. Althusser mounts a careful study of Rousseau's notions of contract, alienation, and general will, showing their internal contradictions, which he ultimately attributes to the author's denial of the primordial existence of class interests. For Althusser, the substitution of the myths of the general interest, on the one hand, and the particular interests of individuals, on the other, for the reality of the interest of social groups, betrays the ideological nature of Rousseau's political theory. In his view, Rousseau obscures the existence of social classes struggling for their interests as he defines the objective of politics as the promotion of the general interest over individual interests. This denial of the class struggle is said to show the hidden articulation between his theory and 'the juridical ideology of the society in which Rousseau lives'.[10] This is a surprising formula, insofar as, for Marx, juridical ideology corresponds to the superstructure of bourgeois society since 1789, and not to the *ancien régime* of 1762. So, could it be that Althusser was here amalgamating Rousseau and his political heirs, the Jacobins? The fact remains that his criticism largely overlaps with that of Marx's critique of the men responsible for the Terror: the 'flight into ideology' to resolve social contradictions and the 'regression' to archaic forms of economic egalitarianism that Althusser attributes to Rousseau are criticisms that Marx also aims against Robespierre, Saint-Just and their supporters.

Althusser's analyses of Enlightenment authors are thus, in many ways, a defence and illustration of Marxian hypotheses on the eighteenth century. The

---

10   Althusser 2006.

same cannot be said of Albert Soboul's historical work on the French Revolution, or more precisely on the popular movement of Year II, the subject of his doctoral dissertation in 1958. Soboul was the first to attempt an in-depth and systematic class analysis of the Parisian revolutionary movement under the Terror. He here implicitly built on the insights of the libertarian communist Daniel Guérin on the contradictions at work within Jacobinism – a movement that Guérin characterised as popular at its base and petty-bourgeois at its head.

Soboul's works shed light on the diverse aspirations of the various protagonists of the 'Jacobin party': egalitarian utopias, the republic of virtue, radical agrarian reform... They played a pioneering role in the development of a new approach to the French Revolution, which several other historians (notably Maurice Dommanget, Michel Vovelle, Florence Gauthier, Françoise Brunel, and Claude Mazauric in France, but also Walter Markov in the German Democratic Republic) showed the internal tendency for the sans-culotte movement in the big cities and the peasant movement in the countryside to go beyond purely bourgeois objectives.

The concept of a 'bourgeois revolution with popular support' (Michel Vovelle) thus made it possible to account theoretically for the originality of the French revolutionary path. It also allowed for the introduction of the idea that the French Revolution had been, in certain respects, a 'permanent revolution' in the Marxian sense; namely, that it had been the bearer of a dynamic that tended to carry it – beyond the limits imposed by its bourgeois leadership – towards egalitarianism or socialism. In this sense, these historians' work was undeniably the bearer of a new *Marxist* interpretation of the great revolution, taking on and seeking to overcome the difficult problems not resolved by Marx himself.

4   An Ambiguous Relationship

The relationship of Marx and then of the Marxists to eighteenth-century France is fraught with theoretical and political problems. For the Germans of the nineteenth century, this relationship was determined by their consciousness of the urgency of the German revolution, be it conceived as bourgeois or proletarian. For many people at the time, this dilemma translated into the question: should we start 1789 all over again – or perhaps 1793? Subsequently, among the French Marxists, analysis of the eighteenth century was linked to their relationship with the Republic, definitively established in 1871. Two currents emerged within the Socialist and then Communist movement, which continue to this day: a majority tradition which followed in the footsteps of Jean Jaurès and claimed the heritage of Jacobinism as compatible with Marxism; and a minority tendency which rejected republicanism in the name of the class struggle, being much more critical of the actors of the century of the Enlightenment and of the 'bourgeois' Revolution.

CHAPTER 18

Marxism and Phenomenology in France

Alexandre Feron

There would appear to be a clear opposition between historical materialism, which stems from the thought of Marx and Engels, and phenomenology, the philosophical current founded by Edmund Husserl. While the former set itself the methodological motto of going beyond the necessarily illusory standpoint of consciousness in order to discover how the individual is conditioned by the objective world, the latter's motto is to stick to 'the things themselves' as they appear, in order to find that the world is relative to consciousness. If historical materialism seeks to really transform the world, phenomenology aims at nothing more than revealing it as it manifests itself and interpreting it in its sense of being. Yet, from the late 1920s until today, there have been countless attempts to articulate these two philosophical traditions. Such a theoretical project was particularly successful in France, especially between the end of World War II and the early 1960s, and can be seen as the core of the first original Marxist philosophical current in France. Until then, there had in fact been few Marxist philosophers in France and their theoretical undertakings were either very isolated (as in the case of the Philosophie group) or simply a reprise of the Marxist vulgate of the Second and Third Internationals.

By 'phenomenology' we refer to a philosophical school that originated with Husserl, which proposes not simply to describe 'phenomena' (what appears), but to bring to light the conditions of possibility of phenomena (the invariant structures or the logic proper to what appears). Phenomenology conceived in this way should not, however, be confused with existentialism. While the two terms were often used as synonyms in the immediate postwar period and French existentialism (mainly represented by Jean-Paul Sartre, Maurice Merleau-Ponty and Simone de Beauvoir) explicitly asserted its descendance from Husserl's philosophy, the existential phenomenology which these latter proposed has its own originality and seeks to critique and go beyond the shortcomings of Husserl's thought. They are not so much interested by the universal structures of consciousness as by the concrete existence of individuals, in its singular, social and historical dimensions. They thus also draw their inspiration from the various currents called the 'philosophy of existence': on the one hand, the philosophical ramifications that have historically stemmed from German idealism (Hegel, Kierkegaard, the young Marx) and, on the other hand, the branch of contemporary German philosophy represented by the works of Jaspers or Heidegger.

The specificity of the French endeavour to articulate Marxism and phenomenology lies in the fact that it is not a simple intraphilosophical attempt to synthesise different philosophical traditions, but a project that puts into question the very status of philosophy and explicitly sets itself a political ambition (in connection with the communist or revolutionary project). Indeed, Marxism affirms the need to go beyond a strictly philosophical mode of discourse in order to confront not only scientific discursiveness (that of political economy or history), but also the practical project of transforming the world. Thus, the various thinkers trained in the phenomenological tradition who seek to articulate phenomenology with Marxism are led to transform their own relationship to philosophy and strive to propose a philosophical practice that takes into account the Marxist demand to transcend philosophy. The articulation between Marxism and phenomenology is therefore not only an attempt at theoretical hybridisation, but also a hybridisation between different types of discourse or rationalities (philosophical exposition, discourse with scientific pretensions, political intervention, and so on) – which contributed to the fertility and dynamism of this Marxist current, particularly between the Liberation and the early 1960s.

Seeking to retrace the history of this theoretical programme, we will first look into its genesis. We will do so by turning back to the particular context of French philosophy in the 1930s and the particular conditions of the simultaneous importing of both Marxism and phenomenology into the French philosophical field. We will then present the great attempts at synthesis proposed during the period of Liberation, when this theoretical project enjoyed its greatest success. We will see how the Cold War profoundly transformed the structuring of the philosophical field that emerged from the Resistance and led to new attempts at articulation that also sought to take into account recent developments in the human sciences. Finally, we will discuss the new directions that the project of hybridising phenomenology and Marxism took after 1960.

1   The Genesis of a Theoretical Project

Before it became a philosophical fashion in 1945, the project of synthesising Marxism and phenomenology was the work of a very small group of young thinkers. It first took form over the very end of the 1930s and the beginning of the 1940s, before spreading to the whole intellectual field after Liberation.

Maurice Merleau-Ponty (1908–61) was its central figure. At the time, he was an *agrégé-répétiteur*[1] at the École Normale Supérieure and came into contact with young philosophers (François Cuzin, Jean-Toussaint Desanti, Yvonne Picard, Pierre Hervé, at the end of the 1930s; Trần Đức Thảo from 1941 onwards). Like him, the had become politically radicalised over the 1930s (most of them were close to Trotskyism, then joined the Communist Party during the Occupation). He introduced them to Husserl's phenomenology, which was little known in France at the time (there was only one text available in French, the *Cartesian Meditations*); but these young thinkers all felt a deep dissatisfaction with the Husserlian project and, more generally, with the classic philosophical posture of standing above all other domains (science and politics). Conversely, in Marxism they found a type of discourse capable of overcoming Husserl's theoretical and practical impasses by getting to grips with the political and historical dimension of existence, while striving to integrate a discourse with scientific pretensions. However, they considered that Marxism lacks a solid philosophical foundation – something that Husserlian phenomenology could provide. This would thus allow for a fruitful encounter between Marxism and phenomenology, with each able to bring the other a missing dimension.

The genesis of such a project can only be fully understood when placed in the historical context of the 1920s and 1930s. In the first place, the historical events of the interwar period led the younger generations of philosophers to violently reject the neo-Kantian and rationalist philosophy that had hitherto been dominant (and politically linked to the Parti Radical-Socialiste). They instead searched for a way of thinking that would be able to grasp 'concrete' historical existence (according to the formula that was a watchword of this generation). This need for philosophical renewal was partly satisfied by various theoretical imports, stemming more or less directly from the Russian revolution. Most important among these was the publication of the texts of the young Marx in Germany and the USSR at the beginnings of the 1930s (the *1844 Manuscripts*, *The German Ideology*), stirring a deep renewal in the possible conceptions of Marxism. Rapidly translated into French (by Costes), these texts enthused the new generation, who thought they had found an existentialist Marx who even anticipated phenomenology in many respects. Secondly, the articulation between Marxism and phenomenology benefited from what is usually called the 'Hegelian revival' of the 1930s: Hegel's *Phenomenology of Spirit*, which Alexandre Kojève and Alexandre Koyré (two Russian émigrés) commented on in their courses at the École pratique des hautes études, constituted an essen-

---

1   A position roughly equivalent to teaching fellows in the Anglophone countries.

tial theoretical mediation connecting Husserl and Marx. Finally, a third decisive factor owed to the fate of Husserlian phenomenology in Germany. Having
become 'stateless' (with the exclusion of Husserl and his disciples from the
academy under the Nazi regime, and the exfiltration of Husserl's unpublished
manuscripts to Belgium in 1938) phenomenology was 'naturalised' as French
during the Occupation, as young French philosophers (most importantly Jean
Cavaillès, Maurice Merleau-Ponty and Trần Đức Thảo) devoted their attentions
to the unpublished manuscripts deposited at the University of Leuven. The
appropriation of Husserl's work during the Occupation, much like the appropriation of Marx's work, was not that of just any other author in the philosophical tradition, but that of a forbidden author.

2   The 'Existentialist' Synthesis between Phenomenology and
         Marxism

The moment of Liberation is often associated with the fashion for existentialism: yet, in reality, existentialism's success is inseparable from Marxism's own,
the debate between the two (which flourished in countless conferences, discussions and issues of journals), as well as the attempts at synthesis between
Marxism and phenomenology which proliferated in this period. Behind the two
front-rank figures Jean-Paul Sartre (1905–80) and especially Maurice Merleau-
Ponty (associated with *Les Temps modernes*), we find a very large number of
young thinkers who fit into this perspective (Jean Beaufret, Ferdinand Alquié,
Jean Domarchi, Trần Đức Thảo...).

    At the time, Husserl's work (like that of Heidegger) was barely known in
France, meaning that the discussions mainly concerned the possibility of articulating Sartrean existentialism (as set out in *Being and Nothingness* and popularised in 'Existentialism is a Humanism') with Marxism. However, if Raymond Aron proclaimed the fundamental incompatibility between existentialism (as a philosophy of freedom) and Marxism (as a deterministic philosophy), Sartre, instead sought to take up and refound the Marxist/commun-
ist revolutionary project on the basis of existentialist philosophy. Thus, in
'Materialism and Revolution', he violently rejected Marxist philosophy and
dialectical materialism, instead proposing that the Communists should con-
vert to existentialism, the only philosophy capable of providing a foundation for their militant revolutionary practice.[2] Such a position could not but

---

2   Sartre 2003.

draw the hostility of the Communists, who launched a vast ideological struggle against Sartrean existentialism.

Merleau-Ponty, the 'political director' of *Les Temps modernes*, took a quite different position. While most of his close associates were members of the Communist Party, Merleau-Ponty sought to promote what he called 'Western communism'. In his view, this was a Marxist movement that would succeed in recovering the true meaning of Marxism (that of Marx and Lenin), against the Stalinist deformation, and which would be autonomous from the USSR from both a political and theoretical point of view. Such a 'Western Marxism' (according to a formula he uses in *Adventures of the Dialectic*) would find its inspiration in György Lukács's *History and Class Consciousness* – with whom Merleau-Ponty exchanged views in the immediate postwar period and whose work he sought to make known in France. The 'Lukácsian' synthesis between Marxism and phenomenology that Merleau-Ponty proposed was expounded in a series of articles collected in *Humanism and Terror* (1947) and *Sense and Non-Sense* (first published in 1948). The specificity of Merleau-Ponty's approach lay in the importance that he attached to Marxism as a political analysis, that is, to the analyses of Lenin and Trotsky in particular. Indeed, according to Merleau-Ponty, phenomenology made it possible to theorise the specificity of Marxist situational analysis, and in particular its perceptive dimension: only a phenomenology of perception can thus account for the Marxist practice of 'concrete analysis of the concrete situation'.

One of the merits of Marxist phenomenology is the importance that it attributes to the description of subjective perception and situational experience, thus proposing a rigorous conception of ideology (which Marxism supposedly only sketched out). This is notably what the young Vietnamese philosopher Trần Đức Thảo (1917–93) – at the time close to Merleau-Ponty and involved in the struggle for Indochina's independence – sought to do in the 1940s. In 'Sur l'Indochine', he mobilised a theoretical framework inspired by Husserl's *Krisis* to show that the economic and social structure of colonialism led the French and the Indochinese to have two radically alien conceptions of the world, which rendered impossible any conciliation between the two sides. The attention paid to the lived dimension of existence thus enabled the existentialists and *Les Temps modernes* in particular to be at the cutting edge of many issues that were then often neglected by orthodox Marxism: anti-colonial struggles, antisemitism, racism, but also abortion and the situation of homosexuals.

The postwar period saw a considerable flurry of attempts to reach a synthesis between existentialism and Marxism. Such a theoretical perspective corresponded to the desire to translate the syncretic hopes of the Resistance onto a theoretical level. But these attempts were still very often based on juxtaposing quotations extracted from their context, taking them from works that remained poorly known (because of the absence of translations or the only few commentaries that existed). These first theoretical syntheses were soon reworked according to historical events, but also with regard to the internal difficulties encountered.

3   Marxism and Phenomenology at the Heart of the Cold War

The onset of the Cold War directly challenged the existentialist synthesis between phenomenology and Marxism. The sharpness of political cleavages had an immediate influence on the intellectual and philosophical field, where everyone was commanded to take a stand for Washington or Moscow. Rejecting such an alternative, the proponents of Marxist existentialism sought to participate in attempts to find 'third ways' between liberalism and communism. Sartre was particularly active in the formation of the Rassemblement démocratique révolutionnaire (RDR), which was both revolutionary and non-Communist. The failure of these experiments at the end of the 1940s revealed both the extent of their isolation and the impossibility of translating their theoretical synthesis into political action.

The crisis that Marxist existentialism now underwent led the authors to reinvent their thought and to transform the relationship that they sought to establish between Marxism and phenomenology. This an evolution that often goes overlooked, when the thought of Sartre or of Merleau-Ponty is reduced to that which they proposed in 1945. It was also a mutation that worked in two directions: on the one hand, by seeking to integrate the human sciences, and in particular the nascent structuralism of Claude Lévi-Strauss or Roman Jakobson, into the synthesis of Marxism and phenomenology; on the other hand, by proposing a critical analysis of Marxism with the aim of developing an understanding of how Marxism had 'become Stalinist' and the political regime that emerged from the Russian revolution. These two axes came together in the new desire to give a proper place to approaches in terms of structures – though, unlike the structuralism of the 1960s, the aim here was to study structures from the point of view of their genesis.

The emblematic work of this period was *Phenomenologie and matérialisme dialectique*,[3] which condensed a large part of the theoretical and practical issues of this era, and played a decisive role in the critique of the postwar exist-

---

3   Trần Đức Thảo 1951.

entialist synthesis. As against the highly individual appropriations of Husserl to be found in Sartre or Merleau-Ponty, Trần Đức Thảo offered a rigorous presentation of the evolution of the thought of the founder of phenomenology, which still today remains one of the best introductions to his work. In it, he clearly distinguished Husserl's phenomenology from French existentialism. Trần Đức Thảo's interest lay in the 'genetic' phenomenology of the later Husserl (who is said to have arrived 'at the threshold of dialectical materialism'), whose analyses he sought to integrate into a dialectical-materialist framework influenced by Engels's later work (*Dialectics of Nature, Anti-Dühring*). The book attempts to articulate phenomenological analyses of subjectivity with behaviour structures in living beings, in order to develop a dialectical-materialist psychology. Phenomenological and Marxist conceptualities are thus mobilised in order to integrate analyses from the human sciences (sociology, anthropology) or experimental sciences (biology, psychology), and to understand the genesis of structures (be they biological, social or historical). Trần Đức Thảo left France for North Vietnam in 1952, but his work, throughout the 1950s, influenced the formation of the generation of philosophers who dominated the subsequent decades (Michel Foucault, Jacques Derrida, Louis Althusser, and so on).

When tracing the evolution of existentialist thinkers during the 1940s, the crucial importance of *The Second Sex*[4] often goes overlooked. Although it appears to take up Sartre's existentialist conceptual framework, Simone de Beauvoir (1908–86) actually transforms Sartre's concepts in order to incline them toward Marxism, in a manner in many ways similar to Merleau-Ponty. Beauvoir thus anticipated the important inflection of Sartre's thought that led him to the *Critique of Dialectical Reason*. Whereas Sartre had hitherto insisted above all on the freedom and responsibility of the individual, Beauvoir showed that the existentialist framework can account for a fundamental alienation that is played out from early childhood with the child's internalisation of parental projects (themselves conditioned by the surrounding society). If, in the following years, Merleau-Ponty (in his lectures at the Sorbonne) and Sartre (especially in *Saint Genet, Actor and Martyr*) so strongly emphasised the importance of childhood as a moment of inscription of the individual in society (through the mediation of the family), this largely owed to De Beauvoir's positive influence. It was also De Beauvoir who invited them to read Lévi-Strauss's existentialist theory – which she reviewed in *Les Temps modernes* in 1949 and discussed in *The Second Sex* – and who opened up existentialism to a reflection on anthro-

---

4 De Beauvoir 2015.

pology, notably by discussing the theses set out by Engels in *The Origin of the Family, Private Property and the State.*

Throughout the 1940s and 1950s, Merleau-Ponty continued his dialogue with Marxism, seeking to rethink in depth the way in which Marxism and phenomenology could be articulated. Influenced by his reading of studies of linguistics (Ferdinand de Saussure, Roman Jakobson), and of Lévi-Strauss, Merleau-Ponty henceforth strove to articulate these two currents by way of concepts coming from the philosophy of language. However, he gradually abandoned the hope of achieving a 'Western communism' and, from the mid-1950s onwards, established an almost exclusively philosophical relationship with Marxism. By meditating on Marx's work as the oeuvre of a 'classic author', Merleau-Ponty brought to light (in *Adventures of the Dialectic* and in his various lectures at the Collège de France) an ontological 'unthought' of Marx – that of the lack of elaboration of the concepts of 'matter' (or 'nature') and 'dialectic'. The dialectical ontology that Merleau-Ponty endeavoured to theorise in the latter part of the 1950s sought to respond to these difficulties, which originated in his reading of Marx – an undertaking that was, however, brutally interrupted by the philosopher's death in May 1961. Merleau-Ponty's last word would thus remain his preface to *Signes*, a text in which he acknowledged the split that would henceforth exist between philosophy and politics: for him, all that was left was to read Marx as a philosopher, while abandoning the political and historical project.

This was precisely what Sartre refused to do. Throughout the 1950s, he sought to produce a critical analysis of Marxism, in order to bring it out of the deep crisis into which Stalinism, he said, had immersed it. The *Critique of Dialectical Reason*, a true masterpiece of the project for an articulation between phenomenology and Marxism, thus claimed to provide the philosophical extension of the vast movement of de-Stalinisation launched on a worldwide scale in 1956. This work condensed all the reflection carried out since 1945 by proposing what Sartre called a 'structural and historical anthropology', a concept developed in parallel with Levi-Straussian structural anthropology and whose proximity to the latter certainly helped to stretch the hitherto friendly relations between the two intellectuals. The aim was to integrate the results at which phenomenology and existentialism had arrived into a broader Marxist framework, while in return founding Marxism on a *praxis* to which existentialism provided the key. The *Critique of Dialectical Reason*, however, never enjoyed a reception commensurate with its ambitions. The beginning of the 1960s marked an abrupt turn in the intellectual and philosophical conjuncture. While the intellectual field had been dominated since 1945 by the project of articulating Marxism and phenomenology, it was now the project of articulating Marxism and structuralism that prevailed, thus making the *Critique of Dialectical Reason* appear already outdated.

4   Heideggerian-Marxist Explorations After 1960

The beginning of the 1960s saw a profound restructuring of the philosophical field, which led to the marginalisation of the project of articulation between phenomenology and Marxism. Henceforth, Marxism was dominated by the structural programme put forward by Althusserism, whereas French phenomenology turned away from Marxism and embarked upon what Dominique Janicaud called its 'theological turn'. But the marginalisation of the project did not mean its outright disappearance. The main heir of the postwar theoretical project was doubtless Jean-Toussaint Desanti (1914–2002): he proposed a critique of the Husserlian phenomenological project,[5] while seeking to develop a theory of the social that would tie together phenomenological and Marxist inspirations, starting from the concept of *praxis*. This undertaking, which also aimed to give a proper place for scientific and especially mathematical discourse, was strongly inspired by the Sartrean conceptuality of *Critique of Dialectical Reason*.[6] However, Desanti's theoretical project appears an exception in the post-1960 philosophical landscape, in its desire to maintain connections between philosophical, scientific and political discourse.

The attempts to hybridise Marxism and phenomenology that developed in these years were characterised by two major shifts compared to the previous period. In the first place, if Marxism had hitherto been set in relation with Husserlian phenomenology, it was now Heidegger's philosophy that predominated, and in particular his 'second philosophy', developed from the mid-1930s onward. The articulation between Marxism and phenomenology was increasingly anchored in ontological-type reflection and proposed an understanding of the modern world that puts Marxism in relation with the Heideggerian analysis of technique. This is what we especially find among the thinkers around the journal *Arguments*, who seek to produce a critique of Stalinism by revisiting Marxism, in order to allow it to account for the contemporary world. Kostas Axelos (1924–2010), who belonged to the small circle of Heideggerians gathered around Jean Beaufret, tried to convince the others (Edgar Morin, Patrick Fougeyrollas, François Châtelet, Henri Lefebvre) that this new form

---

5   Desanti 1994.
6   Desanti 2008a, 2008b.

of Marxism had to be articulated with Heidegger's thought. Giving a privileged importance to the thought of the very young Marx (especially his doctoral thesis), Axelos combined the idea of a 'becoming-world of philosophy' with the Lukácsian concept of totality and the Heideggerian concept of Being, to develop what he calls a 'planetary thought'. Axelos then played an important role in the reconfiguration of the Marxist philosophical landscape in France, both through the journal *Arguments* and through the 'Arguments' collection that he directed at Éditions de Minuit – connections in the publishing world that made it possible to disseminate not only the texts of the thinkers who wrote for the journal, but also numerous translations of Marxist (Lukács, Trotsky, Carr, Wittfogel, Korsch, Marcuse, Broué, Hilferding, Adorno) or phenomenological texts (Fink, Beaufret, Heidegger). Starting from a completely different perspective, Gérard Granel (1930–2000) was also part of this Heideggerian-Marxist movement: rejecting the Althusserian epistemological break, Granel argues that the unity of Marx's thought (from the *1844 Manuscripts* to *Capital*) is to be found in his ontology, which, he claims, succeeded in discovering that the true sense of Being is to be found in production.[7] The research of Jean Vioulac and Franck Fischbach in the 2000s was also situated in this Heideggerian perspective.

The second shift concerned the ever-less political character of philosophical elaborations, thus confirming the Merleau-Pontyian diagnosis of a split between philosophy and politics. Although these works did sometimes have a political intention, the mode of intervention and writing was now strictly philosophical and addressed to philosophers, unlike in the cases of Sartre or Merleau-Ponty (in the immediate postwar period) who sought to give an immediately political dimension to their texts. This refocusing on philosophy can be seen in particular in the importance taken on by reflection on the very status of philosophy – a central theme of the *Arguments* group's research – as Axelos's rewriting of the 11th thesis on Feuerbach testifies: 'The technicians only transform the world in different ways ... the important thing is now to *think* it and to interpret the transformations in depth, by grasping the difference that unites being with nothingness'.[8] This philosophical inflection made attempts at synthesis between the two traditions increasingly personal and idiosyncratic. The reading proposed by Michel Henry (1922–2002) was symptomatic of the now-open possibility a non-political appropriation of Marx. Right from the preface of his 1976 book, he proposed to put the whole of Marxism (as a political appropriation of Marx) in parentheses, to make Marx a thinker of life (and subjectiv-

---

7   Granel 2014.
8   Axelos 1958.

ity) and even a Christian thinker. His original reading of the whole of Marx's oeuvre is thus a projection of his personal phenomenology onto Marx's texts. The approach of Paul Ricoeur (1913–2005), a philosopher close to the journal *Esprit*, was much more academic: although he never wrote a book on Marx, he took part in the international workshops held in Dubrovnik from 1975 to 1978 on the subject of 'Phenomenology and Marxism' and devoted many articles to the articulation between the two currents of thought,[9] as well as a year-long course on the question of ideology. Jacques Derrida (1930–2004) was also part of this constellation: strongly influenced in the 1950s by the texts of Trần Đức Thảo, throughout his life he pursued an underground dialogue with phenomenology and Marxism, as evidenced by his ENS lectures, *Specters of Marx* and a number of interviews.[10] After 1960, the project of hybridisation between phenomenology and Marxism continued to nourish research, but this research was now almost exclusively in the realm of philosophical discourse and had largely abandoned the initial ambition to go beyond philosophy in contact with Marxism.

5   The First Original Marxist Current in France

For nearly twenty years, the project of articulating Marxism and phenomenology had a structuring role in the intellectual and philosophical field. It gave rise to what can be considered the first original Marxist current in France (before passing the baton to the Althusserian current) and was a driving force behind one of the most fruitful periods of French philosophy in the twentieth century. Its originality lay in the fact that it was not a strictly philosophical movement, but rather in its desire to go beyond and transform the conception of philosophy, particularly by entering the political domain. Refusing to become 'party philosophers' (who merely relayed a political line), the proponents of a synthesis between Marxism and phenomenology nevertheless sought to give a political, even militant, dimension to their theoretical endeavour. This is what distinguished this first great sequence from the attempts at synthesis between Marxism and phenomenology that continued after 1960. Thus, after having been a fundamentally important cultural movement, Marxist phenomenology henceforth became a relatively limited current. Even if the project of hybridising these two traditions of thought can still inspire fruitful and stimulating research, these remain singular and strictly philosophical undertakings.

---

9   Ricoeur 1997.
10   Derrida 1994, 2011.

CHAPTER 19

The Structuralist Marx

Frédérique Matonti

In 1965, two works by the philosopher Louis Althusser were published by Éditions Maspero: *For Marx*, a collection of his articles, and *Reading Capital*, a collective volume devoted to Marx's work. These texts are part of a series of publications which were issued in short succession: Roman Jakobson's *Essais de linguistique générale* (Minuit, 1963), *The Raw and the Cooked*, the first volume of Claude Lévi-Strauss's *Mythologiques* (Plon, 1964), Michel Foucault's *Words and Things* (Gallimard, 1966), the *Writings* of Jacques Lacan (Seuil, 1966), *Criticism and Truth* by Roland Barthes (Seuil, 1966), *Théorie de la littérature*, made up of texts by the Russian formalists collected by Tzvetan Todorov and presented as inspiring structural linguistics (Seuil, 1966) and *Figures* by Gérard Genette (Seuil, 1966). These texts by Althusser were also part of a series of political-intellectual disputes involving the philosopher, within the French Communist Party (PCF).

These two series have one thing in common: structuralism, or at least what was labelled structuralist by the critical reception in academic and intellectual journals, in the rapidly expanding news magazines and among readers, whose educational level had never been higher. Yet, among part of the Communist intellectuals and the PCF leadership group, this current and its authors were perceived as contradicting Marxism. This was, of course, not the first time that they had spoken out against a theoretical current liable to compete with Marxism, or more precisely with the French interpretation of Marxism, which they intended to monopolise. Since the Liberation, existentialism had been the object of a comparable offensive: far from the humanism it claimed to be, existentialism was seen as one of the reactionary bourgeoisie's Trojan horses in its bid to undermine Marxism. Unlike Sartre's writings, the so-called 'structuralist' theoretical hybrids seduced even the ranks of Communist intellectuals, starting with Althusser and his students at the École Normale Supérieure, many of whom were members of the Union of Communist Students (UEC) and editors of two journals, the *Cahiers Marxistes-Léninistes* and the *Cahiers pour l'Analyse*.

Marx was not at the heart of the pantheon of authors mobilised by authors labelled structuralist. Lévi-Strauss and Barthes linked Marx to their formative years. After discovering him in his early teens, Lévi-Strauss devoted his graduate thesis to Marx, while he was still destined for a political career in the French Section of the Workers' International (SFIO).[1] In *Sad Tropics*, he nonetheless lists Marxism among his three 'schoolmistresses', along with psychoanalysis and geology, and throughout his career he remained interested in Marx's vision of history as well as in his historical texts. Barthes, for his part, cited Marx in his *Roland Barthes par Roland Barthes*, as one of the three authors (with Jean-Paul Sartre and Bertolt Brecht) of the intertext for his works until 1961. But his reading of Marx was hardly orthodox, since it came by way of a Trotskyist militant he met in a sanatorium, Georges Fournié.[2] His discovery of Brecht, during the 1954 visit to Paris by the Berliner Ensemble – the theatre company created by the playwright – was at the origin of a sort of 'return to Brecht' in his work, just as there Althusser made a 'return to Marx', Lévi-Strauss a 'return to Mauss', and Lacan a 'return to Freud' – in short, each of them invented and reread, or even 'structuralised' a classic author. But the discovery of Brecht further distanced him from the PCF and orthodox Marxism, as the author was at that time considered too 'German' by Communist theatre critics, starting with Elsa Triolet.[3] Foucault, a short-lived member of the PCF during the 1950s, more bluntly rejected Marx in the interviews he gave at the time of the publication of *Words and Things*: 'Marxism,' he wrote and repeated, 'is in nineteenth-century thought like a fish in water, that is to say that everywhere else it ceases to breathe' – remarks which Althusser deemed 'ridiculous', despite their friendship.[4]

Here, we will first look at the conditions for the reception of a theory such as structuralism within the Communist world, then at certain attempts to reconcile Marxism and structuralism, before finally focusing on one of the most important: Althusser's.

1   The PCF and Theoretical Production

The transformation of political parties may have banished this from the memory, but some of them, at least until the end of the 1970s, really were concerned with intellectual theories, thinking about how consistent these were with their body of doctrine. Moreover, while Marxism in France is not limited to the PCF alone, this party – despite the earthquake of 1956 (the revelations at the Twentieth Congress and the repression of the Budapest uprising) and the political

---

1   Loyer 2015.
2   Roger 1996; Samoyault 2015.
3   Matonti 2005b.
4   Althusser 1998.

recomposition brought about by the establishment of the Fifth Republic – non-etheless constituted the Left's centre of gravity in the years that we are dealing with, here. That is, the PCF was the party in relation to which, or in opposition to which, the other parties or groups defined themselves. This is why, in order to examine the relationship between structuralism and Marxism, we will focus on the positions taken by Communist intellectuals and journals and by the PCF leadership group before May '68 – meaning, at the time that so-called 'structuralist' productions enjoyed greatest visibility. Moreover, before May, the intellectual reviews in dialogue with Marxism, such as *Socialisme ou Barbarie* (1949–65), or *Arguments* (1956–62), which was born out of the critique of the PCF, were hardly interested in structuralist productions – they disappeared, moreover, a little before the period in which structuralism enjoyed its most striking success. After May, on the other hand, the recomposition of the balance in the intellectual and political field led to the emergence of other critiques, with the devaluation of the 'structuralist' label, on the one hand, and the PCF's gradual loss of centrality, to the benefit of far-left movements and of the Socialist Party (PS), refounded in 1969.

From the end of the Algerian war, the PCF entered into what was later described – with reference to the reforming Vatican II council – as a process of *aggiornamento*. This was a complex movement in which the search for electoral alliances on the Left (with Socialist forces, themselves undergoing a recomposition process), the relative opening up of a previously exclusively working-class leadership group, and theoretical renovation, all exerted a pull on each other. This logic of renewal also had its effects on the status of Communist intellectuals. During the Cold War – one of whose characteristics was the cadreisation of this intellectuals – they had little choice but to take one of two *public* positions: either to adopt the watchwords of the international Communist movement in the field of intellectual and artistic production (starting with Zhdanovism and Lysenkoism), or else to leave the PCF. From the 1960s onwards – and perhaps even from the Twentieth Congress of the CPSU and the resulting modification of the 'truth regime' within the international Communist movement[5] – the imperative of theoretical renovation required the presence and work of 'institutional scribes'[6] whose function was to produce – *a posteriori* and *ad hoc* – the theory intended to support the strategic changes decided by the leadership group, or more precisely by the dominant fraction within it.[7] In March 1966, the Argenteuil Central Committee codified the role of intellectuals and defined

5   Pudal 2009.
6   Pudal 1989.
7   Matonti 2005a.

the freedoms that they were granted: there was complete liberty with regard to artistic production and the 'hard' sciences (as the PCF officially broke from the errant paths of Zhdanovism and Lysenkoism), and a monitored freedom for the human and social sciences (to which 'structuralist' output belonged). Hence, 'controversial problems must be examined within the regular Party bodies themselves', when the divergent 'positions' 'directly affect the political line of the Party', as the General Secretary Waldeck Rochet established in his 'Conclusions'.[8] The Communist Party had at its disposal a whole galaxy of national and regional magazines and newspapers, though their number had already decreased since Liberation. These publications addressed each segment of its audience (from children to peasants to the young adults of the baby-boom), highlighted the whole range of its programmatic offer and array of demands, and addressed all the sensitivities of its electorate (from *L'Humanité*, which targeted its core – workers and party cadres – to the intellectual journals competing for the monopoly of *aggiornamento*, such as *Les Lettres françaises*, *La Nouvelle Critique* or *Démocratie nouvelle*). These publications took stances on all manner of subjects, including intellectual and artistic production, with a view to popular education and informing its audience. They often did this in order to evaluate how compatible a given product was with the PCF's own doctrinal corpus, itself frequently recomposed. Marx was sometimes described as a 'wax nose' by Communist intellectuals, who thus emphasised the plasticity of his thought in the light of its successive interpretations. Lenin was a reservoir to draw from according to the requirements of the moment, whereas Stalin and Mao were, of course, prosecribed in this period marked by the *aggiornamento*, the 'thaw' in the USSR and the Sino-Soviet schism. Many of these Communist intellectuals, especially the younger ones, were also pursuing professional careers (as students at the École Normale Supérieure, doctoral students, assistants and lecturers, teachers in preparatory classes, and so on). The stances they took in journals in the orbit of the PCF were thus also a way of reconciling the readings and tastes of their distinct professional and militant universes.

For the PCF leadership group and for those who aspired to be part of it – for example, in the case of philosophers, those (such as Lucien Sève, regularly called upon to intervene in debates) who coveted the position of 'party philosopher', which was still held by Roger Garaudy – the evaluation was more directly political: the question 'what kind of politics can be done with structuralist Marx?' seemed to have guided their way of evaluating theoretical products.[9]

8   Martelli 2017.
9   Matonti 2005a.

This mode of evaluation was underpinned by the relationship to philosophy within the party as an institution. In the interwar period the PCF developed a training system for its cadres and leaders who had not been able to study at *lycée* or still less go to university. Philosophy was taught there, with the same function as in the school system: to explain other knowledge and practices, as a crowning discipline,[10] but it was also redefined in accordance with the schemas of the Communist universe. In their introduction to the philosophy course given at the central school (the highest level of training for PCF cadres), some of the 'teachers' reread the eleventh thesis on Feuerbach as 'the philosophers have interpreted the world so that we can transform it' – a rereading which was also Althusser's own.[11] Thus, philosophy was entirely oriented towards action, or even produced for this purpose. This schema of evaluation was at the heart of the Communist relationship to structuralism, and all the more so within the leadership group.

'Man is the product of structure, which means that I am not, for example, master of my speech, because the words I use do not only have the meaning that *I* want, but also the meaning they have because they are defined only in relation to other words, that is to say, a linguistic system which, as structural linguistics has taught us, functions by distinctive oppositions'.[12] This summary of the aims of structural linguistics helps us to understand what, at first sight, made 'structuralism' difficult to reconcile with the theoretical choices and strategic obligations of the leadership group – if it was, indeed, to be evaluated on political grounds. How can a politician not imagine being able to master their own speech? Other reductions to the political level were constantly invoked against structuralism, for example its supposed ignorance of history and the class struggle, rendering it a philosophy of despair (as Roland Leroy, the cadre in charge of intellectuals at the time, apparently put it). That is, it was deemed incompatible with political action.

We can also see which elements of structuralism could seduce a reader of Marx, or at least resonate with such a reader. Was this theoretical position ever so different from the rejection of the 'illusion' that consists in believing that it is 'consciousness that determines life', whereas it is, instead, 'life that determines consciousness', as Marx and Engels put it in *The German Ideology*? In fact, lines of inquiry – those of Maurice Godelier, Lucien Sebag and Althusser, for example – often regarded the relations between Marx's 'superstructures' and the 'structures' of structuralism.

---

10   Fabiani 1988.
11   Althusser 1992.
12   Maniglier 2005.

2   Confronting/Reconciling Marxism and Structuralism

In many areas of the humanities and social sciences, Marxist and/or Communist intellectuals found themselves confronted with 'structuralist' productions, and possibly with the most orthodox of their peers, when they tried to elaborate a reading compatible with their own both intellectual and political demands. One of the most visible attempts at a confrontation/reconciliation between Marxism and structuralism was that mounted by Lucien Sebag, a CNRS researcher and author of *Marxisme et Structuralisme*, published by Payot in 1964. A former member of the PCF, expelled after 1956, and a former contributor to *La Nouvelle Critique*, he became a regular contributor to *Les Temps modernes*. A student of Lévi-Strauss, in analysis with Lacan, he had plans to write a book on the 'analysis of discourse during psychoanalysis'[13] before committing suicide in 1965. With Marx, Sebag shows, 'the science of man [has] reached ... an unprecedented degree of elaboration'. But 'Marxism remains deeply attached to the idea that explanation rests in the first place on the unveiling of the continuum of history itself'.[14] For him, this is a 'shortcoming' that only structural anthropology and, even more so, Lacanian psychoanalysis can fill, precisely because neither of them presupposes an answer.

Maurice Godelier, a member of the PCF between 1952 and 1968, Claude Lévi-Strauss's assistant at the Collège de France and, like Sebag, a member of the Laboratoire d'anthropologie sociale,[15] also proposed to articulate Marxism and structuralism. Asked by *Les Temps modernes* to contribute to an issue devoted to the 'problems of structuralism', in November 1966, he sought to reread *Capital* 'from the point of view of anthropological structuralism' and thereby raise Marxism to the rank of a science of man.[16] This article drew a first response from Lucien Sève in *La Pensée* ('Méthode structurale et méthode dialectique'), sparking a 'dispute' that continued over several years. As when confronted with other attempts to reconcile Marxism and structuralism, Lucien Sève set about denouncing his interlocutor's misreadings and generally denounced the 'anti-historicism of structuralism, [its] abandonment of dialectics', and the 'anti-humanism of anthropologists'. This critique ran parallel to the one he simultaneously pursued in *La Nouvelle Critique*, in his March 1967 article 'Marxisme et sciences de l'homme': for him, structuralism was part of a 'break, not an epistemological one [an allusion, of course, to

---

13   Leavitt 2005.
14   Karsenti 2005, pp. 99, 104.
15   Boursier 2010.
16   Lamy 2016.

Althusser's reading], but a political one, which the entire effort of the bourgeoisie ... aims to maintain between the world of thought and the working
class'.

Given the rulings passed at Argenteuil, specialists in literary criticism and
linguists were freer to work on reconciling the two perspectives; their disciplines, after all, stood at the intersection of literature and the humanities (and
thus of the free and the monitored). Particularly at stake, among the Communist journals competing to monopolise the *aggiornamento*, was control over the
modernity of structural linguistics. At the same time, given the concern to discuss the repression of the Soviet avant-gardes, *Les Lettres françaises* director
Louis Aragon and editor-in-chief, Pierre Daix gave wide coverage to the Russian
formalists, who were now presented as the precursors of structural linguistics. They interviewed Philippe Sollers, whose journal *Tel Quel* was one of the
vectors of this rediscovery.[17] At the end of 1967, partly in reaction to this, *La
Nouvelle Critique* began a cooperation with *Tel Quel*, which was then engaged
in the discovery of *literaturnost* and the scriptural level of texts – an alliance
that survived and was even strengthened through May '68, lasting until 1971,
when the journal turned to Maoism.[18] It was in this context of competition
with the Aragonian clan on the one hand, and alliance with the literary avant-
garde on the other, that *La Nouvelle Critique* devoted itself to organising two
conferences in Cluny. With the first one, 'Littérature et linguistique', in April
1968, it sought to take on board what the figure responsible for this event –
Michel Apel-Muller, then a professor at the École normale de Mâcon – called
'the richness and complexity of the work on the problems of language, both
in France and abroad (the *nouveau roman*, Barthes and the *Tel Quel* group,
Chomsky, Jakobson, Lévi-Strauss, Mounin, and so on)'. A preparatory note by
Jean Peytard, then a lecturer at Besançon,[19] emphasised the need to 'free' the
methods of structural linguistics from what must be called the 'structuralist
ideology'. Despite this precaution, these two conferences made La *Nouvelle
Critique* appear to be the privileged partner of *Tel Quel*, thus weakening its
position within the Communist space and ultimately forcing it to return to
a more classical conception of literary criticism. This was particularly true
of the second conference, 'Littérature et idéologie', which led to a near-brawl
between the members of *Tel Quel* and *Change*. This latter group, founded by
Jean-Pierre Faye (a *Tel Quel* dissident), Jean Paris, Jacques Roubaud and Léon

---

17   Matonti 2009.
18   Matonti 2005a.
19   Mondini 2010.

Robel, sought to go beyond the supposedly over-rigid structural linguistics, to move from Jakobson to Chomsky and, to this end, to reread the Russian formalists.[20]

3   Political Readings: Althusser and Structuralism

Althusser was undoubtedly at the heart of the most visible Communist attempt to reconcile Marxism and structuralism – and the most perilous, since it also touched on philosophy. His teaching at the ENS at the rue d'Ulm bore the traces of this attempt, for he alternated between seminars on Marx (on the 'Young Marx' in 1961–2 and on *Capital* in 1964–5) and seminars on the themes revisited by structuralist authors (on the origins of structuralism, Foucault and Lévi-Strauss, in 1962–3, and then on psychoanalysis, and thus necessarily on Lacan, in 1963–4). He regularly hosted these same theorists at the ENS, starting with Lacan who, in the midst of building his own psychoanalytical movement, abandoned his seminar at the Hôpital Sainte-Anne to give it at Ulm, from 15 January 1964.

Althusser's correspondence with his mistress Franca Madonia – translator into Italian of Maurice Merleau-Ponty, Claude Lévi-Strauss, Gérard Genette, and soon of *For Marx* – provides a good observation post on Althusser's readings and of the uses he intended to make of them for his own theoretical elaborations. In autumn 1962, he described the *History of Madness* as a 'capitally important book',[21] 'amazing, astonishing, brilliant'. When he mentioned the goal of his seminars, he explained that he wanted to think about the 'relationship between structuralist thought and Marxism', and 'above all ... the essence of superstructures' – pointing back to the resemblance mentioned above. Similarly, he read Lévi-Strauss in order to 'untangle the imposture and the fruitful elements', that is, to 'nourish the concepts in me waiting to be charged', more seduced by *Structural Anthropology* than by *Wild Thought*. Four years later (when structuralism was most in vogue), his relationship with all these authors changed. Althusser had definitively distanced himself from the work of Lévi-Strauss and Barthes, and decried, as has been said, [Foucault's] 'ridiculous interviews on Marx'. Only Lacan seemed to be entirely free from criticism. But was it only the latter's structuralism that attracted Althusser – or, much more likely, what it allowed him like the early Foucault to see in madness? 'Freud et

20   Matonti 2011.

21   Althusser 1998.

Lacan' – published in *La Nouvelle Critique* in 1964 after many reversals – was, to Althusser's eyes, 'an article written with a little life, a little blood, and a lot of death'.[22] As François Matheron has shown, it was indeed written at the time of his friend Jacques Martin's suicide.[23] Besides the fact that 'Freud et Lacan' gave back some room for psychoanalysis – banished from the Communist intellectual space at the time of the Cold War – and returned, much like the preface to *For Marx*, to the errant paths of the Stalinist period, Althusser here applied the reading deployed in *Reading Capital*: in it he distinguished between a 'young Freud' and a mature Freud (just as there is a 'young Marx' from before the epistemological break). Here, he also compared Lacan's endeavours and his own project of constituting a Marxist philosophy.

Yet, Althusser's attempt to reconcile Marxism and structuralism, which culminated in the two 1965 books and in his students' journals, could not but pose a problem, especially given the persistent accusation of Maoism levelled against the philosopher. It was in *La Pensée* – a Communist journal founded just before the war and whose sensibility followed in line with the materialist and rationalist tradition of the Enlightenment as well as with the republican strategy of bringing the left together, that Althusser faced the first criticisms directed against his texts, some of which were taken up in *For Marx*. In *The Future Lasts Forever*, Althusser even describes as a 'theoretical trial' the meetings that took place at *La Pensée* every Saturday for a month and a half.[24] One of the keys to this controversy was the fact that Althusser defended the right to use Mao's texts (notably on contradiction). The 'Chinese pot' tied to Althusser by Georges Cogniot (the director of *La Pensée*) and the philosopher Lucien Sève – if we are to believe the words of the editor-in-chief of *La Nouvelle Critique*, Jacques Arnault[25] – had an effect on Althusser's position and resources within the PCF. This meant difficulty in being published (only *La Nouvelle Critique* welcomed his texts during this period), his decision to establish several collections at Maspero and not at Éditions sociales (a 'natural' outlet for a Communist intellectual), involvement in the journals of his students, themselves caught up in the crisis of the UEC, in some cases leaning toward Maoism with the foundation of the UJC(ml) – Union des jeunesses communistes (marxiste-léniniste). Althusser found himself being pushed toward heterodoxy; all his actions and positions were henceforth evaluated by this yardstick. It is therefore with this heterodoxy in mind and the generalised competition of com-

---

22   Althusser 1998, p. 521.
23   Althusser 1993.
24   Althusser 1992.
25   Matonti 2005a.

munist philosophies that we must understand the reception of the texts on humanism published by Maspero and *La Nouvelle Critique*.

What has been called the 'debate on humanism' began in March 1965 with the publication in *La Nouvelle Critique* of two texts by Althusser and an article by Jorge Semprún, who had just been expelled from the Spanish Communist Party. While Althusser sought to proceed with a scientific reading of Marx and to base political practice on it, Semprún's objective – overcoming Stalinism – led him to the acceptance of a Marxist humanism. Despite the absence of the term 'epistemological break' (though the elements that the term would come to cover are already present), Althusser's texts are very close to *Reading Capital* and *For Marx*. Semprún's text is fairly representative of what were then termed 'Italian theses' (in reference to the early attempt at *aggiornamento* by the Italian Communist Party). The suggestion, in 'Marxisme et humanisme', of a theoretical antihumanism in Marx stood at the heart of the controversy: it is based on the hypothesis of a 'radical', 'unique' break (the future 'epistemological break', a notion taken from Georges Canguilhem), with the 'young Marx' of before 1845 and his concept of alienation. After 1845, on the other hand, 'the essence of man,' writes Althusser, 'is defined as an ideology [i.e. an illusion]'.

The quarrel led to a 'philosophers' debate' at Choisy-le-Roi in January 1966 (Althusser, who was ill, was not present), and then fed into the dynamic that led to the Central Committee meeting at Argenteuil. The dispute now pitted 'Althusserians' against the 'Garaudists', including Aragon, a member of the Central Committee. At Choisy-le-Roi, Garaudy argued that Althusser 'substitutes the bourgeois science/proletarian science divide for the science/ideology divide' and practised a 'conceptual purification'. Moreover, Althusser's 'symptomatic reading', in supposedly questioning the 'gaps, blanks, and shortcomings of rigour in Marx's discourse' was held to be 'in fact [a] long polemic against Marx'. In Argenteuil, Aragon was particularly virulent in his opposition to Althusser, denouncing his 'references to authors who are beyond the Europe of homelands, well, I mean, beyond the Urals' – that is, the Chinese – and his 'influence' on a part of the 'intellectual youth'.[26] Even if this dual consignment to left-wing sectarianism (both Stalinist and Maoist) could have led to Althusser's exclusion, the Central Committee at Argenteuil settled the quarrel by proposing a median theory, 'Marxist humanism', of which Lucien Sève became the main promoter, both against Garaudy and against Althusser's 'left-wing structuralism' (to use Foucault's formula).

---

26   Martelli 2017.

With this episode in Argenteuil, any possibility of a theoretical rethinking of Marxist philosophy within the PCF, based on the contributions of structuralism, was closed off. On the other hand, in linguistics, as in the field of literary criticism, journals and intellectuals were able for a time to reconcile their professional interests and political affiliations. But, in the post-'68 period, the main attempts to reconcile Marxism and structuralism would above all come from the side of Lacanian psychoanalysis, and not without difficulties.

CHAPTER 20

Marx, an Avant-Gardist?

Frédéric Thomas

'Spinoza, Kant, Blake, Schelling, Proudhon, Marx, Stirner, Baudelaire, Lautréamont, Rimbaud, Nietzsche: this list of names alone is the beginning of your disaster.' This footnote to the October 1925 tract *La Révolution d'abord et toujours* seems to be Surrealism's first reference to Marx. This way of entering the scene, with the German revolutionary embedded in a series of other names – poets and philosophers – is a good indicator of the dynamics and conditions of Marx's apprehension among the avant-gardes.

By 'avant-garde' we mean, as per Peter Bürger's definition, those 'historical movements'[1] which have distinguished themselves primarily through artistic self-criticism and the attempt to overturn the established separation between art and life. In this sense, only Dada, Surrealism and the Situationist International (SI) in France – and, at least in part, the groups that gravitated around them – belong to this category. The temporal spectrum which they covered with greatest intensity runs from World War I to 1968 (the SI dissolved in 1972, while surrealist activity continued with great difficulty). The French panorama presented here – necessarily a synthetic overview – should not, however, obscure the international character of these groups. We will follow a largely chronological path, before identifying the constants and specificities of the figure of Marx within these movements.

1   When the Surrealists Met Marx

Unlike in the case of German Dadaism, Dada's work of eroding morals in Paris did not result in a re-commitment to revolutionary politics. Significantly, in the game played in 1921 in *Littérature* (founded by the future Surrealists Aragon, Breton and Soupault), which consisted of giving marks from +25 to -25 to a series of personalities, Marx's name does not appear, unlike those of Marat, Robespierre, Hegel, Jaurès, Bernstein, Lenin and Trotsky. Marx was only understood or read via the French and Russian revolutionaries or else Hegel: he was not drawn on in any specific way.

---

1   Bürger 1984.

The Surrealist group built itself around André Breton's 1924 *Surrealist Manifesto*. Very quickly, the political character of the movement became clear. Years later, looking back on the path that they had taken in order to demonstrate its relevance, the Surrealists foregrounded two major historical events that were at the origin of their orientation: World War I and the Russian Revolution. However, it was during another war, the French colonial campaign in the Moroccan Rif, that the movement's politicisation crystallised.

Signed by the surrealist groups *Clarté*, *Philosophie* and *Correspondance* (a Belgian surrealist group), the tract *La Révolution d'abord et toujours* juxtaposes various concepts of revolution, including the *Communist Manifesto*'s own, without synthesising them – an ambivalence that would encourage tensions and contradictions. The tract seals surrealism's leap into politics and thus marks the end of the polemic that had opposed Aragon to *Clarté* a short time previously. Aragon, who had been reproached for his use of the expression 'Moscou-la-gâteuse' ('a senile Moscow'), had responded by refusing 'a lesson in the name of a social dogma, even that of Karl Marx'.

The tract brought together various groups, which would constantly intermingle in the subsequent period, within a space where Marx was in union with other figures considered (equally) revolutionary. The Moroccan war had provided a catalyst, but it was through the 'things of the spirit' – on the poetic terrain – that the Surrealists arrived at Marx. The tract expressed an understanding of Marx shaped by a both romantic and pessimistic prism. This meant going against the grain of the PCF and exposing themselves to its attacks. Didn't the Communist leader Paul Vaillant-Couturier say, at the beginning of 1926: 'To me, what seems grave about the Surrealists is their pessimism about the passivity of the European proletariat'?[2]

If, as in Breton's account, upon contact with *Clarté* the Surrealists rushed 'perhaps too hurriedly, or at least very avidly',[3] into Marx's writings – especially his early, more philosophical texts – this does not mean that they had a thorough or all-embracing understanding of them. Breton admitted that their knowledge of Marx was precarious, and that they were hardly equipped for the critique of political economy.

References to and quotations from Marx would henceforth proliferate across the Surrealists' texts, especially from the pen of the most 'political' among them: Maxime Alexandre, Louis Aragon, André Breton, René Crevel, Benjamin Péret, André Thirion... But this also prompted difficulties and tensions within

---

2   Cited in Bonnet 1988.
3   Breton 1969.

the group. Illustrative in this sense is Prévert's statement, during their 1926 discussions over whether to join the PCF: 'I was a revolutionary at seven years of age. I am completely incapable of opening a book by Marx, it pisses me off. On that score, I'll leave it up to others'.[4] So, while there was a consensus among the Surrealists that Marx was interesting, important and original, his appropriation and dissemination within their ranks required effort, if not necessarily throwing themselves into it.

Like the French Communists, the Surrealists read Marx through the Leninist prism of the Russian Revolution. They would, nonetheless, engage in a labour of reading and educating themselves. But they sought to *make use* of Marx, at least as much as they worked to really familiarise themselves with him. They used his name in an offensive and even polemical spirit. Through him, they put forward a style, a method, and watchwords. They appreciated his feel for pithy formulas and the sharpness of his assertions, whose form they reproduced (in 1946, Breton partly attributed the polemical tone of the *Second Manifesto* of Surrealism to this 'formal influence'). The reference to Marx was used as a method, as against individualism and the inconsequence of an intellectual milieu complicit in the reigning order – hence the abundance of references to ideology, bourgeois morality and class culture. Finally, the Surrealists looked to Marx for their watchwords – first and foremost, 'more consciousness' and 'transforming the world', which sketched out a programme common to both surrealism and the author of *Capital*. This way of embracing Marx also expresses the all-encompassing character of their adoption of Marxist concepts. These concepts were neither defined nor discussed, but rather served as weapons and instruments for radicalising the Surrealist offensive.

Which of Marx's writings did the Surrealists lay their hands on, read and refer to? The most oft-cited texts are *The Holy Family*, the *Theses on Feuerbach*, the *Communist Manifesto* and the *Poverty of Philosophy*, in addition to which was Engels's *Anti-Dühring* and *The Origins of the Family* (the latter having been read by a number of Surrealists in 1931, according to Thirion). There were also sporadic references to Paul Lafargue's *Right to Be Lazy*, as well as to articles from the Communist press – especially, from *L'Humanité*, the pieces by Jean Fréville concerning art and literature – and publications of somehow communist bent (*La Critique sociale*, *La Revue marxiste*, *Lutte des classes*, and so on). We know that Breton's library included – in addition to the *Communist Manifesto* and a collection of texts by Engels and Marx on literature and art published by Éditions sociales internationales (1936) – four books by Engels, another four

---

4 Cited in Bonnet 1988.

by Marx (including two volumes of *Capital*, with some passages underlined, from the 1872–5 Librairie du Progrès edition) and three by Lafargue (on Marx's thought). Most of these books were in editions from the 1920s–30s.

The Marx that emerges from Surrealist discourse is a fundamentally Hegelian figure. The Surrealists never ceased to insist on this filiation – one shared by Surrealism, which also started from Hegel and 'the "colossal abortion" of the Hegelian system'.[5] This origin, and the importance of the dialectic, was used by the Surrealists to counter the PCF's elementary materialism and vulgar Marxism. For example, issue 8 of *La Révolution surréaliste*, from December 1926, features a cover montage, with the quote from Engels: 'What all these gentlemen lack is dialectics.'

' "Transform the world" said Marx, "change life", said Rimbaud; for us these two watchwords are one': in 1935, this famous formula definitively pinned down the Surrealist's Marx. It encapsulated the Surrealists' attraction to the revolution. Marx was already present in the 1925 tract, and was also present in 1930 in the Second Manifesto of Surrealism, which highlighted 'Hegel, Feuerbach, Marx, Lautréamont, Rimbaud, Jarry, Freud, Chaplin, Trotsky'.[6] Finally, it heralded – on a political basis, and in the name of Marx – the break with the PCF, which several Surrealists had joined in 1927. It is true that the Surrealists, both before and after this split, reaffirmed their adherence to dialectical materialism. But these demonstrations of 'orthodoxy' went hand-in-hand with the continuous assertion of the inadequacy of Marx, which had to be corrected, filled in, by creating a superior montage in which he would have to be inseparably combined with other names, Rimbaud, Lautréamont and Freud first among them. The 1935 formula defined Surrealism's own particular space, at the crossroads of poetry and revolution. The other historical avant-garde movements would develop and recognise themselves in this space, even if that meant reconfiguring its contours.

2   Calling on Marx to Go beyond Surrealism?

During World War II, the dispersion of the Surrealist group, the exile from Europe of several of their number (including Breton and Péret), the rallying of others (including Paul Éluard) to the *parti des fusillés* (the party of the executed partisans), the arrival of a new generation and the growing might of the PCF,

---

5 Breton 1977.
6 Ibid.

crowned by its role in the Resistance, brought a recomposition of forces. In the first few years following the Liberation, surrealism was the object of intense debate and bitter polemics, and even of a generalised settling of accounts.

Breton's discovery of the work of Charles Fourier – to whom he dedicated a poem in 1947, the *Ode à Charles Fourier* – was at once the consequence, the marker, and the catalyst of Surrealism distancing itself from Marx. To the eyes of the Belgian Surrealists and the 'Revolutionary Surrealists' who affirmed their commitment to communism, this recourse to pre-Marx utopian socialism was proof that Surrealism had had its day. They sought to react to this turn by upholding Marx's materialism in opposition to Fourier's idealism (Christian Dotremont, a member of the Revolutionary Surrealists, wrote an *Ode à Marx* in response to Breton), or in some cases to Breton's mysticism itself.

The Revolutionary Surrealists' July 1947 tract *La cause est entendue*, was a response to the position taken by the new Surrealist group formed around Breton. After insisting upon the 'absolute determination of Surrealism by dialectical materialism', it lay special emphasis on a quotation from the *Anti-Dühring*. This was a way of striking two blows at once, since it was a quotation already used in Breton's *Les Vases communicants* and in Crevel's *Le Clavecin de Diderot*, both published in 1932. This was to oppose the analysis of Engels (and Marx) to Surrealism's present wanderings, but also the interwar Surrealist choices to the ones taken in 1947.

The reference to Marx allowed for a three-fold positioning, which either converged or diverged in relation to surrealism, in relation to the PCF and in relation to the revolution. The configuration was the same for 'Lettrism', which purported to take over from 'historical' Surrealism, to correct and complete Marx, according to another conception of revolution.

For all that, these debates and polemics did not lead to any real effort to reinterpret Marx. It was as if, on all sides, the way in which he had been appropriated and fixed in place by the USSR and the PCF was taken as read, whether this was to be celebrated or bewailed. Marx was less actually *read* than he was *used* to distance oneself from Surrealism – cast as a failure – and to provide for its overcoming.

3   Had the Surrealists Tired of Marx?

In 1949–50, in the course of several interviews and speeches, Breton for the first time expressed doubts about the correctness of Marx's thought; the fault, according to the Surrealist, lay with Hegel's *Philosophy of Right*, to which Marx supposedly remained subordinate. From then on, the Surrealist group (in which there remained hardly any members of the first generation, apart from Benjamin Péret), united around Breton, now only spoke of Marx with increasing distance. The November 1953 game *Ouvrez-vous?* Is revealing in this sense: to the question 'Would you open the door for Marx?', Breton replies 'No, out of exhaustion'. The great majority of the group (but not Péret), answered the same way; this contrasted, paradoxically, with the answers they gave for Lenin, and even more so with the hearty welcome reserved for Fourier ...

During the 1950s, the few references to Marx were linked to the discussion of the dialectic, or served the purposes of comparison with other thinkers or currents. But this remained a very general and superficial reading. Even the political positions that the group took (on the Algerian war, on the Budapest uprising in 1956, on the Cuban revolution in 1959, and so on) were not based on Marx. It seemed that the group stuck to the minimalist bedrock of fighting 'the exploitation of man by man', on the basis of ethics.

Benjamin Péret was the exception, in this regard. Continuing to draw on Marx, he nevertheless also began to foreground his limits, the dated and outdated part of some of his ideas, the fatalism that can emerge from some of his quotations, and even his errors. For Péret, these errors are encapsulated in the dialectic of the strengthening of the state before its supposed withering away, and in the notion of the 'nationalisation of the means of production'. According to the Surrealist, this latter constituted one of the main causes of the failure of Russian revolutionary experience and of the blindness of present-day Marxists (including Trotsky, whose action and life Péret analysed in a long article in 1953). But, interesting as this hypothesis is, Péret did not develop it further, nor did he discuss Marx's writings.

4   The Fourth Period of Marxist Thought?

It is doubly significant that it was around Rimbaud – upon the centenary of his birth, in 1954 – that the Surrealists and the Lettrist International (LI; itself a split from Lettrism) collaborated for the first time, and that Marx was the pretext for the break. Indeed, the Surrealists had problems with a sentence that the Lettrists wanted to include on a joint leaflet, because of its 'Marxist sound': 'In a society based on class struggle, there can be no impartial literary criticism'.[7] In reality this is a detourned phrase from Lenin. The divisive use of Marx by the Lettrists (who could not, at the time, claim to have a better know-

---

7   Duwa 2008.

ledge of his thought) and the coldness of the Surrealists are both revealing. In the collection of Surrealist tracts published by José Pierre, he goes so far as to comment on this polemic, evoking 'the 'Marxist' trap' that was set by the Lettrists.

It was shortly afterwards that Guy Debord, one of the main theoreticians of the LI and soon (in 1957) founder of the SI, began a work of reading and appropriating Marx. Thanks to the research of Patrick Marcolini and Anselm Jappe, as well as the Debord collection held at the BNF, it is now possible to have a more precise idea of the knowledge that Debord and, more generally, the SI had of Marx. Based on the 'Marxism' file (consisting of reading cards and notes) in the Debord collection, Jappe concluded that he had 'a fairly extensive knowledge of the writings of Hegel and Marx, as well as of many authors following in their footsteps', based on a targeted, even utilitarian, reading, especially attentive to the 'young' Marx.[8] This dossier contains an 82-page notebook in which Debord takes large extracts from Marx's philosophical texts – especially from *The Holy Family*.

But this dossier also reflects a more general reconfiguration, conducive to a rereading of Marx. In the pages devoted to Karl Korsch's *Marxism and Philosophy*, Debord takes up the three-part periodisation of Marxist thought as distinguished by the author (from 1843 to the first third of the twentieth century). But Debord then adds: 'The "fourth", it seems, begins in the 1950s: East Berlin, Budap[est], Marxology, the SI, and the crumbling of the revo[lutionary] image.' This new phase thus corresponds to the crisis of Stalinism, to the revolts in the East, linked to a renewal of the interpretation of Marx, of which the SI and Maximilian Rubel, in 1959 founder of *Études de marxologie*, were among the participants. This also makes it possible to situate Debord's rereading of Marx within a wider context, whose bounds are marked by the writings of György Lukács, Henri Lefebvre, Maximilien Rubel, and so on.

The case of Maximilien Rubel provides a good illustration of this 1950s–60s encounter between Marx and the avant-gardes. A Marx specialist and editor of his works, Rubel's close collaborator was Louis Janover, who quickly passed through surrealism and founded the journal *Front noir* in 1963. The latter attempted a re-examination of the Surrealist movement, published Rubel's theses and took up his ethical reinterpretation of Marx. Rubel was also read – and discussed – by the Surrealists and the Situationist International. Finally, he occasionally contributed to the journal *Arguments* (1956–62) which, though the target of numerous attacks by Debord (who nevertheless read it attent-

---

8 Jappe 2018.

ively), occupied a central place in this movement of reinterpretation and reappropriation of Marx by the avant-gardes. Indeed, authors such as André Frankin, Henri Lefebvre and Maximilien Rubel, linked to historical avant-garde movements, were *Arguments* collaborators, and issue 21 of this journal (from 1961), devoted to 'Love-as-Problem', pays tribute to the Surrealists as an original 'modern revolutionary current'. Moreover, it was probably in these pages that these movements discovered the texts of György Lukács and Karl Korsch, of Theodor Adorno and Herbert Marcuse, who, in turn, bore definite influence on them.

Central to this 'avant-garde' re-reading of Marx was the emphasis placed on the concepts of alienation and reification. The SI would go furthest in the reinterpretation of these concepts. But, to a lesser extent, they also reoriented *Front noir*'s Marxist reading (notably by way of a long article by Paul Mattick). In the second half of the 1960s the Surrealist group would sketch out a return to Marx, which took place partly through reading Marcuse. Indeed, in issue 8 of the Surrealist journal *La Brèche*, in November 1965, Claude Feraud devoted a long analysis to Ferdinand Alquié's book, *Philosophie du surréalisme* (1955), based on Rubel's *Pages choisies de Marx* (1948) and the *1844 Manuscripts* in which Marx developed 'the famous theory of social alienation'. He concluded that 'surrealist and Marxist ambitions ... complement each other in the affirmation of a human totality and of its irreducible value'.

5   Intermediaries

It is near-certain that, at the turn of the 1950s, access to these concepts was first gleaned through second-hand readings of Marxism. The main mediators in this sense were Lucien Goldmann (who published a long article 'La réification' in *Les Temps modernes* at the beginning of 1959), Lukács (from 1957, as *Arguments* presented chapters of *History and Class Consciousness* for the first time in French, before the translation of the book itself was published in 1960), Joseph Gabel (who wrote regularly in *Arguments* and published *La Fausse Conscience: essai sur la réification* in 1962) and Henri Lefebvre (who, having broken from the PCF, published several important works between 1958 and 1961).

In the rereading of Marx, the SI had the advantage of benefiting from the contributions of Frankin and especially Lefebvre, as well as from Debord's brief passage by way of *Socialisme ou Barbarie*. Neither a simple calque nor a brilliant reinvention, the notion of 'spectacle' that the SI developed attempted to update and redeploy the concept of commodity fetishism. The first chapters of *The Society of the Spectacle* (1967) are largely based on a synthesis and *détournement* of the texts of Hegel, Marx and Lukács. More generally, it can be pointed out by way of illustration that in late 1964 Debord had outlined a reading programme 'to become a revolutionary thinker, at the present stage'. Of the fifteen or so works mentioned, four were by Marx (the philosophical works, the *Communist Manifesto*, *Class Struggles in France* and the *Civil War in France*). There were also titles by Lefebvre, Marcuse and Reich, as well as *Marx et les marxistes* by Kostas Papaïoannou.[9] A few of the avant-gardes' fellow travellers also contributed to the reading of Marx. Among these were Victor Crastre (a member of *Clarté*) and Dyonis Mascolo (who was close to the Surrealists, and whose notes Debord mentions as having 'confused sit[uationist] tendencies'), though Henri Lefebvre was undoubtedly the main intermediary, in terms of both his career and his writing. As a member of the *Philosophies* group, he signed the tract *La Révolution d'abord et toujours*, and remained linked to the Surrealists for some time, before entering into conflict with them. He then became involved with the PCF, and from the 1930s onwards, with *Morceaux choisis de Marx* (1934) and *La Conscience mystifiée* (1936), he offered a reading of Marx that was critical of Marxism and which also drew on Romanticism. This reading had an important role for Marx's philosophical writings, and put forward concepts (totality, alienation, praxis, everyday life, the unity of theory and practice, and so on) that would be at the heart of the avant-gardes' rereading of Marx.

Lefebvre's *Critique of Everyday Life*, in 1947, was welcomed and read with interest, first among the ranks of the revolutionary Surrealists and then within the SI. He became friends with Debord at the very start of the 1960s (having recently been expelled from the PCF), and for several years they had fruitful exchanges, notably on Marxism, Romanticism and everyday life. Breton and especially Debord read many of his books, and it is likely that it was from *Critique of Everyday Life* that Debord first became acquainted with Marx's philosophical writings and the theory of alienation.

6   With Marx, against Reification

If Carole Reynaud Paligot remarked that the political culture of the Surrealists 'remained weak', and that 'references to Hegel or Marx ... were more like professions of faith than a real and solid political philosophy',[10] such an assess-

---

9   Brun 2014.
10   Reynaud Paligot 2010.

ment ought to be given some qualification and put into perspective. The avant-gardes' reading and knowledge of Marx would develop and become more precise in the course of their history. Moreover, while a lack of knowledge of Marx's texts was surely a handicap for surrealism, it was also an asset: it sharpened an uninhibited gaze, and allowed for unexpected convergences, based on montages and détournements, telescoping Marx with Rimbaud, Freud and Lautréamont. This thus opened up a space whose shape was configured by both poetry and revolution.

But ultimately, what passageways did these historical avant-gardes open up within Marxism – and what does the Marx who emerges from them look like? A Marxism centred on the critique of alienation (Jappe), a romantic one (Löwy), or an anthropological one (Benjamin)? In any case, a heterodox Marxism, based on a partial, critical and selective reading, centred on the philosophical writings of Marx's youth (with next to no references to his writings on the history of class struggles in France). This meant a Marxism that strove to correlate the Marxian rupture with a series of other caesuras – within philosophy as well as at other levels (poetry, love, sexuality, and so on) – of which the avant-gardes would be the extension, the synthesis and the guarantor.

The avant-gardes' use of Marx was thus always plural, associated with other figures, taken from a constellation of other names and other fields (mainly those of poetry, desires, dreams and sexuality), short-circuiting any specialisation or fixed certainties. Marx was moreover used as an offensive weapon, mainly driven by the critique of capitalist civilisation and anti-colonialism, which also served to mark the difference within the intellectual field, and even among the avant-gardes themselves.

Within this space common to the historical avant-gardes, there were inflections and different framings: while Feuerbach and Hegel remained central references, Engels was above all read by the Surrealists of the interwar period. These latter, moreover, adopted a more pessimistic vision than the SI did of the proletariat's 'historical mission'. Similarly, these various groups claimed, albeit to varying degrees, to be revolutionary romantics (the title of a 1958 article by Lefebvre), and would see in the demonstrations of May 1968 the confirmation of their theses. While they all agreed on the need to shake up the boundaries between art and politics, the scales sometimes tipped to one side, sometimes to the other.

But the central axis around which all these movements gathered, when it came to their readings of Marx, lay in their radical critique of reification. In Marx, they found confirmation of what they had drawn from certain poetic experiences: in today's society, everything is against poetry, and capitalism distorts all problems, 'poetic problems as well as others, or rather poetic problems before all others'.[11] It was through poetry and in the name of poetry that the avant-gardes arrived at Marx, read him and used him, making shifts and distortions, establishing connections and montages, in order to alter the coordinates of the revolution and to place it in service of an overhaul of the world and of life itself.[12]

11   Blanchot 1949.
12   Thomas 2007.

CHAPTER 21

Post-'68 Intellectuals and Marx: A Fascination with 'Farewells'

Antoine Aubert

'All this has come to an end, as it has for ten years or so now. Among French intellectuals, something akin to a sobering-up has occurred'.[1] These words of François Furet's provide an exemplary illustration of how Marxism's trajectory in France after May 1968 has generally been summarised. After intellectuals' massive adherence to the different variants of the revolutionary project primarily inspired by Marx's writings – an 'intoxication', according to Furet, and an 'opium' or 'secular religion', according to Aron – it would seem that at the end of the 1970s these same intellectuals suddenly became conscious of the set of illusions carried forth by Marxism. In this version of events, Marxist production – and the revolutionary project with it – now came to an abrupt halt, in the very moment that François Mitterrand reached the summit of the state along with the Socialists and Communists. If this is true, then the 1980s marked the final death of Marx, seen as a desirable as well as natural development.

Of course, Furet's statement is that of a repentant former Communist and is largely performative in nature. But it coincides with the dominant analyses of post-'68 French intellectual history, which emphasise three phenomena: the inevitable decline of radical ideas towards the end of the 1970s; the advent of a neoliberal conservative revolution largely owing to repentant ex-leftists; and finally, the rise of modern individualism, as a direct result of May–June '68.[2]

On the whole, it can be said that this observation regarding the supposed collapse of Marxism has never been measured or really substantiated, but rather posited as a fact. Here, we propose to discuss and qualify this reading, through an approach based on the social history of political ideas,[3] analysing the constraints that influenced the production and circulation of ideas during this period.

---

1 Furet 1987.
2 Jeanpierre and Martin 2013.
3 Matonti 2005a.

First, we will briefly discuss the discourse on the crisis of Marxism and the revolutionary project that took hold at the end of the 1970s, after the boom period for radical ideas following 1968. We will then return to this crisis, which, while real and multiple, was neither total nor attributable solely to internal impasses in the revolutionary project and, consequently, in Marxian thought itself. Only through an analysis of the whole set of transformations which affected the intellectual field in this period can we grasp the transformations which, even before the collapse of the USSR, affected Marxist ideas. Lastly, we will return to the years following this major political event to show that the reference to Marx, though weakened and rarefied, has indeed persisted.

1   From Abundance to Crisis: Marxism in the 1970s

1.1   *A Flurry of Political Books*

In May–June 68, France was the scene of a major political crisis. The revolutionary perspective, which had up till then largely been an ideal, became a plausible horizon. At the same time, the ideas of Marx (or ideas claiming to be Marxist) were widely disseminated. Their spread owed above all to militant publishers, such as Éditions sociales, Maspero and Anthropos. While these ideas were, of course, already in circulation before 1968, the events of May–June made people buy books – if not necessarily read them – especially as many political publishing houses were then being created, at the same time as other more generalist publishers, such as Gallimard or Le Seuil, began to build up specifically political collections.

It must be said that there was a considerable 'supply' of Marxism at the time, especially from the currents opposed to the established Communist Party which, though they had a long existence in France, had enjoyed little visibility up till this point. For these currents, the novelty of the post-'68 period was two-fold: on the one hand, the support coming from intellectuals was both more massive in scale and more broadly transmitted; on the other hand, the PCF had partly been discredited by its cautious wait-and-see position during the events of May–June, making *gauchiste* ideas all the more audible.

Lastly, this flowering of Marxism took place in a context of the '1968 years' – a boom period for struggles not only in France, but also in other parts of the world, when 'the revolution was knocking on the door again, from Cuba to Vietnam, from Portugal to Nicaragua'.[4]

---

4 Bantigny 2016.

1.2   *A Political and Theoretical Crisis*

Conversely, the 1970s saw the emergence of a diagnosis of a crisis of Marxism and of hopes of revolution. At the international level, if May '68 muffled the impact of the Soviet invasion of Prague in August, the same cannot be said of the growing testimonies of the Communist regimes' crimes. From Solzhenitsyn's accounts of the USSR to the defeat for Solidarność in Poland, via the gradual discovery of the reality of the Chinese Cultural Revolution or the Khmer Rouge genocide in Cambodia, the whole revolutionary myth was negatively affected.

At the same time, the socio-economic changes experienced by Western countries after 1945 had caused major difficulties for Marxist theory as well as the parties that claimed to be based on it. The revolutionary subject par excellence, the Western working class, saw its standard of living rise, and managers took on increasing importance in society (as did the cadres of the Communist Party itself). The PCF tried to adapt its doctrine to these realities: the thesis of 'absolute immiseration' was abandoned at the party's Seventeenth Congress in 1964; the Argenteuil central committee in 1966 granted intellectuals greater freedom of action; the Twentieth Congress in February 1976 rejected the very idea of a 'dictatorship of the proletariat'. However, despite these developments, the attitude of the PCF's leadership remained uncertain: it never ceased to evolve, between openness and closure, between the Argenteuil central committee and the end of the Common Programme in 1977, as a deeply divided PCF withdrew into itself.[5] It was precisely at this moment that the rebellion among the Communist intellectuals became a mass phenomenon. Some of Louis Althusser's former pupils, like many others, left the party; such was the case of Étienne Balibar, who in a 1981 article in *Le Monde* denounced the 'errors' of the PCF and the 'astonishing cult of personality around Georges Marchais'. This haemorrhaging of intellectual support symbolised the beginning of the PCF's electoral decline and the beginning of the Parti Socialiste's hegemony over the Left.

But if there was above all a crisis of the PCF, this was also a crisis of Marxisms, given how far political and the theoretical stakes were intertwined. In his 1978 *Ce qui ne peut plus durer dans le Parti communiste*, Althusser considered that there was a 'general crisis of Marxism', which was an 'ideological, political and theoretical crisis'. This question was also posed among the Marxisms that stood in opposition to the PCF. For example, the economist Bernard Chavance, then a Maoist, published under a pseudonym, in 1980, a text signific-

---

5   Pudal 2009.

antly entitled 'Crisis of the revolutionary perspective' in which he attempted to draw a balance-sheet;[6] André Gorz made his 'farewell to the working class' in 1980, in a resounding book. In the same years, other intellectuals from Marxism publicly raised the question of the relationship between Marx, Marxisms and the crimes committed in his name. In *The Crisis of Marxism*, Lucio Colletti[7] averred that 'one cannot close one's eyes to what has happened and pretend that nothing has happened'.

But can we deduce, from the crisis of Marxisms, their outright disappearance – positing a simple and unilateral causality? Should we not ask, in parallel, about the more general transformations of the intellectual field that allowed the idea of the collapse of Marxisms to take hold? We can do this, without denying that such a phenomenon exists. If the study of ideas remains paramount, an analysis of Marxism's trajectory in 1980s France cannot do without an examination of all the transformations that affected the intellectual field at that time, given that 'in the production of symbolic goods, the institutions apparently responsible for circulation are an integral part of the production apparatus, which must produce both the product and the belief in the value of its own product'.[8]

2   For A Social History of the Decline of Revolutionary Ideas

2.1   *The Anti-Totalitarian Offensive*

On 27 May 1977, the 'new philosophers' made their first TV appearance on the programme *Apostrophes*, hosted by Bernard Pivot. Bernard-Henri Lévy and André Glucksmann, both former leftists, came to present *La Barbarie à visage humain* and *La Cuisinière et le mangeur d'hommes*, in which they directly attributed the paternity of Stalinist totalitarianism to Marx. Along with others, Lévy and Glucksmann's books were part of 'anti-totalitarian ideology'. This made the 'gulag effect' a force in French intellectual and political debate, notably through issues of the journal *Esprit* and several news magazines (such as *L'Express* and *Le Nouvel Observateur*). The proclaimed equality between any form of Marxism and totalitarianism, at a time when the Common Programme and the Socialist-Communist alliance represented a considerable challenge, thus constituted a 'vaccine' against the illusions of Marxisms.[9] Implicitly or explicitly, any form of

---

6   Chavance 1980.
7   Colletti 1984.
8   Bourdieu and Delsaut 1975.
9   Christofferson 2004.

radical political project was condemned, just before the tenth anniversary of May '68, which saw the generalisation of discourse condemning the 'desire for radical systemic change'.[10]

Beyond its strictly ideological content, the offensive by the new philosophers testified to a change in the rules of the intellectual field, with the growing importance of audiovisual media, sealing the 'prevalence of the image over the word' and, consequently, a change in the power balance in intellectual debates.[11] Finally, the new philosophers' clamorous arrival on the scene lent credence to the idea of a massive reconversion of former revolutionary militants, which Guy Hocquenghem subjected to virulent criticism in 1986 in his *Lettre ouverte à ceux qui sont passés du col Mao au Rotary*.

2.2   *Transformations in the Academic and Publishing Arenas*

Important changes also took place in the universities. In some locations like Vincennes, political commitment was a prerequisite for all recruitment and all intellectual pretensions. But a profound professionalisation process in the humanities and social sciences, coupled with disciplinarisation, led both to the promotion of the principle of axiological neutrality – contradicting Marxism's 'scientific' status – and to a withdrawal within disciplinary limits. The image of the Tower of Babel well encapsulates this shift from a hitherto common language – Marxism – to a more selective, disciplinary one. The closure of Vincennes in 1980 was also strongly emblematic: the University of Paris-VIII moved to Saint-Denis and fell into line, with the return of the 'national accreditation' of its degrees, earlier withdrawn by the education ministry on account of the 'Marxist-Leninist' character of the teaching there.

At the same time, there were other transformations affecting the publishing sector. Indeed, the arrival of the liberal Valéry Giscard d'Estaing as president in 1974 led to a redefinition of editorial independence. The tendency toward concentration beginning in the postwar period accelerated in the 1960s and 1970s. While 7 percent of publishing houses accounted for 55 percent of the sector's total turnover in 1962, this same proportion held 63 percent of the market in 1971 and 68 percent in 1993. This phenomenon was encouraged by the economic situation of the publishing sector. Indeed, despite its vitality in the 1960s and 1970s, the poor figures of 1980 and especially 1981 considerably weakened this craft. At the same time, the whole chain of publishing was evolving. Hachette launched its new circulation/distribution mechanism in

---

10   Ross 2008.
11   Hourmant 2012.

1972, followed a year later by Presses de la Cité. The opening of the first branch of Fnac in 1974 and the discount policy at supermarkets such as Leclerc, where books were sold 20 percent cheaper, jeopardised the traditional bookshop, an ally of independent publishing. Through the Monory decree of 23 February 1979, d'Estaing supported this market logic by abandoning the previous 'recommended' book prices.

In short, the very structure of the publishing field was transformed, making the end of the 1970s a pivotal moment for the world of political books. However, it was not yet time to give up, and François Maspero stated in 1980 in his internal bulletin that he wanted to continue 'with a programme that remains in line with [Maspero's] choices across the past twenty years: constant research in the fields of politics, the humanities, the social sciences and literature'. However, he eventually handed over the reins in 1982. The sociologist Camille Joseph explains that despite this publisher's Marxist past, its successors, who renamed it after one of its collections, La Découverte, 'promoted a "critical" publishing style more focused on social sciences and popular science for students'. Despite this, 'La Découverte never strayed from a [politically] committed vision of publishing'.[12] Similarly, critical houses such as Anthropos or Le Sycomore stopped producing while other '68er voices, such as Christian Bourgois, turned their focus to literature.

2.3   A Professional Stigma?

This transformation of the context had an impact on intellectuals themselves. On the one hand, radical thinkers' very possibilities of being published were narrowing. On the other hand, the link between radical political commitment and professional integration was becoming more complicated. If we study the development of Maspero's authors over the 1980s, we can see three main kinds of journey. Some moved to the right wing of the political spectrum. Others – those who bore the least educational capital – remained on the fringes, for instance Denis Langlois, a lawyer involved in the Ligue des droits de l'homme and author of several books published by Maspero. He tells of how his persistent revolutionary commitment brought him 'face to face with a censorship that [he] could not have imagined', adding that he had 'paid dearly for his fidelity to [his] political positions'. As for the third group – those most endowed with academic resources, such as the *normaliens* – they would, in general, now have a 'slow career'. In other words, they became university professors late in life and spent a good part of their career outside Paris. If factors linked to the state of

---

12   Joseph 2010.

the academic field must be taken into account, at a time when assistants were very numerous and tenured positions became increasingly rare, the slowness of these careers cannot be separated from this 'stigma against revolutionaries'. Sometimes, political stigma directly forbade access to academic positions. But, more often, the delay in these academics' careers owed to their considerable political activism in the post-'68 years which them not to play the game of professionalisation, at least for a while. In 1986, Félix Guattari described the general context of this decade, which saw the shrinking of revolutionary possibilities, as the 'winter years'.

3   The 1980s: A Moment of Marxist Renewal

3.1   *1983: A Half-Hearted Centenary*

1983 occupies a decisive place in the study of the 1980s. This was the year of the Mitterrand government's 'austerian' turn, and also the moment of a debate on the 'silence' of the intellectuals, with the passing of Jean-Paul Sartre, Michel Foucault and many others within just a few years. This year was also the centenary of Marx's death. His legacy was the subject of a tense episode of *Apostrophes* in August, with guests Georges Labica, Jean-Pierre Lefevre, Claude Mazauric and Maximilien Rubel. Similarly, several conferences devoted to the author of *Capital* were organised and their proceedings published. The speakers took seriously the idea of a 'crisis of Marxism', but without abandoning Marx. Bernard Chavance wrote that 'if Marx is not the unsurpassable horizon of our time, he cannot be relegated to a simple chapter, now closed, in the history of ideas'.[13] Jean-Claude Delaunay explained his 'refusal of the "new right's" noisy attempts to kill Marxism' and called for an 'update of Marxist economic theory'.[14] Georges Labica wanted to 'show that it is now possible everywhere to do away with dogmas, fetishes and schools, and to open the way to a free research, indifferent to labels'.[15] Henri Lefebvre averred that 'Marx's work stands in relation to our time in much the same way as Newton's physics stands in relation to modern physics. In order to arrive at the latter, one must go through the former, take its concepts, modify them, complete them, transform them by adding other concepts ... Neither fetishising Marx nor putting him on the scrapheap!'[16]

---

13   Chavance 1985.
14   Delaunay 1986.
15   Labica 1985.
16   Lefebvre 1986.

3.2   Theoretical Hybridisations

All these intellectuals shared common problematics and contributed to a kind of updating of Marxism. Marx remained the main point of reference, but within the framework of multiple hybridisations; meanwhile, the question of what in Marxism had become outdated was still unanswered. There was agreement that Marx and Engels's philosophy of history – at least, the idea that scientific socialism merely follows historical development and is a 'process of natural history', as Marx states in *Capital* – was no longer operable. Similarly, the idea that the proletariat alone still constituted the revolutionary subject was largely abandoned, in favour of an analysis of the evolutions in the working class as well as the transformations of capitalism. New themes, such as ecology, also appeared, at a time when the Green Party, founded in 1984, was foregrounding this political question. A complex process of confrontation of Marx's thought with that of other thinkers then took place: the hybridisation of Marx with Marcel Mauss, Karl Polanyi, and even John Rawls allowed for a certain intellectual renewal.[17]

The trajectory of Antonio Negri is exemplary in this respect. A figure of Italian *operaismo* in the 1960s and 1970s, he befriended Guattari, Althusser, Gilles Deleuze and Yann Moulier-Boutang during his stays in France. But Negri was arrested in 1979 and sentenced to seventeen years in prison for his alleged intellectual proximity to the Red Brigades, responsible for the murder of Aldo Moro. It was in prison that he wrote *The Savage Anomaly*, his first major text devoted to Spinoza. Setting Spinoza into relation with Marx, Negri drew on the French philosophical context of the 1960s and 1970s: on Alexandre Matheron, an (oppositionist) member of the PCF who published his *Individu et communauté chez Spinoza* with Minuit in 1969; on Althusser, who sought to renew Marxism using Spinoza during the 1960s, and then at the moment when he was added to the syllabus for the *agrégation* in philosophy in 1972–3; and on Deleuze's courses at Vincennes, which Negri attended when he was in France. It was from Spinoza that Negri drew the concept of 'multitude', which allowed him to progressively update Marxism by breaking out of the workerist framework and by expanding the revolutionary subject to include 'all those who work under the rule of capital'.[18] Negri's trajectory also fitted into a more collective phenomenon where, from the 1980s onwards, Spinoza came to Marx as a subversive author. The vision of Spinoza as a radical atheist, an anti-contractualist democrat and, more generally, precursor of the materialist tradition, can be

---

17   Hauchecorne 2009.
18   Hardt and Negri 2005.

found in the first issue of the *Cahiers Spinoza*, published in 1977 and devoted to the links between Marx and Spinoza.

3.3   *New Spaces of Reflection*

Yet, if these Marxisms were renewed, they remained little-visible in the early 1980s. Their publication owed to small publishers such as L'Harmattan and relayed by elite media, such as *Le Monde diplomatique* or *France Culture*. However, new editorial havens appeared, such as the *Cahiers Georges Sorel*, created in 1983 with an issue on Sorel and Marx, or the *Bulletin du MAUSS*, which was launched in 1981 around Alain Caillé, Serge Latouche and other intellectuals with a Marxist past. This latter was characterised in this period by 'its reluctance to cut too many bridges with central Marxian aspirations, its refusal to throw the baby of radical hope – or rather of the hope of a certain radicalism – out with the bath waters of totalitarianism'.[19] *L'Autre Journal* was founded in 1984 by Michel Butel, a former Maoist. 1986 saw the appearance of *M, mensuel, marxisme, mouvement*, its first issue including an interview with Henri Lefebvre.

The situation remained difficult, at a time when the right returned to power in 1986 with a radical free-market programme. However, other spaces continued to be created. The journal *Actuel Marx* published its first issue, devoted to the state of Marxism, in 1987. It was linked to the work of Nanterre university's philosophy department, mainly around Georges Labica, Jacques Texier and Jacques Bidet, but also other communist intellectuals who had left the PCF at the end of the 1970s, such as Étienne Balibar, André Tosel, Michèle Bertrand and Christine Buci-Glucksmann. In 1982 this latter group had already been at the origin of the *Dictionnaire critique du marxisme* published by Presses universitaires de France. Alongside this there was also the review *Futur antérieur*, created in 1989 by Antonio Negri and Jean-Marie Vincent, a historical Trotskyist and founder of the political science department at Vincennes in 1968. This journal brought together many intellectuals who had passed through heterodox Marxism in the 1970s.

These spaces allowed Marxist thought to continue to develop while forming a new intellectual generation, such as Yves Sintomer and Stathis Kouvelakis, doctoral students of Georges Labica's at Nanterre. A certain spirit of May '68 thus continued to blow through the air, despite the collapse of the communist world.

---

19   Caillé and Dzimara 2009.

4   Marx after Marxisms

The start of the 1990s was marked by one major fact: the end of the Cold War. In 1992, Francis Fukuyama prophesied the 'end of history', the result of a generalised consensus on the superiority of liberal democracy, while François Furet continued his work on the revolutionary idea and communist ideology, in which he saw the 'passing of an illusion'.[20] Yet against this, the resistance was also getting organised. Jacques Derrida, in his *Specters of Marx* published in 1993, criticised 'the media parade of current discourses on the end of history and the last man [which] most often resembles a boring anachronism', and called for lessons to be taken from Marx 'so long as we take into account what Marx and Engels themselves said'. Henri Maler and Denis Berger, for their part, attacked François Furet who 'traps communism in a one-sided version in order to strangle its history with one hand and pull it to the floor'.[21]

With the movements of 1995, there seemed to be a renewed period of social rebellion. This allowed radical ideas to gain visibility, aided by the creation of collectives such as Attac and Acrimed. New 'critical independent' publishers such as Agone and La Fabrique emerged at the end of the 1990s. Daniel Bensaïd, who had published *Marx l'intempestif: Grandeur et misère d'une aventure critique* in 1995, launched *Contretemps* in 2001, finding its place alongside other journals such as *Vacarme*, *Mouvements* (which succeeded *M*) and *Multitudes*, itself the result of a split within *Futur antérieur*. This renewed interest in Marxist-inspired critique can also be seen in the success of certain radical thinkers whose trajectory is rooted in the '1968 years'. Slavoj Žižek, Antonio Negri, Étienne Balibar, Jacques Rancière and Alain Badiou formed a kind of international and politically radical intellectual collective that delved into the legacy and the vigour of the 'idea of communism' in the twenty-first century.[22]

5   Is Marx Still Alive?

This overview of the post-1968 destiny of Marx in France – the fate of an inseparably intellectual and political figure – shows that, although there was initially a form of fascination and then a significant decline in reference to Marx among French intellectuals, no 'farewell' took place. Albeit fewer in number from the

---

20   Furet 1999.
21   Berger and Maler 1996.
22   Badiou and Žižek 2010.

end of the 1970s onwards, some intellectuals did remain attached to the German thinker and, with him, to a project which, since the 1990s and 2000s, has been presented more as 'critical' or 'emancipatory' than as 'revolutionary' or 'Marxist'. Taking into account all the constraints weighing on radical ideas allows us to question and shed light not on the 'end of the blindness', but on an evolution and hybridisation of Marxisms. The study of the 1980s and 1990s reveals new, more open and critical relations to Marx, the product of 'a new era in which Marx has become a "great thinker" who can be studied without believing that he is the bearer of "social truth"'.[23] However, beyond this newfound status as a 'great thinker', through the critical scope of his writings themselves, Marx remains indispensable for those who want to continue thinking about emancipation.

23   Lindenberg 2004.

CHAPTER 22

Feminisms, Marxism, And Their Contentious Links

Sylvie Chaperon and Florence Rochefort

The links between feminisms and Marxism have always been contentious, both at the level of theory and in political practice. The question of autonomy occupies a primary place at the heart of this conflict. What is the specificity of women's oppression – and what place can be given to a struggle for gender equality when the priority is to eliminate capitalism? On the feminist side of things, the challenge is to take into account the class struggle and the social inequalities that divide women, while preserving the goal of individual and collective emancipation. These strong tensions have not prevented the emergence, ever since the 1890s, of currents that have attempted to combine feminism and Marxism. Since the end of the 1960s, a few women theorists have seized on Marxism and transformed it to nourish a materialist feminism, a current that is becoming influential again today.

1 The First Links Between Feminism and Marxism, from the 1860s to the 1920s

In the early days of Marxism, doctrine took little interest in the question of women as such, even though it had been on the agenda since the French Revolution and then in the women's clubs of 1830 and 1848. In the *Communist Manifesto* of 1848, the female worker is only the wife of the proletarian, and there is no reference to her enfranchisement or emancipation – key words among the utopian socialists whom Marx and Engels severely condemned. While the ideology of the bourgeois family was denounced as hypocritical – treating women as mere instruments of production, or even prostitution – women were not seen as a political force.

During the popular meetings of 1868, when a mobilisation for women's rights was again on the rise in France, there were heated debates around women working. While feminists such as Paule Minck held this to be an essential right, most Proudhonians were still marked by the anathema 'housewife or courtesan'. In the First International, if the Marxists were somewhat favourable to women's work, this was with a view to strengthening the proletariat, not to dealing with their specific condition.

Throughout the Third Republic, several feminists created socialist women's groups, such as Léonie Rouzade and her short-lived Women's Union in 1880, but they did not manage to establish themselves in the mysterious male world of political activism. Despite some success in getting pro-equality motions passed at congresses, they bore only very limited influence. These votes had to be reiterated over and over (Dr Madeleine Pelletier again obtained votes of principle in 1906 and 1907), and they did not lead to any action, either to attract women into the movement or to defend their rights. It was not easy to make a feminist voice heard at the theoretical level, either. Aline Valette, a feminist militant and member of Jules Guesde's Parti Ouvrier (POF), tried to propose a theoretical synthesis in her newspaper L'Harmonie sociale. Organe des droits et intérêts féminins (1892–3).[1] She was inspired in particular by August Bebel's analysis of Woman in the Past, Present and Future (1879), translated in 1891, from which she published large extracts in her paper, and by Dr Bonnier's theory of 'sexualism'. Despite a certain confusion and maternalism which limited its scope, sexualism presented an effort to take into account – following Bebel as well as Engels's The Origin of the Family, Property and the State (1884, translated in 1886) – not only the double exploitation of women as producers and reproducers, but also the 'masculinism' which they suffered in addition to capitalist oppression. Thus, the class struggle was associated with the struggle between the sexes and the idea of a 'sex class'. Women – and feminism, according to Aline Valette – were thus tasked with solving the 'sexual question', the feminist counterpart of the Marxian 'social question'. However, the emancipation of women remained first and foremost conditional on the abolition of capitalism, and for socialists no alliance with bourgeois women was possible. Aline Valette did not succeed in convincing the feminists, either.

Early twentieth-century initiatives by socialist feminists had little greater impact.[2] While many of them belonged to both feminist and socialist groups, a few tried to create a common current. Each time, the difficulties proved insurmountable. The condemnation of 'bourgeois feminism' became increasingly widespread within international socialism, from the criticisms of the German activist Clara Zetkin in 1893 to the motion at the Stuttgart Congress in 1907, which forbade any rapprochement with the women's rights movement, perceived as a competitor. French socialism especially struggled to open up to women, unlike its German counterpart. The interest that left-wing republican feminists, for instance the journalist Marguerite Durand or the lawyer Maria

---

1   Sowerwine 1978; Klejman-Rochefort 1989.
2   Rochefort 2004.

Verona showed in all the forms of women's work; their in-depth investigations into working conditions, wage inequality and the struggles of women workers; their financial solidarity during strikes; and their willingness to encourage and defend women's trade unionism, as in the famous Couriau affair (1913) – all this intensely irritated those who saw it as nothing more than bourgeois reformism. The idea that there could be common interests concerning all women and that male domination was not only the preserve of the bourgeoisie was intolerable for most socialists. Louise Saumoneau, who headed the socialist-feminist group founded in 1899, thus obstructed any attempt at rapprochement and denounced the aspiration to individual emancipation, which she considered incompatible with the liberation of the proletariat. She also blocked the 1913 attempt to form a new socialist-feminist grouping within the French Section of the Workers' International (SFIO). This conflict was not only a matter of repudiating themes such as neo-Malthusianism and free motherhood – causes which rallied the minority of radical feminists – but also had to do with the very legitimacy of an autonomous feminism. The schoolteacher Hélène Brion was one of those who defended the dual struggle, in socialism as in trade unionism, where the battle to get a hearing for feminist demands was just as tough. The 1914–18 war and the influence of the Russian Revolution led to a radicalisation of left-wing feminist activists, who joined the Third International with real hope.

2   The Communist Party and Women, from the 1920s to the 1990s

In the interwar period, the links between the feminist and Marxist movements were redefined by the birth of the French Communist Party, which claimed to embody Marxism and represent the working class. Although the party strongly defended equality between the sexes, it constantly denigrated feminists. For their part, while radical feminists were able to see in this new party a hope for change, they rapidly came up against the sectarianism and dogmatism of a Bolshevised PCF.

In the 1920s, the PCF was undoubtedly the most feminist of all French parties. It defended gender equality, political rights and the repeal of the 1920 law banning contraception (though most feminists approved of this). The party took care of propaganda and work directed women, thanks to its weekly *L'Ouvrière*, the 'Women' page of *L'Humanité* and the International Women's Week, around 8 March. It stood women candidates for municipal elections, and women representatives momentarily took office before being barred. Finally, Communist MPs voted for bills for women's suffrage. Radical feminists such as Madeleine Pelletier, Hélène Brion, Louise Bodin, Lucie Colliard and Marthe Bigot found a place in the party for a while, but the Bolshevisation of the PCF pushed them toward the door. Disappointed or excluded, they often found a place in far-left circles. Marthe Bigot joined the Trotskyist reviews *La Vérité* and then *La Révolution prolétarienne*, while Lucie Colliard joined Marceau Pivert's Workers' and Peasants' Socialist Party (PSOP) in 1938.[3] The communist CGTU defended women's right to work, equal pay and women's strikes. There were also active Feminist Secular Education Groups, until their disappearance in 1932.[4]

The popular-frontist strategic turn transformed the PCF's positions on women. Now a defender of the family and mothers, if not forgetting women workers, the party put off questions of 'sexual reform' and the fight against the 1920 law. It now supported pro-natalist policies and family allowances. The 'Women' page of *L'Humanité* became 'Women and Children', while 8 March was neglected. Turning its back on the combined organisations which had been promoted up till that point, the party set up satellite associations in order to encourage the recruitment of women and to nurture a broad anti-fascist front: the Fraternal Union of Women against Imperialist War (created in 1927) in 1934 became the World Committee of Women against War and Fascism, headed by Gabrielle Duchêne and Bernadette Cattanéo.[5] The founding congress of the French Girls' Union was held in December 1936. Directed by Danielle Casanova, it published a monthly magazine, *Jeunes Filles de France*, and had around 20,000 members in 1939.

The Communist Party emerged from World War II strengthened by its major contribution to the Resistance. It was equipped with a new mass women's association, the French Women's Union (UFF), itself a product of the Communist women's Resistance. Its first congress was held in June 1945 at La Mutualité in Paris. A month later, the founding congress of the Women's International Democratic Federation, with delegates from 45 countries, also met in Paris. The UFF was not feminist and routinely characterised feminists as bourgeois who diverted women from the correct revolutionary struggle. However, the women designated or elected by the PCF or the CGT, like the leaders and activists of the UFF, defended women's rights, first in the Consultative Assembly in Algiers and then in the first National Assemblies. They worked for the abrogation of legal reductions in women's wages (obtained in July 1946 largely thanks to

---

3   Bard and Robert, 1998.
4   Sohn 1977.
5   Tardivel 1993.

the actions of Marie Couette); for the declaration of gender equality in the new Fourth Republic's constitution; and for the reform of the civil code; while celebrating women's participation in the Resistance each 8 March. The PCF ran more women candidates than any other party and elected the most women representatives at all levels. However, it continued to promote pro-natalist policies and the generous family policy introduced by the early postwar governments. The UFF reached out to all progressive women and opened the pages of its weekly magazine *Femmes françaises* to numerous personalities such as Dominique Aury, Clara Malraux, Françoise d'Eaubonne, Édith Thomas and Françoise Dolto.[6]

The Cold War brought this first period to a halt, with the PCF abandoning the promotion of women's rights in favour of highlighting the role of mothers in pacifist movements, support for children's literature and the benefits of painless childbirth in the Soviet Union. Many intellectuals left the party and the UFF and tried to combine feminism and Marxism in other ways. Édith Thomas regained her freedom at the time of the Tito affair, and wrote numerous books on women's activity in the socialist movement. It was not until 1954 that a women's rights commission was created in the UFF, under the leadership of Andrée Marty-Capgras and Suzanne Kieffé. This committee especially worked for the reform of the system of laws governing marriage.

In 1949, Simone de Beauvoir scrutinised Marxism's contribution to women's liberation in *The Second Sex*, also criticising it for reducing the human being to 'Homo economicus'. A great admirer of *Capital*, in her memoirs she would admit that reading this work, at the beginning of the 1930s, revealed to her that labour is indeed 'the source and substance of values'. She drove Jean-Paul Sartre to the recognition that the ontological freedom of consciousness is always limited by a historical and social 'situation'. Subsequently, like Sartre, she drew closer to the Communist Party. She then invited women not to form groups of their own but to join men in the socialist struggle. She would remain faithful to this viewpoint until her encounter with the militants of the Women's Liberation Movement (MLF).

At the moment of *The Second Sex*'s publication, the Communist press joined in chorus with conservative intellectuals such as François Mauriac, who strongly criticised the book. Marie-Louise Barron in *Les Lettres françaises*, Jean Kanapa and then Jeannette Prenant in *La Nouvelle Critique*, and an anonymous reviewer in *Action*, all took turns to cast Beauvoir, the 'suffragette of sexuality', as a bourgeois diversion from the righteous struggle against capitalism and

---

6   Fayolle 2005.

US imperialism. 'While we are told about love, we are not told about peace or wages', was Marie-Louise Barron's summary. This polemic expressed the Communist rejection of existentialism, condemned as idealism by György Lukács in his book *Existentialism or Marxism?* published in 1948. But it also revealed the party's hostility towards the sexual liberalisation which Beauvoir called for. Conversely, many left-wing intellectuals, progressive Christians and contributors to *Les Temps modernes* defended her arguments. For instance, in her 1951 essay *Le Complexe de Diane*, Françoise d'Eaubonne, a Communist until 1956, mounted a critical synthesis of Marxism and Freudiansm and called on women to form autonomous groups.[7] When the Maternité heureuse ('Happy Motherhood') association was created in 1956 with the aim of repealing the 1920 law, the party proved just as dogged. On International Women's Day, Marie-Claude Vaillant-Couturier condemned 'neo-Malthusian and petty-bourgeois' propaganda. Jeannette Vermeersch in *France nouvelle* and Maurice Thorez in *L'Humanité* insisted on the need to fight 'for the right to motherhood and the future of France', though this was not enough to stop many Communists from supporting the demand for free contraception. After Thorez's death, the party demanded the repeal of the 1920 law within the context of the union of the left.

3   The Women's Liberation Movement and the Revival of Marxism,
       from the 1960s to the 1990s

In the 1960s, Althusser, the Frankfurt School and Freudo-Marxism breathed new life into Marxism, albeit without paying great attention to the feminist question. For its part, the feminist movement regenerated itself, influenced by a new generation of activists. Small groups appeared, such as Féminin Masculin Avenir (1967) within the women's democratic movement, a sort of women's New Left, or the Vincennes group around Antoinette Fouque and Monique Wittig (1968). These groups became more radical and joined forces after 1968, even as they passionately debated Marxist and psychoanalytical theories. A few public events, as well as the publication of feminist articles in the far-left press, led to the emergence of a women's movement in autumn 1970, soon baptised by the media as the Women's Liberation Movement (MLF). This movement consisted of a multitude of initiatives, groups, publications and autonomous events in all France's main cities.

---

7 Chaperon 2000.

In schematic terms, there were two major tendencies in this movement that fed on and identified with Marxism: materialist feminism and class-struggle feminism. As early as 1970, in the first theoretical opus of the new MLF – entitled 'Libération des femmes année zéro' and published in the review *Partisans* by Maspero – Christine Delphy provided a contradiction of Marxist theses, while also taking them up on behalf of feminism. She demonstrated that the oppression of women is neither secondary nor due to capitalism. For Delphy, patriarchy, which in the domestic mode of production extorts the work done by women, is the 'main enemy'. She thus transposed the key concepts of historical materialism to the situation of women (gender class, the domestic mode of production, unpaid labour), to demonstrate the importance of their exploitation and the necessary autonomy of their struggle. In a 1975 article published in *L'Arc*, she called for a 'materialist feminism', tasked with demonstrating the material oppression of women in all fields. This programme was pursued in the journal *Questions féministes*, founded in 1977 under the patronage of Simone de Beauvoir, with contributions by Christine Delphy, Colette Guillaumin, Nicole-Claude Mathieu, Colette Capitan, Emmanuelle de Lesseps, Monique Wittig, and so on. Together – and with the help of Paola Tabet, an Italian anthropologist of the same persuasion – they went beyond merely highlighting the exploitation of women's labour to assert the collective male appropriation of their bodies and their fertility – a comprehensive relationship of domination that Colette Guillaumin calls 'sexing'.

The other tendency regarded far-left activists concerned with linking feminist struggles to popular struggles. They led numerous neighbourhood groups, went to meet striking women workers – very numerous in the 1970s – and were particularly involved in the Movement for the Liberation of Abortion and Contraception (MLAC) and against domestic and sexual violence. Their twofold struggle was difficult, prompting reticence among both feminists – who saw them as leftists subservient to their party – and party militants who did not understand their feminist demands. The Elisabeth Dimitriev Circle of activists of the Revolutionary Marxist Alliance or the newspapers *Les Pétroleuses* and then *Les Cahiers du féminisme* (founded within the Revolutionary Communist League, LCR, in 1977, notably by Josette Trat) illustrate this tendency.

Within the Socialist Party, the Communist Party and the CGT, feminist sensibilities tried, with some difficulty, to get a hearing. Current 3 (which proposed gender parity on electoral lists) and the magazine *Elles voient rouge*, produced by PCF feminists, were criticised as bearers of so many 'fractional activities'. The CGT's dismissal in May 1982 of the editorial board of *Antoinette*, a women's (and increasingly, feminist) magazine attached to the confederation, also illustrates these difficulties.[8] The feminist *aggiornamento* of the PCF took place in the 1990s. At the Thirtieth Congress in 1999, the individual and no longer the working class was set at the heart of its logic, while feminisms partly moved away in part from the neo-Marxist analytical framework.

4   New Feminist Paradigms and Marxism in the 2000s

The 2000s were marked by the success of new paradigms – queer, postcolonial and intersectional theories – which reshaped feminist issues and shattered the supposed homogeneity of the category 'woman' and the idea of sisterhood. This conceptual splintering corresponded to the emergence of new social forces and contradictions, as well as to the waning impact of a feminism centred on women's rights and liberation, which nevertheless remained active. The gay and lesbian (LGBT+) movements encouraged the introduction to France of work on queer theories from North America. In particular, Teresa de Lauretis and Judith Butler proposed a radical deconstruction of the notion of 'sex' and of the heteronormativity that shapes all gender thinking, understood as a normative system that constructs gendered categories. Femininities and masculinities were analysed as performances, pointing to the profound instability of identities and their possible transgression as a politics of subversion. Transgender figures became the object of particular attention, both in fighting against the discriminations affecting them (compulsory operations, the refusal to change their civil status ...), but also to highlight their potential to destabilise gender norms. These analyses were initially the subject of severe criticism from the leading lights of 1970s materialist feminism; they were especially criticised for privileging discourses over the materiality of oppressions and bodies.[9] The American Nancy Fraser's criticisms of an excessive focus on identity, recognition and the politicisation of sexualities disconnected from socio-economic contexts also found an echo in France.[10] She defended an anti-capitalist and anti-neoliberal feminism capable of recovering its insurrectionary spirit and its critical potential against 'capitalist androcentrism'; this meant integrating demands for recognition, but articulated to a politics of redistribution. Judith Butler, for whom the struggle against heterosexism is anti-capitalist in its essence, saw Fraser as a neo-conservative Marxist. At the heart of their dis-

---

8   George 2011.

9   Cervulle and Clair 2017.

10   Fraser 2012.

pute was the question of priorities and the articulation between different types of oppression that had marked the polemics (notably around rape) in the 1970s.

A new generation of feminists, formed by their reading of *Gender Trouble* (published in the United States in 1990, but only translated into French in 2005), has shown renewed interest in materialist feminism; in Marxism as reformulated by this current and by Anglo-American intellectuals; and in the Gramscian concept of hegemony.[11] The challenge from Black feminism, which reached France a few years after its emergence in the United States and Great Britain, has also fuelled reflection on the limits of universalism and the need, for feminists in particular, to take into account ethnic minorities and racism.[12] A new feminist current, headed by Christine Delphy, defended girls who wanted to wear the Islamic headscarf against the 2004 law banning it in schools; more recently it has supported Afrofeminism, which has begun to take organised form.[13] The conceptual triad 'gender, race and class' has a long history, often overlooked by activists. This is no longer, as in the 1970s, a way of integrating class and race into a patriarchal system considered all-encompassing and to have an existence that precedes the class system. Rather, it is a way of understanding the interdependence and multidimensionality of these systems of domination. This makes it possible, from a theoretical point of view at least, to transcend the question of priorities.

Reviving an analysis of class domination and forms of labour exploitation does not mean an explicit adherence to Marxian doctrine. Some activists and researchers have, nevertheless, laid claim to this latter by advocating – in the journal *Période* and in certain books[14] – a 'feminism of totality', which prioritises the critique of capitalism enriched by the contributions of feminisms, the gay and lesbian movements and postcolonial analyses. Particular focus is placed on the evolution of women's wage labour and on a women's liberation in rich countries which implies the exploitation and commodification of migrant women in domestic services, care work and prostitution. This new Marxist and feminist current puts a primary emphasis on denouncing modes of economic exploitation, consumerism and inequalities between North and South. It seems that despite the determination to analyse oppressions in terms of cosubstantiality or coextensivity (inspired by the sociologist Danièle Kergoat), or intersectionality, it remains difficult to go beyond a more structural and traditionally Marxist vision of relations of oppression.

---

11 Dorlin 2007; Arruzza 2016; Noyé 2014.
12 Dorlin 2008.
13 Nouvelles Questions féministes 2006.
14 Boggio Éwanjé-Épée et al. 2017.

PART 5

Seen from Elsewhere

∴

CHAPTER 23

Marx Seen from the Right: When French Economists Discovered Marx's *Capital*

Jacqueline Cahen

The history of Marx's reception has long been considered only in the political and intellectual contexts of Marxism itself.[1] In a country where Marxist references have left a lasting impression on the major left-wing organisations, what could be more logical than to try to understand how Marx influenced the political world? Yet, socialist militants and self-proclaimed Marxists were not the only ones in France to read *Capital* closely, nor even likely the first. In fact, it was outside Marxist circles that Marx's master work was first discussed. While some scholars have previously noted this paradox,[2] there has never been a close study of the attention that figures outside of the organised workers' movement paid to *Capital* Volume I, at a time when Marxists close to Jules Guesde and Paul Lafargue were less interested in this work's theoretical and economic dimensions than its more immediately political ones, and the demands of propaganda.[3]

In the afterword that Marx wrote for the second German edition of *Capital* in January 1873, he noted that 'the method employed in Capital has been little understood, as the contradictory conceptions of it suffice to show'. It is these reactions in the French context that we wish to examine here, with particular focus on responses among the liberal economists and the 'university-chair socialists' – theorists of a conservative socialism, opposed to any idea of revolution.

---

1 This text was put together by Jean-Numa Ducange and Guillaume Fondu based on the manuscript for the unfinished dissertation (supervised by Christophe Prochasson) by Jacqueline Cahen, who sadly passed away in 2015.

2 Bernstein 1933; Dommanget 1969.

3 Prochasson 2004.

1   Liberals and Socialists: The Conduits of an Encounter

In July 1872, the leading journal of French liberalism, the *Journal des économistes*, published a long critical essay on *Capital* by Maurice Block. Before returning to the surprising attention which he devoted to Marx, it is necessary to set it in its wider historical perspective. Indeed, in many respects, liberal and socialist theories developed in parallel, in a play of oppositions that makes the history of one inseparable from the history of the other.

Since the first half of the nineteenth century, there has been a long tradition of critical analysis of socialist theories. The milieu of French economists took form at the same time that socialist and communist conceptions were emerging, in the 1830s and 1840s – a period when rebellions by workers (such as the *canut* revolts of 1831–4) were also of increasing concern to politicians. For liberal economists, it was necessary to fight against all protectionist notions and against any propensity toward state economic intervention to solve the problems posed by working-class destitution. Much like their socialist counterparts, the champions of liberal ideas moved to organise – and coalesced into a real political 'lobby'.[4]

Within this context, we can distinguish three rallying points for the liberal economists: Guillaumin, the publisher founded in 1835; the famous *Journal des économistes* founded in 1841 (whose first director was the economist Adolphe Blanqui), and lastly, starting in 1842, the *Société d'économie politique*, the forerunner of modern think tanks, where industrialists and politicians met, discussed the problems of the modern world and worked out concrete solutions to counteract the rise of socialist propaganda. This influential group published numerous texts against 'utopia', deemed pernicious and negative, to which it counterposed an economic 'science' based on unshakeable natural laws.

Indeed, it was an economist – Louis Reybaud – who first grouped together personalities such as Saint-Simon, Fourier and Owen under the term 'socialists', in order to banish them from the field of political economy where they had hitherto enjoyed a right of place. His *Études sur les réformateurs ou socialistes modernes* – first published in 1841 and repeatedly reissued – provides a model of works in this anti-socialist key.

This interplay of oppositions between liberals and socialists explains why the liberal economists – already-well organised and with a seemingly well-honed set of arguments against socialism – were the first to 'discover' Karl Marx

---

4   Le Van-Lemesle 2004.

and his monumental critique of political economy, even before socialists themselves took an interest in it.

2   Reading and Commenting on *Capital*

If these liberal economists' attentive concern for socialism must be analysed in a longer historical perspective, one major event, which shortly preceded the first French edition of *Capital*, led these economists to take an interest in Marx especially: namely, the Paris Commune of March–June 1871.[5]

Indeed, for these men, the Commune revealed that socialism was a real danger, not least given that there were several factors that demonstrated the enduring vitality of this doctrine despite the repression of the Paris insurgents. One was the existence of the International Working Men's Association (the IWMA, the 'First International', founded in 1864), in which Marx was highly active (the conservative press, overestimating his influence, described him as the 'great leader of the International'), attesting to the progress made in organising the 'subversive' currents in several countries. Moreover, and more specifically, the growing strength of German socialism never ceased to cause concern.[6] As an 'economic chronicle' in the *Journal des économistes* put it: 'All these misfortunes, all this delirium, all this suffering, all these disasters, all these horrors, have in large part their primary cause in ignorance of sound notions of social organisation'. And it was the liberal economists' task to defend these 'sound notions'.

The early French reception of Marx is of particular interest insofar as it provided the occasion for a debate between two economists with antagonistic political and epistemological positions (albeit ones who shared a robust hostility to Marx), Maurice Block (1816–1901) and Émile de Laveleye (1822–92). Block, despite his meandering trajectory a typical representative of the liberal school, was a staunch opponent of the 'university-chair socialism' defended by Laveleye from 1874 onwards. Their two articles on *Capital*, published in 1872 and 1876 respectively, set out the broad outlines of Marx's reception among economists. While this reception was deepened and depoliticised from 1880 onwards, it would long bear the impression of these two contributions. They further attest to the difficulty that economists of the time had in getting to grips with a work that so defied their expectations, since it was so atypical both for a 'socialist' work and for a work of 'political economy'.

---

5   Rougerie 1971.
6   Droz 1972.

So, who were these first attentive readers of *Capital*? Block, born in Berlin in 1816 and naturalised in France in 1848, was a former employee of the French administration (he rose to the rank of deputy head of the Statistics office), from which he resigned to devote himself to his work on economics. His knowledge of German enabled him to write numerous articles on the economic debates taking place on the other side of the Rhine. He expressed a lively interest in these questions, doubtless linked to his own past: in his review he mentions that in 1844, at the time of the *Deutsch–Französische Jahrbücher*, he had met with Marx, of whom he still had 'the memory of a man who was as learned as he was pleasant'. As a regular and important contributor to the *Journal des économistes*, he thus read and critiqued *Capital* from his position as an avowed exponent of French liberal economics.[7]

In July 1872, Block published his review of *Capital* in the *Journal des économistes*, under the title: 'Les Théoriciens du socialisme en Allemagne. I. Système de M. Karl Marx'. He worked using the German version (as did Laveleye), and made no mention of the French translation (which only began to be published from August, and remained very marginally used by economists). His argument was based on categories inherited from Jean-Baptiste Say, constitutive of liberal thought at the time: economics, the science of natural economic laws, was opposed to socialism and its intrinsic artificiality, consistent with nothing apart from the political project of social reform or revolution. But *Capital* posed a problem in this context. It is not a purely socialist text, insofar as its content and references place it directly in the history of political economy, as Block himself underlines. But, on the other hand, its critical and political dimension (further accentuated by the fact that Block was writing just after the Commune) prevent it from being a pure and simple contribution to political economy. *Capital*, according to Block, 'is a remarkable work. With this book, Mr. Marx ranks among the most eminent analytical minds, and we have only one regret, that he followed a wrong direction'.

Block pulled off an operation which would greatly influence the subsequent reception of Marx among French economists: namely, to distinguish, within *Capital*, between what pertained to economic analysis and what pertained to history. This amounted to cutting the link that Marx had established between the study of the capitalist structure and that of its historicity, meaning, the dynamic study of the contradictions of capital. Refusing to situate the debate on this terrain, Block ends up identifying Marx with Proudhon and more generally with all the theories (described as 'eccentric doctrines') which see labour

---

7   Laurent and Marco 1996.

alone as the factor of production which allows one to claim a right over the product. This re-reading of *Capital* within the theoretical framework of the remuneration of the factors of production allows Block to repeat the liberal arguments against this monopoly role for labour.

3   'University-Chair Socialism' and Marx

Émile de Laveleye's trajectory led him to read *Capital* from a completely different perspective. At first a philosophy and then a law student, in 1856 he had to give up his doctorate in public and administrative law because he was considered too subversive by the professors at Ghent University. It was after his studies of rural economics that he was awarded the chair of political economy at the University of Liege in 1864. But what distinguished him from the French economists mentioned above was his Christian convictions, making him sensitive to social problems as well as historical developments, seen through an evangelical teleology which counselled preparing in this world the kingdom of God to come. It was in this perspective that he published, in 1873, his great work *De la propriété et de ses formes primitives*, which consisted of a historical and comparative study of the different forms of property. In an 1875 article in *Revue des deux Mondes*, he reviewed the 'new trends in the economy and socialism'. It was only the following year that he got directly to grips with *Capital*, after a lively exchange with Block on the epistemology of political economy.

Laveleye laid claim to an anti-Marxist socialism, called the 'socialism of the university chair'. Its appearance in Germany (*Kathedersozialismus*), taking the form of an association with the Verein für Sozialpolitik (Social Policy Association) founded in 1872, was to change things somewhat. This socialism was the work of a number of economics professors, all linked to the German historical school and concerned about the social tensions caused by the sudden development of capitalism in Germany. Their epistemology, both historicist and comparative, was placed in service of reflection on the different institutions that could integrate the working class into the national economy in order to keep it away from the revolutionary temptation (represented at the time by the growing Marxist social democracy) and to strengthen the national community. In the French context, the founding of this current represents a second oddity, demanding alterations to the usual categories, since it included not only socialist economists but also statist economists, politically opposed to any idea of revolution. In his article on 'Les tendances nouvelles de l'économie et du socialisme', Laveleye provided an account of the formation and the ideas of this current, declaring his own identification with these notions, while simultaneously attacking French liberalism, which he criticised for its profoundly contradictory character. According to Laveleye, the radical naturalism that it advocates ought to forbid it from having any political and militant perspective, even though this did historically represent a constitutive dimension of the French liberal current. Only a theory of economics as a 'moral science' made it possible to imagine a political combat in favour of certain economic ideas, even if that meant liberal ones.

For Laveleye, Marx did not represent a kind of ideal-type of German socialism. Rather, because of the naturalism he continued to uphold, he constituted an exception to this socialism. Laveleye's reading of Marx allows us to understand the gap between the revolutionary political dimension of Marx and the perspectives of university-chair socialism. This is what Laveleye set out to demonstrate in the second major article in French devoted to *Capital*, which was published in the *Revue des deux Mondes* on 1 September 1876 under the title: 'Le Socialisme contemporain en Allemagne. 1. Les théoriciens'. Like Block's piece, Laveleye's article – which also deals with Marx's book only in a roundabout way – offered an exposition of Capital followed by a critique. The author's intellectual training led him to refer to and discuss Marx's historicisation of capitalism much more than Block did. But here again, the central question of the motor of this historicity is left aside and simply analysed as a 'contradiction' of Marx's: by confusing nature and history, Marx locks himself into an incoherent fatalism instead of recognising moral progress and legislative activity as the true dynamic element of any society. This moral evolutionism makes it possible to imagine – and defend – a form of socialism built on political (and gradual) reforms of property, which Laveleye had explored in his 1873 book. In fact, behind this opposition between nature and history, we find the liberal opposition between naturalness and artificiality; Block, tellingly, considered Laveleye's own article as revealing of the artificiality of socialism, whether revolutionary or reformist.

4   Marx or the Confusion among Genres

So, behind these debates, we can see the difficulties that contemporary economists had in leaving behind the naturalist paradigm and thinking a science of history. This latter's epistemological status is, indeed, ambiguous and would be addressed only later, when French sociology emerged and gave rise to more philosophically endowed readings of Marx. But, beyond this conjunctural problem – the horizon of expectations among these economists, as early readers of Marx – the question of the true status of *Capital* had an importance of its own, which was being debated in Germany, Italy, Russia, and beyond in this same era. Indeed, in seeking to dialectically study the contradictions of the capitalist system and the necessity of their outcome in socialism, Marx outlined a perspective that was certainly new but also very problematic, and which remains the subject of debate even today. Confronted with this, it is understandable that the two rival economic perspectives that were then emerging – liberalism and institutionalism – rose up against what they saw as confusion and used Marx to delegitimise their own doctrinal opponents. In the first case, the liberals took Marx as revealing of the revolutionary consequences of historicism; in the latter (among the university-chair socialists), he was the most perfect expression of naturalist fatalism, insofar as he refused to see the economic world as the sole harmony of interests – a perspective manifestly contradicted by the social tensions of the time.

5   A Reception-in-Development

Despite the interest of these early comments, which raise important questions about the reception of *Capital* in France, it should not be forgotten that the representation of Marx as an economist remained very marginal in the 1870s and 1880s. He still enjoyed only weak notoriety and a rather indistinct image, even among the ranks of economists. The few lines of the obituary that appeared in the *Journal des économistes* in 1883 are testament to this. The journal's editor, Gustave de Molinari, a devotee of pure liberalism, presented Marx as 'a notable theorist of socialism' who contributed to the foundation of the First International. He mentions *The Poverty of Philosophy* and his disputes with Proudhon, and ends abruptly: 'His main work is *Capital* (1867), which is considered the Gospel of collectivism, that final incarnation of communism.' Here, we might note his ignorance of the *Communist Manifesto* (though it is also true that no French translation had yet been published) and above all of Marx's texts providing a socio-historical analysis of France. Of course, this also implies ignorance of Marx's historical and political theory. Above all, not a word is said to suggest that Marx's works have anything to do with political economy. Rather, he appears as a political activist of the past, no longer frightening and thus no longer worthy of attention.

In fact, it was not until the mid-1890s that academics took an interest in Marx's work, both in greater numbers and across a variety of disciplines. The political growth of the organised labour movement obviously contributed to this, while socialist theorists such as Labriola and Sorel published critiques of dogmatic Marxism in journals read by academics.[8] It was Marx's conception of history, which had been much neglected until then, that attracted attention, particularly in the sociological milieu, which was now taking more structured form. A new representation of the author of *Capital* was being constructed – that of the sociologist, which at the turn of the century tended to supplant the figure of the economist. However, it was economists who played the role of precursors, in this slow and still limited discovery of Marx's thought by French intellectuals.

8   Sorel 2007.

CHAPTER 24

Marx Seen from the Right: Raymond Aron, Marxism and Communism

Gwendal Châton

It is true that I have never been a Marxist, but it is also true that I began my research in social philosophy by reading *Capital*. I long tried to convince myself that Marx was right, because I saw great advantages in that on other grounds. I couldn't do it. So, I didn't become a Marxist. That said, there is no author whom I have read as much and who has shaped me as much as Marx, about whom I have never stopped speaking ill[1]

• • •

If anti-communism consists in overlooking the virtues of militants, in ignoring the adherence of a majority of the working class to communist hope, in forgetting the social reforms whose necessity the workers' parties rightly repeat, we are not anti-communists. But if, in order to avoid the accusation of anti-communism, we have to approve all methods of action, resign ourselves to a totalitarian regime, believe that Stalin is always right ... then we will accept the accusation and we will claim the rights of free thought[2]

∙ ∙
∙

There is a story often told by many of the philosophers and sociologists who attended the École normale supérieure in the 1960s. Anxious to learn about Marxism, they came along to the oracle Althusser to ask him which books they should read. It is said that the *caïman* of the rue d'Ulm would invariably give

---

1 Aron 2002.
2 Aron 1946.

them the same answer: 'Go read Aron!' The anecdote, which is more profound than it appears, reveals that even the liberal thinker's opponents granted him the status of a great reader of Marx. It should be said that Raymond Aron had very early in his journey begun a dialogue with the author of the *Communist Manifesto* that he would continue throughout his life – a dialogue that formed the bedrock on which he built his thinking.

There was a political reception of Marx in the Socialist camp from the end of the nineteenth century: the 'Jaurès-Guesde moment' provides the proof of this. We can then observe the Marxist reference point being imported into the human sciences from the 1920s. It was at the crossroads of these two worlds that Aron – a young philosopher of bourgeois origin, vaguely socialist and passionately pacifist – embarked upon his own study of Marxism, a project that occupied him from the early 1930s until his death in 1983. For half a century, he pursued a demanding discussion with Marxism and Marxists, even if, after 1945, this initially purely scholarly interest was also coupled with his anticommunist commitment. In this sense, like Janus, the liberal thinker presents the observer with two faces: we cannot understand 'Aron the Tocquevillian' without paying attention to 'Aron the Marxian'.

Aron's heterodox reception of Marxism is first of all remarkable on account of its precociousness. This was in fact connected to a certain sacrifice he made: the ritual of having a spell in Germany, at the time a necessity for a French philosopher of any ambition. This opened the way to a singular reading of Marx – and indeed one that ought to be taken seriously, for it is based on a close analysis of the texts. This, lastly, leads us to examine Aron's answer to a question that has occupied the most eminent Marxians for many decades: what link should be established between Marx's thought and 'actually-existing socialism'? The study of Aron's case is thus essential for those who want to understand how Marx could be read from the right, and how this reading served as a basis for a liberal anti-communism seeking to oppose the 'communist hypothesis'.

1   Aron, a Precocious Reader of Marx

As Max Likin has emphasised, Aron's reading evolved between 1930 and 1983.[3] It is thus useful to look back at the genesis of what Aron often described as a fascination for Marx. He began to study him during his German period, between

---

3   Likin 2008.

1930 and 1933; more precisely, it was in 1930–1 that he read *Das Kapital* for the first time. At this point, Aron two ideas in mind: to look for confirmation of the socialist orientation which he had inherited from his family; and to find therein an explanation of the 1929 crisis, whose effects were then beginning to make themselves felt in France. In 1931–2, he became acquainted with Marx's early writings, the famous *1844 Manuscripts* and *The German Ideology*, which had just been published in German. And he did not settle for reading Marx: he also immersed himself in all the debates that agitated the Germany of the early 1930s by reading Karl Mannheim, Herbert Marcuse and György Lukács. Yet even in this period, Aron cultivated a certain distance from his object of study: in 1932, he explained that 'the enslavement of consciences to Marxism is unattractive', while at the same time he was indignant against 'the perpetual hypocrisy or naivety of bourgeois politics'.[4] It is clear that Marxism was no longer the definitive philosophical horizon of Aron's time, thus explaining his yearning for attempts to go beyond it, such as Henri de Man's.

The first text in which Aron undertook an in-depth discussion of Marxism dates to 1937. This was an essay written at the time of the Popular Front, in which he showed his concern to grasp the true complexity of Marx's thought. At the time, he was preoccupied by the question of the links between politics and economics: this was a central question for Aron, who would argue his own posiition after the war in his books on industrial societies.[5] Having mounted a comprehensive analysis, Aron concluded that there was no single universally valid first cause: Marxism was thus wrong to consider that the economy can constitute a determinism 'in the last instance'. Consequently, only in vain does historical materialism claim to give the final word on history: 'there is no "primus movens" of the total historical becoming'.[6] The attentive reader will notice that Aron also smuggled some political remarks into this sociological discussion. He mentioned the Soviet case and denied that the USSR had become a classless society. Further, he worried about the possibility of the dictatorship of the proletariat developing in an autocratic direction: 'Unfortunately, the intermediate regime is likely to assert itself more and more as the definitive regime, with the classless society combining with the dictatorship of one party or even of one man'.[7] There was thus no trace in the young Aron of the philo-communism that characterised an intellectual milieu then very susceptible to the charms of the 'fatherland of socialism'.

---

4 Aron 1932.
5 Aron 1963, 1964, 1965a.
6 Aron 2005a.
7 Aron 2005a.

The following year, Aron defended a landmark thesis.[8] It dealt with the philosophy of history and was largely based on a line of interrogation resulting from his reading of Marx. In it, he undertook a thorough critique of the 'metaphysics of history', whether they were inspired by Hegelian-Marxist ideas or heirs to lightning bolts from Nietzsche. This led him to defend several ideas that would go on to structure his thought: no science can deliver the secrets of history, no prophet can predict the final destination of humanity, no determinism can relieve men of the burden of freedom, and no philosophy can prevent the individual from committing himself without certainty about the truth. In a word, Aron here asserted himself as a philosopher of history without a philosophy of history, as a rationalist who refused to disguise his convictions as truth, as a reformist who considered that revolutions do not necessarily improve the organisation of society. It is clear that this book closed a first stage of Aron's dialogue with Marx.

By this point, Aron was already recognised as one of the best French Marxologists. A text published in 1939, devoted to the notion of class, attests to this. In it, Aron discussed the Marxist conception of class, drawing on the aid of several arguments: a class is never homogeneous; an individual can belong to several classes if he possesses mixed sources of income; a class is always crisscrossed by divergent individual interests; the immiseration of the proletariat seems to be contradicted by the facts. It therefore seems to Aron 'impossible to rigorously define the class interests whose contradiction is supposed to lead to a permanent struggle'. Nevertheless, he recognised that Marx had grasped something essential: the fact that 'the attitude of groups in economic conflicts is closely linked to the place they occupy in the production process'. Aron thus outlines a kind of non-economic theory of class struggle: for this attentive reader of Vilfredo Pareto, the lever of this confrontation is above all political in nature.[9] Two central ideas of Aron's thought – the relative autonomy of politics and its existential primacy; and the centrality and positivity of conflict in social life – are thus closely linked to his dialogue with Marx. This text also reveals a particular relationship with Marx's oeuvre: for Aron, it was necessary to critique it, but at the same time to preserve what constitutes its share of the truth at the scientific level.

---

8   Aron 1938.
9   Aron 2005b.

2   Aron, a Critical Reader of Marx

During World War II, Aron no longer wrote on Marxism: Nazism and communism were now his main focuses. The discussion with Marx did not resume until after 1945 and essentially took two forms. The first was a critique of the 'hybrid' Marxisms that were developing in France. It was essentially aimed at two targets: Sartre's existentialised Marxism and Althusser's structuralised Marxism. In both cases, he attacked what he considered a partial vision of Marx's work. On the one hand, Aron rejected Sartre's reduction of Marxism to the 'young Marx', a philosopher of alienation still influenced by Hegel – a path on which Sartre was preceded by Lukács in his *History and Class Consciousness*. On the other hand, Aron challenged the pertinence of the 'epistemological rupture' introduced by Althusser and his disciples, who concentrated on the mature Marx while sweeping aside his youthful writings. For Aron, these are two sides of the same coin – and, in this case, it was in counterfeit currency, since it was based on the denial of the obvious fact that one cannot understand the post-1848 economist and sociologist Marx without studying the philosopher and historian Marx who went before him. In the 'return to Marx' that characterised the France of the 1960s, Aron saw only 'imaginary Marxisms' that repeated the error of many Marxists of the 1930s, with the effect of impoverishing a thought whose interest lies precisely in its complexity.[10]

The second way in which he continued his discussion with Marx was his Sorbonne lectures. Aron was appointed at the Sorbonne in 1955 and devoted his first lectures to questions that constantly brought him back to Marxism. How to think about modern industrially based societies? How to analyse the social stratification in the East and the West? What meaning should be given to the clash between the political regimes on either side of the Iron Curtain? The famous trilogy on industrial societies can thus be read as the implementation of a Marxist method in order to demonstrate both its fruitfulness and its limits.[11] But we find his reading set out in detail above all in a course for the *agrégation* given in 1962–3.[12] It is obviously impossible to give an account of such a detailed analysis in a few pages, but we shall nevertheless try to identify the main points.

First of all, what was the method followed by Aron? It was a history of ideas that we would today call 'classical', that is, centred on the texts and not claim-

---

10   Aron 1970.

11   Châton 2017.

12   Aron 2002.

ing to understand Marx better than he understood himself: in short, this means 'taking Marx at his word'. So, what was Aron trying to do in this course? To show that Marx's thought must be studied by distinguishing two periods – 1835–48 and 1848–83 – which must nevertheless be thought of as a continuum, even if the early writings are of secondary importance in relation to *Capital*: they are important as milestones in a trajectory that leads to the critique of political economy. The mature Marx, the sociologist and economist of capitalism, was born in 1848 with the *Manifesto*, and his master work is *Capital*, which Aron does not hesitate to describe as a 'brilliant endeavour'. What is the central characteristic of Marxism, which explains its incredible success? For Aron, it is its equivocality, the fact that Marx's texts 'have the necessary qualities to be endlessly commented on and transfigured into orthodoxy'.[13]

To enable students to 'enter into' Marx's work, Aron always uses the same procedure: he starts from the concept of 'critique', for him the central notion of the Marxist construct. Marx's primary contribution is indeed the critique of the false consciousness of the world, and thus the need for a deconstruction of religious, political, moral and cultural illusions, which all stem from a primary illusion concerning the economic structure. Aron's originality is thus to want to apply his own method to Marx by 'criticising the critique'. Here, we can identify two angles of attack. The first was to subject *Capital* to the criticism of an economist and a sociologist: Aron emphasised the fragility of the theory of surplus-value and the analysis of exploitation; he pointed out the limits of the law of the tendency of the rate of profit to fall; he challenged the thesis of the immiseration of the proletariat; he methodically unpicked the prophecy of the final self-destruction of capitalism. In a word, he upheld the idea that the history of Marxism is that of a grandiose ambition which had nevertheless ended in failure, because not only had capitalism not disappeared, but it even seemed, despite its crises, to be improving situation of the working class more effectively than 'actually existing' communism. The second line of attack was not on a technical level but a philosophical one. Aron sought to highlight three limits inherent to Marxism: the difficulty of producing an external critique of capitalism (in this sense it remains Schumpeterian); the lack of rigour of postulating an economic determinism 'in the last instance'; the absence of a real analysis of politics, which cannot be summed up as a superstructure whose form is conditioned by the economic base.

---

13   Aron 1967.

Much more would need to be said to do justice to this reading.[14] Let us simply add, as a counterpoint, that Aron also remained very sceptical of the economism of the neoliberals of his time, to whom he was ultimately much less close than he was to the German Social Democrats of the post-Bad-Godesberg period.[15] So, we ought to take him seriously when he explains that 'We have all become Marxists in a sense: men are responsible for circumstances and they must change these circumstances insofar as these deprive certain individuals of the means considered indispensable for a decent life'.[16] This adherence to the moral demand upheld by Marx – to respect human dignity by improving living conditions – did not prevent Aron from severely denouncing its use as a doctrine of government. This observation leads us straight to examine his answer to one of the most difficult questions posed by twentieth-century history: is there a link between Marx's work and the tormented history of the Soviet Union? And if so, is Stalinism, if not the highest stage of Marxism, at least one of its logical outcomes?

3   From Marx to the Gulag?

Aron did not only devote so much time to studying Marxism because he wanted to try to unravel the mysteries of *Capital*: it was also because it served as the foundation of the ideology that supported the Soviet regime. In this respect, Aron can easily be considered the archetypal intelligent anti-communist, that is, one who does not throw the baby Marx out with the bathwater. Unlike Marx, who conceived of communism as the 'riddle of history finally resolved', Aron sees it as a 'secular religion' that served as a justification for a new type of domination: totalitarianism.[17] It is this great gulf between propaganda and facts that justifies a resolute anti-totalitarian commitment.

From the 1950s onwards, Aron became one of the central figures in the French anti-communist movement and, beyond that, one of the leading figures in the 'anti-communist international' built around the Congress for Cultural Freedom.[18] Aron was thus involved in four journals, which admittedly had different political orientations and were built on specific networks, but which all defined themselves as anti-communist: the Gaullist intellectual journal *Liberté*

---

14   Mahoney 2003; Mesure 2015.
15   Châton 2016a.
16   Aron 1965b.
17   Aron 1944.
18   Grémion 1995.

de l'esprit; *Le Contrat social*, at whose helm was the former Bolshevik Boris Souvarine; the information bulletin *Est&Ouest*, created by Georges Albertini and Claude Harmel, two socialists who had made their way via wartime collaboration; and finally, *Preuves*, the vehicle of a social-democratic anti-communism. When *Liberté de l'esprit* stopped appearing in 1954, Aron became involved in *Preuves*, which was to play a decisive role in the crystallisation of a European anti-totalitarian milieu. However, in 1969, when this review ceased publication, this current was abruptly deprived of a voice. It was then that the Aronian journal *Contrepoint* was created, based on social ties that had developed in Aron's seminar. It published 27 issues between 1970 and 1976. Although its creation stemmed from the opposition to the May '68 movement, it nevertheless benefited from the networks that gravitated around Preuves, and it is clear that anticommunism provided its guiding thread.[19] The sudden end of *Contrepoint* finally led to the creation of *Commentaire*, in January 1978, in the context of the political battle between the free-market right and the left united around the Programme commun.[20] This highly composite but continuous anti-totalitarian lineage was able to draw on Aron's thought, while at the same time taking its cue from his political engagement, which – he readily told those who joined him – was a lifetime's struggle.[21]

This anti-totalitarian commitment did not, however, lead Aron to establish – as many less refined anti-communists would – a continuity between Marx, Lenin, Stalin and the Gulag. Aron examined this weighty question as early as 1951 in *Les Guerres en chaîne*. In a chapter entitled 'From Marxism to Stalinism', he explains that once democratic centralism and the theory of the revolutionary party had been introduced, the transition from Leninism to Stalinism seemed almost logical. Thus, for Aron it is Leninism that explains why the Russian Revolution 'went astray'. It is interesting to note, in this respect, that Aron interprets this deviation as a distancing of the USSR from the Western matrix and – in correlation to this – a rapprochement with the Eastern one: Aron speaks of a Soviet society 'descended from Byzantium'. However, we also know that he always strongly emphasised that Marx's thought followed in the wake of the Enlightenment: he often repeated that Marx was a humanist and a liberal exasperated by the gap between the modern project and the realities of his time. So, Aron did not resort to the easy option of making Marxism into the cause of the errors of 'actually existing communism', of reducing Marx to

---

19   Châton 2007.
20   Châton 2006.
21   Châton 2016b.

the rank of supply officer for the Gulag. He explicitly steered clear from this in the 1962–3 course, explaining that Marx's vagueness as to what socialism would look like does not provide justification for such an argument: 'There are certainly relations between the regimes that claim to be based on Marx's thought and Marx's thought, but they are much more complicated than they appear at first sight'.[22] If the communist regimes were heirs to Marx, this was not because they implemented this or that technical measure – planning, land collectivisation, and so on – but rather because they were the heirs of the three tendencies of Marxism identified by Karl Popper: prophetism, utopianism and revolutionism. For all that, Aron is not Popper, and he does not endorse some of the latter's highly reductive statements: in a 1973–4 lecture, he explains that the logician attributes, in *The Open Society and its Enemies*, 'excessive responsibility [to Hegel and Marx] for the catastrophes that have afflicted humanity in the twentieth century'.[23]

Shortly after this nuanced judgement, the French intellectual mood changed drastically: with the 'anti-totalitarian turn' the establishment of a direct link between Marx and the Gulag became one of the *topoi* of the 'new philosophy'.[24] Did this affect Aron's hitherto carefully judged position? In Aron's 1976–7 lecture on Marx at the Collège de France, he suggested a link between the theorisation of capitalism based on the commodity-form and the policy followed by the Bolsheviks during war communism and Lenin's positions regarding trade and property: in communism, 'it is ultimately the very category of the economic that must be abolished', he explained.[25] In 1977, Aron published *Plaidoyer pour l'Europe décadente* in which we can again see a questioning of Marx's responsibility for the tragedies of the twentieth century. In it he deployed a concept that had long remained in the background in his work: that of 'ideocracy'. Following Hannah Arendt, Alexander Solzhenitsyn, Andrei Sakharov and Alain Besançon, he insists on the centrality of ideology in the general architecture of the Soviet regime. Marxism had been able to turn into an ideology because Marx's thought itself operates 'the junction of an analysis-condemnation of capitalism on the one hand, and a prophetism-socialist utopia on the other': He thus considers that 'the mystification begins with Marx himself when he baptizes his prophetism as science'.[26] Aron had never seemed so close to questioning Marx's responsibility for the dramas of communism. This much harsher

---

22   Aron 2002.
23   Aron 1991.
24   Christofferson 2004.
25   Aron 2002.
26   Aron 1977.

judgement was later confirmed in his *Mémoires*. Aron did not totally abandon the equanimity which he had always shown towards Marxism, but he no longer hesitated to write that Marx was both a great economist and a cursed sophist:

> Specialists know an economist named Marx, who is much richer, more subtle and interesting than the author of *Capital* alone. But the useful Marx, if I may say so, the one who perhaps changed the history of the world, is the one of false ideas; the rate of surplus value that he suggests gives reason to believe that the nationalisation of the means of production will make it possible to recover for the workers enormous quantities of value that have been monopolised by the owners of the means of production; socialism or, at least, communism eliminates the category of the 'economic' and the 'sordid science' itself. As an economist, Marx remains perhaps the richest, most exciting economist of his time. As an economist-prophet, as the putative ancestor of Marxism-Leninism, he is a cursed sophist who bears his share of responsibility for the horrors of the twentieth century.[27]

4   From Marx to Tocqueville

For Aron, the problem posed by Marx's thought can be easily summarised: he perfectly identified the fundamental difficulties of modern societies but formulated them in such a way that they appear as insoluble contradictions that can only be overcome by revolution.[28] We know Marx's famous formula, in Hegel's *Critique of the Philosophy of Right*, according to which 'to be radical is to take things by the root'. It is precisely this radicalism that Aron criticises him for: while recognising the importance of the discrepancy, rightly pointed out by Marx, between the ideals and the reality of modern societies, Aron for his part always preferred to speak of conflicts rather than contradictions, thus leaving open the possibility of a resolution that could do without the recourse to redemptive violence. This is also what he criticised Sartre for, setting this latter in the lineage of thinkers attached to violence as the 'midwife of history'. This philosophy of fruitful conflicts – which cannot fail to evoke the Machiavelli of the *Discorsi*, of which Aron was an informed reader – enabled him to argue

---

27   Aron 1983.
28   Aron 2002.

for a reformist perspective. His rejection of revolutionism also helps us understand why he became increasingly attached to the figure of Tocqueville, to the point of spearheading a 'French Tocqueville revival'.[29] Thus Aron was not, as has sometimes been written, a 'right-wing Marxist'. But, at the end of this journey, we can better understand why this label has sometimes been attached to him.

29   Le Strat and Pelletier 2005; Audier 2005.

CHAPTER 25

French Catholics and Marxism, From the 1930s to the '1968 moment'

Denis Pelletier

The reception of Marx can be analysed as a vantage point on French Catholicism in the twentieth century. Unlike most Protestants who – like Charles Gide, Paul Ricœur or even Jacques Ellul – took an interest in Marxism, Catholics read Marx *as Catholics*. Their reading certainly responded to an intellectual ambition, but it also fed into an internal project with a strong social and political component, which led them to question the Church and its place in modernity.

The 'hand extended' by Maurice Thorez in April 1936, the Worker Missions of the postwar years, the sequence opened up by the Vatican II Council (1962–5) and continued through the '68 moment' mark out this history. It is also linked to the reception of Marx in France, itself marked by the translation of the *1844 Manuscripts* in the 1930s, then by the breakthrough of the structuralist paradigm in the 1960s, following Louis Althusser's works.

This combination of defining moments sets out a periodisation (1930s, the first postwar decade, 1968), whose main contours are retraced here. The philosophical reception of Marx by Catholic intellectuals was marked by a double heterodoxy, vis-à-vis the vulgate disseminated by the PCF and vis-à-vis the religious authorities. Contrary to popular belief, this heterodoxy does not make it a marginal reading: in a still overwhelmingly Catholic, country where the confrontation over secularism weighs heavily on intellectual debate, Catholic readings of Marx have played a role underestimated by the historiography.

1   The 1930s: An Interrupted Encounter

The absence of a Catholic reception of Marx until the beginning of the 1930s owed to a double blockage. On the one hand were the condemnations coming from Rome, which struck at socialism and communism in general: Leo XIII opened *Rerum Novarum* (1891) with a critique of the socialist doctrine of collective property, and Pius XI built part of *Quadragesimo Anno* around the denunciation of an atheistic and materialistic communism. Yet neither of them mentioned Marx's name or the details of his doctrine. The founders of 'Catholic sociology', at the beginning of the twentieth century, sometimes quoted Marxist texts, but this was still internal to a presentation of 'socialist doctrines' as a current of thought and social policies that ran through the contemporary world. On the other hand, after World War I, the PCF, undergoing a process of 'Bolshevisation', had little interest in religion, except within the framework of a base/superstructure dialectic directly derived from the Plekhanovite vulgate which represented the norm in Party schools. Between the 'opium of the people' on the one hand and the 'thought from the belly' on the other, there was hardly any room for mutual understanding.

1.1   The Conditions for a First Reception

Things nevertheless began to move discreetly, under the effect of three new events. The first was the entry into the discussion of the Russian philosopher and theologian Nicolas Berdyaev (1874–1948). In his youth he had rallied to Marxism – he was a member of the Kiev social-democratic committee – before in 1904 becoming one of the actors of the Russian-Orthodox 'new religious consciousness' movement. Exiled to France in 1922, he settled in Paris where he founded the review *Put'* (*The Way*), and soon took part in the meetings organised in his villa in Meudon by the philosopher Jacques Maritain, whose wife Raisa was of Russian origin. Through the Meudon Circle, Berdyaev came into contact with the two components, Thomist and Personalist, of the Catholic intellectual renewal of the interwar period.[1] In two decisively important texts, 'Un nouveau Moyen-Âge', published in 1927 in the 'Le Roseau d'or' collection directed by Maritain at Plon, and 'Vérité et mensonge du communisme', which appeared in 1932 in the first issue of *Esprit*, he highlighted the messianic, quasi-religious foundation of Russian communism. This opened the way to a reading of communism as a mysticism in competition with Christianity, based on the thought of Marx. He also emphasised the need to free the reading of Marxism from the reality of the Soviet regime.

The second event was the 'hand extended' to Catholics by Maurice Thorez in 1936 as part of the Popular Front strategy. It was overwhelmingly refused, with the exception of the four MPs from La Jeune République and a small fringe of Christian socialists, Catholics and Protestants (the young Paul Ricœur was one of them), who founded the journal *Terre nouvelle* around Maurice Laudrain.[2] But the outstretched hand, then the victory, of the Popular Front and the work-

---

1   Chenaux 1999.
2   Rochefort-Turquin 1986.

ers' strikes that followed it posed a challenge to Catholics involved in winning back working-class France, in a context marked by the search for an alternative to *Action française*, condemned by Rome in 1926, and by the rise of *Action catholique spécialisée*.

The 1930s finally saw the emergence of a heterodox reading of Marx on the French left, centred on his early writings. In 1933, in the short-lived journal *Avant-Poste*, the Philosophie group (Henri Lefebvre, Georges Politzer, Norbert Guterman) published the first translation of extracts from the *1844 Manuscripts*, of which a reputedly complete (but in fact still very partial) edition appeared in 1937 with Costes.[3] Between these two dates, Auguste Cornu published his thesis on *La Jeunesse de Marx* (1934) with Félix Alcan, and the Cercle de la Russie neuve published, under the title *À la lumière du marxisme* (1935), a collection of essays in which René Maublanc posed the question of the relationship between Marx and Hegel.[4] Finally, between 1933 and 1939, Alexandre Kojève held his seminar on *The Phenomenology of Spirit* at the École pratique des hautes études (EPHE). His reading was centred on the dialectic of master and slave, leading many of his audience to gain an understanding of Marx in his confrontation with Hegel.[5] This marked the beginning of a cycle of 'Hegelian reception' of Marx in France, and this would remain at the heart of the dialogue between Catholics and Marxists until the 1960s, after the break marked by Occupation.

1.2   *The Young Marx, between Hegel and Thomas Aquinas*

The first works on this moment of Catholic reception of Marx owe to the British historian David Curtis.[6] A first group of readers can be situated in the Hegelian line of descent. The Jesuit Gaston Fessard discovered Hegel in 1926, through the German text. His project for translating the *Phenomenology of Spirit* and rethinking Christianity by way of the Hegelian dialectic came up against hostility among the authorities of his order. In *La Main tendue? Le dialogue catholique-communiste est-il possible?* (1937), he challenged Maurice Thorez's 'extended hand' proposal by analysing Marxism as a betrayal of Hegelianism. He then followed Kojève's seminar at the EPHE and engaged in a discussion with the latter on the possible parallel between the master-slave dialectic and the Christian dialectic of pagan and Jew.[7] A polytechnician and business-

---

3   Trebitsch 1986.
4   Carlino 2015.
5   Filoni 2008; Fourcade 2014.
6   Curtis 1997, Curtis 2000.
7   Petrache 2017.

man, close to both the surrealists of the rue Blomet and the Christian democrats of the journal Politique, Marcel Moré became fascinated by Marxism
after attending a screening of Eisenstein's *The General Line*.[8] Oriented towards
Emmanuel Mounier, he published six articles on Marx in *Esprit* between 1934
and 1936, four of which were devoted to his youth.

A second group was part of the revival of Thomistic studies following the
encyclical *Aeterni Patris* (1879), by which Leo XIII imposed a return to Thomas
Aquinas in Catholic higher education and the major seminaries. The condemnation of Action Française did indeed dispel the spectre of the modernist crisis
of the early twentieth century. The philosopher Jacques Maritain, who interpreted Charles Maurras's condemnation of 'politics first' from the perspective
of 'The Primacy of the Spiritual', (1927), thus devoted the second chapter of
Humanisme intégral (1936) to the discussion and refutation of Marx, using the
tools forged by Thomas Aquinas and by his own friend Berdyaev.[9] Under the
title 'A New Humanism' he analysed Marxism and Christianity as two competing mysticisms, while acknowledging the critical value and sincerity of Marx's
humanism. At the same time, Paul Vignaux devoted several texts to Marx in
the journal *Politique*. Founded in 1928 at Éditions du Cerf by the Dominican
Marie-Vincent Bernadot in order to contribute to the fight against Action française, in 1937–8 *La Vie intellectuelle* published – in response to the strikes of
spring 1936 and the war in Spain – a series of texts with revealing titles: 'Marx
and the Problem of Man' (Paul-Louis Landsberg), 'Marxist Man' (Jean Lacroix),
'Dialectical Materialism' (Ambroise Gardeil), 'The Spring of Marxist Dialectics:
Alienation' (Paul Vignaux), and 'Some Aspects of Marx's Life after 1845' (Daniel
Villey).

The new Regent of studies at the *studium* of Le Saulchoir, which trains young
Dominicans in provincial France, Father Marie-Dominique Chenu was the first
to introduce Marx to the teaching he gave to his students. He also intervened
among the activists of the Jeunesse ouvrière chrétienne (JOC) confronted with
the strikes of spring 1936. In 1938, Father Louis-Joseph Lebret, leader of a fish-
ermen's union movement, the Mouvement de Saint-Malo, read and annotated
Capital in Molitor's translation published by Costes: the notes in the margins of
the text reveal the seductive effect of Marx's sociology on this Dominican friar,
who had been fed on the Catholic social tradition and who was a follower of
the method of investigation inherited from Le Play.[10]

---

8   Fouilloux 2015.
9   Chenaux 2006.
10   Pelletier 1996.

Maritain's work is important, for *Humanisme intégral* soon became a work of reference for the Catholic Action movements and for part of the Christian-Democratic current, in French-speaking countries (France, Belgium, Canada, and so on) as well as in Latin America. It immediately gave a certain number of authors the freedom to speak, notably – among the younger generation of Jesuits – Jean Daniélou and Henri de Lubac. In 1938, the former published two articles in the Chronique sociale de France on 'La foi en l'homme chez Marx' ('Faith in Man in Marx'), which also provided an opportunity to respond to *La Crise du progrès*, which Georges Friedmann had just published. The latter, a few years older than him, was influenced by the philosophy of Maurice Blondel, like Henri Lefebvre, who was his pupil, and like Gaston Fessard, according to whom Blondel was 'our Hegel'. In *Catholicisme. Les aspects sociaux du dogme* (1938), Lubac was one of the first to delve into the theory of alienation starting from the confrontation between Marx and Feuerbach, but he also discusses Guterman and Lefebvre's *La Conscience mystifiée*.[11]

This first encounter was doubtless marginal. Moreover, it was quickly hampered, first by the 1938 encyclical *Divini Redemptoris*, then by the sanctions imposed on the weekly of the 'Christian Reds', *Sept*, and on Father Chenu at Le Saulchoir, and finally by the war and the Occupation. But this was only the appearance of a halt, and work continued discreetly. In fact, the framework for thirty years of dialogue between Christianity and Marxism had already been established. This was a socio-political framework posed in terms of 'reconquering the working class', thus involving a *political* competition with the PCF milieu, and *theoretical* competition with Marxism. It was also a philosophical framework: most often, we read a young Marx, a philosopher, grappling with Hegel; a humanist Marx, a communitarian Marx, a theorist of alienation, liable to have echoes within the Catholic tradition. This reading was done by 'theologians in suits', such as Maritain and Vignaux, that is, laymen who occupied a position at the interface between the Catholic magisterium and intellectual life; it was also carried out by 'serving theologians', as Étienne Fouilloux put it, meaning by clerics whom the rise of Action catholique handed a role of training up lay activists.[12] The reception of Marx thus accompanied a discrete but essential change in the conditions of theological research in France.

---

11   Curtis 2000.
12   Fouilloux 1998.

2   The Reception of Marx during the Period of Christian Progressivism (1944–56)

2.1   *A Renewed Intellectual Context*

Contrary to the received wisdom, it was in the aftermath of the Liberation, and not during the 1968 period, that the dialogue between Christianity and Marxism reached its peak in France. The links forged in the Resistance with the Communists opened the way to a form of fellow-travelling spearheaded by the Union des chrétiens progressistes, founded in 1947 around André Mandouze, Jean Verlhac and Marcel Moiroud. Its periodical, *Action*, pursued political alignment with the PCF rather than intellectual debate. Beyond this small group, the domination of the PCF on the Left and the debates on trade-union unity made knowledge of Marxism an important question for those who wanted to combat the CGT: the *Chronique sociale de France* published a study 'Autour du marxisme' aimed at militants in March–April 1945, and *Documentation catholique* published a 'Bibliographie sur le communisme' in July 1949.

Another innovation as compared to the prewar period was the arrival of existentialism as a 'third party' between Christianity and Marxism. This facilitated the debate by preventing it from being reduced to a matter of confrontation or alignment. There was, indeed, a Christian existentialism, of which Gabriel Marcel and Lyon's Jean Lacroix – philosopher for *La Chronique sociale de France*, regular contributor to *Esprit* and critic for *Le Monde* – were good representatives. Like its Sartrean counterpart, this existentialism was marked by the phenomenological tradition, and was attentive to the issues of consciousness and freedom, thus giving rise to a way of thinking about vocation, or 'availability', which echoes Sartre's 'commitment'. After the founding of the Centre catholique des intellectuels français in 1945, the 'Semaine des intellectuels catholiques' became an interlocutor and a competitor to the Communist intellectuals' own such discussions.[13] The journal *Esprit*, where Emmanuel Mounier had shown an early interest in Marx, published a special issue in May–June 1948, on *Marxisme ouvert contre marxisme scolastique* ('Open Marxism versus Scholastic Marxism'), in which almost all those interested in the question took part.

Finally, the Catholic reception of Marx fitted into the double context of the Worker Missions and the extension of the model of Action catholique to the whole system of activism. Both confronted the 'theologians of service' not only with youth movements, but also with a public of adults, notably within the

---

13   Toupin-Guyot 2002.

Mouvement populaire des familles (MPF), the oldest branch of the Jeunesse ouvrière chrétienne de France (JOCF), involved in a process that would lead many of its militants to join the New Left from the 1950s onward. The same applies to the minority in the CFTC trade union, grouped around the *Reconstruction* bulletin, which militated in favour of the deconfessionalisation of this Catholic union.

For the likes of Henri-Charles Desroches, Marie-Dominique Chenu, Albert Bouche and Maurice Montuclard – all four of whom were Dominicans – reading Marx served a dual purpose of mediation. On the one hand, they relied on it to give words to field experience, to formalise it in terms with which activists could identify. On the other hand, they also tried to express this experience in a way acceptable to Rome and the bishops. In 1946, *Masses ouvrières* – the organ of the chaplaincies of the Worker Missions, founded the previous year – published a series of articles on Marx written by Albert Dominique, a pseudonym chosen by Father Bouche in reference to Thomas Aquinas and his master Albert the Great. In the journal *Économie et Humanisme*, founded by Father Lebret in 1942, Desroches launched a series of in-depth articles on Marx, combined with a translation of unpublished works by Guillaume Dunstheimer, a German anarchist who had taken refuge in France. The journal also organised a series of educational sessions on Marxism for activists. The *Cahiers de jeunesse de l'Église* (Maurice Montuclard) and *La Quinzaine*, founded in 1950 around Ella Sauvageot, were part of the same effort at a critical reading.

2.2 *Between Hegel and Thomas Aquinas, a Heterodox and Conflicting Reception*

For this fringe of French intellectual Catholicism, a parallel can be drawn between the thirteenth century, confronted with the urban revolution and the return to the West of Aristotle's thought via Averroes and Arab philosophy, and the contemporary era, grappling with the Industrial Revolution and the breakthrough of a modern philosophy of which the Marx-Hegel couple was the paragon. In this perspective, the 'return to Thomas Aquinas' advocated by Rome since 1879 should not be limited to the recourse to scholasticism as a lens for understanding modernity, as the conservative neo-Thomists thought. On the contrary, Thomas Aquinas was first and foremost the figure who had been able to Christianise the thought of Aristotle, the 'modern' philosophy of the thirteenth century, by freeing it from the Averroist burden. This was the gesture that had to be reproduced, by removing Marx and Hegel from the grip of atheistic materialism and Soviet communism: 'Aristotle is still besieging Christianity', wrote Father Chenu in *Économie et Humanisme* in 1945.

A simple path was then opened up – indeed, the one most widely shared among Christian readers of Marx because it made it possible to tie in with certain analyses of the Church's social doctrine. It consisted in freeing Marx's sociology from his philosophy. Marx then became the figure who had been able to put words and a history to the phenomena of domination and inequalities that are at the very heart of a capitalist order that social Catholics oppose in the name of justice. It was thus possible to speak of the class struggle and join with the militants of the CGT on the terrain of social struggles. Unity could be built in the name of Christ the worker who inspired the priests' commitment in the factories, while keeping at bay Marx's atheism and materialism.

But it was also possible to go further and to engage in a properly philosophical dialogue. 'The grandeur of communism is that it is not a simple economic technique, nor even a social anthropology, but a philosophy of man and humanity', wrote Chenu, with the effect that 'it would be too summary a move to accept its purely economic theses while rejecting its atheism'. In a perspective that built on the reflections of the 1930s, a certain number of Thomistic concepts were then mobilised, pointing to the humanism of the young Marx. Here, Thomas's realism provided a meeting ground with Marxist materialism; the Thomistic dialectic of nature and grace echoed the Marxist conception of history as the completion of human nature; Thomas's *communitas* related to class consciousness, both making it possible to understand the worker-solidarities discovered in the factory by the worker-priests, and even to rethink the Church on the basis of them, in a gesture subverting traditional ecclesiology.

All these themes are present in the book *Signification du marxisme*, published by Father Desroches with Éditions ouvrières in 1949. In it, he took up a series of texts that had previously appeared in Christian left-wing reviews, and added a remarkable critical bibliography of the works of Marx and his successors. Composed by his friend Guillaume Dunstheimer under the pseudonym Charles-François Hubert, the neglect of this text by the French Marxist tradition is perplexing. Desroches was linked to Roger Garaudy, Maximilien Rubel, Henri Lefebvre and the linguist Georges Mounin, who was regularly sent by the PCF to meetings of Christians debating Marxism. Le *Signification du marxisme* was a great success but – published the day after the decree by which the Holy Office condemned collaboration between Catholics and Communists in July 1949 – it provoked a polemic followed by an investigation in Rome, and the second edition had to be withdrawn from the market in the autumn of 1950. A few months later, Father Desroches left the Dominican order.[14] After

---

14   Pelletier 1997.

taking back his family name Henri Desroche, which he had abandoned during his Dominican career, he continued his career at the CNRS and became one of the pioneers in France of the sociology of religion, and later of the sociology of cooperation.

Jesuit readings of Marx were more critical. In 1945, in *Le Drame de l'humanisme athée*, Henri de Lubac systematised his critique of Marx through a reading of Feuerbach. However, he was a central figure in the Jesuit school at Fourvière, which profoundly renewed French theology through a rereading of the Church Fathers and the medieval tradition. He, too, soon found himself in trouble with Rome. Another pioneer of the 1930s, Fessard was, during the Occupation, the author of the manifesto of the *Cahiers du Témoignage chrétien*, entitled *France, prends garde de perdre ton âme* ('France, Take Care Not to Lose Your Soul'). It was in the name of the same 'spiritual resistance' that he condemned the dialogue with Marx in *France, prends garde de perdre ta liberté* ('France, Take Care Not to Lose Your Freedom', 1946), and then combatted Desroches and the progressive Christians. His critique of Marx was closely linked to his own use of the Hegelian dialectic, put at the service of an eschatological conception of history and actuality: dialectical materialism was, in his eyes, a betrayal of Hegel by Marx, making it incompatible with Christianity. Finally, in 1956, the Jesuit Yves Calvez published his thesis on *La Pensée de Karl Marx* ('Karl Marx's Thought'), a real scholarly tome whose last chapter constitutes a 'return to order', denouncing the way in which progressive Christians had allowed themselves to be deceived by the mirages of the young Marx. A similar reading is found among his colleagues Pierre Bigo (*Marxisme et Humanisme. Introduction à l'œuvre économique de Karl Marx*, 1953) and Henri Chambre (*Le Marxisme en Union soviétique. Idéologie et institutions*, 1955).

As we can see, the Catholic reception of Marxism was marked by conflicts, and the polemics cannot be reduced to an opposition between 'innovators' and 'traditionalists', even if they were part of the debates around Christian progressivism. In fact, there was a common culture shared by all of these authors, which can be seen in the place occupied by the concept of alienation. 'The philosopher Marx will be critical because reality bears the marks of alienation: alienation is even the object of his critique, and the latter has the exclusive task of reducing it', Calvez wrote in 1956.

The writings of Marx's youth served to construct Marxism as a philosophy of alienation, that is, as a thought on consciousness that made it possible to tackle Jean-Paul Sartre and existentialism, as Mounier did in *Qu'est-ce que le personnalisme?* (1946) and in the texts collected soon after his death in *Feu la chrétienté?* (1950). Jean Lacroix used a similar interpretative lens in *Marxisme, Existentialisme, Personnalisme. Présence de l'éternité dans le temps*, published in 1955. Later, Raymond Aron made the interest in the notion of alienation the trademark of Christian readings of Marx.[15] It would be difficult to challenge him on this score. The concept of alienation made it possible to refer to the long Christian tradition of 'divided consciousness', born with the writings of St Paul and St Augustine, and which runs from Pascal to Mauriac via Maine de Biran. 'In the first look we take at twentieth-century man, Marx and Pascal, existentialism and personalism, come together. He is profoundly alienated, he must be returned to himself and to his destiny', wrote Mounier.

Far from being exclusively collective, alienation is first and foremost individual, lodged in the intimacy of each consciousness. Thus, the debate between the young Marx and his Catholic readers plays out around the 'human person', as a consciousness open to the contradictions that run through society. It is as if the encounter with Marx were the last episode in a long struggle against the secularisation of the very idea of consciousness.

3   The 1968 Years: The End of the Philosophical Dialogue

The story, once again, ended badly: between 1949 and 1955, French Catholicism was plagued by the so-called crisis of 'Christian progressivism'. The worker-priests had to stop their work in the factories in 1954; there were several condemnations surrounding this ban against press organs or Christian theologians engaged in dialogue with Marxism. These notably included Fathers Desroches, Montuclard and Bouche, who soon left the priesthood, and Father Chenu, who was condemned to silence in 1954 along with several of his colleagues who were like him involved in the Worker Missions. The debate on – and with – Marxism nevertheless continued in a muted fashion, in *Témoignage chrétien* under the direction of Georges Montaron and above all in the monthly *Lettre*. It took up the torch of dialogue in 1959, under the pens of Gilles Ferry, Claude Tresmontant and Claude Cuénot, and opened up to the work of the Protestant philosopher Pierre Burgelin.[16]

3.1   *Between the Council and Structuralism*
Not until the mid-1960s would the question of the Christian reception of Marxism again regain importance. The Vatican II Council opened up new perspectives for encounters with modern thought and gave its blessing to a philosoph-

---

15   Aron 1976.
16   Sevegrand 2011.

ical and political pluralism that the bishops of France confirmed in 1972 by publishing the text 'Église, politique et foi', which showed a new openness to Marxist vocabulary and to the human sciences. The recomposition of the French left allowed for dialogue between left-wing Christians on the one hand, and those disappointed with the SFIO and the PCF on the other, first within the framework of the PSU, and then within that of the new PS and the Union of the Left. Finally, the events of May 1968 opened the way for the expression of a Christian leftism whose critiques of institutions was directed simultaneously against the Church and the Fifth Republic. Readings of Marx were embroiled in the Catholic crisis of the 1968 years, during which the debates on the implementation of the Vatican II Council intersected with the wider questioning of systems of values and meaning that was at the heart of the 'leftist moment' in French society.[17]

Now there began another cycle in the reception of Marx. This was marked by an ecumenical approach where, in the wake of the conciliar *aggiornamento*, a new generation of Catholic authors rubbed shoulders with clerics such as Jean Cardonnel, Paul Blanquart, Giulio Girardi and Jean-Yves Jolif; lay figures such as Jean Guichard; and Protestant authors such as Pastor Joseph Casalis, theorist of a 'world theology' open to Marx's legacy. But philosophical dialogue, while still possible in the early 1960s with Roger Garaudy[18] or Gilbert Mury before his move to Maoism, soon came up against the breakthrough of the structuralist paradigm on the heels of Louis Althusser (*For Marx*, 1965) and his disciples, notably Pierre Macherey and Jacques Rancière (*Reading Capital*, 1965). Althusserian structuralism posed two obstacles to dialogue with Christians. By defining Marxism as a theoretical anti-humanism, Althusser disqualified the search for a humanism, which was common both families of thought. By highlighting, upon Émile Bottigelli's new translation of the *1844 Manuscripts* by (1962), the 'epistemological break' – at the end of which Marx became himself only by renouncing the philosophy of his youth in favour of a 'scientific' materialism – the Althusserians cut short the debate on the relation between Marx and Hegel and the theory of alienation.

3.2   *The Instrumentalisation of Concepts*

In this context, the 1968 years paradoxically marked the end of Catholics' strictly philosophical reception of Marx. It gave way to a type of reading that developed in three main ways. On the one hand, for a few years in the wake

---

17   Pelletier 2005.
18   Gugelot 2009.

of 1968, the leadership bodies and some of the activists of movements such as Mouvement rural de la jeunesse chrétienne in 1969 – after a few lectures by the Dominican Jean-Yves Jolif – or the La Vie nouvelle movement – at the instigation of its leader Philippe Warnier in 1971 – adopted Marxism as a lens for reading reality. This phenomenon of 'conversion' to Marx gave an important role to a certain body of manuals intended for militants, in particular explaining the success of Jean Guichard's book (*Le Marxisme. Théorie et pratique de la révolution*, 1968), whose fourth edition, published in 1976, announced that 30,000 copies had been sold. In 1972, Jean Guichard, an associate professor of Italian politically involved in the PSU, published a work with a real theoretical content, but subordinated to the immediate demands of a struggle that was both internal to Catholicism and involved in the revolutionary project of the French far left.

A second mode of reception consisted in the instrumentalisation of Marxist concepts in service of a subversion of the Church as an institution. The Christian Marxists of *Lettre* and *Cité nouvelle* thus seized on the Althusserian notion of the 'ideological state apparatus' to formulate a radical critique of the instituted Church and to articulate political revolution and revolution in the Church. The concept of 'praxis' allowed for a rethinking of theological work, at a time when French theology was dominated by the encounter with the human sciences. A structural semantics of Marxist inspiration fed into the work of rereading the scriptural tradition, notably in Fernando Belo (*Lecture matérialiste de l'Évangile de Marc*, 1974) and within the context of ecumenical study groups where research on the Bible ('having Mark read by Marx', as Belo put it) nourished a struggle for revolution both within and outside the Church.[19]

Finally, the Marxist theory of imperialism (Lenin, Bukharin, dependency theories) provided for a third mode of borrowing from Marxism, placed in service of a Christian Third Worldism. In this vein, the 'theology of revolution' of the Salesian Giulio Girardi and the Dominican Jean Cardonnel served as a prelude to the first reception in France of Liberation Theology during the 1970s. Through these three configurations, the properly philosophical dialogue with Marxism gave way to a strategy of borrowing from it and even its instrumental use. Marxism was no longer an interlocutor, but rather operated as a theoretical referent, a sort of scientific umbrella for revolutionary Christian politics. For some years, this movement withstood the decline of the reference to Marx in France from the mid-1970s onwards.

---

19   Tranvouez, 2015.

The historian Jean Baubérot, a leading figure in the revolt by young Protest-ants in the 1960s, was surprised by this in 1977: 'There is perhaps something paradoxical in affirming so strongly that one is a Marxist and a "materialist" at a time when the plurality of Marxisms makes Marxism problematic, when the far left perceives flaws in "materialism" and no longer lays claim to it so much'.[20]

Tellingly, it was at some distance from the Christian left that in 1976 the philosopher Michel Henry proposed an original reading of Marx, centred on the analysis of individual subjectivity, on the basis of a return to Husserl's phe-nomenology and to his Christian heritage (*Marx*, book I: *Une philosophie de la réalité*, book II: *Une philosophie de l'économie*). At the time, his work went almost unnoticed,[21] but it was a prelude to the 'theological turn in phenomen-ology' for which its author and some others would be reproached in the 1990s. In fact, the Catholic reference to Marx was then caught up in the turmoil of the 'crisis of ideologies' and its aftermath, before it died out in the face of the policy of restoring order under John Paul II's pontificate. At the same time, Marx's work seems to have departed from the French philosophical horizon.

20   Baubérot 1977.
21   Corcuff 2014.

CHAPTER 26

Marx in French-Speaking Africa

Françoise Blum

The reception and dissemination of Marx and Marxism by French-speaking Africans – nationals of the French African Empire or the French Union until 1958 (Guinea) and 1960 – is a relatively recent object of study. The discovery and appropriation of Marx and Marxism in Africa was initially the doing of Africans living in France – intellectuals and/or students (some of them French citizens, as in the case of Léopold Sédar Senghor) – before it took on a more autonomous life on African soil. The French Communist Party (PCF), from its creation, and in its ambiguous support for colonised peoples, was one of the vehicles of this transmission of Marx to Africa, with the École coloniale, the Centre d'études et de recherches marxiste (CERM), the Université nouvelle and, on African soil, the creation of the Groupes d'études communistes upon the initiative of Raymond Barbé. Works published by Éditions sociales, alongside the volumes issued by the Moscow or Beijing publishers and distributed in France, enabled generations of Africans to familiarise themselves with the great Marxist texts (or digests of them) and thus to make Marxism – a doctrine of progress – the theoretical tool of their liberation.

It is thus difficult to separate the study of the reception of Marx in Africa from the reception of Marx in France, for there are many connections between the two. As we shall try to demonstrate in these pages, the reception of Marx in France is also the reception of Marx in Africa.

From the foundation of the Communist International, the promulgation of the 21 conditions (and in particular the eighth condition on oppressed peoples), and the 1924 congress which affirmed the International's support for independence movements – and, in the French case, from the foundation of the Communist Party at the Tours Congress – links were forged between Communists and colonised peoples. This is evidenced by the 1921 creation of the Intercolonial Union, then of the League against Imperialism, which held its first congress in Brussels in February 1927. The leaders of the so-called 'negro movements',[1] Senegal's Lamine Senghor[2] and Mali's Tiémoko Garan Kouyaté,

---

1 Dewitte 1985.
2 Murphy 2015.

flirted with the Communist world in an often ambiguous relationship, made up of conjunctural alliances, compromises, more or less strategic agreements, and sometimes ruptures, as was the case for Kouyaté, who was expelled from the Communist Party and the Union of Negro Workers in 1933. In this relationship, attraction often competed with dissatisfaction. Indeed, what David Murphy writes about Lamine Senghor is valid for many other African figures: 'The evolution of Lamine Senghor's political thought expressed frustration with the limits of a communism that was supposed to be global but was primarily focused on European interests'.[3] This type of relationship would endure, with ups and downs, until these countries won their independence. This provided the backdrop against which the relationship between Marxism and African intellectuals was built.

1   From World War II to Independence

1.1   *The First African Readings of Marx*

The first African students in France, in particular the intellectuals of the *Négritude* movement, read Marx and developed a constructive critique of him from the 1930s onwards. But only after World War II would the founding texts of an African reading of Marx appear. The most famous of these is undoubtedly Léopold Sédar Senghor's article published in 1948 in the *Revue socialiste*, 'Marxisme et humanisme'.[4] In it, the future president of Senegal laid the foundations of his doctrine of African socialism, opposing the humanism of the young Marx to the doctrine of the mature economist. To this end he drew on texts published in 1927–38 by Éditions Costes and in 1946 by Éditions sociales. 'The Marx that Senghor adopts and on which his spiritualist socialism would be based is precisely the philosopher of alienation, not the economist of surplus value'.[5] Thus Senghor wrote:

> What profit is to be gained from these youthful works! They also contain the principles of Marx's ethics, which propose to us, as the object of our practical activity, the total liberation of man. We should mention here: 1844: *Contribution on the Jewish Question*; 1845: *The Holy Family or the Critique of Critical Criticism* (in collaboration with Engels); 1847 [sic – the theses on Feuerbach date from 1845]: *Eleven Theses on Feuerbach*; 1844: *Political Economy and Philosophy*, from which we should compare the

---

3 Murphy 2015.
4 Senghor 1971.
5 Diagne 2013.

manuscript published in the *Revue socialiste* (February 1947) under the title 'Le Travail aliéné et l'idéologie allemande' ['Alienated Labour and the German Ideology'] (1845, 1846, in collaboration with Engels).[6]

Building on this first reading, Senghor later popularised his intellectual relationship with the founding fathers in a short text published under the title *Pour une relecture africaine de Marx et d'Engels* ('For an African Re-Reading of Marx and Engels').[7] In it, he challenged certain Marxist concepts, first among them class struggle, and claimed that it should be d theoretically by the opposition between 'affluent peoples and proletarian peoples': 'The major problem of socialism is not so much the elimination of class inequalities within the same nation as those between affluent peoples and proletarian peoples, between "developed countries" and "developing countries".'[8]

The problem that Marxism poses for many African readers is its atheism. Either one can ignore this aspect of Marxism, or try to reintroduce God into it, in one way or another. Senghor developed his reading of Marx in the light of that by Father Teilhard de Chardin. He reintroduced religion by judging that 'in reality, Marx's protest against religious alienation is the very one that could be formulated in "a reaction of Christian origin against the deviations of the historical forms of Christianity" which "still less undercut the very essence of religion seeing as the idea of alienation is itself religious in essence".'[9] It should be emphasised that the articulation of Marx and Teilhard is not unique to the future president of Senegal. It can be found, for example, in the co-founder of the Rassemblement démocratique africain (RDA), Gabriel d'Arboussier,[10] or in the Rwandan Christian democrat Grégoire Kayibanda.

The years 1945–50 saw African students accomplish a real labour of reading Marxist thought, appropriating it in a specific fashion and hybridising it, in parallel with the publication of a series of texts by Éditions sociales. These thoughtful readings were the main focus of the Groupement africain de recherches économiques et politiques (GAREP), in which the Senegalese Abdoulaye Ly and Ahmadou Mokhtar Mbow, the Dahomean Solange Faladé and a few others discussed Marx, but also Lenin, Karl Kautsky and Rosa Luxemburg. They translated into French *Towards Colonial Freedom* by the Ghanaian leader Kwame

---

6   TN: Senghor cites non-standard French titles for these works, and they are translated here accordingly.
7   Senghor 1976.
8   Senghor 1976.
9   Diagne 2013.
10   Arboussier 1967.

Nkrumah who, in his major theoretical work, *Consciencism*, also – timidly – reintroduced God into scientific socialism. Abdoulaye Ly published a kind of condensed version of the GAREP theses under the title *Les Masses africaines et l'actuelle condition humaine* ('The African Masses and the Present Human Condition'), which is 'a critique of Kwame Nkrumah's conception of imperialism inherited from Lenin'. 'Certainly,' writes Ly, 'one does not overlook Marxism with impunity, one does not validy condemn it, one understands it; one situates it as a historical phenomenon'.[11]

Senegal's Cheikh Anta Diop also had his own reading of Marx. The work of this figure, a kind of master thinker for generations of African intellectuals, was rather marked by culturalism. But Cheikh Anta Diop never rejected Marxism and, as a prelude to his masterpiece *Nations nègres et cultures*, he criticised that 'intellectual who has forgotten his Marxist training or the one who has rapidly studied Marxism in the absolute without ever having considered its application to the particular case that is the social reality of his own country'.[12] These are non-dogmatic, thoughtful and open readings of Marx.

Nor can we ignore the great influence of Aimé Césaire – although he was not himself African – on students of Africa. All of them have read the 'Letter to Maurice Thorez' in which he broke with the PCF even while granting a role to Marxism and calling for 'A form of organization in which Marxists would not be drowned, but rather play their role of leavening, inspiring, and orienting, as opposed to the role which, objectively, they play at present: of dividing popular forces'.[13]

1.2   *Access-Routes to Marx*

In parallel, on African soil, Marx was introduced through different channels. The main one was undoubtedly the Groupes d'études communistes (GEC) set up from 1943 to 1951 under the responsibility of the Communist Raymond Barbé. The GECs, which brought together Europeans and Africans from one end of French-speaking Africa to the other – particularly in Senegal, French Sudan, Ivory Coast, Congo and Cameroon – were places for introductory talks on Marxism, conceived as a kind of philosophy of liberation. A circular from Raymond Barbé, dated 20 July 1948 and addressed to the GECs, lays down the bases of the Marxist – and/or Communist – doctrine applied to Black Africa, with many quotations from Stalin: 'For countries which have little or no pro-

---

11   Ly 1956.
12   Cheikh Anta Diop 1954.
13   Césaire 1956.

letariat of their own and are not at all developed industrially ... For countries where the bourgeoisie has no reason to split into revolutionary and conciliatory parties, the task of the Communist elements is to take all measures to create a single national front against imperialism'.[14]

Amady Aly Dieng, who was president of the Fédération des étudiants d'Afrique noire en France (FEANF) in 1961–2, offers a portrait of the activist's library,[15] made up of books taken from the catalogues of Éditions sociales, Progress Publishers, the Beijing Foreign Languages Press and, from 1959, Éditions Maspero. There were no works by Marx, although it should be noted that the Éditions sociales published *Capital* in 1954 (Volume I) and 1959 (Volume II), making it easily accessible. Lenin, Stalin and Mao were the main authors: Lenin's *Imperialism, Highest Stage of Capitalism* and *What Is to Be Done*; Stalin's *Foundations of Leninism* and *Marxism and the National and Colonial Question*; Rosa Luxemburg's *The Mass Strike, the Political Party and the Trade Unions* and *The Accumulation of Capital*; Mao Zedong's *On Contradiction, On Practice* and *On New Democracy*. Georges Politzer's *Elementary Principles of Philosophy* was also read. African students shared these readings with French Communist students, but had a particular fondness for the Stalin of *Marxism and The National and Colonial Question* and for the writings of Mao. Marxist study circles were not uncommon. Amady Aly Dieng himself started a reading circle on *Capital*, which he continued once he had returned to Dakar. Students thus pursued real work on the oeuvre of Marx and Engels, but also on the texts of Lenin, Stalin and Mao, in accordance with the publications being issued in French, which were multiplying in this period.

1.3 *An African Marxist Party*

In Senegal, a new stage was reached with the creation, in 1957, of the African Independence Party (PAI), the first Marxist party in West Africa, which was to have sections in all the countries of French West Africa, before being banned in most cases: 'The African Independence Party, a party of a new type, a party armed with the theory of scientific socialism, a party of the struggle for independence and national sovereignty, a party for the construction of African socialist society'.[16] It is important to emphasise the leading role which the PAI attributed to the proletariat in an Africa where this latter remained largely in the minority. This was a core issue, which also set a dividing line: not all African

---

14   Suret-Canale 1994.
15   Dieng 2009.
16   Manifesto, quoted in Camara 2013.

Marxists, or self-declared Marxists, recognised the existence of classes in Africa. The question of classes and class struggle was at the heart of the debate over the invention of an African Marxism, and not an object of consensus. The theoretical positions adopted by some leaders would play a role when it came to defining the structure and vocation of the single party, an instrument of national construction set up after independence in all the countries of the continent. Would the party be a mass party, such as the one established under the rule of Sékou Touré in Guinea (Sékou Touré himself theorised the 'people-class')? Or would it be a minority and vanguard party in the hands of a conscious elite (or class)? What changed with the PAI was the role now assigned to scientific socialism. Marxism appeared as a tool for the subversion of the colonial world, but also for the construction of a future socialist state, and thus a tool of government.

2   After Independence

2.1   *From Critical Discourse to Official Discourse?*
After independence, Marxism remained a language of social revolt, in more or less developed forms. In Madagascar, the newspaper Andry Pilier, for example, undertook a Malagasyisation of Marxist concepts: the 'little people' d the proletariat as the agent of history. But it also becomes a government programme. In Congo-Brazzaville, the 1963 revolution known as the *Trois Glorieuses* brought to power a youth that decreed scientific socialism as the official doctrine of government. Similarly, in Dahomey, Marxism-Leninism was declared the official doctrine of the regime that emerged from the October 1972 coup d'état which brought Mathieu Kérékou to power. In his speech of 30 November 1975, he confirmed its adoption as a principle of government. Even if one did not officially proclaim oneself to be a 'Marxist-Leninist', this did not rule out calling on the services of Marxist experts, particularly in the field of planning. Such was the case with the French economist Charles Bettelheim who worked in Mali and Guinea.[17]

Apart from the royal road of state control, there were still many paths to Marxism in post-independence Africa. Educational initiatives were created, such as the Guinean workers' university,[18] organised by the World Federation of Trade Unions (WFTU), with a view to training up cadres. It is difficult to meas-

---

17   Denord and Zunigo 2005.
18   Blum 2013.

ure the impact of these courses, but they did contribute to the dissemination of a watered-down Marxist vulgate – one with particular emphasis on humanity's stages of development – which was, in any case, widespread across the globe. Another example is the teaching of Marxism-Leninism to African students in the USSR and in the People's Democracies, although this type of training seems to have been rather counterproductive.[19]

2.2 Producing an African Marxism

Much more serious theoretically were the attempts by African intellectuals to adapt or translate Marxism into specifically African terms. The Franco-Egyptian economist Samir Amin has had a strong influence in Francophone Africa. His oeuvre consists of de-Europeanising Marxism, by trying to take into account what, in Marx, seems to him to be insufficiently dealt with: 'the polarisation and destruction of peoples conquered by capitalism', or, in other terms, the global character of capitalism. Close to Amin, Amady Aly Dieng defines himself as 'a student who is a pure tropical product of the Renaissance, the Enlightenment and the twentieth century dominated by the thought of Marx'.[20] In *Hegel, Marx, Engels et les problèmes de l'Afrique noire* and in *Le Marxisme et l'Afrique noire : bilan d'un débat sur l'universalité du marxisme*,[21] he clearly poses the question of the usefulness or necessity of adapting Marxism to a continent with a very underdeveloped working class. But, unlike Samir Amin, he quotes extensively from *Capital* precisely in order to show that Marx's great work, based on the analysis of capitalism in Europe and North America, hardly concerns Africa.[22] Another Senegalese, Babacar Sine, challenged the thesis of the 'radical Europeanism of Marxism' and of *Capital*.

In France, at the same time, Marxian analysis had its moment of glory in the Africanist sciences, with Jean Suret-Canale, Claude Meillassoux, Emmanuel Terray, Jean Copans, Catherine Coquery-Vidrovitch and a few others, whose research had as its main contribution 'the recognition of the autonomy of African historical processes'.[23] Although this Africanist historiography was produced in Europe, it was also read in Africa. Nevertheless, very few academics in French-speaking Africa claimed to be Marxists, for reasons that sometimes owed to prudence.

---

19 Katsakioris 2015.
20 Dieng 2011.
21 Dieng 1978, Dieng 1985.
22 Dieng 1978.
23 Jewiesiwicki 1985.

2.3   A Marxist Library in Mali

In order to understand the spread of Marxism in Africa, it is important to know what literature was available to individuals on the African continent. We are fortunate to have an inventory of the library of a Malian militant: Amadou Seydou Traoré, a partner of Modibo Keita. This inventory was drawn up by the historian Ophélie Rillon, through direct access to the library. Amadou Traoré, who died in 2016, called himself a Marxist. Before independence, he founded a bookshop, L'Étoile noire, which he donated to Modibo Keita's regime, which gave him responsibility for three state-owned firms: the Librairie populaire, the Éditions Imprimeries du Mali and the Office cinématographique national du Mali (OCINAM). These functions as a bookseller-publisher explain the importance of a library that has been preserved to this day, despite the ins-and-outs of the political context. This library contains more than a thousand volumes. As a bookseller-publisher and as a socialist activist, Amadou Traoré was the recipient of all the literature disseminated by the networks active in the Communist world, and all the Marxist or related literature disseminated through them. Unsurprisingly, we find volumes from Éditions sociales (Paris), Progress Publishers (Moscow), the foreign-language presses of both Moscow and Beijing, and the Novosti press agency. The lion's share of the works are not by Marx and Engels, by Lenin and Mao. Nevertheless, there is an edition of volume I of *Capital* published by Éditions sociales in 1960 and volumes I and II published by the same publisher in 1983–4. Curiously, there is only one copy of the *Communist Manifesto*, in German. On the other hand, the library contains eighteen volumes of Lenin's works published by Éditions sociales between 1958 and 1977, as well as a few other texts from Progress Publishers, the Moscow Foreign Languages Publishing House and the Novosti press agency published between 1954 and 1984. Mao Zedong is also well-represented, with four volumes of selected works published by Éditions sociales between 1955 and 1959, and fourteen volumes from the Peking Publishing House in foreign languages between 1955 and 1967. Stalin's essential text, *Marxism and the National and Colonial Question*, published by Éditions sociales in 1949, stands alongside two other works by the same author. Lastly, in this library we find the complete works of Kim-Il-sung, coming directly from the Pyongyang Foreign Languages Publishing House (1975–84), a volume of the selected works of Trotsky, some texts by Hô Chi Minh and Georgi Dimitrov.

Traoré was no simple activist: as a bookseller and publisher/printer, he was also a 'smuggler' of literature across borders. This bookshop-library threw its doors open wide, and anyone could get information and borrow the books collected there. Amadou Traoré's books were not only for his own use and if one was in Bamako and interested in the corpus of Marxist literature, it was to him that one should come. No Marxist publications in African languages are to be found on Amadou Traoré's shelves. If there had been any African editions, they would not have found a readership. Judging by the catalogue of the library of the former Marx–Engels–Lenin Institute in Moscow, there were very many translations of Marx into Arabic but very few in African languages: the *Manifesto* has, however, been translated into Malagasy, Amharic, Hausa and Swahili. Of these languages, only Hausa is spoken in West Africa. But Swahili is spoken in Central Africa and Malagasy can find a readership.

3   Marx, on Loan from the Colonisers?

The history of Marxism in Africa, or of African Marxisms, is perhaps above all the paradoxical history of the borrowing from the coloniser's culture of theoretical weapons useful for the fight against colonisation. African rebels found a theory of liberation in this European culture, of which Marxism was initially a part. But this did not prevent the development of a specifically African reading of Marx, aimed at filling in the gaps, thinking about the blind spots, erasing the overly Eurocentric aspects, and producing a critical reading, while at the same time setting it within twentieth-century modernity and the confrontation between North and South. Marx inspired both oppositions and programmes of government. To sum up, one could say that the history of Marxism in Africa is that of the reception, translation – or hybridisation – of cultures. It is also the history of anti-colonial struggles and hopes for a better world. And it is sometimes, as it has been on other continents, a history of repression and authoritarianism.

CHAPTER 27

Learning Marxism in Paris: Chinese Communist Students in France (1919–25)

Kaixuan Liu and Wenrui Bi

In the first half of the 1920s, about two thousand young Chinese students stayed in France (and other Western European countries) as part of the 'Work-Study' (*qingong jianxue*, literally 'diligent work, frugal study') programme. About a hundred of them became communists, including several top leaders of the Chinese Communist Party (CCP) of the People's Republic of China (PRC), such as Zhou Enlai, Deng Xiaoping, Chen Yi, and others. They became much more active and successful in the CCP than those students from China who were introduced to communism in Japan. Here, we will try to explain this by studying their learning of Marx's texts in France and the characteristics of their Marxism.

1 Reasons for Leaving

Most of these students were between 16 and 25 years old in 1919–20. For this generation, the choice to leave for France was justified by both personal and political reasons. On the one hand, the profound transformations of Chinese society since the end of the nineteenth century had opened up new horizons for young people, the most ambitious of whom looked to the outside world for new opportunities for personal advancement.[1] On the other hand, politically, these young people belonged to the 'May Fourth' generation, its name referring to the May–June 1919 students' and workers' demonstration against the Chinese signature of the Treaty of Versailles, which handed the Japanese the former German concessions in China. But the political stakes facing this generation extended far beyond the question of the Treaty of Versailles. From then on, the whole socio-cultural tradition of China, perceived as incapable of facing up to the great foreign powers, was called into question in public debate. While they had not all participated in the demonstrations in Beijing or Shanghai, the

---

1 Wang 2002.

students who later went to France were looking for a way to put China on a better footing and restore its place among the great nations of the world.

The 'Work-Study' programme seems to have responded to both these needs. The Chinese initiators of this programme, such as Li Shizeng and Wu Zhihui, had been students in Paris at the start of twentieth century. Anarchist followers of the ideas of Pierre Kropotkin and Élisée Reclus, they advocated the abolition of the state, mutual aid and the combination of manual and intellectual labour, seen as the means of access to modernity and progress. As early as 1912, they set up reception and coordination organisations in China and France to facilitate the departure of students for French shores. The aim of the programme was to provide students from modest backgrounds with an opportunity to study in France – considered by Chen Duxiu to be 'the origin of modern Western civilisation' – in frugal material conditions. Factory work was not compulsory but provided an indispensable source of income for students who had no other resources.

Did all these students share in an anarchist outlook? Certainly, anarchism was a very influential political current among the more politicised Chinese intellectuals of the time, and it is quite likely that these young students sympathised with anarchist ideas. The early Chinese Communists, including Mao Zedong himself, all more or less made their way to the Marxist school via mutualist anarchism. But after the May Fourth movement, anarchism began to lose ground to Marxism for two main reasons. Anarchism proved inadequate to address the particular concerns of the working class, which entered politics with the strikes of June 1919; and student activists were frustrated by anarchist pacifism, which was unable to cope with government repression and transform their ideals into real action.[2] No doubt these young Chinese students in France were aware of all these debates.

2   The Encounter with Capitalism

The Chinese emigrants arrived in France by boat: there were twenty departures between March 1919 and December 1920, with the last of them disembarking in Marseille in January 1921. They spent the first months of their stay in France in favourable conditions. The students who had no financial worries enrolled in colleges to learn the language and technical trades. Students who had to work had an easy time of finding jobs in French factories, given the postwar labour

2   Dirlik 1989.

shortages. The Chinese Patronage Association aided them in their endeavours. French institutions were welcoming: special classes for Chinese students were organised in colleges (particularly in Montargis, Melun and Fontainebleau), while some of the Chinese students working in factories found French bosses and engineers very hard-working, respectful and friendly.[3]

But disillusionment was not long in coming, mainly because of the rise of cyclical unemployment from 1920 onwards. It was even harder for the student workers to find work because the vast majority of them did not speak French and lacked the technical skills for industrial jobs. Many had only received a general secondary education in China.[4] Those who did manage to find a job had little time, or especially energy, to devote to their studies, causing great frustration among these students. Faced with the impossibility of studying and/or working, these Chinese youths looked for the reason for the failure of the work-study project. The most radicalised among them identified it in the nature of capitalism, and would gradually turn to theories that critiqued this system – notably the theories of Karl Marx. He Guo, who worked at the Schneider factory in Harfleur, wrote in October 1920:

> Labour is not a commodity to be sold, it has its true value ... My time, my energy, my mind, my brain, all that is worth only fourteen francs a day? ... All this worthless work, why do we do it, what is the point! ... Life is not only material, but also intellectual. A just work must satisfy intellectual desire in addition to material desire.[5]

For Chen Yi, it was already clear:

> The enemy of human values is capitalism. ... In conclusion, my pain for the past two years has been that of selling my working time for money, and this money cannot satisfy my [intellectual] desire .... In a word, it is the fault of the social system.[6]

The encounter with capitalist reality facilitated the conversion to communism. Some student-workers arrived in France more politicised and radicalised than others. Among those who lived in Montargis was Cai Hesen. A classmate and friend of Mao Zedong, in Changsa in 1918 he founded, together with him and

---

3   Qinghua 1980.
4   Wan 2002.
5   Qinghua 1980, Vol. II.
6   Qinghua 1981, Vol. III.

a dozen comrades, a 'New Citizens' Study Society', whose objective was to find ways to transform China. The members of this society who had a spell in France did not give up on this objective. In July 1920, a dozen of them met in Montargis to discuss, among other things, a collective project for political studies. They did shared readings; among the few titles mentioned (our source is in Chinese, and it is difficult to match all the Chinese translations with the original titles), we find, in no particular order, *L'Humanité*, *The Federative Principle and the Need to Reconstitute the Party of Revolution* and *La Voix des femmes*, as well as the publications of the Second and Third Internationals.

Reading these political texts – in the context of the debate in France on whether the SFIO should rally to the Comintern – had a decisive influence on these young socialists. Cai Hesen arrived in France in February 1920. He initially set out to understand, during his first two years there, 'the socialist parties and trade unions of each country, the Comintern, socialism, syndicalism, anarchism and democracy'.[7] That same August he made a 'great leap forward' politically: he wrote to Mao that it was necessary to form a Soviet-style Communist Party to lead the proletarian revolution, which was the only possible way to change China. From what he observed of the European workers' movement, he concluded that the Socialists were traitors: it was therefore necessary to adopt the Bolshevik model.

All that was needed was a trigger for the students to form a Communist Party. Three clashes between the student-workers and the Chinese and French authorities (represented respectively by the Student Patronage Association, the Chinese embassy and the French police) in the course of 1921 played this role: the first concerning the Chinese government funding of their studies; the second, a secret loan between France and China; and the third, the most spectacular, over the conditions of entry to the Franco-Chinese Institute in Lyon. This series of events revealed to student-workers the hypocrisy of the 'Work-Study' project, the collusion between the Chinese and French governments, and the need for political regroupment. The first communists began to get organised in 1921. Finally, in June 1922, eighteen young Chinese living in Europe met in the Bois de Boulogne to proclaim the constitution of the Chinese Communist Youth Party.[8]

---

7   Cai 1980.
8   Wang 2002.

3   A Marxism of Class Struggle

With the foundation of this party organisation, we have a press organ, published in Chinese, on which basis to study these young Communists' theoretical
understanding. Their first periodical was called *Shaonian* ('The Youth'), which
appeared monthly between August 1922 and December 1923. In February 1924,
the magazine changed its name to *Chiguang* ('The Red Rays') and became a
fortnightly. Its publication stopped temporarily in June 1925. Between 1928 and
1930, *Chiguang* reappeared in Paris, then in Berlin. Zhou Enlai, Chen Yannian,
Deng Xiaoping, Ren Zhuoxuan (who became a member of the Kuomintang and
an anti-communist theorist in the 1930s) and Cheng Fangwu were, in turn, the
main figures responsible for these publications.

How did these young Chinese Communists understand Marx? According to
Cai Hesen, 'Marx's thought is composed of three principles: in history, historical materialism; in economics, *Capital*; in politics, class war. By combining the
three, we get revolutionary Marxism'.[9] But their publications contain very little
discussion of the first two elements. For them, Marx's thought boiled down to
one thing: the class struggle. This struggle is first of all, of course, that between
the proletariat and the bourgeoisie. In the second issue of *Shaonian*, Zhou
Enlai published a theoretical article entitled 'Communism and China: The Economic Arguments of Wu Hao' (his pen name). For Zhou, neither capitalism nor
'state socialism' would allow China to simultaneously accumulate the capital
necessary for industrialisation, protect itself against foreign imperialism and
enrich the workers materially and intellectually. 'The origin of our ills is private
property' which allows the bourgeoisie to monopolise economic and political
power; the only solution is communism, in which Marx's economic theory, in
which the abolition of private property and the seizure of power by the proletariat 'occupy an extremely important place'.

Who were the proletarians and bourgeois in China? Did the Chinese economic and political system fit into the Marxist scheme of a society that could
fall prey to proletarian revolution? For the Chinese Communists in France, the
entire Chinese population, with the exception of a few warlords and big capitalists, belonged to the proletariat. The Chinese bourgeoisie was economically and
politically weak and subject to domination by the big international capitalists.
The struggle between the proletariat and the bourgeoisie was not forgotten, but
the essential problem was to be located at the international level: the condition
of China was also that of all colonial and semi-colonial countries. To use a for-

---

9   Qinghua 1981.

mula of Ren Zhuoxuan's, the class struggle is situated *at the same time* between the proletariat and the bourgeoisie and between oppressed and the oppressor nations (*Shaonian*, 1 May 1923). In short, what these Chinese Communists were above all looking for, in the existing political thought in Europe, was a tool to change the face of China. This vision of Marxism was shared by Communists in China itself:[10] it is significant that access to the documents available in France and in Europe does not reveal any notable difference.

It is difficult to compile a list of all the titles mentioned in the 'recommended reading'. However, it should be noted that the original texts of Marx, Engels and Lenin that Chinese émigrés used in their publications almost exclusively concerned the class struggle. In fact, the articles published in *Shaonian* and *Chiguang* rarely cited the original texts directly. In the 1 April 1923 *Shaonian*, Yin Kuan (who became a Trotskyist in the late 1920s) 'quoted' nine whole paragraphs from the *Communist Manifesto* at the end of the article 'Marxist Morality' to make the case for communist revolution, and he inserted eleven paragraphs from Lenin's *State and Revolution* into another article, 'A Dialogue between an Anarchist and a Communist', to emphasise the necessity of revolution if the repressive state was to be overthrown. These quotations are very little integrated into the argument: when Yin Kuan cites the texts, he does so almost without comment. As for Zhou Enlai's articles, which were essentially theoretical, they never mentioned their sources.

In this context, translations of texts by Marx and Engels were rare. The 1 July 1923 *Shaonian* published a short passage from Engels's 'On Authority' on its cover, which opposes a simple seizure of power without a dictatorship of the proletariat. The first article in this issue is Yin Kuan's translation of Marx's 5 March 1852 letter to Weydemeyer (the translator's title is 'History is for the Dictatorship of the Proletariat'), originally published in the *Correspondance internationale* (the Comintern's main publication in French). But the translator wrongly presents it as an extract from *The Civil War in France*. The first page of the 15 August 1923 *Shaonian* features the last paragraph of Engels's *Socialism: Utopian and Scientific* on 'the historical mission of the modern proletariat', an 'act of universal emancipation'. Issue 13 of *Shaonian* published the full translation of 'On Authority' under the title 'The Principles of Power'. These are not, however, all good-quality transitions: compared to the other articles in these reviews, the language used in the translation of 'On Authority' is extremely difficult for today's readers to understand.

---

10   Yang 2010.

What explains this lack of direct reference to Marx's writings? Firstly, an insufficient level of foreign-language and social-sciences training among the young Communists probably left them unable to read Marx's original texts. Secondly, they did not consider reading him an absolute necessity. Indeed, except for the Chinese version of the *Manifesto*, no title by Marx or Engels appears in the political and theoretical educational programme of the Chinese Communists in Europe (this programme was a collective system of reading, correspondence and meetings on the classics and the textbook works of Marxism and Leninism). On the other hand, French-language translations included Lenin's *State and Revolution*, Nikolai Bukharin's *ABC of Communism* and 'Leninism' (probably the text written by Grigori Zinoviev).[11]

It is not surprising, therefore, that the Chinese Communists' publications in France granted much more room to the Soviet Union. For them, the experience of the October Revolution counted for more than Marx's works. Their seemingly anodyne assessments of the merits of Marx and Lenin reflected their conceptions. For them, Marx was 'only' a great theoretician who turned communism from a utopia into a science, while Lenin was an extraordinary revolutionary leader, who turns the dream of communism into reality. On 1 May 1923, *Shaonian* published a commemorative article for the 105th anniversary of Marx's birth. The author believed that Marx's thoughts were 'to be greatly cherished and respected', and that the anniversary of Marx's birth and death 'should be and deserves to be commemorated'. But when Lenin died, the 1 February 1924 *Chiguang* devoted its entire front page to the event, presenting the Bolshevik leader as 'the great and beloved leader of the oppressed peoples of the whole world'. The magazine's editors could 'not find words to describe [their] sadness and [Lenin's] accomplishments'.

Texts from the Soviet Union and the Comintern played an important role in the publications of the Chinese young Communists. Lenin's 'Tasks of the Youth Leagues' is published in full in the first four issues of *Shaonian*. Other texts, such as the directives of the Executive Committee of the Comintern, and the writings of Trotsky, Zinoviev, Bukharin and Stalin are present in all the issues of these magazines, in contrast to the writings of Marx, commentaries on world events and reports on the situation in China.

The experience of the Russian revolution and the building of the Soviet Union was *the* source of inspiration and example for young Chinese Communists. The 1 December 1922 *Shaonian* was entirely devoted to the fifth anniversary of the October Revolution, and it is the only special issue among all the issues

---

11   Xianyu 2003.

that we could find. In most of the articles praising the achievements of the Soviet Union, there are also paragraphs concerning the Chinese situation. In this special issue, the anonymous author of an article comparing the Russian and Chinese revolutions draws lessons from the February revolution, to remind Chinese revolutionaries that a bourgeois republic (such as the Chinese Republic, founded in 1911) cannot the dictatorship of the proletariat.

4   The Chinese Communists' Marx

What were the specifically French sources of the young Chinese Communists's Marxism? The French language itself represented a decisive aspect: for they got into the habit of explaining theoretical terms directly in French, sometimes using the *Larousse* dictionary. They drew on the works of French Socialists and Communists, for example Amédée Dunois, Paul Lafargue, Gaston Monmousseau and Charles Rappoport. When Xue Shilun used Marx's notion of 'an association, in which the free development of each is the condition for the free development of all', he quoted it indirectly from Rappoport's *La Philosophie de l'histoire comme science de l'évolution* without indicating its original source – that is, the *Communist Manifesto* itself.[12]

On the other hand, direct contacts between Chinese and French Communists were rather limited. The Chinese Communists' political activity focused on the Chinese community, even if a few meetings took place beyond that: Nie Rongzhen remembers their participation in the *'L'Humanité* evening class', an opportunity for a secondary school teacher, a member of the PCF, to make friends with them.[13] On 7 June 1925, a meeting was organised by the Chinese Communists to protest against the repression of the workers of Shanghai. Alfred Costes, Jacques Doriot and André Marty took part and, in the name of the PCF, invited the Chinese 'to organise themselves solidly in order to make their revolution, which is only in its infancy, and promised them moral and material support'.[14] Following this anti-imperialist meeting – and probably because of the participation of PCF members in it – the Chinese Communists were subjected to increased police surveillance. At the same time, the CCP decided to repatriate its members from France to increase its strength back home. Communists gradually left France to return to China or to complete their training in Moscow.

---

12   Qinghua 1981.
13   Nie 1986.
14   Wang 2002.

As compared to their counterparts in Japan, who did not have the experience of working in factories, the Chinese students' life in France provided them with a few rudiments of doctrine, based on quotations from Marx. This may have been a summary assemblage of fragments, but it echoed their daily struggles. And it provided a Marxist basis for the great adventure which lay ahead of them – leading some of them to the highest responsibilities.

References

Aglietta, Michel 1976, *Régulation et crises du capitalisme. L'expérience des États-Unis*, Paris: Calmann-Lévy.

Aglietta, Michel and André Orléan 1982, *La Violence de la monnaie*, Paris: PUF.

Agulhon, Maurice 1973, *1848 ou l'apprentissage de la République*, Paris: Seuil.

Alexander, Jeffrey C. 1995, *Fin de Siècle Social Theory: Relativism, Reduction, and the Problem of Reason*, London: Verso.

Althusser, Louis 2003, *Montesquieu, la politique et l'histoire*, Paris: PUF.

Althusser, Louis 2005a, *For Marx*, London: Verso.

Althusser, Louis 2005b, 'Contradiction and Overdetermination', in *For Marx*, London: Verso.

Althusser, Louis 2006, *Politique et Histoire, de Machiavel à Marx. Cours à l'école normale supérieure 1955–1972*, edited by François Matheron, Paris: Seuil.

Althusser, Louis 2012, *Cours sur Rousseau*, Pantin: Le Temps des cerises.

Amin, Samir 1988, *Eurocentrism*, London: Zed Books.

Amossy, Ruth (ed.) 2005, 'Analyse du discours et sociocritique', *Littérature*, 140: 4.

Anderson, Perry 1979, *Considerations on Western Marxism*, London: Verso.

Aprile, Sylvie 2010, *Le Siècle des exilés. Bannis et proscrits, de 1789 à la Commune*, Paris: CNRS Éditions.

Arboussier, Gabriel d' 1967, *Intime réflexion*, unpublished manuscript.

Arena, Richard 2000, 'Les économistes français en 1950', *Revue économique*, 51, 5: 969–1007.

Aron, Raymond 1932, 'Lettre d'Allemagne', *Libres propos*, February.

Aron, Raymond 1938, *Introduction à laphilosophie de l'histoire. Essai sur les limites de l'objectivité historique*, Paris: Gallimard.

Aron, Raymond 1946, 'Le Parti communiste français', *Combat*, April

Aron, Raymond 1963, *Dix-huit Leçons sur la société industrielle*, Paris: Gallimard.

Aron, Raymond 1964, *La Lutte de classes*, Paris: Gallimard.

Aron, Raymond 1965a, *Démocratie et totalitarisme*, Paris: Gallimard.

Aron, Raymond 1965b, *Essai sur les libertés*, Paris: Hachette.

Aron, Raymond 1967, *Les Étapes de la pensée sociologique*, Paris: Gallimard.

Aron, Raymond 1970, *Marxismes imaginaires. D'une sainte famille à l'autre*, Paris: Gallimard.

Aron, Raymond 1976, *Les Étapes de la pensée sociologique*, Paris: Gallimard.

Aron, Raymond 1977, *Plaidoyer pour l'Europe décadente*, Paris: R. Laffont.

Aron, Raymond 1980, *Mémoires. Cinquante ans de réflexion politique*, Paris: R. Laffont.

Aron, Raymond 1990 [1944], 'L'avenir des religions séculières', in *Chroniques de guerre. La France libre, 1940–1945*, Paris: Gallimard.

Aron, Raymond 1991, *Leçons sur l'histoire*, Paris: Le Livre de Poche.

Aron, Raymond 2002, *Le Marxisme de Marx*, Paris: De Fallois.

Aron, Raymond 2005a [1937], 'Politique et économie dans la doctrine marxiste', in *Les Sociétés modernes*, Paris: PUF.

Aron, Raymond 2005b [1939], 'Le concept de classe', *in Les Sociétés modernes*, Paris: PUF.

Arruzza, Cinzia 2016, 'Vers une "union queer" du marxisme et du féminisme ?', *Contretemps*, 10 October.

Audier, Serge 2006, *Tocqueville retrouvé. Genèse et enjeux du renouveau tocquevillien français*, Paris: Vrin/Éditions de l'EHESS.

Aunoble, Éric 2016, *La Révolution russe, une histoire française*, Paris: La Fabrique.

Axelos, Kostas 1958, 'Thèses sur Marx', *Arguments*, 7

Axelos, Kostas 1961, *Marx penseur de la technique*, Paris: Minuit.

Badia, Gilbert 1978, 'Défense et illustration de [la] "plus-value"', *La Pensée*, 200, 128–32.

Badiou, Alain and Slavoj Žižek (eds.) 2010, *The Idea of Communism*, London: Verso.

Balibar, Étienne and Jean-Pierre Lefebvre 1978, 'Plus-value ou survaleur?', *La Pensée*, 197: 32–42.

Bantigny, Ludivine 2016, 'Flux et reflux de l'idée révolutionnaire' in Christophe Charle and Laurent Jeanpierre (eds.), *La Vie intellectuelle en France*, Paris: Seuil.

Barberis, Pierre 1970, *Balzac et le mal du siècle : contribution à une physiologie du monde moderne*, Paris: Gallimard.

Barberis, Pierre 1990, 'La sociocritique', in *Méthodes critiques pour l'analyse littéraire*, Paris: Bordas.

Bard, Christine 1995, *Les Filles de Marianne. Histoire des féminismes 1914–1940*, Paris: Fayard.

Bard, Christine and Jean-Louis Rober 1998, 'The French Communist Party and Women, 1920–1939: From "Feminism" to Familialism', in Helmut Gruber and Pamela Graves (eds.), *Women and Socialism, Socialism and Women. Europe between the two World Wars*, New York: Berghahn Books.

Barthes, Roland 1975, 'Texte (Théorie du)', *Encyclopaedia Universalis*.

Barthes, Roland 2013, *Mythologies*, New York: Hill and Wang

Bartoli, Henri 1950, *La Doctrine économique et sociale de Karl Marx*, Paris: Seuil.

Baubérot, Jean 1977, *À gauche ces chrétiens*, Paris: Stock.

Baudelot, Christian and Roger Establer 1971, *L'École capitaliste en France*, Paris: Maspero.

Baudelot, Christian, Roger Establer and Jacques Malemort 1974, *La Petite Bourgeoisie en France*, Paris: Maspero.

Beauvoir, Simon de, Yves Berger, Jean-Pierre Faye, Jean Ricardou, Jean-Paul Sartre and Jorge Semprún 1965, *Que peut la littérature ?*, Paris: 10/18.

Beauvoir, Simone de 2015 [1949], *The Second Sex*, London: Vintage.

Benetti, Carlo 1976, *Valeur et répartition*, Grenoble: Presses universitaires de Grenoble.

Benetti, Carlo and Jean Cartelier 1981, *Marchands, salariat et capitalistes*, Grenoble: Presses universitaires de Grenoble.

Bensaïd, Daniel 2015, *An Impatient Life: A Memoir*, London: Verso.

Berger, Denis and Henri Maler 1996, *Une certaine idée du communisme*, Paris: Éditions du Félin.

Bergounioux, Alain and Gérard Grunberg 1992, *Le Long Remords du pouvoir. Le Parti socialiste français. 1905–1992*, Paris: Fayard.

Bergounioux, Alain and Gérard Grunberg 2005, *L'Ambition et le Remords. Les socialistes français et le pouvoir*, Paris: Fayard.

Bernis, Gérard Destanne de 1966, 'Industries industrialisantes et contenu d'une politique d'intégration régionale', *Économie appliquée*, 3–4, 415–73.

Bernstein, Samuel 1933, *The Beginnings of Marxism in France*, New York: Elliot Publishing.

Berstein, Serge 2006, *Léon Blum*, Paris: Fayard.

Bertrand, M. 1985, 'La réception de l'œuvre de Marx dans l'Église de France (1945–1978)', in Georges Labica (ed.), *1883–1983 : L'Œuvre de Marx un siècle après*, Paris: PUF.

Bettelheim, Charles 1964, *Planification et croissance accélérée*, Paris: Maspero

Binoche, Bertrand, *Critiques des droits de l'homme*, Paris: PUF.

Blanchot, Maurice 1949, 'Réflexions sur le surréalisme', in *La Part du feu*, Paris: Gallimard.

Bloch, Marc 2015, *Strange Defeat: A Statement of Evidence Written in 1940*, London: Folio.

Bloch, Marc and Lucien Febvre 2004, *Correspondance*, Vol. 2: *De Strasbourg à Paris (1934–1937)*, Paris: Fayard.

Blum Françoise 2013, 'Une formation syndicale dans la Guinée de Sékou Touré : l'université ouvrière africaine, 1960–1965', *Revue historique*, 667: 661–91.

Boccara, Paul 2009, 'La traduction par "plus-value" de "Mehrwert" de Marx et sa portée', *Économie et Politique*, 658–9.

Boggio Éwanjé-Épée, Félix et al (eds.) 2017, *Pour un féminisme de la totalité*, Paris: Amsterdam/Période.

Bois, Guy 1984, *The Crisis of Feudalism. Economy and Society in Eastern Normandy c. 1300–1550*, Cambridge: Cambridge University Press.

Bolle de Bal, Marcel 2004, 'Georges Friedmann, père-fondateur d'une "autre" sociologie', *Cahiers internationaux de sociologie*, 116, 55–76.

Bonnet, Marguerite 1988, *Vers l'action politique. De "La Révolution d'abord et toujours !" (juillet 1925) au projet de "La Guerre civile" (avril 1926)*, Paris: Gallimard.

Bottomore, Tom H. 1968, 'Marxisme et sociologie', *L'Homme et la société*, 10, 5–11.

Bouffard, Alix, Alexandre Feron and Guillaume Fondu 2017, 'Les éditions françaises du Capital', in *Ce qu'est le Capital*, Paris: Éditions sociales.

Bouglé, Célestin 1908, 'Marxisme et sociologie', *Revue de métaphysique et de morale*, 16, 6: 723–50.

Bouglé, Célestin 1918, 'L'alliance intellectuelle franco-allemande', in *Chez les prophètes socialistes*, Paris: Alcan.

Bouju, Marie-Cécile 2010, *Lire en communiste: les maisons d'édition du PCF, 1921–1968*, Rennes: Presses universitaires de Rennes.

Boulland, Paul, Nathalie Ethuin and Julian Mischi 2008, 'Les disqualifications des gauchistes au sein du PCF. Enjeux sociologiques et stratégiques', *Savoir/Agir*, 6: 29–39.

Bourdieu, Pierre 1975, 'La lecture de Marx. Quelques remarques critiques à propos de "Quelques remarques critiques de *Lire le Capital*"', *Actes de la recherche en sciences sociales*, 5–6: 65–79.

Bourdieu, Pierre 1984, 'Le champ littéraire. Préalables critiques et principes de méthode', *Lendemains*, 9, 36, 5–20.

Bourdieu, Pierre 1985, 'The Social Space and the Genesis of Groups', *Theory and Society*, 14, 6: 723–44.

Bourdieu, Pierre 1987, 'Fieldwork in Philosophy', *Choses dites*, Paris: Minuit.

Bourdieu, Pierre 2010, *Outline of a Theory of Practice*, Cambridge: Cambridge University Press.

Bourdieu, Pierre and Yves Delsaut 1975, 'Le couturier et sa griffe: contribution à une théorie de la magie', *Actes de la recherche en sciences sociales*, 1: 7–36.

Bourdieu, Pierre, Jean-Claude Chamboredon and Jean-Claude Passeron 1991, *The Craft of Sociology: Epistemological Preliminaries*, Berlin: De Gruyter.

Bourrinet, Philippe 1987, *Aux origines du courant communiste international des conseils: la Gauche communiste hollandaise (1907–1950)*, doctoral dissertation in history, Université Paris-I.

Breton, André 1969, *Entretiens*, Paris: Gallimard.

Breton, André, 1977, *Manifestes*, Paris: Gallimard

Bruhat, Jean 1966, 'Marx et la Révolution française', in *La Pensée socialiste devant la Révolution française*, Paris: SER.

Brun, Éric 2014, *Les Situationnistes. Une avant-garde totale*, Paris: CNRS éditions.

Bürger, Peter 1984, *The Theory of the Avant-Garde*, Manchester: Manchester University Press.

Burles, Jean 1981, 'Le PCF et la société française, 1964–1972', in Roger Bourderon et al., *Le PCF. Étapes et problèmes, 1920–1972*, Paris: Éditions sociales.

Cahen, Jacqueline 1994, 'La réception de l'œuvre de Karl Marx par les économistes français (1871–1883)', *Mil neuf cent*, 12, 19–50.

Cahen, Jacqueline 2011, 'Les premiers éditeurs de Marx en France 1880–1901', *Cahiers d'histoire. Revue d'histoire critique*, 114, 285–94.

Cai, Hesen 1980, *Cai Hesen wenji*, Beijing: Renmin chubanshe.

Caillé, Alain and Sylvain Dzmira 2009, 'De Marx à Mauss, sans passer par de Maistre ni Maurras', *Revue du MAUSS*, 34: 65–95.

Calvié, Lucien 1989, *Le Renard et les Raisins. La Révolution française et les intellectuels allemands*, Paris: EDI.

Camara, Sadio 2013, *L'Épopée du parti africain de l'indépendance (PAI) au Sénégal (1957–1980)*, Paris: L'Harmattan.

Candar, Gilles 2007, *Jean Longuet. 1876–1938. Un internationaliste à l'épreuve de l'histoire*, Rennes: Presses universitaires de Rennes.

Canguilhem, Georges 1998, 'The Decline of the Idea of Progress', *Economy and Society*, 27, 2–3: 313–29

Carlino, Fabrizio 2015, 'Lectures de Hegel "à la lumière du marxisme" et genèse de la "coupure épistémologique"', *Cahiers du GRM*, 8.

Cartelier, Jean and Michael de Vroey 1989, 'L'approche de la régulation: un nouveau paradigme?', *Économies et Sociétés*, 11: 63–87.

Castagnez, Noëlline and Gilles Morin 2000, 'Le parti issu de la Résistance', in Serge Berstein et al. (eds.), *Le Parti socialiste entre Résistance et République*, Paris: Publications de la Sorbonne.

Castoriadis, Cornelius 1973, *La Société bureaucratique*, book 1, Paris: UGE.

Cavalhés, Jean 1979, *Les Réponses des marxistes à la question agraire*, research documents, École nationale supérieure des sciences agronomiques de Dijon (Enesad).

Cépède, Frédéric 2000, 'Les socialistes sur les bancs. Des écoles aux universités d'été des socialistes (1958–1999)', *Cahiers d'histoire*, 79.

Cervulle, Maxime and Isabelle Clair 2017, 'Lire entre les lignes: le féminisme matérialiste face au féminisme poststructuraliste', *Comment s'en sortir?*, 4: 1–22.

Césaire, Aimé 1956, *Lettre à Maurice Thorez*, Paris: Présence africaine.

Chambarlhac, Vincent 2011, 'L'orthodoxie marxiste de la SFIO. À propos d'une fausse évidence (1905–1914)', *Cahiers d'histoire*, January–March: 39–50.

Chaperon, Sylvie 2000, *Les Années Beauvoir 1945–1970*, Paris: Fayard.

Châton, Gwendal 2006, *La Liberté retrouvée. Une histoire du libéralisme politique en France à travers les revues aroniennes "Contrepoint" et "Commentaire"*, doctoral dissertation in political science, Université Rennes-I.

Châton, Gwendal 2007, 'Désaccord parfait. Le *Contrepoint* libéral dans la configuration intellectuelle des années 1970', in Jean Bauduoin and François Hourmant (eds.), *Les Revues et la dynamique des ruptures*, Rennes: Presses universitaires de Rennes.

Châton, Gwendal 2016a, 'Libéralisme ou démocratie? Raymond Aron lecteur de Friedrich Hayek', *Revue de philosophie économique*, 17, 1: 103–34.

Châton, Gwendal 2016b, 'Taking Anti-Totalitarianism Seriously. The Emergence of the Aronian Circle in the 1970s', in Iain Stewart and Stephen W. Sawyer (eds.), *In Search of the Liberal Moment. Democracy, Anti-totalitarianism, and Intellectual Politics in France since 1950*, London: Palgrave Macmillan.

Châton, Gwendal 2017, *Introduction à Raymond Aron*, Paris: La Découverte.

Chaunu, Pierre 1974, 'Conjoncture, structure, systèmes de civilisation', in *Conjoncture économique, structures sociales. Hommage à Ernest Labrousse*, Paris: Mouton.

Chavance, Bernard (ed.) 1985, *Marx en perspective*, Paris: Éditions de l'EHESS.

Chavance, Bernard 1980, 'La crise de la perspective révolutionnaire', *Communisme*, 5/6.

Chenaux, Philippe (ed.) 2006, *'Humanisme intégral' (1936) de Jacques Maritain*, Paris: Éditions du Cerf.

Chenaux, Philippe 1999, *Entre Maurras et Maritain. Une génération intellectuelle catholique (1920–1930)*, Paris: Éditions du Cerf.

Chenu, Alain 2002, 'Une institution sans intention. La sociologie en France depuis l'après-guerre', *Actes de la recherche en sciences sociales*, 141–2: 46–61.

Chi, Miao, Olivier Dard, Béatrice Fleury and Jacques Walter (eds.) 2017, *La Révolution Culturelle en Chine et en France*, Paris: Riveneuve éditions.

Christofferson, Michael Scott 2004, *French Intellectuals Against the Left: The Antitotalitarian Moment of the 1970s*, New York: Berghahn Books.

Colletti, Lucio 1984, *Le Déclin du marxisme*, Paris: PUF.

Colliot-Thélène 1990, *Max Weber et l'histoire*, Paris: PUF.

Corcuff, Philippe 2014, 'Le Marx hérétique de Michel Henry: fulgurances et écueils d'une lecture philosophique', *Actuel Marx*, 55: 132–143.

Cordillot, Michel 2010, 'Un article sur Karl Marx dans L'Illustration', in *Aux origines du socialisme moderne*, Ivry-sur-Seine: L'Atelier.

Cornillet, Gérard, Laurent Francatel-Prost and Lucien Sève 2010, 'Annexe sur la traduction du mot "Mehrwert"', in Karl Marx, *Le Chapitre VI – Manuscrits de 1863–1867*, Paris: Éditions sociales.

Cornu, Auguste 1962, *Karl Marx et Friedrich Engels. Leur vie et leur œuvre*, book 3: *Marx à Paris*, Paris: PUF.

Cornu, Auguste and Adam Schaff 1972, 'Pour mettre fin à la discussion sur la traduction des "Thèses sur Feuerbach" de Karl Marx', *L'Homme et la Société*, 26: 249–51.

Crastre, Victor 1963, *Le Drame du surréalisme*, Paris: Les Éditions du Temps.

Curtis, David 1997, *The French Popular Front and the Catholic Discovery of Marx*, Hull: University of Hull Press.

Curtis, David 2000, 'True and False Modernity: Catholicism and Communist Marxism in 1930s France', in Kay Chadwick (ed.), *Catholicism, Politics and Society in Twentieth-Century France*, Liverpool: Liverpool University Press.

Cuvillier, Armand 1936, *Introduction à la sociologie*, Paris: Armand Colin.

Cuvillier, Armand 1948, 'Durkheim et Marx', *Cahiers internationaux de sociologie*, 4: 75–97.

Delaunay, Jean-Claude 1986, 'Le marxisme et la politique économique, aujourd'hui', in *Marx ou pas … ? Réflexions sur un centenaire*, Paris: Études et documentation internationale.

Dembélé, Demba Moussa 2015, *Samir Amin: intellectuel organique au service de l'émancipation du Sud*, Dakar: Nouvelles éditions numériques africaines.

Denis, Henri 1941, *La Corporation*, Paris: PUF.

Denis, Henri 1950, *La Valeur*, Paris: Éditions sociales.

Denis, Henri 1957, 'Science marxiste et critique catholique', *Économie et Politique*, 36.

Denis, Henri 1966, *Histoire de la pensée économique*, Paris: PUF.

Denis, Henri 1980, *L'Économie de Marx, histoire d'un échec*, Paris: PUF.

Denord, François and Zunigo 2005, ' "Révolutionnairement vôtre". Économie marxiste, militantisme intellectuel et expertise politique chez Charles Bettelheim', *Actes de la recherche en sciences sociales*, 158: 8–29.

Derrida, Jacques 1994, *Specters of Marx*, New York: Routledge.

Derrida, Jacques 2011, *Politique et Amitié. Entretien avec Michael Sprinker autour de Marx et d'Althusser*, Paris: Galilée.

Desanti, Jean-Toussaint 1994 [1963], *Introduction à la phénoménologie*, Paris; Gallimard.

Desanti, Jean-Toussaint 2008a [1976], *Le Philosophe et les Pouvoirs (et autres dialogues)*, Paris: Hachette Littératures.

Desanti, Jean-Toussaint 2008b [1982], *Un destin philosophique ou Les Pièges de la croyance*, Paris: Hachette Littératures.

Dewitte, Philippe 1985, *Les Mouvements nègres en France, 1919–1939*, Paris: L'Harmattan.

Di Maggio, Marco 2013, *Les Intellectuels et la stratégie communiste. Une crise d'hégémonie (1958–1981)*, Paris: Éditions sociales.

Diagne, Souleymane Bachir 2013, *Bergson postcolonial: l'élan vital dans la pensée de Léopold Sédar Senghor et de Mohamed Iqbal*, Paris: Éditions du CNRS.

Diaz, Delphine 2014, *Un asile pour tous les peuples? Exilés et réfugiés étrangers dansla France du premier xixᵉ siècle*, Paris: Armand Colin.

Dieng, Amady Aly 1978, *Hegel, Marx, Engels et les problèmes de l'Afrique noire*, Dakar: Sankoré.

Dieng, Amady Aly 1985, *Le Marxisme et l'Afrique noire. Bilan d'un débat sur l'universalité du marxisme*, Paris: Nubia.

Dieng, Amady Aly 2009, *Les Grands Combats de la FEANF. De Bandung aux indépendances*, Paris: L'Harmattan.

Dieng, Amady Aly, 2011, *Mémoires d'un étudiant africain, vol. 2. De l'Université de Paris à mon retour au Sénégal (1960–1967)*, Dakar: Codesria.

Diop, Thierno 2010, *Léopold Sédar Senghor, Majhemout Diop et le marxisme*, Paris: L'Harmattan.

Diop: Cheikh Anta 1954, *Nations nègres et cultures*, Paris: Éditions africaines.

Dirkx, Paul 2015, 'Bourdieu et les études littéraires', in Catherine Leclercq, Wenceslas Lizé and Hélène Stevens (eds.) *Bourdieu et les sciences sociales. Réception et usages*, Paris: La Dispute.

Dirlik, Arif 1989, *The Origins of Chinese Communism*, Oxford: Oxford University Press.

Dommanget, Maurice 1969, *L'Introduction du marxisme en France*, Lausanne: Rencontre.

Dorlin, Elsa (ed.) 2008, *Black Feminism. Anthologie du féminisme africain américain*, Paris: L'Harmattan.

Dorlin, Elsa 2007, 'Le Queer est un matérialisme. Entretien avec Elsa Dorlin par Gabriel Girard', in *Femmes, genre, féminisme*, Paris: Syllepse.

Dosse, François 2010, *L'Histoire en miettes*, Paris: La Découverte.

Dosse, François 2011, *Pierre Nora, homo historicus*, Paris: Perrin.

Droz, Jacques 1972, *Histoire générale du socialisme*, Paris: PUF.

Druon, Maurice 2000, *La France aux ordres d'un cadavre*, Paris: De Fallois.

Ducange Jean-Numa and Serge Wolikow 2017, 'Le siècle du léninisme', *Actuel Marx*, 62: 11–25.

Ducange, Jean-Numa 2014, 'Friedrich Engels and the first steps of the French Socialist Movement', *Beiträge zur Marx-Engels Forschung*.

Ducange, Jean-Numa 2015, 'Marx, le marxisme et le "père de la lutte de classes" Augustin Thierry', *Actuel Marx*, 58: 12–27.

Ducange, Jean-Numa 2020, *Jules Guesde: The Birth of Socialism and Marxism in France*, London: Palgrave Macmillan.

Ducange, Jean-Numa and Isabelle Garo (eds.) 2015, *Marx politique*, Paris: La Dispute.

Ducange, Jean-Numa, Julien Hage and Jean-Yves Mollier (eds.) 2014, *Le Parti communiste et le livre. Écrire le politique au XXᵉ siècle*, Dijon: Éditions universitaires de Dijon.

Duchet, Claude (ed.) 1979, *Sociocritique*, Paris: Nathan.

Duchet, Claude 1971, 'Pour une socio-critique, ou variation sur un incipit', *Littérature*, 1, 1: 5–14.

Duchet, Claude and Isabelle Tournier 1994, 'Sociocritique', in Béatrice Didier (ed.), *Dictionnaire universel des littératures*, vol. 3, Paris: PUF.

Ducoulombier, Romain 2010, *Camarades! La naissance du Parti communiste en France*, Paris: Perrin.

Duménil, Gérard and Dominique Lévy 2014, *La Grande Bifurcation. En finir avec le néolibéralisme*, Paris: La Découverte.

Durkheim, Émile 1970, *La Science sociale et l'action*, Paris: PUF.

Duwa, Jérome 2008, *Surréalistes et Situationnistes. Vies parallèles*, Paris: Dilecta.

Ebguy, Jacques-David and Boris Lyon-Caen 2015, 'Débat critique : Pierre Barbéris aujourd'hui ?', *Romantisme*, 2, 168: 105–27.

Elbe, Ingo 2008, *Marx im Westen: die neue Marx-Lektüre in der Bundesrepublik seit 1965*, Berlin: Akademie Verlag.

Engels, Friedrich 1941, *Ludwig Feuerbach and the Outcome of Classical German Philosophy*, New York: International Publishers.

Ethuin, Nathalie 2006, *À l'école du Parti : l'éducation et la formation des militants et des cadres du Parti communiste français (1970–2003)*, dissertation in political science, supervised by Christian-Marie Wallon-Leducq, Université de Lille-II.

Fabiani, Jean-Louis 2010, *Qu'est-ce qu'un philosophe français?*, Paris: Éditions de l'EHESS.

Fayolle, Sandra 2005, *L'UFF, une organisation de masse du PCF (1945–1965)*, doctoral dissertation, Université Paris-I.

Febvre, Lucien 1930, 'La Guerre des paysans d'Engels', *Annales*, 7: 437–8.

Febvre, Lucien 1948, *Annales E.S.C.*, 3, 2.

Febvre, Lucien 1962, *Pour une histoire à part entière*, Paris: SEVPEN.

Filloux, Jean-Claude 1970, 'Introduction' in Durkheim 1970.

Filoni, Marco 2008, *Le Philosophe du dimanche. La vie et la pensée d'Alexandre Kojève*, Paris: Gallimard.

Fischbach, Frank 2007, 'Présentation', in Karl Marx, *Manuscrits économico-philosophiques de 1844*, Paris: Vrin.

Forlin, Olivier 2006, *Les Intellectuels français et l'Italie: 1945–1955, médiation culturelle, engagements et représentations*, Paris: L'Harmattan.

Fougeyrollas, Pierre 1979, *Sciences sociales et marxisme*, Paris: Payot.

Fouilloux, Étienne 1998, *Une Église en quête de liberté. La pensée catholique entre modernisme et Vatican II (1914–1962)*, Paris: Desclée de Brouwer.

Fouilloux, Étienne 2015, *Christianisme et Eschatologie. Dieu Vivant (1945–1955)*, Paris: CLD éditions.

Fourcade, Marion 2009, *Economists and Societies. Discipline and Profession in the United States, Britain and France, 1890s to 1990s*, Princeton, NJ: Princeton University Press.

Fourcade, Michel 2014, 'Kant, Hegel et Compagnie', in Étienne Fouilloux and Frédéric Gugelot (eds.), *Jésuites français et sciences humaines (années 1960). Chrétiens et sociétés*, 22.

Fraser, Nancy 2012, *Le Féminisme en mouvements. Des années 1960 à l'ère néolibérale*, Paris: La Découverte.

Frédéric Gugelot 2009, 'Un dialogue avec l'humanisme athée', in Dominique Avon and Michel Fourcade (eds.), *Un nouvel âge de la théologie? 1965–1980*, Paris: Karthala.

Fulla, Mathieu 2016, *Les Socialistes français et l'économie (1944–1981). Une histoire économique du politique*, Paris: Presses de Sciences Po.

Furet, François 1975, 'Faut-il brûler Marx?', *Le Nouvel Observateur*, 28 July.

Furet, François 1987, 'Préface', in Tony Judt, *Le Marxisme et la gauche française*, Paris: Hachette.

Furet, François 1988, *Marx and the French Revolution*, Chicago: University of Chicago Press.

Furet, François 1999, *The Passing of an Illusion*, Chicago: University of Chicago Press.

Gaudin, François 2014, *Maurice Lachâtre, éditeur socialiste*, Limoges: Lambert-Lucas.

George, Jocelyne 2011, *Les Féministes de la CGT. Histoire du magazine* Antoinette *(1955–1989)*, Paris: Delga.

Georgi, Frank (ed.) 2003, *Autogestion. La dernière utopie?*, Paris: Publications de la Sorbonne.

Gleize, Joëlle and Philippe Roussin (eds.) 2009, *La "Bibliothèque de la Pléiade": travail éditorial et valeur littéraire*, Paris: Éditions des archives contemporaines.

Gobille, Boris 2005, 'La guerre de Change contre la "dictature structuraliste" de Tel Quel. Le "théoricisme" des avant-gardes littéraires à l'épreuve de la crise politique de Mai 68', *Raisons politiques*, 2, 18: 73–96.

Goebel, Michael 2017, *Paris capitale du tiers-monde. Comment est née la révolution anticoloniale*, Paris: La Découverte.

Goldmann, Lucien 1955, *Le Dieu caché. Étude sur la vision tragique dans les Pensées de Pascal et dans le théâtre de Racine*, Paris: Gallimard.

Gouarné, Isabelle 2013, *L'Introduction du marxisme en France. Philosoviétisme et sciences humaines, 1920–1939*, Rennes: Presses universitaires de Rennes.

Grandjonc, Jacques 1974, *Marx et les communistes allemands à Paris*, Paris: Maspero.

Granel, Gérard 2014 [1969], *Incipit Marx. L'ontologie marxiste de 1844 et la question de la "coupure"*, Mauvezin: Éditions TER.

Grémion, Pierre 1995, *Intelligence de l'anticommunisme: le Congrès pour la liberté de la culture à Paris (1950–1975)*, Paris: Fayard.

Groh, Dieter 1973, *Negative Integration und revolutionärer Attentismus: die deutsche Sozialdemokratie am Vorabend des Ersten Weltkrieges*, Berlin: Propyläen Verlag.

Guichard, Bruno, Julien Hage and Alain Léger (eds.) 2009, *François Maspero et les paysages humains*, Lyon: À plus d'un titre/La Fosse aux ours.

Hage, Julien 2010, *Feltrinelli, Maspero, Wagenbach, une nouvelle génération d'éditeurs politiques. 1955–1982, histoire comparée, histoire croisée*, doctoral dissertation in contemporary history, supervised by Jean-Yves Mollier, Université de Versailles Saint-Quentin-en-Yvelines.

Hardt, Michael and Antonio Negri 2005, *Multitude: War and Democracy in the Age of Empire*, London: Penguin.

Haubtmann, Pierre 1981, *Proudhon, Marx et la pensée allemande*, Grenoble: Presses universitaires de Grenoble.

Hauchecorne, Mathieu 2009, 'Libéral-communiste? Chiche! Les usages des "théories de la justice" chez les intellectuels marxistes français', *Regards sociologiques*, 37–8: 107–22.

Haupt, Georges 1980, *L'Historien et le mouvement social*, Paris: Maspero.

Heilbron, Johan 1985, 'Les métamorphoses du durkheimisme, 1920–1940', *Revue française de sociologie*, 26, 2: 203–37.

Heilbron, Johan 1991, 'Pionniers par défaut? Les débuts de la recherche au Centre d'études sociologiques (1946–1960)', *Revue française de sociologie*, 32, 3: 365–79.

Heilbron, Johan 2015, *French Sociology*, Ithaca, NY: Cornell University Press.

Henry, Michel 1976, *Marx*, Paris: Gallimard.

Heredia, Mariana 2014, *À quoi sert un économiste*, Paris: La Découverte.

Hobsbawm, Eric 1968, *The Pelican Economic History of Britain. From 1750 to the Present Day. Industry and Empire*, London, Penguin Books.

Hobsbawm, Eric 2012, *How to Change the World: Reflections on Marx and Marxism*, New Haven: Yale University Press.

Hourmant, François 2012, 'BHL, un entrepreneur intellectuel au temps de la médiasphère', in François Hourmant and Arnaud Leclerc (eds.), *Les Intellectuels et le Pouvoir: déclinaisons et mutations*, Rennes: Presses universitaires de Rennes.

Huard, Raymond 1984a, 'Avant-propos', in Karl Marx, *Les Luttes de classes en France*, Paris: Éditions sociales.

Huard, Raymond 1984b, 'Avant-propos' in Karl Marx, *Le 18 Brumaire de Louis Bonaparte*, Paris: Éditions sociales.

Jappe, Anselm 2018, *Guy Debord*, Oakland, CA: PM Press.

Jaurès, Jean 1983 [1903], 'Discours à la chambre des députés' (27 November 1903), in Charles-Olivier Carbonell and Georges Livet (eds.), *Au berceau des Annales*, Toulouse: Presses de l'IEP.

Jeanpierre, Laurent and Laurent Martin 2013, '1968–1986: la "révolution conservatrice" de la pensée française à l'épreuve des rencontres de Cerisy', *Histoire@Politique*, 20: 1–10.

Jewsiewicki, Bogumil 1985, *Marx, Afrique et Occident: les pratiques africanistes de l'histoire marxiste*, Montreal: McGill University.

Joseph, Camille 2010, *Les éditions La Découverte: la gestion d'un héritage éditorial*, doctoral dissertation in sociology, EHESS, Paris.

Jousse, Emmanuel 2017, *Les Hommes révoltés. Les origines du réformisme en France*, Paris: Fayard.

Judt, Tony 1976, *La Reconstruction du Parti socialiste. 1921–1926*, Paris: Presses de la FNSP.

Judt, Tony 1986, *Marxism and the French Left: Studies on Labour and Politics in France, 1830–1981*, Oxford: Clarendon Press.

Kalinowski, Isabelle 2005, 'Leçons wébériennes sur la science et la propagande', in Max Weber, *La Science, profession et vocation*, Marseille: Agone.

Karady, Victor 1976, 'Durkheim, les sciences sociales et l'Université: bilan d'un semi-échec', *Revue française de sociologie*, 17, 2: 267–311.

Katsakioris, Constantin 2015, *Leçons soviétiques: La formation des étudiants africains et arabes en URSS pendant la guerre froide*, dissertation, Paris: École des hautes études en sciences sociales.

Kaufmann, Vincent 2011, *La Faute à Mallarmé. L'aventure de la théorie littéraire*, Paris: Seuil.

Kautsky, Karl 1947, *Les Trois Sources du marxisme: l'œuvre historique de Marx*, Paris: Spartacus.

Keucheyan, Razmig 2014, *The Left Hemisphere: Mapping Critical Theory Today*, London: Verso.

Klejman, Laurence and Florence Rochefort 1989, *L'Égalité en marche. Le féminisme sous la Troisième République*, Paris: PFNSP/Éditions des femmes.

Kouvelakis, Stathis 2019, *Philosophy and Revolution: From Kant to Marx*, London: Verso.

Kriegel, Annie 1985, *Les Communistes français dans leur premier demi-siècle, 1920–1970*, Paris: Seuil.

Kristeva, Julia 1969, *Sēmeiōtikē. Recherches pour une sémanalyse*, Paris: Seuil.

Kristeva, Julia 1974, *La Révolution du langage poétique*, Paris: Seuil.

Labica, Georges (ed.) 1985, *1883–1983: L'Œuvre de Marx un siècle après*, Paris: PUF.

Labrousse, Ernest 1980, 'Entretiens', *Actes de la recherche en sciences sociales*, 32–3: 111–27.

Lacroix, Bernard 1976, 'La vocation originelle d'Émile Durkheim', *Revue française de sociologie*, 17, 2: 213–47.

Lafargue, Paul 2009, *Paresse et Révolution*, Paris: Tallandier.

Lafon, François 1989, 'Structures idéologiques et nécessités pratiques au congrès de la SFIO en 1946', *Revue d'histoire moderne et contemporaine*, 36, 4: 672–94.

Laurens, Sylvain 2019, *Militer au nom de la science. Une socio-histoire des mouvements rationalistes en France (1931–2005)*, Paris: Éditions de l'EHESS.

Laurent, Évelyne and Luc Marco 1996, 'Le *Journal des économistes* ou l'apologie du libéralisme (1841–1940)', in Luc Marco (ed.) *Les Revues d'économie en France (1751–1994)*, Paris: L'Harmattan.

Lazar, Marc 1990, 'Damné de la terre et homme de marbre. L'ouvrier dans l'imaginaire du PCF des années trente à la fin des années cinquante', *Annales. Économies, sociétés, civilisations*, 45, 5: 1071–96.

Lazar, Marc 1992, *Maisons rouges: les partis communistes français et italien de la Libération à nos jours*, Paris: Aubier.

Le Bras, Laurence and Emmanuel Guy (eds.) 2016, *Lire Debord*, Paris: L'Échappée.

Le Moullec-Rieu, Aude 2015, *Maximilien Rubel, éditeur de Marx dans la "Bibliothèque de la Pléiade" (1955–1968)*, dissertation for archivist-palaeographer diploma, École nationale des chartes.

Le Strat, Claire and Willy Pelletier 2005, *La Canonisation libérale de Tocqueville*, Paris: Syllepse.

Le Van-Lemesle, Lucette 2004, *Le Juste ou le Riche. L'enseignement de l'économie politique, 1815–1950*, Paris: Comité pour l'histoire économique et financière de la France.

Lebaron, Frédéric 2000, *La Croyance économique. Les économistes entre science et politique*, Paris: Seuil.

Lebaron, Frédéric 2001, 'Toward a New Critique of Economic Discourse', *Theory, Culture and Society*, 18, 5: 123–9.

Lefebvre, Henri 1948, 'Marxisme et sociologie', *Cahiers internationaux de sociologie*, 4, 48–74.

Lefebvre, Henri 1986, 'Lettre', in *Marx ou pas ...? Réflexions sur un centenaire*, Paris: Études et documentation internationale.

Lefebvre, Jean-Pierre 1982, 'Introduction', in Karl Marx, *Le Capital: critique de l'économie politique*, Paris: Éditions sociales.

Lefebvre, Jean-Pierre 2017, 'Introduction de l'édition de 1983', in Karl Marx, *Le Capital*, Paris: Éditions sociales.

Lévy, Louis 1931, Comment Ils Sont Devenus Socialistes, Paris: Le Populaire.

Likin, Max 2008, '"Nothing fails like success". The Marxism of Raymond Aron', *French Politics, Culture & Society* 26, 3: 43–60.

Lindenberg, Daniel 1979, *Le Marxisme introuvable*, Paris: 10/18.

Lindenberg, Daniel 2004, 'Le marxisme au xxᵉ siècle', in Jean-Jacques Becker and Gilles Candar (eds.), *Histoire des gauches en France*, Vol. 2: *xxᵉ siècle, à l'épreuve de l'histoire*, Paris: La Découverte.

Lordon, Frédéric 1997, 'Le désir de "faire science"', *Actes de la recherche en sciences sociales*, 119, 27–35.

Löwy, Michael 1992, 'Figures du marxisme wébérien', *Actuel Marx*, 11: 83–94.

Luxemburg, Rosa 2013, *Le Socialisme en France*, Marseille: Agone.

Ly, Abdoulaye 1956, *Les Masses africaines et l'actuelle condition humaine*, Paris: Présence africaine.

Magazine Littéraire 1982, 'Georges Duby. Le style et la morale de l'histoire', November.

Mahoney, Daniel 2003, 'Aron, Marx, and Marxism. An Interpretation', *European Journal of Political Theory*, 2, 4: 415–27.

Mainfroy, Claude 1980, 'Sur le phénomène radical. L'approche de Marx et Engels dans les années 1871–1895', *Cahiers d'histoire de l'IRM*, 1: 8–51.

Mainfroy, Claude 1983, 'Avant-propos', in *Marx/Engels et la Troisième République*, Paris: Éditions sociales.

Mainfroy, Claude 1985, *Sur la Révolution française. Écrits de Marx et Engels*, Paris: Éditions sociales.

Marcel, Jean-Christophe 2001, 'Georges Gurvitch: les raisons d'un succès', *Cahiers internationaux de sociologie*, 110: 97–119.

Marcellesi, Jean-Baptiste 1971, *Le Congrès de Tours*, Paris: Le Pavillon.

Marchal, Jean 1955, *Deux Essais sur le marxisme*, Paris: Éditions M.-T. Génin.

Marcolini, Patrick 2013, *Le Mouvement situationniste. Une histoire intellectuelle*, Paris: L'Échappée.

Martelli, Roger 1981, 'L'année 1956', in Roger Bourderon et al., *Le PCF. Étapes et problèmes, 1920–1972*, Paris: Éditions sociales.

Martelli, Roger 2017, *Une dispute communiste. Le Comité central d'Argenteuil sur la culture*, Paris: Éditions sociales.

Marx, Karl 1963, *Œuvres: Économie I*, book 1, Paris: Gallimard, 'Bibliothèque de la Pléiade' [further printings in 1965, 1968, 1972, 1977, 1994]

Marx, Karl 1968, *Œuvres: Économie II*, Paris: Gallimard, 'Bibliothèque de la Pléiade' [further printings 1972, 1979].

Marx, Karl 1982, *Œuvres: Philosophie*, Paris: Gallimard, 'Bibliothèque de la Pléiade'

Marx, Karl 1994, *Œuvres: Politique I*, Paris: Gallimard, 'Bibliothèque de la Pléiade'

Massa, Patrick 1993, 'Les classes moyennes vues par le PCF et le PSU', *Vingtième Siècle*, 37: 45–54.

Massa, Patrick 2010, 'La Chine maoïste vue par Socialisme ou Barbarie: l'œuvre méconnue de Pierre Souyri', *Dissidences*, 8, *Prochinois et maoïsme en France*, Lormont: Bord de l'eau.

Mathiez, Albert 1964, *The French Revolution*, New York: Grosset & Dunlop.

Matonti, Frédérique 2005a, *Intellectuels communistes. Essai sur l'obéissance politique. La Nouvelle Critique (1867–1980)*, Paris: La Découverte.

MauBlanc, René 2011 [1934], 'Marx et Durkheim' (20 December 1934), *Durkheimian Studies/Études durkheimiennes*, 17: 3–7.

Mauger, Gérard 2012, 'Bourdieu et Marx', in Frédéric Lebaron and Gérard Mauger (eds.), *Lectures de Bourdieu*, Paris: Ellipses.

Mauger, Gérard 2015, 'Le style de pensée de Pierre Bourdieu', in Catherine Leclercq, Wenceslas Lizé and Hélène Stevens (eds.) *Bourdieu et les sciences sociales. Réception et usages*, Paris: La Dispute.

Mauss, Marcel 2011, 'Introduction', in Émile Durkheim *Le Socialisme. Sa définition, ses débuts, la doctrine saint-simonienne*, Paris: PUF.

MEGA 1999, *Marx-Engels Gesamtausgabe. IV/ 32. Die Bibliotheken von Karl Marx und Friedrich Engels*, Berlin: De Gruyter.

Mehring, Franz, 1981, *Karl Marx: The Story of His Life*, Brighton: Humanities Press.

Merleau-Ponty, Maurice 1964, *Sense and Non-Sense*, Evanston, IL: Northwestern University Press.

Merleau-Ponty, Maurice 1974, *Adventures of the Dialectic*, London: Heinemann.

Merleau-Ponty, Maurice 2001, *Humanism and Terror*, Boston: Beacon Press. Merleau-Ponty, Maurice 1964, *Sense and Non-Sense*, Evanston, IL: Northwestern University Press.

Merlin, Eléonore 2002, *Le CERES, de l'autogestion à la République: 1966–1986*, masters dissertation in history, Université Paris-1.

Mesure, Sylvie 2015, 'Aron and Marxism: the Aronian Interpretation of Marx', in José Colen and Élisabeth Dutartre-Michaut (eds.) *The Companion to Raymond Aron*, London: Palgrave Macmillan.

Mischi, Julian 2014, *Le Communisme désarmé: le PCF et les classes populaires depuis les années 1970*, Marseille: Agone.

Mollier, Jean-Yves 2014, *Édition, presse et pouvoir en France au xxe siècle*, Paris: Fayard.

Moner Frédéric 2016, *Léon Blum. La morale et le pouvoir*, Paris: Armand Colin.

Mossé, Claude 1998, 'Rencontre avec M.I. Finley: l'histoire économique et sociale dans l'œuvre de Pierre Vidal-Naquet', in François Hartog, Pauline Schmitt Pantel and Alain Schnapp (eds.) *Pierre Vidal-Naquet, un historien dans la cité*, Paris: La Découverte.

Murphy, David 2015, 'Tirailleur, facteur, anticolonialiste : la courte vie militante de Lamine Senghor (1924–1927)', *Cahiers d'histoire. Revue d'histoire critique*, 126.

Musto, Marcello 2017, 'Le dernier voyage de Marx : éléments pour une biographie intellectuelle', Actuel Marx, 61: 106–23.

Nie, Rongzhen 1986, *Nie Rongzhen huiyilu*, Beijing: Jiefangjun chubanshe, *Nouvelles Questions féministes*, 2006, 25, 1.

Noyé, Sophie 2014, 'Pour un féminisme matérialiste et queer', *Contretemps*, 17 April.

Olivera, Philippe 1996, 'Le sens du jeu. Aragon entre littérature et politique (1958–1968)', *Actes de la recherche en sciences sociales*, 111–12: 76–84.

Ollivier, Anne-Laure 2011, *Gaston Defferre. Un socialiste face au pouvoir, de Marseille à l'élection présidentielle de 1969*, doctoral dissertation in history, ENS Cachan.

Orléan, Andre 2011, *L'Empire de la valeur. Refonder l'économie*, Paris: Seuil.

Paquot, Thierry 1980, *Les faiseurs de nuages : essai sur la genèse des marxismes français (1880–1914)*, Paris: Le Sycomore.

Pelletier, Denis 1996, *Économie et Humanisme. De l'utopie communautaire au combat pour le Tiers-Monde 1941–1966*, Paris: Éditions du Cerf.

Pelletier, Denis 1997, '*Signification du marxisme* (1949). Histoire d'un livre', in Émile Poulat and Claude Ravelet (eds.), *Henri Desroche : un passeur de frontières*, Paris: L'Harmattan.

Pelletier, Denis 2005, *La Crise catholique. Religion, société, politique en France (1965–1978)*, Paris: Payot-Rivages.

Petrache, Ana 2017, *Gaston Fessard, un chrétien de rite dialectique ?*, Paris: Éditions du Cerf.

Politzer, Georges 1938, *Les Grands Problèmes de la philosophie contemporaine. La pensée française et le marxisme*, Paris: Bureau d'éditions.

Pollak, Michael 1988, 'La place de Weber dans le champ intellectuel français', *Droit et société*, 9: 189–201.

Porshnev, Boris Fedorovich (1972), *Les Soulèvements populaires en France au xviie siècle*, Paris: Flammarion.

Poster, Mark 1975, *Existential Marxism in Postwar France: From Sartre to Althusser*, Princeton, NJ: Princeton University Press.

Pouch, Thierry 2001, *Les Économistes français et le marxisme. Apogée et déclin d'un discours critique (1950–2000)*, Rennes: Presses universitaires de Rennes.

Préteceille, Edmond 1989, 'Les marxistes et la question urbaine', interview by Jean-Louis Briquet, *Politix*, 7–8: 24–29.

Prochasson, Christophe 2004, 'L'introduction du marxisme en France', in Jean-Jacques Becker and Gilles Candar (eds.), *Histoire des gauches en France*, Paris: La Découverte.

Pudal, Bernard 2004, 'Pour une histoire de l'"intellectuel collectif" communiste avec et contre les enseignants (1920–2000)', in Jacques Girault (eds.) *Les Enseignants dans la société française au xxᵉ siècle*, Paris: Publications de la Sorbonne.

Pudal, Bernard 2009, *Un monde défait. Les communistes français de 1956 à nos jours*, Paris: Éditions du Croquant.

Pudal, Bernard and Claude Pennetier 2017, *Le Souffle d'octobre 1917. L'engagement des communistes français*, Ivry-sur-Seine: L'Atelier.

Qinghua Daxue Zhonggong Dangshi Jiaoyanzu (ed.) 1979–81, *Fufa qingong jianxue yundong shiliao*, Beijing: Beijing chubanshe.

Racine, Nicole and Michel Trebitsch 1992, 'Sociabilités intellectuelles : lieux, milieux, réseaux', *Cahiers de l'Institut d'histoire du temps présent*, 20, March.

Ragona, Gianfranco 2003, *Maximilien Rubel (1905–1996) : etica, marxologia e critica del marxismo*, Milan: Franco Angeli.

Rebérioux, Madeleine 1977, 'Jean Jaurès et le marxisme', in Dominique-Antoine Grisoni (ed.), *Histoire du marxisme contemporain*, Paris: 10/18.

Reybaud, Louis 1841, *Études sur les réformateurs ou socialistes modernes. Saint-Simon, Charles Fourier, Robert Owen*, Paris: Guillaumin.

Reynaud Paligot, Carole 2010, *Parcours politique des surréalistes 1919–1969*, Paris: CNRS éditions.

Ricœur, Paul 1997 [1978], 'Le questionnement à rebours (Die Rückfrage) et la réduction des idéalités dans la Krisis de Husserl et L'Idéologie allemande de Marx', *Alter*, 5: 315–30.

Rioufreyt, Thibaut 2012, *La Traduction du néo-travaillisme britannique dans la gauche socialiste française (1997–2008)*, doctoral dissertation in political science, Université Lyon-II.

Robert, Jean-Louis (ed.) 2016, *Édouard Vaillant 1840–1915. De la Commune à l'Internationale*, Paris: L'Harmattan.

Robin, Régine 1973, *Histoire et Linguistique*, Paris: Armand Colin

Rochefort-Turquin, Agnès 1986, *Front populaire. Socialistes parce que chrétiens*, Paris: Éditions du Cerf.

Rochefort, Florence 2004, 'Les féministes', in Jean-Jacques Becker and Gilles Candar (eds.), *Histoire des gauches en France*, Vol. 2: *xxᵉ siècle, à l'épreuve de l'histoire*, Paris: La Découverte.

Roger, Philippe 1996, 'Barthes dans les années Marx', *Communications*, 63, 1: 39–65.

Ross, Kristin 2008, *May '68 and its Afterlives*, Chicago: University of Chicago Press.

Rougerie, Jacques 1971, *Paris libre 1871*, Paris: Seuil.

Rubel, Maximilien 1960, *Karl Marx devant le bonapartisme*, Paris: Mouton.

Rubel, Maximilien 1974, *Marx critique du marxisme*, Paris: Payot.

Rubel, Maximilien 2012, *Marx et les nouveaux phagocytes*, introduction and postface by Louis Janover, Paris: Sandre.

Sartre, Jean-Paul 2003 [1949], 'Matérialisme et révolution', *Situations, III. Lendemains de guerre*, Paris: Gallimard.

Sartre, Jean-Paul 2004 [1960], *Critique of Dialectical Reason*, London: Verso.

Sassoon, Donald 2014, *One Hundred Years of Socialism. The West European Left in the Twentieth Century*, London: I.B. Tauris.

Schaff, Adam 1971, 'Au sujet de la traduction française de la VIe thèse sur Feuerbach de Marx', *L'Homme et la Société*, 19: 157–67.

Seidel, Jutta 1982, *Deutsche Sozialdemokratie und Parti ouvrier 1876–1889. Politische Beziehungen und Theorische Zusammenarbeit*, Berlin: Akademie Verlag.

Senghor, Léopold Sédar 1971, *Liberté 2. Nation et voie africaine du socialisme*, Paris: Seuil.

Senghor, Léopold Sédar 1976, *Pour une relecture africaine de Marx et d'Engels*, Paris: Nouvelles éditions africaines.

Sève, Lucien 1971, 'Mise au point', *L'Homme et la Société*, 20: 264–7.

Sevegrant, Martine 2011, *Temps Présent. Une avant-garde catholique*, tome II: *1950–1968*, Paris: Temps Présent.

Sine, Babacar 1983, *Le Marxisme devant les sociétés africaines contemporaines*, Paris: Présence africaine.

Skornicki, Arnault and Jérôme Tournadre, La Nouvelle Histoire des idées politiques, Paris: La Découverte.

Soboul, Albert 1958, *Les Sans-Culottes parisiens en l'An II*, Paris: Clavreuil.

Sohn, Anne-Marie 1977, 'Exemplarité et limites de la participation féminine à la vie syndicale: les institutrices de la CGTU', *Revue d'histoire moderne et contemporaine*, 24, 3: 394–474.

Sommier, Isabelle 2008, 'Les Gauchismes', in Dominique Dammame, Boris Gobille, Frédérique Matonti and Bernard Pudal, *Mai-juin 68*, Ivry-sur-Seine: L'Atelier.

Sorel, Georges 2007, *Essais de critique du marxisme*, Paris: L'Harmattan.

Soulage, Vincent 2012, 'L'intégration des chrétiens au Parti socialiste: d'Épinay à Metz', in Denis Pelletier and Jean-Louis Schlegel (eds.), *À la gauche du Christ. Les chrétiens de gauche en France de 1945 à nos jours*, Paris: Seuil.

Souyri, Pierre 1970, *Le Marxisme après Marx*, Paris: Flammarion.

Souyri, Pierre 1983, *La Dynamique du capitalisme au xxe siècle*, Paris: Payot.

Sowerwine, Charles 1978, *Les Femmes et le Socialisme*, Paris: PFNSP/Éditions des femmes.

Sperber, Jonathan 2014, *Karl Marx: A Nineteenth-Century Life*, New York: Liveright.

Stedman Jones, Gareth 2016, *Karl Marx. Greatness and Illusion*, London: Allen Lane.

Steiner, Philippe 2000, 'La Revue économique 1950–1980. La marche vers l'orthodoxie académique', *Revue économique*, 5: 1009–58.

Streiff, Gérard 2002, *Jean Kanapa, 1921–1978: une singulière histoire du PCF*, Paris: L'Harmattan.

Stuart, Robert 1992, *Marxism at Work. Ideology, Class and French Socialism during the Third Republic*, Cambridge: Cambridge University Press.

Suret-Canale, Jean 1994, *Les Groupes d'études communistes* (GEC) *en Afrique noire*, Paris: L'Harmattan.

Tardivel, Jacqueline 1993, *Des pacifistes aux résistantes, les militantes communistes en France, dans l'entre-deux-guerres*, doctoral dissertation in history, Université Paris-VII.

Tavernier, Yves, Michel Gervais, and Claude Servolin 1972, *L'Univers politique des paysans dans la France contemporaine*, Paris: Colin.

Teroni, Sandra and Wolfgang Klien 2005, *Pour la défense de la culture: Les textes du congrès international des écrivains*, Dijon: Éditions universitaires de Dijon.

Thomas, Frédéric 2007, *Rimbaud et Marx. Une rencontre surréaliste*, Paris: L'Harmattan.

Thompson, Edward Palmer 1963, *The Making of the English Working Class*, London: Gollancz.

Topalov, Christian 2013, 'Christian Topalov, chercheur et militant', interview by Louis Weber and Laurent Willemez, *Savoir/Agir*, 4, 26: 63–75.

Tosel, André 2009, *Le Marxisme du 20ᵉ siècle*, Paris: Syllepse.

Toupin-Guyot, Claire 2002, *Les Intellectuels catholiques dans la société française. Le Centre catholique des intellectuels français (1941–1976)*, Rennes: Presses universitaires de Rennes.

Tracol, Matthieu 2015, *La Rigueur et les Réformes. Histoire des politiques du travail et de l'emploi du gouvernement Mauroy (1981–1984)*, doctoral dissertation in history, Université Paris-I.

Trần Đức Thảo 1946a, 'Marxisme et phénoménologie', *La Revue internationale*, 2: 168–74.

Trần Đức Thảo 1946b, 'Sur l'Indochine', *Les Temps modernes*, 5: 878–900.

Trần Đức Thảo 1949, 'Existentialisme et matérialisme dialectique', *Revue de métaphysique et de morale*, 58, 3–4: 317–29.

Trần Đức Thảo 1951, *Phénoménologie et matérialisme dialectique*, Paris: Minh Tân.

Tranvouez, Yvon 2015, 'Les idées du ciel ne tombent pas juste. La division théologique des chrétiens de gauche', in Denis Pelletier and Jean-Louis Schlegel (eds.), *À la gauche du Christ. Les chrétiens de gauche en France de 1945 à nos jours*, Paris: Seuil.

traoré S. (1983), *Les Intellectuels africains face au marxisme*, L'Harmattan, Paris.

Trebitsch, Michel 1986, 'Le renouveau philosophique avorté des années 1930. Entretien avec Henri Lefebvre', *Europe*, 683.

Trebitsch, Michel 1987, 'Le Groupe Philosophies, de Max Jacob aux surréalistes (1924–1925)', *Les Cahiers de l'*IHTP, 6.

Various authors 1971, *Traité marxiste d'économie politique. Le capitalisme monopoliste d'État*, Paris: Éditions sociales

Vatin, François 2004, 'Machinisme, marxisme, humanisme: Georges Friedmann avant et après guerre', *Sociologie du travail*, 46: 205–23.

Verdès, Jeannine 1966, 'BA 1175. Marx vu par la police française 1871–1883', *worl*, S, 10: 83–120.

Vigreux, Jean 2000, *Waldeck Rochet: une biographie politique*, Paris: La Dispute.

Vilar, Pierre 1982, *Une histoire en construction. Approche marxiste et problématiques conjoncturelles*, Paris: Seuil.

Vovelle, Michel 1982, *Idéologies et Mentalités*, Paris: Maspero.

Wang, Nora 2002, *Émigrations et Politique: les étudiant-ouvriers chinois en France 1919–1925*, Paris: Les Indes savantes.

Wieviorka, Annette 2010, *Maurice et Jeannette: biographie du couple Thorez*, Paris: Fayard.

Wilfert, Blaise 2003, *Paris, la France et le reste: importations littéraires et nationalisme culturel en France, 1885–1930*, doctoral dissertation in history, supervised by Christophe Charle, Paris-I Panthéon-Sorbonne.

Willard, Claude 1965, *Le mouvement socialiste en France (1893–1905): les guesdistes*, Paris: Éditions sociales.

Wittfogel, Karl 1957, *Oriental Despotism: A Comparative Study of Total Power*, New Haven: Yale University Press.

Wolikow, Serge 2010, *L'Internationale communiste (1919–1943): le Komintern ou le rêve déchu du parti mondial de la révolution*, Ivry-sur-Seine: L'Atelier.

Wolikow, Serge 2017, 'The Comintern as a World Network', in Silvio Pons (ed.), *The Cambridge History of Communism*, Cambridge: Cambridge University Press.

Wurmser, André 1950, 'Chronique artistique: réponse à Francis Jourdain', *La Pensée*, 32, 127–32.

Xianyu, H. 2003, 'Lun Zhonggong lv'ou dangtuan zuzhi de neibu xunlian', *Journal of Southwest University for Nationalities (Philosophy and Social Sciences)*, 24, 2.

Yang, Kuisong 2010, '"Zhongjian didai" de geming: guoji dabeijing xia kan Zhonggong chenggong zhidao', Taiyuan: Shanxi renmin chubanshe.

Ymonet, Marie 1984, 'Les héritiers du *Capital*. L'invention du marxisme en France au lendemain de la Commune', *Actes de la recherche en sciences sociales*, 55: 3–14.

Yon, Karel 2005, 'Modes de sociabilité et entretien de l'habitus militant. Militer en bandes à l'AJS-OCI', *Politix*, 2, 70: 137–67.

Yon, Karel 2011, 'Que faire de la théorie au Parti socialiste? La carrière écourtée du marxisme de Convergences socialistes', *Sociétés contemporaines*, 81: 81–105.

Zévaès, Alexandre 1947, *De l'introduction du marxisme en France*, Paris: Marcel Rivière.

Index

www.ingramcontent.com/pod-product-compliance
Lightning Source LLC
Chambersburg PA
CBHW071136130626
46553CB00004B/1393